札幌
さっぽろ

青森
あおもり

秋田
あきた

盛岡
もりおか

山形
やまがた

新潟
にいがた

仙台
せんだい

福島
ふくしま

東京
とうきょう

横浜
よこはま

千葉
ちば

①	北海道地方 ほっかいどう ち ほう
②	東北地方 とうほく ち ほう
③	関東地方 かんとう ち ほう
④	中部地方 ちゅうぶ ち ほう
⑤	近畿地方 きん き ち ほう
⑥	中国地方 ちゅうごく ち ほう
⑦	四国地方 し こく ち ほう
⑧	九州地方 きゅうしゅう ち ほう

NAKAMA 1

INTRODUCTORY JAPANESE: *COMMUNICATION, CULTURE, CONTEXT*

Second Edition

Yukiko Abe Hatasa
Hiroshima University

Kazumi Hatasa
Purdue University
The Japanese School, Middlebury College

Seiichi Makino
Princeton University

HEINLE
CENGAGE Learning

Australia • Brazil • Japan • Korea • Mexico • Singapore • Spain • United Kingdom • United States

Nakama 1: Introductory Japanese: Communication, Culture, Context, Second Edition
Yukiko Abe Hatasa, Kazumi Hatasa, Seiichi Makino

Publisher: Beth Kramer

Acquisitions Editor: Nicole Morinon

Development Editor: Kim Beuttler

Editorial Assistant: Sara Dyer

Media Editor: Laurel Miller

Marketing Manager: Mary Jo Prinaris

Marketing Coordinator: Janine Enos

Senior Marketing Communications Manager:
    Stacey Purviance

Senior Content Project Manager: Margaret Park Bridges

Print Buyer: Betsy Donaghey

Production Service: Inari Information Services

Photo Manager: Jennifer Meyer Dare

Cover Design Director: Tony Saizon

Cover image: Harold Burch, New York City

Compositor: Inari Information Services

For product information and technology assistance, contact us at

Cengage Learning Customer & Sales Support, 1-800-354-9706

For permission to use material from this text or product,

submit all requests online at **cengage.com/permissions**

Further permissions questions can be emailed to

permissionrequest@cengage.com

Library of Congress Control Number: 2007926500

Student Edition

ISBN-13: 978-0-495-79818-7

ISBN-10: 0-495-79818-5

Heinle

20 Channel Center

Boston, MA 02210

USA

Cengage Learning is a leading provider of customized learning solutions with office locations around the globe, including Singapore, the United Kingdom, Australia, Mexico, Brazil, and Japan. Locate your local office at: **international.cengage.com/region**

Cengage Learning products are represented in Canada by Nelson Education, Ltd.

For your course and learning solutions, visit **www.cengage.com**

Purchase any of our products at your local college store or at our preferred online store **www.ichapters.com**

Photographs unless otherwise noted courtesy of the authors.
Page 31: © Kayte M. Deimoa/PhotoEdit; Page 45: © Christine Schneider/zefa/Corbis; Page 83: © Gary Conner/PhotoEdit; Page 134: © Kenneth Hamm/Photo Japan; Page 176: © Teruyo Shimizu/Photo Japan; Page 177: © Kenneth Hamm/Photo Japan; Page 220: © Jeremy Hoare/Alamy; Page 221: © Jeremy Hoare/Alamy; Page 263: © Hugh Threlfall/Alamy; Page 294: © D. Hurst/Alamy; Page 294: © Hugh Threlfall/Alamy; Page 294: © Hugh Threlfall/Alamy; Page 294: © D. Hurst/Alamy; Page 294: © Bloomimage/Corbis; Page 294: © Lew Robertson/Corbis; Page 295: © Kenneth Hamm/Photo Japan; Page 308: © Kenneth Hamm/Photo Japan; Page 308: © Kenneth Hamm/Photo Japan; Page 350: © Kenneth Hamm/Photo Japan; Page 350: © Kenneth Hamm/Photo Japan; Page 381: © Kenneth Hamm/Photo Japan; Page 396: © Joeri DeRocker/Photo Japan; Page 396: © Chad Ehlers/Alamy; Page 413: © Stefan Zaklin/epa/Corbis; Page 423: Handout/Getty Images; Page 438: © Kenneth Hamm/Photo Japan; Page 438: © Kenneth Hamm/Photo Japan; Page 439: © Kenneth Hamm/Photo Japan; Page 471: © Barry Lewis/Alamy; Page 487: © Kenneth Hamm/Photo Japan

Printed in the United States of America
1 2 3 4 5 6 7 13 12 11 10 09

ABOUT THE AUTHORS

Professor Yukiko Abe Hatasa received her Ph.D. in linguistics in 1992 from the University of Illinois at UrbanChampaign. She is known nationwide as one of the premier Japanese methodologists in the United States and as an experienced coordinator of large teacher training programs. She has served as the coordinator of the Japanese language program at the University of Iowa and is currently a professor at Hiroshima University, where her primary responsibilities are teacher training and SLA research.

Professor Kazumi Hatasa received his Ph.D. in education in 1989 from the University of Illinois at UrbanChampaign. He is currently a professor at Purdue University and Director of the Japanese School at Middlebury College. He is recognized internationally for his work in software development for the Japanese language and distributes most of his work as freeware over the Internet.

Professor Seiichi Makino received his Ph.D. in linguistics in 1968 from the University of Illinois at UrbanChampaign. He is an internationally prominent Japanese linguist and scholar who is recognized throughout the world for his scholarship and for his many publications. Before beginning his tenure at Princeton University in 1991, he taught Japanese language, linguistics and culture at the University of Illinois while training lower division language coordinators. He is an experienced ACTFL oral proficiency trainer in Japanese and frequently trains Japanese instructors internationally in proficiency-oriented instruction and in the administration of the Oral Proficiency Interview. Professor Makino has been the Academic Director of the Japanese Pedagogy M.A. Summer Program at Columbia University since 1996. He also directs the Princeton-in-Ishikawa Summer Program.

CONTENTS

CHAPTER 4: JAPANESE CITIES

CHAPTER 5: JAPANESE HOMES

CHAPTER 6: LEISURE TIME

CHAPTER 7: FAVORITE THINGS AND ACTIVITIES

CHAPTER 10: MY FAMILY

CHAPTER 11: SEASONS AND WEATHER

TO THE STUDENT

Nakama 1 is based on the principle that learning another language means acquiring new skills, not just facts and information—that we learn by doing. To achieve this goal, *Nakama 1* systematically involves you in many activities that incorporate the language skills of listening, speaking, reading, and writing. We believe that culture is an integral component of language, too. To help you become familiar with Japanese culture, your text includes high-interest culture notes and relevant communication strategies. New to this edition, an appealing story line video, featuring a Japanese-American exchange student in Tokyo, bring chapter dialogues to life.

ORGANIZATION OF THE TEXTBOOK

Nakama 1 consists of twelve chapters in two parts. In Chapter 1, you will learn the sounds of the Japanese language and a set of Japanese syllabary symbols called **hiragana**. You will also learn basic greetings and classroom instructions. A second Japanese syllabary called **katakana** is presented after Chapter 2. Chapters 2 through 12 each focus on a common communicative situation and contain the following features:

- Chapter Opener: Each chapter opens with a theme-setting photograph and chapter contents by section. Keeping in mind the objectives listed at the top of the opener will help you focus on achieving your learning goals.

- Vocabulary: The vocabulary is presented in thematic groups, each followed by a variety of communicative activities and activities in context. Supplemental vocabulary is also provided throughout the chapter, but you are not expected to retain it. All active vocabulary is listed by function at the beginning of each chapter, except for Chapter 1, where the list appears last, after you've learned to read **hiragana**.

- Dialogue: The lively dialogues center on Alice Ueda, a Japanese-American college student, who is spending two years studying in Japan. Through the dialogue and accompanying video, you will get to know a series of characters and follow them through typical events in their lives. The video, related activities, and interactive online practice will all reinforce your understanding of the content, discourse organization, and use of formal and casual Japanese speech styles.

- Japanese Culture: Up-to-date culture notes in English explore social, economic, and historical aspects of Japanese life that are essential to effective communication.

- Grammar: Clear, easy-to-understand grammar explanations are accompanied by sample sentences and notes that help you understand how to use the grammar appropriately. In-class pair and group activities let you practice immediately what you've learned. As there is a high correlation between successful communication and grammar accuracy, this section is especially important.

- Listening: Useful strategies and pre-listening activities for general comprehension precede the section's main listening practice. Post-listening activities concentrate on more detailed comprehension and apply what you have learned to other communicative purposes.

- Communication: This section will provide you with knowledge and practice of basic strategies to accelerate your ability to communicate in Japanese.

- **Kanji:** Chapters 4 through 12 introduce a total of 127 **kanji** (Chinese characters). The section begins with useful information such as the composition of individual characters, word formation, and how to use Japanese dictionaries. The presentation of each character includes stroke order to help you master correct stroke orders when writing in Japanese and to prepare you for the reading section.

- Reading: Each reading passage begins with a reading strategy, and includes pre- and post-reading activities designed to help you become a successful reader of Japanese. From Chapter 2, the text is written in all three scripts: **hiragana, katakana,** and **kanji. Hiragana** subscripts (**furigana**) are provided for **katakana** through Chapter 3, and for unfamiliar **kanji** throughout the textbook. The readings include a small number of unknown words to help you develop strategies for understanding authentic texts.

- Integration: Integrated practice wraps up every chapter using discussion, interviewing, and role-play activities that interweave all the skills you've learned in the current and previous chapters.

STUDENT COMPONENTS

- Student Text: Your Student Text contains all the information and activities you need for in-class use. It is divided into two parts encompassing twelve chapters plus a special chapter following Chapter 2 that introduces **katakana.** Each regular chapter contains vocabulary presentations and activities, a thematic dialogue and practice, grammar presentations and activities, cultural information, reading selections, writing practice, and ample communicative practice. Valuable reference sections at the back of the book include verb charts, a **kanji** list, and Japanese-English and English-Japanese glossaries.

- In-Text Audio CD: The In-Text Audio CD contains recordings of all the listening activities in the text as well as all active chapter vocabulary. The audio activity clips are also available as MP3 files and the vocabulary pronunciations can be found in the flashcards on the student website. These audio materials are designed to maximize your exposure to the sounds of natural spoken Japanese and to help you practice pronunciation.

- Student Activities Manual (SAM): The Student Activities Manual (SAM) includes out-of-class practice of the material presented in the Student Text. Each chapter of the SAM includes a workbook section, which focuses on written vocabulary, grammar, **kanji** and writing practice, and a lab section, which focuses on pronunciation and listening comprehension, including Dict-Conversation dictation activities.

- SAM Audio Program: The SAM Audio Program corresponds to the audio portion of the SAM and reinforces your pronunciation and listening skills. You may listen to this material in the lab or on CD. The audio is also available as MP3 files from the passkey-protected area of the student website.

- DVD: New for the second edition, the two-tiered Nakama video program includes a story line video, where the experiences of a Japanese-American exchange student, Alice Ueda, featured in the chapter dialogues are brought to life. A series of cultural segments that depict everyday situations are tied to the theme of each chapter. You will be able to view the video in class, on DVD, on the student website as MP4 files, or while working on video comprehension activities found on the passkey-protected area of the site.

- Student companion site: You will find a variety of resources on the student companion site. A wealth of interactive exercises and games give you further practice with chapter topics. Vocabulary and grammar quizzes, audio flashcards for vocabulary, and **kanji** and pronunciation review help you monitor and assess your progress. MP3 files for the text listening activities can also be downloaded from the site. The website is accessible at www.cengage.com/japanese/nakama.

ACKNOWLEDGMENTS

The authors and publisher thank the following people for their recommendations regarding the content of *Nakama 1*. Their comments and suggestions were invaluable during the development of this publication.

Noriko Akatsuka
Aloysius Chang
Len Grzanka
Hiroko Harada
Masako Hamada
Janet Ikeda
Mieko Ishibashi
Noriko Iwasaki
Kimberly Jones
Sarachie Karasawa
Hiroko Kataoka
Yukio Kataoka
Michiya Kawai
Chisato Kitagawa
Lisa Kobuke
Chiyo Konishi
Junko Kumamoto-Healey
Yukari Kunisue
Yasumi Kuriya
John Mertz
Masahiko Minami
Akira Miura
Shigeru Miyagawa
Seigo Nakao
Hiroshi Nara
Machiko Netsu
Catherine Oshida
Yoko Pusavat
Yoshiko Saito-Abbott
Haruko Sakakibara
Kitty Shek
Ritsuko Shigeyama
Satoru Shinagawa
Zenryu Shirakawa
Shizuka Tatsuzawa
Miyo Uchida
Alexander Vovin
Paul Warnick
Yasuko Ito Watt
Kikuko Yamashita

The authors and publisher also thank the following people for field-testing *Nakama 1*. Their comments contributed greatly to the accuracy of this publication.

Nobuko Chikamatsu
Fusae Ekida
Junko Hino
Satoru Ishikawa
Yoshiko Jo
Sayuri Kubota
Yasumi Kuriya
Izumi Matsuda
Junko Mori
Fumiko Nazikian
Mayumi Oka
Amy Snyder Ohta
Mayumi Steinmetz
Keiko Yamaguchi

The authors are also grateful to the following people at Houghton Mifflin for their valuable assistance during the development of this project: Rolando Hernández, Glenn Wilson, Eileen Bernadette Moran, Lorreen Pelletier, Judith Bach, Kim Beuttler, Charline Lake, and Margaret Bridges.

They are especially grateful to Yoshiko Jo and Margaret Hines for copyediting, to Satoru Ishikawa, Bill Weaver, and Yoshiko Jo for proofreading, and to Michael Kelsey of Inari Information Services, Inc. Finally, profound thanks go to Noriko Hanabusa for her work on the Student Activities Manual and to Kazuko Yokoi for her work on the illustrations in this edition.

Chapter 1

だ い い つ か

The Japanese Sound System and Hiragana

I. Introduction

Japanese is usually written with a combination of three types of script: **hiragana, katakana,** and **kanji** (Chinese characters). Individually, **hiragana** and **katakana** represent sounds, and **kanji** represent words. **Hiragana** is used for function words (words such as *in*, *at*, and *on*) and for inflectional endings (indicating sound changes used to express tense, negation, and the like), and for some content words as well. **Katakana** is used for words borrowed from other languages, for example, **keeki** (cake), for onomatopoeic words expressing sounds, such as **wanwan** (the Japanese word for *bow-wow*), and for some scientific terms, such as the names of animals and plants in biology textbooks. **Kanji** are characters of Chinese origin, and each **kanji** represents a morpheme or a word and is used for content words, such as nouns, verbs, and adjectives.

Hiragana

Like the individual letters in the English alphabet, **hiragana** represent sounds, but each **hiragana** character represents a vowel or a combination of a consonant and a vowel, such as **a, sa, ki, tsu, me,** and **yo**. **Hiragana** evolved through the simplification of Chinese characters during the Heian period (794–1185).

Having no writing system of their own, the Japanese began importing Chinese characters (**hanzi**) to write their own language in the late fourth or early fifth century. They employed two adaptation strategies to do so. One was based on meaning and the other was based on sound. The meaning-based strategy involved using an individual **kanji** to write a Japanese word that was synonymous with the Chinese word the **kanji** represented. For example, the Japanese word for "wave" was expressed using the Chinese character with the same meaning, 波. Its pronunciation in Chinese, *puâ*, was replaced with the pronunciation of the corresponding Japanese word, **nami**.

The sound-based strategy, by contrast, used Chinese characters to represent Japanese sounds rather than meanings. For instance, the character 波 in this context was used to represent the syllable *ha* because of its close resemblance to the sound *puâ* in Middle Chinese. (The character is currently pronounced [ha], but it was pronounced as [pa] in classical Japanese, similar to the middle Chinese [puâ].) In this usage, the meaning of the character 波 was completely ignored. This was a cumbersome system, however, because Japanese words usually contain several syllables and Chinese characters represent only one sound. In order to overcome this problem, Chinese characters were gradually simplified until they reached the forms used in present-day **hiragana**. These simplified characters appear in many women's literary works, including the famous *Tale of Genji*, and for this reason **hiragana** was once called **onna de** (*women's hand*).

Hiragana as written today consists of 46 characters (Figure 1). Two diacritical marks in the shapes of two dots ゛ or a small circle ゜ are used to show voiced consonants (Figure 2). The basic syllabary can also be used to represent *glides*, which are combinations of characters that represent more complex sounds (Figure 3).

Look at Figure 1 and pronounce each character by repeating it after your instructor and/or the accompanying audio. This chart should be read from top to bottom and right to left. Japanese may be written vertically in this manner or horizontally, from left to right, as in English.

Figure 1

n	w	r	y	m	h	n	t	s	k	
ん	わ	ら	や	ま	は	な	た	さ	か	あ a
		り		み	ひ	に	ち	し	き	い i
		る	ゆ	む	ふ	ぬ	つ	す	く	う u
		れ		め	へ	ね	て	せ	け	え e
	を	ろ	よ	も	ほ	の	と	そ	こ	お o

(handwritten: ち-"chi" フー"tsu")
(handwritten: ふっ-"fu")

Figure 2

p	b	d	z	g	
ぱ	ば	だ	ざ	が	a
ぴ	び	ぢ	じ	ぎ	i
ぷ	ぶ	づ	ず	ぐ	u
ぺ	べ	で	ぜ	げ	e
ぽ	ぼ	ど	ぞ	ご	o

(handwritten: ぱんだ パンダ Panda)

Figure 3

p	b	d	z	g	r	m	h	n	t	s	k	
ぴゃ	びゃ	ぢゃ	じゃ	ぎゃ	りゃ	みゃ	ひゃ	にゃ	ちゃ	しゃ	きゃ	ya
ぴゅ	びゅ	ぢゅ	じゅ	ぎゅ	りゅ	みゅ	ひゅ	にゅ	ちゅ	しゅ	きゅ	yu
ぴょ	びょ	ぢょ	じょ	ぎょ	りょ	みょ	ひょ	にょ	ちょ	しょ	きょ	yo

(handwritten: りょう)
(handwritten: しゃっくり Shakkuri, Small tsu)
(handwritten: なっと natto)

II. Hiragana あ〜そ

In this section, you will learn fifteen **hiragana** and their pronunciation. The following charts show both printed and handwritten styles.

Note that some lines that are connected in the printed style are not connected in handwriting. For example, the vertical diagonal curved lines in the printed forms of き [ki] and さ [sa] are connected, but they are not connected in handwriting (き and さ). Also, the character そ [so] is written as a single stroke in the printed style, but as two strokes in handwriting (そ), where the diagonal line at the top is not connected with the rest of the character.

Printed style

	s	k		
さ	か	あ	a
し	き	い	i
す	く	う	u
せ	け	え	e
そ	こ	お	o

Handwritten style

	s	k		
さ	か	あ	a
し	き	い	i
す	く	う	u
せ	け	え	e
そ	こ	お	o

Learning hiragana

The mnemonic pictures and keys below have been provided to help you memorize the **hiragana** characters. Remember that the mnemonic pictures are not accurate representations of the shapes or the sounds of the characters.

a	あ	あ	あ is similar to [ah] but is shorter.	*Ah!* Ann is good at ice-skating.
i	い	い	い is similar to the vowel sound in *ear* but is shorter.	I have big *ears*.
u	う	う	う is similar to the vowel sound in [ooh] but is shorter and the lips are not as rounded.	*Ooh!* This is heavy.
e	え	え	え is similar to the first vowel sound in *exercise* but the mouth is not opened as widely.	I need *exercise*.

o	お	お	お is similar to the vowel sound [o] in *on* as the British pronounce it, but the lips are slightly more rounded.	The ball will land *on* the green.
ka	か	か	か is a combination of [k] and [a]. The Japanese [k] sound is less forceful than the English sound.	*Karate* kick.
ki	き	き	き is similar to *key* but the vowel sound is shorter.	This is *a key*.
ku	く	く	く is similar to the first syllable of *cuckoo* but the lips are not as rounded.	This is a *cuckoo*.
ke	け	け	け is similar to the sound [ca] in *cane*, but without the [y] sound.	A man with a *cane*.
ko	こ	こ	こ is similar to the sound [co] in *coin* without the [y] sound.	A ten yen *coin* is worth about a dime.
sa	さ	さ	さ is a combination of [s] and [a]. The Japanese [s] sound is not as strong as the English [s] sound because less air is forced out between the teeth.	Don't drink too much *sake*.
shi	し	し	し is similar to *she* but is shorter and the lips are spread wider. Japanese does not have the sound [si] as in *sea*.	This is how *she* wears her hair.
su	す	す	す is a combination of [s] and [u].	*Swimming* is fun in the summer.
se	せ	せ	せ is similar to the sound of *se* in *señor*.	Hello, *Señor* García.
so	そ	そ	そ is similar to *so* but is shorter.	This character zigzags *so* much.

Reading hiragana

Read the following words, paying attention to intonation and devoiced (whispered) sounds. Characters with a bar over them (for example, いけ) should be pronounced with a higher pitch than those without a bar. The [i] and [u] in き , く , し , す , ち , つ , ひ , and ふ may be devoiced between two voiceless consonants or at the end of a word. Characters with a small circle under them (き) contain a devoiced [i] or [u].

え	picture	いけ	pond
おかし	confectionery	いす	chair
き	tree	きく	chrysanthemum
かお	face	さけ	sake
あし	leg	えき	station
せかい	world	そこ	bottom
あさ	morning	しお	salt
あかい	red	あかい かさ	red umbrella
あおい	blue	あおい いす	blue chair

Useful Expressions

1. Forms of address

The Japanese always use a title to address people other than family members. Young people, however, sometimes refer to their close friends by name only, without using titles.

se n se e せんせい　　　　～せんせい　　　～さん

professor, teacher　　　Professor ～　　　Mr./Mrs./Miss/Ms. ～

Example:　たなかせんせい　　　やまださん

Professor Tanaka　　　Mr./Mrs./Miss/Ms. Yamada

NOTES

- The せい in せんせい (**sensee**) is pronounced by stretching the [e]. You will learn more about long vowels in a later section.

- It is customary to address an instructor simply as せんせい .

- The literal meaning of せんせい is "born ahead," which by extension means "honorable master." For this reason, it is used to refer to other people but never to oneself. Further, it can be used to address people in professions other than teaching, especially when the person in question has recognized expertise and performs a mentoring function. Patients refer to their medical doctors as せんせい. But せんせい should never be used in reference to oneself.

- The Japanese usually address each other using last names and titles, even when they have known each other for a long time. First names are used primarily among family members and close friends.

- 〜さん is a generic term, but you cannot use it when referring to yourself or to someone who should be addressed with a title such as せんせい.

2. Introducing yourself

はじめまして。　〜 です。どうぞ よろしく 。

How do you do? I am 〜 . Pleased to meet you.

(The English translation here is not a literal equivalent of the Japanese.)

Example:　A: はじめまして。やまだ です。どうぞ よろしく。

B: はじめまして。すみす です。どうぞ よろしく。

Mr. Smith　　　　**Mr. Yamada**

まも

いり

さち ほ

はろ る

ラリルレロ

NOTES

- The little circle at the end of each sentence represents a period in written Japanese.
- You cannot use a title or さん when speaking of yourself.

はなして みましょう   Conversation Practice

1. Today is the first day of Japanese class. Introduce yourself to your classmates. Listen to your classmates as they introduce themselves and try to remember their names.

2. Did you greet your classmates with a bow? If you didn't, greet them again, and bow. If you don't know how to bow properly, ask your instructor to show you.

III. Hiragana た～ほ

In this section, you will learn fifteen more **hiragana** and their pronunciation. Note that the right side of な [na] consists of a single connected line in the printed style, but consists of two strokes in the handwritten style な [na].

Printed style

	h	n	t	
	は	な	た	a
	ひ	に	ち	i
	ふ	ぬ	つ	u
	へ	ね	て	e
	ほ	の	と	o

Handwritten style

	h	n	t	
	は	な	た	a
	ひ	に	ち	i
	ふ	ぬ	つ	u
	へ	ね	て	e
	ほ	の	と	o

Learning hiragana

| ta | た | 　 | た is a combination of [t] and [a]. The Japanese [t] sound is produced by touching the upper teeth and gum with the tip of the tongue. The Japanese [t] sound is not as strong as the English [t] because less air is forced between the teeth. | ta | The letters *t* and *a* make *ta*. |

chi	ち	ち	ち The sound is [chi] as in *cheer*. There is no [ti] sound in Japanese.	Being a *cheerleader* isn't easy.
tsu	つ	つ	つ is similar to the sound [t's] in *cat's*.	A *cat's* tail.
te	て	て	て is similar to the first syllable of *table*, but without the [y] sound.	Fruit on a *table*.
to	と	と	と is similar to the sound of *toe* but the [t] is softer.	I've got a thorn in my *toe*.
na	な	な	な is similar to the sound of [na] in *nap* in British pronunciation, but the vowel sound is more like [a] as in *ah*.	This person is taking a *nap*.
ni	に	に	に is similar to the sound of *knee*, but the vowel sound is shorter.	Look at my *knees*.
nu	ぬ	ぬ	ぬ is similar to the first syllable of *noodle*, but the vowel sound is shorter.	*Noodle*s and chopsticks.
ne	ね	ね	ね is similar to the sound of *ne* in *net*.	I caught a fish in my *net*.
no	の	の	の is similar to the sound of the English *no*, but the vowel sound is shorter and the lips are not as rounded.	See the *no* smoking sign.
ha	は	ば	は is a combination of [h] and [a]. The Japanese [h] sound is much softer than the English equivalent.	I bought a *house*.
hi	ひ	ひ	ひ is similar to the sound of *he*, is but the vowel sound is shorter.	This is Mr. Hill. *He* is strong.

fu	ふ	ふ	ふ is a combination of [f] and [u]. The initial consonant [f] is produced by bringing the lips together as if blowing out a candle.	Mt. *Fuji* is beautiful.
he	へ	へ	へ is similar to the sound of *head*, without the final [d] sound.	I have a *head-ache*.
ho	ほ	ほ	ほ is similar to the initial part of *home*, without the [u] sound.	A house isn't a *home* without TV.

Reading hiragana

Read the following words, paying attention to devoiced sounds and intonation.

て	hand	にく	meat
つき	moon	ひと	person
おなか	stomach	ねこ	cat
はな	nose	いぬ	dog
くち	mouth	ふえ	flute
たき	waterfall	ほし	star
たな	shelf	うち	house
たかい	high, expensive	たかい にく	expensive meat
ひくい	low, flat	ひくい こえ	low voice

Useful Expressions

Daily greetings

Greeting people properly is important in all cultures. In Japanese, the phrases used when greeting people vary according to the time of day.

In the morning:

o ha yoo   go za i ma su

おはよう　ございます。

Good morning. / Hello. (formal speech)

o ha yoo

おはよう。

Good morning. / Hello. (casual speech)

Examples: Student A: ^{o h a y o o} おはよう。

Student B: ^{o h a y o o} おはよう。

Student: ^{o h a y o o   g o z a i m a s u} おはよう　ございます。

Teacher: ^{o h a y o o} おはよう。

Acquaintance A: ^{o h a y o o   g o z a i m a s u} おはよう　ございます。

Acquaintance B: ^{o h a y o o   g o z a i m a s u} おはよう　ございます。

In the afternoon:

ko n ni chi wa

こんにちは。

Good afternoon./ Hello.

Example: A: ^{k o n n i c h i w a} こんにちは。

B: ^{k o n n i c h i w a} こんにちは。

In the evening:

ko n ba n wa

こんばんは。

Good evening./Hello.

Example: A: ^{k o n b a n w a} こんばんは。

B: ^{k o n b a n w a} こんばんは。

NOTES

- The よう in おはよう　ございます [**ohayoo gozaimasu**] is pronounced by stretching the [o]. You will learn more about long vowels in a later section.

- In general, these phrases are used in both casual and formal situations. The expression おはよう　ございます [**ohayoo gozaimasu**], however, has a less formal version, おはよう [**ohayoo**], which may be used with friends or family members. It is considered rude if used with superiors or in formal situations.

- If you see the same person more than once on the same day, using these phrases each time you meet would sound rather silly. In such cases, you should just bow slightly or talk about something else.

- The は in こんにちは [**konnichi wa**] and こんばんは [**konban wa**] is pronounced [wa] rather than [ha].
- こんにちは [**konnichi wa**] and こんばんは [**konban wa**] are not used among family members.

はなして みましょう   Conversation Practice

1. It is morning. You meet an elderly neighbor on the street. Greet him/her.
2. Imagine that class is about to begin in the morning. Greet your instructor and classmates, nodding slightly rather than bowing.
3. Greet a friend in the morning. Greet your instructor in the afternoon. Greet a friend in the evening.
4. Walk around the classroom. As your instructor announces whether it is morning, afternoon, or evening, greet five classmates with the appropriate phrase. Don't forget to bow slightly.

IV. Hiragana ま〜ん

In this section, you will learn the remaining **hiragana**. Notice that the right side of む [mu] consists of a single connected line in the printed style but has two strokes in the handwritten style む [mu]. Similarly, while ゆ [yu] in the printed style is written in a single stroke with all lines connected, the handwritten style of ゆ [yu] is written in two strokes. In addition, り [ri] in the printed style is written in a single connected line, but り [ri] in handwritten style consists of two vertical lines.

Printed style

n	w	r	y	m	
ん	わ	ら	や	ま	a
		り		み	i
		る	ゆ	む	u
		れ		め	e
	を	ろ	よ	も	o

Handwritten style

n	w	r	y	m	
ん	わ	ら	や	ま	a
		り		み	i
		る	ゆ	む	u
		れ		め	e
	を	ろ	よ	も	o

Learning hiragana

ma	ま	ま	ま is a combination of [m] and [a]. The Japanese [m] sound is like the [m] in *mom*, but is less forceful.	*Mom!* I can't sit any longer.
mi	み	み	み is similar to the sound of *me*, but the vowel sound is shorter.	Who is twenty-one? *Me!*
mu	む	む	む is similar to the sound of *moo*, but the vowel sound is shorter.	Cows *moo*.
me	め	め	め is similar to the first syllable of *medal*.	An Olympic gold *medal*.
mo	も	も	も is similar to the sound of [mo] in *more*.	Catch *more* fish with a hook.
ya	や	や	や is a combination of the [y] and [a] sounds. The sounds [yi] and [ye] do not exist in Japanese.	A *yacht*.

yu	ゆ	ゆ	ゆ is similar to the first syllable of *ukulele*.	Can you play the *ukulele*?
yo	よ	よ	よ is similar to the first syllable of *yo-yo*, but the vowel sound is shorter.	*Yo-yos* were once very popular.
ra	ら	ら	ら The [r] sound in Japanese differs slightly from both the English [l] and [r]. To an English speaker's ears, its pronunciation lies somewhere between [r], [l], and [d]. It is produced by flicking the tip of the tongue against the gum behind the upper set of teeth. It is much lighter than the English [l].	A *rabbit*.
ri	り	り	り is similar to the first syllable of *ribbon*. The position of the tongue is the same as in ら.	A *ribbon*.
ru	る	る	る is similar to the sound of *loop* without the [p] sound, but the vowel sound is shorter. The position of the tongue is the same as in ら.	A *loop* at the end.
re	れ	れ	れ is similar to the sound of *let's* without the [t's]. The position of the tongue is the same as in ら.	*Let's* dance.
ro	ろ	ろ	ろ is similar to the sound *rope* without the [p] sound, but the vowel sound is shorter. The position of the tongue is the same as in ら.	A cowboy with his *rope*.
wa	わ	わ	わ is similar to the English *wah*, but the lips are not as rounded or pointed.	*Wah*!
wo	を	を	を is pronounced like お.	*Oh!* I can ride a unicycle
n	ん	ん	ん The pronunciation of ん changes according to the sound it precedes. It is [n] before [t], [s], [d], [z], [dz], [n], and [r], and [m] before [m], [n], [b]. It is a somewhat more nasal sound [ng], when it comes before [k] or [g], or at the end of a word.	The *end*

Reading hiragana

Read the following words, paying attention to devoiced sounds and intonation.

あたま	head	はれ	clear (weather)
みみ	ear	とり	bird
め	eye	むすめ	daughter
ひる	afternoon	かわ	river
よる	night	やま	mountain
あめ	rain	からし	mustard
ゆき	snow	くすり	medicine
くも	cloud	うま	horse
しろい	white	しろい　とり	white bird
くろい	black	くろい　め	black eyes

(handwritten annotations: 雨 and あめ — candy)

Useful Expressions

Taking leave of friends and instructors

The phrase for good-bye differs according to the person you are addressing.

To instructors or social superiors:

shi tsu ree   shi ma su
しつれい　します。
Good-bye.

Example: Student: sensee shitsuree shimasu
せんせい、　しつれい　します。

Instructor: ja sayonara
じゃ、　さよなら。

NOTES

- The literal translation of しつれい　します is *I am about to commit a rudeness* or *I am about to disturb you*.
- You should nod slightly when you say good-bye.
- しつれい　します can also be used as a polite greeting (similar to "excuse me") when you enter the office of a professor or social superior.

To friends:

^{j a a ma ta}
じゃあ、また。

See you later. (literally, *well then, again*)

Example: Student A: ^{j a a mata} じゃあ、また。

             Student B: ^{j a a mata} じゃあ、また。

NOTE

- The 、 mark represents a comma in Japanese. Unlike English commas, Japanese commas always slant to the lower right.

To someone you do not expect to see for an extended period of time:

^{sa yo o na ra}   ^{sa yo na ra}
さようなら。 / さよなら。

Good-bye.

Example: Friend A: ^{sa yo na ra} さよなら。

           Friend B: ^{sa y o o n a r a} さようなら。

NOTE

- さようなら [**sayoonara**] or さよなら [**sayonara**] is usually used when you do not expect to see the person for an extended period of time, although these phrases, especially the more colloquial さよなら [**sayonara**] can be used more generally as well.

はなして みましょう   Conversation Practice

1. Imagine that class is over. Say good-bye to your instructor and five classmates.
2. You are leaving your professor's office. Say good-bye to him/her.
3. Your friend is moving to a different city. Say good-bye to him/her.

V. Hiragana が〜ぽ : Voiced consonants

The consonants [k], [s], [t], [h] are voiceless, and they have voiced counterparts. The difference between voiceless and voiced consonants is the presence or absence of vibration. For instance, pronounce [k] and [g] one after another. The position of the tongue and the shape of the lips are identical for both sounds. In both cases you touch the back of your mouth with your tongue, then you quickly release the tongue to let the air flow. The only difference between the two is that your vocal chords vibrate when you pronounce [g], but not when you pronounce [k]. Feel the difference by putting your hand on your throat when you pronounce [k] and [g]. A voiced consonant is indicated by two dots (゛) and an unvoiced consonant by a small circle (゜) to the upper right corner of the character. For example, the voiced consonant [b] in ば has its voiceless counterpart [p] in ぱ。

					h		t	s	k	
ん	わ	ら	や	ま	は	な	た	さ	か	あ
		り		み	ひ	に	ち	し	き	い
		る	ゆ	む	ふ	ぬ	つ	す	く	う
		れ		め	へ	ね	て	せ	け	え
	を	ろ	よ	も	ほ	の	と	そ	こ	お

New hiragana

Printed style

p	b	d	z	g (ng)	
ぱ	ば	だ	ざ	が	a
ぴ	び	ぢ	じ	ぎ	i
ぷ	ぶ	づ	ず	ぐ	u
ぺ	べ	で	ぜ	げ	e
ぽ	ぼ	ど	ぞ	ご	o

Handwritten style

p	b	d	z	g (ng)	
ぱ	ば	だ	ざ	が	a
ぴ	び	ぢ	じ	ぎ	i
ぷ	ぶ	づ	ず	ぐ	u
ぺ	べ	で	ぜ	げ	e
ぽ	ぼ	ど	ぞ	ご	o

Note that [g] is sometimes represented as [ng] to reflect the softness of this sound.

Reading hiragana

Read the following words, paying attention to the voiced and voiceless consonants.

ひげ	beard	にほんご	Japanese language
ゆび	finger	かばん	bag
うで	arm	ちず	map
のど	throat	かぎ	key
ひざ	knee	かぜ	wind
からだ	body	えんぴつ	pencil
でんわ	telephone	てんぷら	tempura
ながい	long	ながい うで	long arm
みじかい	short	みじかい ゆび	short finger

Useful Expressions

Thanking, apologizing, and getting attention

Expressions of courtesy are important in every culture. Here are some of the basic ones in Japanese.

ありがとう ございます。

Thank you.

どういたしまして。

You are welcome.

すみません。

I am sorry, excuse me.

（あのう、）すみません。

(Um,) Excuse me.

NOTE

- ございます as in おはよう ございます [ohayoo gozaimasu] and ありがとう ございます [arigatoo gozaimasu] are polite expressions. The more informal おはよう [ohayoo] and ありがとう [arigatoo] are used in casual speech, among peers, but not with older people or with those of a higher social status.

はなして みましょう   Conversation Practice

1. What would you say to your instructor if you forgot your homework?
2. Your instructor is talking to someone. You need to speak to him/her. How would you interrupt the conversation?
3. Your classmates are standing in front of the door. You want to leave the room. What would you say to them?
4. The student sitting next to you picks up the pencil you just dropped. What would you say to him?

VI. Hiragana ああ〜わあ : Long vowels

When the same vowel appears twice consecutively in a word, the two are pronounced as a continuous sound rather than as two separate vowels. This is called a long vowel.

In general, long vowels are written by adding あ to **hiragana** containing the vowel [a], い to **hiragana** containing the vowel [i] or [e], and う to **hiragana** containing the vowel [u] or [o]. Note that when い is added after the vowel [e] it is pronounced as [e]. (See the following chart.) Similarly, when う is added after the [o] sound, it is pronounced as [o]. There are some exceptions in which え and お are added instead of い and う, respectively, but you should not worry about them for now. You can learn them when you learn new vocabulary.

ん	w	r	y	m	h	n	t	s	k		
ん	わあ	らあ	やあ	まあ	はあ	なあ	たあ	さあ	かあ	ああ	aa
		りい		みい	ひい	にい	ちい	しい	きい	いい	ii
		るう	ゆう	むう	ふう	ぬう	つう	すう	くう	うう	uu
		れい		めい	へい	ねい ねえ	てい	せい	けい	えい ええ	ee
	を	ろう	よう	もう	ほう	のう	とう とお	そう	こう こお	おう おお	oo

Reading hiragana

Read the following words, paying attention to long vowels.

せんせい	teacher	がくせい	student
ふうせん	balloon	さとう	sugar
おうさま	king	こうこう	high school
ていねい	polite	とけい	clock, watch
おにいさん	elder brother	いもうと	younger sister
おとうと	younger brother	おとうさん	father
おかあさん	mother	おばあさん	grandmother
おじいさん	grandfather		
ちいさい	small	ちいさい　とけい	small clock, watch

Here are some common exceptions that use え or お for long vowels.

ええ	yes	おねえさん	elder sister
とおり	street	こおり	ice
おおきい	big, large	おおきい　とおり	big street

Useful Expressions

Understanding your instructor's requests

Here are a few common expressions your instructor will use in class. When you hear words you don't understand, try to guess what the teacher is saying from the context or situation or by observing gestures.

きいて　ください。	Please listen.
みて　ください。	Please look.
かいて　ください。	Please write.
よんで　ください。	Please read.
いって　ください。	Please say it/repeat after me.
もう　いちど　いって　ください。	Please say it again.
おおきい　こえで　いって　ください。	Please speak loudly.

はなして　みましょう　Conversation Practice

1. Listen to your instructor's requests and try to determine what he/she wants you to do.
2. Working in pairs, take turns asking each other to perform certain actions, using phrases you know.

VII. Hiragana Small つ : Double Consonants

A small **tsu** つ indicates that the consonant that immediately follows it is preceded by a glottal stop and held for an additional syllable. This is called a double consonant. Double consonants often involve the glottis in speech, but may not necessarily require a full glottal stop. When written in a romanized form, they are indicated by a doubled consonant.

Horizontal writing

Printed style	Handwritten style
っか	っか
っき	っき
っく	っく
っけ	っけ
っこ	っこ

Vertical writing

Printed style			Handwritten style		
っく	っき	っか	っく	っき	っか

Reading hiragana

Read the following words, paying attention to double consonants.

にっき	diary	ざっし	magazine
がっき	musical instrument	せっけん	soap
がっこう	school	はっぱ	leaf
きっぷ	ticket	こっき	national flag
きって	stamp	さっか	writer
ねっとう	boiling water	しっぽ	tail
りっぱな	fine, magnificent	りっぱな　がっこう	fine school

Useful Expressions

Confirming information and making requests

わかりましたか。	*Do you understand (it)?*
はい、わかりました。	*Yes, I understand (it).*
いいえ、わかりません。	*No, I don't understand (it).*

If you have trouble understanding your teacher because he/she speaks too softly or too fast for you, you can make requests using the following phrases.

To hear something repeated:

もう　いちど　おねがいします。

Please say it again. (literally, *Once more, please.*)

> Example: Student :   せんせい、すみません。もう　いちど　おねがいします。
>
> *Excuse me, Professor, could you say that again?*
>
> Teacher: あ、すみません。じゃ、もう　いちど　いいます。
>
> *Oh, sorry. Okay, I'll say it again.*

To hear something spoken more loudly:

おおきい　こえで　おねがいします。

Please speak loudly. (literally, *Loud voice, please*) .

> Example: Student: あのう、すみません。おおきい　こえで　おねがいします。
>
> *Excuse me, Professor, could you say that again a bit louder?*
>
> Teacher: はい、わかりました。
>
> *Okay.*

To hear something spoken more slowly:

もう　すこし　ゆっくり　おねがいします。

Please say it slowly. (literally, *A bit more slowly, please.*)

Example:　Student:　すみません、もう　すこし　ゆっくり
　　　　　　　　　　　おねがいします。

　　　　　　　　　　Excuse me, could you say that once more, a bit more slowly?

　　　　　　Teacher:　はい、わかりました。

　　　　　　　　　　Okay.

NOTES

- These phrases can be used with (あのう、)すみません、which makes your request sound more polite.
- おねがいします is more polite than ～てください (as in いってください) because the latter is a command form. It is more appropriate to use おねがいします with a social superior such as your instructor.

はなして　みましょう Conversation Practice

1. Your instructor says something and checks your comprehension. Respond to him/her.
2. Your instructor says something you don't understand completely because it was spoken too fast, too softly, etc. Make the appropriate request so that you can understand what was said.

VIII. Hiragana きゃ〜ぴょ : Glides

Sounds containing a consonant and [y], such as [kya], [kyu], or [kyo], are called glides. Glides are written with a **hiragana** containing the sound [i] followed by a small や、ゆ、or よ.

ぱ	ば	だ	ざ	が	ん	わ	ら	や	ま	は	な	た	さ	か
ぴ	び	ぢ	じ	ぎ			り		み	ひ	に	ち	し	き
ぷ	ぶ	づ	ず	ぐ			る	ゆ	む	ふ	ぬ	つ	す	く
ぺ	べ	で	ぜ	げ			れ		め	へ	ね	て	せ	け
ぽ	ぼ	ど	ぞ	ご		を	ろ	よ	も	ほ	の	と	そ	こ

[i]

pya	bya	dya	ja zya	gya			rya		mya	hya	nya	cha tya	sya sha	kya
ぴゃ	びゃ	ぢゃ	じゃ	ぎゃ			りゃ		みゃ	ひゃ	にゃ	ちゃ	しゃ	きゃ
pyu	byu	dyu	ju zyu	gyu			ryu		myu	hyu	nyu	chu tyu	syu shu	kyu
ぴゅ	びゅ	ぢゅ	じゅ	ぎゅ			りゅ		みゅ	ひゅ	にゅ	ちゅ	しゅ	きゅ
pyo	byo	dyo	jo zyo	gyo			ryo		myo	hyo	nyo	cho tyo	syo sho	kyo
ぴょ	びょ	ぢょ	じょ	ぎょ			りょ		みょ	ひょ	にょ	ちょ	しょ	きょ

There are some variations in romanization.

Horizontal writing		Vertical writing	
Printed style	**Handwritten style**	**Printed style**	**Handwritten style**
きゃ しゅ ちょ	きゃ しゅ ちょ	き し ち ゃ ゅ ょ	き し ち ゃ ゅ ょ

Reading hiragana

Read the following words, paying attention to glides.

こうちゃ	black tea	きんじょ	neighborhood
でんしゃ	train	ひゃく	one hundred
いしゃ	doctor	さんびゃく	three hundred
しゃしん	photo	りょこう	trip

A glide can be combined with a double consonant.

しゅっぱつ	departure	ちょっかく	right angle
しゃっくり	hiccup	しょっき	tableware

Add あ or う to form a long vowel within a glide.

きょう	today	びょうき	sickness
きゅうり	cucumber	みょうじ	last name
にんぎょう	doll	しょうがつ	New Year's Day
りょう	dormitory	ぎゅうにゅう	milk

Useful Expressions

Asking for Japanese words and English equivalents

1. Asking for a Japanese word

   Look at the objects in your classroom. Is there anything you do not know how to say in Japanese?

If the object is close to you:

これは にほんごで なんと いいますか。
What do you call this in Japanese?

Example: Smith: これは　にほんごで　なんと　いいますか。

What do you call this in Japanese?

Yamada: 「ほん」と／って　いいます。

You call it **hon**.

Smith   **Yamada**

NOTES

- To answer, say　〜と／って　いいます.
- The marks　「」are the equivalent of quotation marks in English.

If the object is close to your interlocutor but at a distance from you:

それは　にほんごで　なんと　いいますか。

What do you call that in Japanese?

Example: Smith: それは　にほんごで　なんと　いいますか。

What do you call that in Japanese?

Yamada: 「いす」と／って　いいます。

You call it **isu**.

Smith   **Yamada**

If the object is at a distance from both you and your interlocutor:

あれは　にほんごで　なんと　いいますか。

What do you call that (over there) in Japanese?

Example: Smith: あれは　にほんごで　なんと　いいますか。

What do you call that (over there) in Japanese?

Yamada: 「でんわ」と／って　いいます。
You call it **denwa.**

Smith   Yamada

Note that これ，それ，and あれ refer only to objects, and never to people.

If you want to know the Japanese word for an object that is out of sight, for something intangible, or for any English word:

〜は　にほんごで　なんと　いいますか。

How do you say 〜 *in Japanese?*

Example: Smith: せんせい、「love」は　にほんごで　なんと　いいますか。

Professor, how do you say "love" in Japanese?

Teacher: 「あい」と／って　いいます。
You say **ai.**

2. Asking for the meaning of a Japanese word or phrase

Do you know what がくせい means? How about だいがく and せんこう？
If you don't understand a Japanese word or expression, ask your instructor or a classmate:

〜って　なんですか。

What does 〜 mean?

Example:　Student:　せんせい、「すいか」って　なんですか。

Professor, *what does* **suika** *mean?*

Teacher:　「Watermelon」です。

It means watermelon.

To give the answer, say 〜です。

はなして　みましょう　Conversation Practice

1. Point at things that you are wearing and ask your instructor how to say them in Japanese.
2. Your instructor is in front of the class and you are sitting at a distance from him/her. What objects are near him/her? Ask your instructor what these objects are called in Japanese.
3. If the classroom has a window, ask your instructor the Japanese word for something you can see outside.
4. Ask your instructor the meanings of the following words: だいがく, せんこう, がくせい, つくえ, こくばん, まど, くるま.

たんご
Vocabulary

Nouns

せんせい	Teacher

Suffixes

～せんせい	Professor ～
～さん	Mr./Mrs./Miss/Ms. ～

Expressions

（あのう、）すみません。   (Um,) Excuse me.

ありがとう ございます。   Thank you.

あれは にほんごで なんと いいますか。 How do you say that (over there) in Japanese?

いいえ、わかりません。   No, I don't understand (it).

いって ください。   Please say it. / Repeat after me.

おおきい こえで おねがいします。   Please speak loudly. (student request)

おおきい こえで いってください。   Please speak loudly. (instructor request)

おはよう。   Good morning. / Hello. (casual)

おはよう ございます。   Good morning. / Hello. (polite)

かいて ください。   Please write.

きいて ください。   Please listen.

これは にほんごで なんと いいますか。   How do you say this in Japanese?

こんにちは。   Good afternoon. / Hello.

こんばんは。   Good evening. / Hello.

さようなら。／さよなら。   Good-bye.

しつれいします。   Good-bye. / Excuse me.

じゃあ、また。   See you later. (literally, Well then, again.)

すみません。   I am sorry. / Excuse me.

それは にほんごで なんと いいますか。   How do you say that in Japanese?

～って なんですか。   What does ～ mean?

～と いいます。／～って いいます。   You say ～, you call it ～.

どういたしまして。   You are welcome.

はい、わかりました。   Yes, I understand it.

はじめまして。　〜です。　どうぞ　よろしく。　　How do you do? I am 〜.

　　Pleased to meet you.

〜は　にほんごで　なんと　いいますか。　　How do you say 〜 in Japanese?

みて　ください。　　Please look at it.

もう　いちど　いってください。　　Please say it again. (instructor request)

もう　いちど　おねがいします。　　Please say it again. (student request)

もう　すこし　ゆっくり　おねがいします。　　Please say it slowly.

よんで　ください。　　Please read.

わかりましたか。　　Do you understand (it)?

Particle

は ＝(わ)

Chapter 2

だいにか

あいさつと じこしょうかい
Greetings and Introductions

Objectives	Meeting people for the first time, introducing people, identifying people, telling time
Vocabulary	Countries, nationalities, languages, year in school and academic status, majors, time expressions
Dialogue	はじめまして *How do you do?*
Japanese Culture	Meeting and greeting people
Grammar	I. Identifying someone or something, using ～は　～です
	II. Asking はい／いいえ questions, using ～は　～ですか
	III. Indicating relationships between nouns with の
	IV. Asking for personal information, using question words
	V. Using も to list and describe similarities
Listening	Listening for key words
Communication	Using あいづち: (attentive feedback) 1; classroom manners
Reading	Using format as a clue

たんご
Vocabulary

Nouns

アジアけんきゅう あじあ	アジア研究	Asian studies
アメリカ あめりか		America, the United States
イギリス いぎりす		England
いちねんせい	一年生	freshman, first-year student (The suffix せい may be dropped.)
いま	今	now
えいご	英語	English
オーストラリア おすとらりあ		Australia
がくせい	学生	student
カナダ かなだ		Canada
かんこく	韓国	South Korea
けいえいがく	経営学	management/business administration
こうがく	工学	engineering
こうこう	高校	high school
ごご	午後	p.m., afternoon
ごぜん	午前	a.m., morning
こちら		this person, this way
さんねんせい	三年生	junior, third-year student (The suffix せい may be dropped.)
しゅっしん	出身	one's native country, hometown, birthplace, alma mater
スペイン すぺいん		Spain
せんこう	専攻	major
だいがく	大学	college, university

だいがくいんせい	大学院生	graduate student
だいがくせい	大学生	college student
たいわん	台湾	Taiwan
ちゅうごく	中国	China
なまえ	名前	name
にねんせい	二年生	sophomore, second-year student (The suffix せい may be dropped.)
にほん	日本	Japan
ビジネス		business
フランス		France
ぶんがく	文学	literature
メキシコ		Mexico
よねんせい	四年生	senior, fourth-year student (The suffix せい may be dropped.)
らいねん	来年	next year
りゅうがくせい	留学生	foreign student
れきし	歴史	history

Pronouns

ぼく	僕	I (normally used by males)
わたし	私	I (used by both males and females)

Copula Verb

です		(to) be

Time Expressions

いちじ	一時	one o'clock
にじ	二時	two o'clock
さんじ	三時	three o'clock
よじ	四時	four o'clock
ごじ	五時	five o'clock
ろくじ	六時	six o'clock

しちじ	七時	seven o'clock
はちじ	八時	eight o'clock
くじ	九時	nine o'clock
じゅうじ	十時	ten o'clock
じゅういちじ	十一時	eleven o'clock
じゅうにじ	十二時	twelve o'clock
はん	半	half past いちじはん 1:30

Question words

どこ		where
どちら		where (more polite than どこ), which way
なに／なん	何	what

Particles

か		question marker
の		noun modifier marker (of), ('s)
は		topic marker
も		similarity marker (also, too)

Prefixes

| お〜 | 御〜 | polite prefix |
| | | おなまえ polite form of なまえ (name) |

Suffixes

〜ご	〜語	language
		にほんご Japanese language
〜じ	〜時	〜 o'clock
〜じん	〜人	-nationality　アメリカじん
〜せい	〜生	-student
		だいがくせい　college student
		いちねんせい　freshman
〜ねん	〜年	year いちねん first year

Interjections

あのう	uh, well . . .
いいえ	no, don't mention it, you're welcome
はい／ええ	yes

Expressions

いいえ、そうじゃありません／ そうじゃないです	No, that's not so
はい／ええ、そうです	Yes, that's so
そうですか	Is that so? I see.
〜から　きました	came from 〜 [casual]
こちらこそ	It is I who should be saying that. Thank you.
〜って　いいます	colloquial version of 〜と　いいます

たんごの　れんしゅう　Vocabulary Practice

A. くに　Countries

Starting with this chapter, loan words (foreign words used in Japanese) will be written in **katakana**. They will have subscripts in hiragana, except for the symbol ー, which indicates a long vowel. For example: コーヒー (*coffee*) is pronounced with an elongated [ko] and an elongated [hi].

B. こくせきと　こくご　Nationalities and languages

Activity 1

In Japanese, identify the countries indicated on the map below, the nationality of the people from each country, and the principal language(s) spoken there.

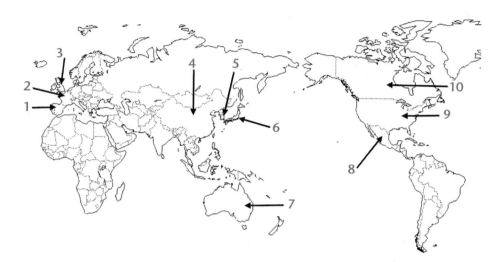

Activity 2

In Japanese, identify the countries represented by the flags below, the nationality of people from each country, and the principal language(s) spoken there.

Activity 3

Identify or guess the language of each of the following greeting phrases.

(a) Good morning.

(b) Bonjour.

(c) Buenos días.

(d) Ni hao?／Zao chen hao.

(e) An nyong haseyo.

(f) おはよう（ございます）。

C. ～ねんせい   Year in school and academic status

1	2	3	4	G
いちねんせい	にねんせい	さんねんせい	よねんせい	だいがくいん せい
freshman	sophomore	junior	senior	graduate student

がくせい	student
りゅうがくせい	international student
だいがく	college
こうこう	high school

Activity 4

Write your answers to the following questions in **hiragana**.

1. いま、なんねんせいですか。 (*Which year are you in now?*)
2. らいねん　なんねんせいですか。(*Which year will you be in next year?*)
3. "high school student" は　にほんごで　なんと　いいますか。
4. "graduate student" は　にほんごで　なんと　いいますか。

D. せんこう   Majors

アジアけんきゅう	Asian studies
けいえいがく	management
こうがく	engineering
ぶんがく	literature
ビジネス	business
れきし	history

Activity 5

Answer the following questions in Japanese.

1. Which of these disciplines are you interested in?
2. Which of these disciplines is the most difficult to learn, in your opinion?
3. Which of these disciplines is the easiest to learn, in your opinion?
4. Do you know how to say your major in Japanese? If not, ask your instructor and write it down.

Supplementary Vocabulary: Academic majors

いがく	医学	medicine (medical science)
おんがく	音楽	music
かがく	化学	chemistry
きょういくがく	教育学	education
けいざいがく	経済学	economics
けんちくがく	建築学	architecture
こくさいかんけい	国際関係	international relations
コンピュータこうがく こんぴゅ　た	コンピュータ工学	computer engineering
しゃかいがく	社会学	sociology
じょうほうかがく	情報科学	information science
じょうほうこうがく	情報工学	information technology
しんりがく	心理学	psychology
じんるいがく	人類学	anthropology
すうがく	数学	mathematics
せいぶつがく	生物学	biology
せいじがく	政治学	political science
びじゅつ	美術	fine arts
ぶつりがく	物理学	physics

E. Time expressions

いちじ　　にじ　　さんじ　　よじ　　ごじ　　ろくじ

しちじ　　はちじ　　くじ　　じゅうじ　　じゅういちじ　　じゅうにじ

じゅうにじはん

You can probably guess how to say the numbers "1" through "12" from the time expressions and academic years presented above. For a complete explanation of Japanese numbers, see Chapter 3, vocabulary practice D (pp. 91–92).

Activity 6

State the time on the following clocks using time + です (*it's ～*).

Example: Q: いま　なんじですか。
What time is it now?

A: いちじです。

1   2   3   4   5

6   7   8   9   10

ダイアローグ
だ い あ ろ ぐ
Dialogue

はじめに　Warm-up

Answer the following questions in English

1. When you meet a Japanese person for the first time, how do you introduce yourself? Do you shake hands?
2. Suppose you have just been introduced to your host family in Japan. What kinds of things would you talk about?

リー　　　アリスうえだ
り　　　　あ り す

はじめまして　*How do you do?*

Alice Ueda, a Japanese-American student, is attending an orientation session at the International Student Center at Joto University in Tokyo. A student sitting next to Ueda speaks to her.

リー：　あのう、すみません。いま　なんじですか。
り

うえだ：　いちじですよ。

リー：　いちじですか。どうも　ありがとう　ございます。
り

うえだ：　いいえ。

リー：　あのう。
り

うえだ：　はい。

リー：　おなまえは　なんですか。ぼく、リーって　いいます。
り　　　　　　　　　　　　　　　　　　　　り

どうぞ　よろしく。

うえだ：こちらこそ　どうぞ　よろしく。わたしの　なまえは

アリス　うえだです。
　　　ありす

リー：ああ、そうですか。ぼくは　たいわんから　きました。
り

うえださんは？

うえだ：シカゴです。わたしは　ウエストサイドだいがくの
　　　しかご　　　　　　　　うえすとさいど

さんねんせいです。

リー：そうですか。ぼくも　さんねんせいです。
り

せんこうは　なんですか。

うえだ：ぶんがくです。リーさんは？
　　　　　　　り

リー：ぼくは　れきしです。
り

An International Student Center staff member and a Japanese man approach them.

りゅうがくせいセンターの　ひと (International Student Center staff member)：
　　　　　　　せんた

うえださんですか。

うえだ：ええ、そうです。

りゅうがくせいセンターの　ひと：すずきさん、こちらは
　　　　　　　せんた

うえださんです。うえださん、こちらは

ホストファミリーの　すずきさんです。
ほすとふぁみり

うえだ：はじめまして。　アリスです。　どうぞ　よろしく。
　　　　　　　　　　ありす

すずき：すずきです。　こちらこそ、よろしく。

DIALOGUE PHRASE NOTES

- The particle よ (*I tell you*) in いちじですよ indicates the speaker's assertion and mild emphasis that he/she is providing information known to him/her but not to the listener.

- どうも can have many meanings. In the dialogue どうも means *very much*, so どうも　ありがとう　ございます (*thank you very much*) expresses a deeper appreciation than ありがとう ございます (*thank you*).

- いいえ means *no*, but in the above dialogue, it means *don't mention it* or *you are welcome*, as in いいえ、どういたしまして. This usage of いいえ is common in Japanese conversation.

- あのう is a hesitation marker. It expresses the speaker's reluctance to bother the person to whom he/she is speaking. This hesitation shows the speaker's respect and consideration for the person he/she is approaching. It can appear by itself as in the dialogue, or with other phrases such as あのう、すみません as in Chapter 1.

- ～と／って　いいます (*[something/someone] is called* ～) was introduced in Chapter 1. This phrase can be used in self-introductions, as in the dialogue.

- ああ、そうですか (*oh, I see*) and そうですか (*I see / is that so?*) is used by the speaker to acknowledge that he/she has understood what has been said. ああ may also be used as a shorter way to convey the same meaning.

ダイアローグの　あとで   Comprehension
だ い あ ろ 　ぐ

Complete the chart with information about Alice and Li.

	くに／まち Country/city	～ ねんせい Year in college	せんこう Major
うえだ			
リー り			

にほんの　ぶんか
Japanese Culture

First name or last name?

How do you address your friends and classmates? How about your professors?

When you meet a Japanese adult for the first time, use your last name when introducing yourself. Also, it is not customary to use a Japanese adult's first name, especially when the person is older or higher in social status. However, it is not uncommon to find close friends calling each other by their first names. Since many Japanese are aware that Westerners usually use first names, a foreign student may be addressed by his/her first name, followed by さん, as in クリスさん . In family settings, older family members address younger ones by their first names, though younger family members do not use the first names of older members. Instead, they use kinship terms such as mother, father, older brother, and older sister. When a foreign student stays with a Japanese host family, the parents will call the student either by his/her first name only, or will use the first name with さん. The host sisters or brothers will most likely use first name + さん. In general, senior members are referred to by kinship terms and junior members by their first name plus さん (unisex), くん (for a young boy) or ちゃん (for small children). When in doubt, ask the members of the host family how they want to be addressed.

Bowing? Shaking hands?

Why didn't Suzuki shake hands with Alice Ueda when he was introduced to her?

To be on the safe side, always bow when meeting a Japanese adult for the first time. Bow with your feet together, bending about fifteen degrees from your waist. Drop your eyes as you bow. You may bow more deeply and more than once if you wish to show greater respect. Shaking hands is not customary in Japan, but if someone extends his or her hand, then respond accordingly. Do not squeeze the person's hand too firmly.

名刺 (business cards)
Who uses めいし*? When and how do people exchange* めいし*?*

In Japan, exchanging business cards is an important part of the ritual of meeting people for the first time. Professionals always have business cards, as do many graduate students. Undergraduate students usually do not have them since they are not considered full-fledged members of adult society. When a person expected to have a card does not have one on hand, he/she usually apologizes for his/her oversight. A person given a name card takes it with both hands. It is important to read the card carefully in order to identify the person's title or position and the name of the organization to which he/she belongs. Such information is considered essential in socializing with the proper degree of formality or politeness.

ぶんぽう
Grammar

I. Identifying someone or something, using 〜は　〜です

The sentences X は Y です (*X is Y*) and X は Y じゃありません／じゃないです (*X isn't Y*) are used to identify or characterize a person or thing. Japanese uses particles in addition to nouns, verbs, adjectives, etc. Particles most often consist of one character (sometimes two), and they are placed immediately after a noun or at the end of a sentence. Those particles that appear after nouns assign a grammatical function to the noun they follow. Those that appear at the end of a sentence indicate the function of the preceding sentence or the speaker's attitudes or emotions. は, which is pronounced *wa*, indicates that the preceding noun X is the topic of the sentence.

Affirmative

Topic		Comment	
Noun	Particle (Topic)	Noun	Copula Verb
たなかさん	は	さんねんせい	です。

Mr. Tanaka is a junior.

Negative

Topic		Comment	
Noun	Particle (Topic)	Noun	Copula Verb
すずきさん	は	りゅうがくせい	じゃありません。 じゃないです。

Mr./Ms. Suzuki is not an international student.

In the above example sentences, the topic Xは represents information already known to both the speaker and the listener. Yです is a comment about the topic. That is, Y represents information concerning the topic X. For example, in the sentence たなかさんは　さんねんせいです。 (*Mr./Ms. Tanaka is a junior.*), たなかさん is what the speaker wants to talk about, or the topic, and さんねんせい is what the speaker wants to say about the topic.

わたしは　いちねんせいです。でも、たなかさんは
　　いちねんせいじゃありません。

I am a freshman, but Ms./Mr. Tanaka is not a freshman.

ロペスさんは　メキシコ じんです。がくせいです。
ろ ぺ す　　　め き し こ

Mr./Ms. Lopez is Mexican. He/she is a student.

モネさんは　だいがくいんせいです。リーさんは
も ね　　　　　　　　　　　　　　　　り

だいがくいんせいじゃありません。

Mr./Ms. Monet is a graduate student, but Mr./Ms. Li is not.

NOTES

- The topic X は can be omitted if the speaker thinks the listener can identify what it is from the context. For example, わたしは is omitted in greetings such as はじめまして　〜です。どうぞよろしく, because it is obvious that the speaker is talking about himself/herself.
- です and じゃありません／じゃないです do not change form according to either the number of persons or things being discussed or the voice (first person, second person, or third person) of the subject. Compare the following Japanese and English sentences.

    わたしは　だいがくせい<u>です</u>。
    I <u>am</u> a college student.

    うえださんは　だいがくせい<u>です</u>。
    Ms. Ueda <u>is</u> a college student.

    わたしたちは　だいがくせい<u>です</u>。
    We <u>are</u> college students.

- じゃないです is more colloquial than じゃありません.
- While the English verb *to be* sometimes indicates location, such as *Tokyo is in Japan*, です and じゃありません／じゃないです do not.

はなして　みましょう　Conversation Practice

Activity 1

Imagine that the following people live in your dormitory. Work with a partner and tell him/her about each person.

Example:　たなかさんは　<u>にほんじん</u>です。
　　　　　　<u>だいがくいんせい</u>です。
　　　　　　せんこうは　<u>かんこくご</u>です。

Name	Nationality	Year in school	Major
たなか	にほんじん	だいがくいんせい	かんこくご
リー り	ちゅうごくじん	だいがくいんせい	アジアけんきゅう あじあ
ブラウン ぶらうん	オーストラリアじん お　すとらりあ	よねんせい	ビジネス びじねす
スミス すみす	アメリカじん あめりか	さんねんせい	こうがく
キム きむ	かんこくじん	にねんせい	フランスご ふらんす
モネ もね	カナダじん かなだ	いちねんせい	ぶんがく

Activity 2

Complete the following chart by circling the appropriate words and by writing in your major (and nationality, if necessary) in Japanese.

Your name	
Status	だいがくせい　だいがくいんせい
Major	
Year	いちねんせい　にねんせい　さんねんせい よねんせい　だいがくいんせい
Nationality	アメリカじん　ちゅうごくじん　かんこくじん あめりか ＿＿＿＿＿じん

Activity 3

Introduce yourself to your partner and describe yourself using the words in Activity 2 and the X は Y です pattern.

Example: はじめまして。   (your name)   です。どうぞ　よろしく。

（わたしは）   (college student/graduate student)   です。
(year)   せいです。

せんこうは ＿＿＿＿＿です。わたしは (nationality) じんです。

Now listen to your partner's self-introduction and complete the following chart.

Partner's name	
Status	
Major	
Year	
Nationality	

Activity 4

Introduce a partner and yourself to another classmate.

Example: わたしは＿＿＿＿＿＿です。＿＿＿＿＿＿じんです。
＿＿＿＿＿＿せいです。

せんこうは＿＿＿＿＿＿です。
こちらは＿＿＿＿＿さんです。

＿＿＿さんは＿＿＿＿＿じゃありません／じゃないです。
＿＿＿＿＿です。

II. Asking はい／いいえ questions, using 〜は　〜ですか

It is very easy to formulate questions in Japanese. All you have to do is add the particle か to the end of the sentence.

Asking the listener's identity

Question				Answer		
	Copula Verb	Particle				Copula Verb
すずきさん	です	か。		はい／ええ、	そう	です。

Are you Mr./Ms. Suzuki?   *Yes, I am.*

Asking about people and things

Question		Particle
キムさんは　かんこくじんです		か。

(きむ)

Is Mr./Ms. Kim Korean? /Are you Korean, Mr./Ms. Kim?

Affirmative Answer				Affirmative Answer		
		Copula Verb				Copula Verb
はい／ええ、	そう	です。		はい／ええ、	かんこくじん	です。

Yes, he/she is. / Yes, I am.   *Yes, he/she is Korean. / Yes, I am Korean.*

(literally, *Yes, it is so.*)

Negative Answer				Negative Answer		
		Copula Verb				Copula Verb
いいえ、	そう	じゃありません。 じゃないです。		いいえ、	イギリスじん (いぎりす)	です。

No, he/she isn't. (literally, *No, it isn't so.*)   *No, I am British.*

おおき：　うえださんですか。   *Are you Ms. Ueda?*

うえだ：　はい、そうです。   *Yes, I am.*

おおき：　うえださんは　にほんじんですか。   *Are you Japanese, Ms. Ueda?*

うえだ：　いいえ、アメリカじんです。   *No, I'm American.*

(あめりか)

NOTES

- The Japanese pronoun あなた, although it is equivalent to *you*, is not used as commonly as its English counterpart. It is more common to use the name of the person being addressed. Thus, アリスさんは　がくせいですか can mean either *Are you a student, Alice?* or *Is Alice a student?* depending on whether you are talking to Alice or someone else.

あ　り　す

- はい／ええ、そうです is an affirmative answer to questions, and means *Yes, I am / you are / it is / he/she is / they are / we are*. いいえ、そうじゃありません／いいえ、そうじゃないです is a negative answer, and it means *No, I'm not / you aren't / it isn't / he/she isn't / they aren't / we aren't*.

はなして　みましょう　Conversation Practice

Activity 1

Answer the following questions, using ええ、そうです or いいえ、そうじゃありません／いいえ、そうじゃないです.

Example:　がくせいですか。　　　ええ、そうです。

1. がっこうは　ウエストサイドだいがくですか。

　　　　　　　　う　え　す　と　さ　い　ど
2. いちねんせいですか。
3. せんこうは　にほんごですか。
4. アメリカじんですか。

　　あ　め　り　か
5. りゅうがくせいですか。
6. せんせいは　にほんじんですか。

Activity 2

Find out how many of your classmates are in the same year of school as you by asking 〜さんは　〜ですか. Also, find out how many have the same major as you.

Example:　A:　<u>たなか</u>さんは　<u>いちねんせい</u>ですか。

　　　　　B:　ええ、そうです。／いいえ、そうじゃありません／
　　　　　　　いいえ、そうじゃないです。

　　　　　A:　そうですか。せんこうは　<u>にほんご</u>ですか。

　　　　　B:　ええ、そうです。／いいえ、そうじゃありません／
　　　　　　　いいえ、そうじゃないです。

Activity 3

Work with a partner. Choose an identity from the chart below, but don't tell your partner. Your partner will try to guess who you are by asking questions using 〜は　〜ですか. Answer with ええ、そうです or いいえ、 そうじゃありません／いいえ、そうじゃないです.

Examples:　A:　にほんじんですか。

B:　いいえ、そうじゃありません。

A:　アメリカじんですか。

B:　ええ、そうです。

A:　せんこうは　えいごですか。

B:　ええ、そうです。

A:　スミスさんですか。

B:　ええ、そうです。

Name	Nationality	Year in school	Major
スミス	アメリカじん	さんねんせい	えいご
ブラウン	アメリカじん	いちねんせい	アジアけんきゅう
ロペス	アメリカじん	にねんせい	ぶんがく
ジョンソン	アメリカじん	だいがくいんせい	ビジネス
ハート	アメリカじん	よねんせい	スペインご
たなか	にほんじん	いちねんせい	スペインご
やまだ	にほんじん	だいがくいんせい	けいえいがく
さとう	にほんじん	にねんせい	こうがく
もり	にほんじん	よねんせい	ぶんがく
すずき	にほんじん	さんねんせい	アジアけんきゅう

III. Indicating relationships between nouns with の

The particle の allows the first noun in a phrase to modify the second noun. Because の can convey a variety of relationships between two nouns, such as possession, group membership, or location, the particle's meaning depends on the context.

とうきょうだいがくの	リーさん	Mr./Ms. Li from Tokyo University
とうきょうだいがくの	がくせい	student at Tokyo University
わたしの	せんこう	my major
れきしの	せんこう	history major
わたしの	せんせい	my teacher
せんせいの	ほん	teacher's book; book written by the teacher
メキシコの	うち	house in Mexico
にほんの	ほん	book about Japan; book from Japan
にほんごの	ほん	book written in Japanese; book about Japanese
とうきょうの	おかださん	Mr./Ms.Okada who lives in Tokyo; Mr./Ms. Okada who is from Tokyo

すずき：はじめまして。すずきです。
How do you do? I'm Suzuki.

きむら：はじめまして。りゅうがくせいセンターの　きむらです。
How do you do? I'm Kimura of the International Student Center.
うえださん、こちらは　うえださんの　ホストファミリーの
すずきさんです。
Ms. Ueda, this is Mr. Suzuki from your host family.

うえだ：はじめまして。アリス　うえだです。どうぞ　よろしく。
How do you do? I'm Alice Ueda. Pleased to meet you.

すずき：こちらこそ。よろしく。
Same here.

たなか：ロペスさんの　せんこうは　ビジネスですか。
Is your major economics, Mr./Ms. Lopez?

ロペス：いいえ。　わたしは　こうがくの　せんこうです。
No. I'm an engineering major.

NOTES

- Possessive pronouns in English consist of one word, as in *my*, but the equivalent forms of Japanese consist of a pronoun followed by の, as in わたし/ぼく＋ の. Also, the semantic relationship between the modifier and the word being modified is not always clear in this structure. The relationship depends on context and the meanings of the two nouns. For example, in the phrase たなかせんせいの ほん, Professor Tanaka may be the author or the owner of the book.
- The appositive relationship can also be expressed with の . The following example is translated into English as *Mr. Suzuki from my host family*. In contrast, すずきさんの ホストファミリー is interpreted as *Mr. Suzuki's host family*.

ホストファミリーの　すずきさん	*Mr. Suzuki, who is in (my) host family*
すずきさんの　ホストファミリー	*Mr. Suzuki's host family*

はなして みましょう　Conversation Practice

Activity 1

Pretend that you are the moderator of a panel discussion on environmental protection. Introduce the following experts using Noun の Noun.

Dr. Yamada University of Chicago

Mr. Kimura ASUKA, Inc.

Dr. Tanaka University of Tokyo

Mr. Sato HAL Japan

Example:　（やまだ）

こちらは　シカゴだいがくの　やまだせんせいです。

Activity 2

You meet a student from another school. Introduce yourself in terms of your school by using Noun の Noun.

Example: はじめまして。（わたしは）_____だいがくの

_____です。

Activity 3

Complete the following dialogue, using the information from the chart below.

Example: A: たなかさんの　せんこうは　えいごですか。

B: いいえ、そうじゃありません。かんこくごです。

Name	School	Major
たなか	とうきょうだいがく	かんこくご
リー り	にほんだいがく	アジアけんきゅう あ じ あ
ケリー け り	UCLA	ビジネス び じ ね す
スミス す み す	ハワイだいがく は わ い	こうがく
キム き む	ヨンセイだいがく よ ん せ い	ぶんがく

1. A: _____の　せんこうは　アジアけんきゅうですか。
   あ じ あ

   B: ええ、そうです。

2. A: ケリーさんは　アジアけんきゅうの_____ですか。
   け り　　　　　　　　あ じ あ

   B: いいえ、ビジネスの　がくせいです。
   　　　　　　び じ ね す

3. A: スミスさんの_____は　ハワイだいがくですか。
   す み す　　　　　　　　　　　　　は わ い

   B: ええ、そうです。

4. A: キム さんは_____の　せんこうですか。
   き む

   B: ええ、そうです。

Activity 4

Use Noun のNoun to tell a classmate your friend's name, school, and major.

Example: _____さんは　わたしの　ともだち (friend) です。

_____さんの　だいがくは_____だいがくです。

せんこうは_____です。

IV. Asking for personal information, using question words

In Japanese, you don't have to change the word order of a sentence to form an information question. All you have to do is to use a question word, such as なん (*what*) or どこ (*where*), for things you want to ask about.

Asking about names and things, using なん

Question			Answer
	Question Word		
おなまえは	なん	ですか。	アリスです。
			あ り す

What is your name?   *I am Alice.*

Question			Answer
	Question Word + Suffix		
キムさんは	なんねんせい	ですか。	さんねんせいです。
き む			

What year are you in, Mr./Ms. Kim?   *I am a junior.*

Question			Answer
	Question Word + Suffix		
いま	なんじ	ですか。	さんじです。

What time is it now?   *It's 3 o'clock.*

> もり ： すみません。いま なんじですか。
> *Excuse me. What time is it?*
>
> すずき ： よじはんですよ。
> *It's 4:30.*
>
> もり ： そうですか。どうも。
> *Oh, is it? Thanks.*
>
> すずき ： いいえ。
> *You're welcome.*

To specify a.m. and p.m., add ごぜん (a.m.) or ごご (p.m.) in front of the time expression.

> とうきょうは　いま　<u>ごぜん</u>　じゅうじです。
> *In Tokyo it is 10 <u>a.m.</u> now.*
>
> ニューヨークは　<u>ごご</u>　ろくじはんです。
> に ゅ よ く
> *It is 6:30 <u>p.m.</u> in New York.*

Using どこ and どちら to ask about places

Question				Answer		
Question word (place)	Particle			Noun (place)	Particle	
どこ	から	きましたか。		にほん	から	きました。

Where are you from?
(literally, *Where did you come from?*)

I'm from Japan.
(literally, *I came from Japan.*)

やまだ： ソフィさんは　どこから　きましたか。
そ ふ ぃ
Sophie, where are you from?

ソフィー： カナダから　きました。
そ ふ ぃ ー　 か な だ
I'm from Canada.

やまだ： そうですか。なんねんせいですか。
I see. What year are you in?

ソフィー： いちねんせいです。やまださんは？
そ ふ ぃ
First year. How about you, Mr./Ms. Yamada?

やまだ： わたしは　にねんせいです。
I am a sophomore.

Notes

- In Japanese, a question word cannot be used as a topic or come before the particle は. It is a part of the です half of the sentence, and replaces the word that is in question. For example:

  やまだ： たなかさんは　なんねんせいですか。
  What year are you in, Mr./Ms. Tanaka?

  たなか： わたしは　いちねんせいです。
  I'm a freshman.

- どこから　きましたか。 is a way of asking about someone's hometown, home state, or native country. から is a particle that means *from*. きました is the past tense form of the verb きます (*come*). In formal situations use the more polite どちらから いらっしゃいましたか (*where are you from*). When answering this more formal question, however, you should always use きました, and not いらっしゃいました.

- To find out the name of someone's school, use どこ. For example,
やまださんの　だいがくは　どこですか。asks for the name of
a school, and not the location of the school.

  A:　やまださんの　だいがくは　どこですか。
  Where do you go to school, Mr./Ms. Yamada?

  B:　とうきょうだいがくです。
  I go to the University of Tokyo.

  Do not use なんですか to ask for the name of a school:

  やまださんの　だいがくは　なんですか。

はなして　みましょう　Conversation Practice

Activity 1

Begin a dialogue by asking a question that corresponds to each of the following answers.

Example:　スミスです。
　　　　　すみす

　　　　あのう、おなまえは　なんですか。

1.　メキシコから　きました。
　　めきしこ

2.　アジアけんきゅうです。
　　あじあ

3.　リーです。
　　り

4.　さんねんせいです。

5.　フランスごです。
　　ふらんす

6.　よじです。

7.　だいがくいんせいです。

8.　じょうとうだいがくです。

Activity 2

Ask your classmates about their majors and hometowns. Is there anyone who is majoring in the same subject as you?

Example:　A:　_____さんの　せんこうは　なんですか。

　　　　　B:　_____です。～さんは？

　　　　　A:　わたしの　せんこうは_____です。

　　　　　B:　ああ、そうですか。

Activity 3

Ask your classmates and your instructor about their majors and hometowns. Find out who comes from the most distant place.

Example: A: ＿＿＿＿＿さんは　どこから　きましたか。

B: ＿＿＿＿＿から　きました。〜さんは？

A: ＿＿＿＿＿から　きました。

B: ああ、そうですか。

Activity 4

Work with a partner. Look at the map of world and ask each other what time it is in various cities.

Example: とうきょう (Tokyo)

A: とうきょうは　いま　なんじですか。

B: ごぜん　じゅういちじですよ。

A: そうですか。

1. ニューヨーク (New York)
   にゅ　よ　く
2. ホノルル (Honolulu)
   ほ　の　る　る
3. シドニー (Sydney)
   し　ど　に
4. モスクワ (Moscow)
   も　す　く　わ
5. バンクーバー (Vancouver)
   ばん　く　　ば
6. ロンドン (London)
   ろ　ん　ど　ん
7. バンコク (Bangkok)
   ばん　こ　く
8. デリー (Delhi)
   で　り
9. カイロ (Cairo)
   か　い　ろ

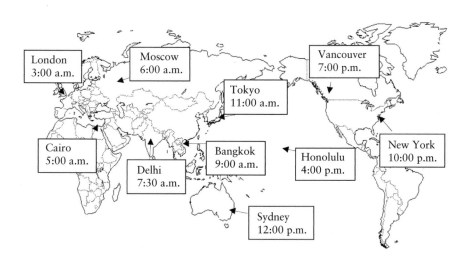

London 3:00 a.m.
Moscow 6:00 a.m.
Vancouver 7:00 p.m.
Tokyo 11:00 a.m.
Cairo 5:00 a.m.
Delhi 7:30 a.m.
Bangkok 9:00 a.m.
Honolulu 4:00 p.m.
New York 10:00 p.m.
Sydney 12:00 p.m.

Activity 5

Work with a partner. You are traveling through a number of cities in the United States. Ask your partner what time it is in the city you are in now. The reference time indicates the current time in the last city you visited. Your partner will have to compute the time for the city you are asking about based on the reference time.

Example: Reference time: 7:30 a.m. EST
City you are in now: Chicago

A: あのう、すみません。いま　なんじですか。

B: ろくじはんですよ。

A: ああ、そうですか。どうも　ありがとうございます。

B: いいえ。

1. 7:30 p.m. EST, Denver
2. 9:00 a.m. CST, Seattle
3. 8:30 p.m. CST, New York
4. 2:30 p.m. MST, Anchorage
5. 1:00 p.m. MST., Atlanta
6. 11:30 p.m. PST, Salt Lake City
7. 1:30 a.m. PST, Honolulu
8. 11:00 p.m. PST, Boston

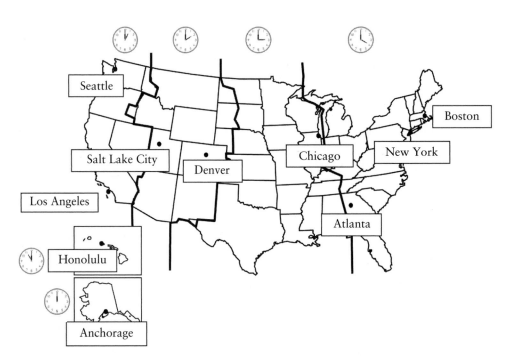

V. Using も to list and describe similarities

The particle も means *also* or *too*, and it is used to show the similarity between what has been just said and what you are saying.

Sentence 1		
	Particle	
わたしの　こうこう	は	ミルズ　ハイスクールです。 みるず　　はいすくーる

My high school is Mills High School.

Sentence 2		
Noun Phrase	Particle	
トムさんの　こうこう とむ	も	ミルズ　ハイスクールです。 みるず　　はいすくーる

Tom's high school is also Mills High School.

うえだ： キムさんは　にほんごの　がくせいですか。
きむ

Are you a Japanese major, Mr./Ms. Kim? (literally, are you a student of Japanese?)

キム： ええ、そうですよ。うえださんは？
きむ

Yes, I am. How about you, Ms. Ueda?

うえだ： わたしも　にほんごの　せんこうですよ。

I am a Japanese major, too.

キム： ああ、そうですか。
きむ

Oh, is that so?

やまだ： すずきさんは　どこから　きましたか。

Ms. Suzuki, where are you from?

すずき： とうきょうから　きました。

I'm from Tokyo.

やまだ： そうですか。ぼくも　とうきょうから　きました。

Is that so? I'm from Tokyo, too.

すずき： ああ、そうですか。とうきょうの　どこですか。

Oh, really. Where in Tokyo?

やまだ： あさくさです。

Asakusa.

はなして みましょう   Conversation Practice

Activity 1

Work with a partner. The following is a list of new students at the International Student Center. Introduce one of the students to your partner, and your partner will then introduce you to a student who shares the trait you have just described in the first introduction. Take turns making the introductions.

Example 1: A: こちらは　キムさんです。キムさんは　フランスごの
がくせいです。

B: こちらは　ロペスさんです。ロペス さんも
フランスごの　せんこうです。

Example 2: A: こちらは　ワットさんです。ワットさんは
イギリスから きました。

B: こちらは　モリスさんです。モリスさんも
イギリスじんですよ。

Name	Country /Nationality	Year in school	Major
キム	かんこく	いちねんせい	フランスご
イー	かんこく	だいがくいんせい	ぶんがく
リー	ちゅうごく	よねんせい	こうがく
チョー	ちゅうごく	にねんせい	かんこくご
ブラウン	オーストラリア	さんねんせい	れきし
スミス	オーストラリア	にねんせい	かんこくご
ロペス	メキシコ	よねんせい	フランスご
ガルシア	メキシコ	だいがくいんせい	こうがく
ワット	イギリス	いちねんせい	れきし
モリス	イギリス	さんねんせい	ぶんがく

Activity 2

Work with the class. Find a person who went to the same high school you attended.

Example: A: わたしの　こうこうは　セントラル　ハイスクールです。
せんとらる　はいすくーる

　　　　　　～さんの　こうこうは　どこですか。

B: わたしの　こうこうも　セントラル　ハイスクールです。
せんとらる　はいすくーる

or　わたしの　こうこうは　ミルズ　ハイスクールです。
みるず　はいすくーる

Activity 3

Work with a partner. Ask your partner the time in the cities on the list.

Example 1:　ペキン (Beijing)　ホンコン (Hong Kong)
ぺきん　　　　　　ほんこん

A: ペキンは　いま　なんじですか。
ぺきん

B: じゅういちじですよ。

A: そうですか。じゃあ、ホンコンは　いま
ほんこん
なんじですか。

B: ホンコンも　じゅういちじですよ。
ほんこん

Example 2:　ペキン (Beijing)　バンコク (Bangkok)
ぺきん　　　　　　ばんこく

A: ペキンは　いま　なんじですか。
ぺきん

B: じゅういちじですよ。

A: そうですか。じゃあ、バンコクは　いま
ばんこく
なんじですか。

B: バンコクは　じゅうじですよ。
ばんこく

1. シドニー (Sydney)　　　グアム (Guam)
　　しどに　　　　　　　　　ぐあむ

2. とうきょう　　　　　　タイペイ (Taipei)
　　　　　　　　　　　　　　たいぺい

3. ペキン (Beijing)　　　タイペイ
　　ぺきん　　　　　　　　たいぺい

4. タイペイ　　　　　　　ホンコン (Hong Kong)
　　たいぺい　　　　　　　ほんこん

5. とうきょう　　　　　　ソウル (Seoul)
　　　　　　　　　　　　　そうる

6. ホンコン (Hong Kong)　バンコク (Bangkok)
　　ほんこん　　　　　　　ばんこく

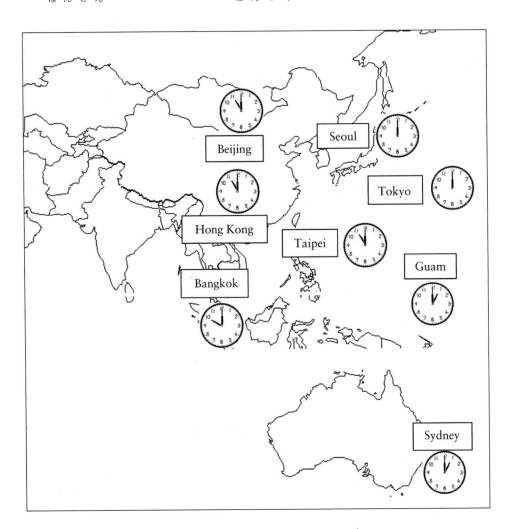

きく　れんしゅう
Listening

じょうずな　ききかた　Listening Strategy

Listening for key words

Listening comprehension passages for this section contain some unknown expressions and words so that you can develop skills to deal with real-life situations in which you may not understand every word. You may be surprised to find that natural speech is very redundant and that it is really not important to understand every single word. Try to focus on key words without worrying too much about the rest. For example, when someone is introduced to you, the most important word to understand is the person's name. Don't worry about the rest; just relax and listen.

きく　まえに　Warm-up

Listen to the dialogue and write the names of the two people who are being introduced

(handwritten:) きむらさん
ブラウンさん

ことばの　リスト　Vocabulary
りすと

むすめ	(speaker's) daughter
ちち	(speaker's) father
はは	(speaker's) mother

れんしゅう Practice

すずきさんの　むすめさん Mr. Suzuki's daughter

Read the statements below, then listen for the key words in the dialogue. Circle はい or いいえ, according to what you understood.

Situation: Remember that Alice and Mr. Suzuki already met in the main dialogue on page 42. Mr. Suzuki's daughter is standing next to him. He introduces her to Alice.

1. The name of Mr. Suzuki's daughter is Michiko.　(はい)　いいえ
2. Mr. Suzuki's daughter is a sophomore at Joto University.　はい　(いいえ)
3. Mr. Suzuki's daughter is majoring in economics.　はい　(いいえ)
4. Alice's father is Japanese.　(はい)　いいえ

ききじょうず　はなしじょうず
Communication

Communication Strategy

Using あいづち (attentive feedback) 1

Being a good listener is one of the most important factors in communicating effectively in any language, but the strategies for being a good listener differ considerably between languages. For example, the Japanese tend to avoid frequent or prolonged eye contact, because they do not think that making eye contact indicates a person's interest in the conversation. A Japanese person will tend to feel intimidated or uneasy after prolonged eye contact, so it's a good idea to look away from time to time. Instead of eye contact, Japanese speakers use various other forms of feedback when they are listening. For example, they nod occasionally to show attentiveness. For this reason, Japanese students often nod in the classroom. Another common type of feedback is the frequent use of ええ or はい, which both mean *yes*. These expressions do not necessarily indicate agreement. They simply mean that the person is listening to you. If the listener remains silent even though he/she is looking at the speaker, the speaker may consider the listener to be impolite, cold, or even uninterested. In Japanese, feedback given to confirm attentive listening is called あいづち.

Classroom Manners

It is considered inappropriate to eat or drink in the classroom in Japan. Equally inappropriate is putting one's feet or legs up on a chair or desk. Japanese instructors who are not used to such behavior may think these acts show a lack of seriousness or boredom on the part of the student.

れんしゅう Practice

1. Listen to your instructor talk about himself/herself. Sit up straight and nod occasionally to indicate interest while listening.
2. Work with a partner. Tell him/her about a friend. While listening, your partner should nod or say ええ or はい between sentences. Avoid making eye contact.

よむ　れんしゅう
Reading

じょうずな　よみかた　Reading Strategy

Using format as a clue

めいし are generally written in **kanji** and **katakana**, and for a beginning student of Japanese, it may seem impossible to make any sense of them. Nevertheless, it is possible to identify a few facts if you know what to look for, and this is a very important first step in improving your reading skills.

The information provided on めいし typically includes name, position or title, the relevant employer or organization, address, phone and fax numbers, e-mail address, and web address. The information always follows a certain format. For example, the name appears in the center, and the organization and title will be next to or above the name.

よむ　まえに　Pre-reading

1. Look at the horizontally formatted card and circle the telephone number and the name of the organization.
2. Look at the other card. Although it is written vertically, the basic format is the same as that of the first card. The second card is read from right to left. Circle the name of the card owner and the address.

インターネット　ジャパン　Inc.

代表取締役
クリシュナ・カーン

1234 Main Street Suite #100, Portland, OR 87654
TEL: (123) 456-7890 FAX: (123)456-7891

帝都大学文学部
英米文学科

教授

山本　太郎

勤務先
東京都八王子市中央一ノ一
電話（〇一二三）三八一五一一番

自宅
東京都八王子市朝日町一〇ノ五ノ一
電話（〇一二三）三八一四六七九番

れんしゅう Practice

ともだち　ぼしゅう　Looking for a friend

Japanese is usually written in **hiragana, katakana,** and **kanji** as appropriate. Printed Japanese is unlike English in that there are usually no spaces between words. The text in the reading section of this book utilizes all three scripts rather than being limited to **hiragana** and **katakana,** so that you can become familiar with normal written Japanese.

The following are short introductory messages placed on a web page for people who are looking for pen pals. Read the messages and answer the following questions.

ことばの　リスト Vocabulary

ネイティブ	native (speaker)
〜を　さがしています	to be looking for 〜

Message 1

はじめまして！　私は東京大学の学生です。なまえはけいこ
です。専攻は英語です。今一年生です。英語のネイティブの友達を
さがしています。どうぞよろしく。

Message 2

はじめまして。僕はたかしです。千葉大学の三年生です。専攻は
アジアとアメリカの歴史です。どうぞよろしく。

Message 3

はじめまして。私はヤン・リーと言います。中国から来ました。京都
の留学生です。日本文学の専攻です。二年生です。友達をさがしてい
ます。よろしく。

Message 4

はじめまして。僕はリチャードです。オーストラリアのシドニーから
来ました。今、大阪大学の四年生です。ビジネスの専攻です。よろしく。

よんだ　あとで　Comprehension

1. Complete the following with information about the four people who posted the messages above. Don't worry about writing **kanji** or **katakana**.

Message 1

Name ___けいこ___

School ___とうきょうだいがく___

Year ___一年生___

Major ___英語___

Hometown/country
 (if mentioned) _____

Message 2

Name ___たかし___

School ___ちば大学___

Year ___三年生___

Major ___アジアとアメリカのれきし___

Hometown/country
 if mentioned) _____

Message 3

Name ___ヤン・リー___

School ___きょとだいがく___

Year ___二年生___

Major ___日本文学___

Hometown/country
 (if mentioned) ___中国___

Message 4

Name ___Richard___

School ___おおさかだいがく___

Year ___4___

Major _____

Hometown/country
 (if mentioned) ___Sydney, Australia___

2. Are there any similarities between you and any of the four people? If there are, describe them.

Example:　　わたしは　いちねんせいです。　けいこさんも
　　　　　　いちねんせいです。

3. Select one person from the list and write a message to him/her to introduce yourself. If you have yet to decide on a major, write (せんこうは)まだ わかりません, meaning "I don't know my major yet."

そうごう　れんしゅう
Integration

インタビュー Interview
いんたびゅ

1. Ask your classmates about their name, major, year in school, hometown, high school, and country of origin. Write the phrase you will use to greet them, and then make a list of questions to ask. Next, ask the questions, speaking with as many people as you can. Fill in the blanks with the information you gather.

   Greeting phrase: <u>はじまして</u>

   Questions:

   なまえ (name) <u>おなまえ は なんですか。</u>

   ～ねんせい (year) <u>なんねんせいですか。</u>

   せんこう (major) <u>せんこう は なんですか。</u>

   ～から　きました (hometown/country) <u>どこ。。どちら</u>

   こうこう (high school) <u>こうこう の なまえ は なん。。。</u>

2. Based on the answers you get, introduce one of your classmates to another classmate. Write down what is said by each person during the conversation.

   Patriciaさん: high school, junior, norway, Vrandensborg
   Kimさん: Harvard, junior, Seoul korea, KMLA
   Tangさん: daigaku freshman, China
   たなか: Harvard freshman, English lit. Tokyo,

   はじめまして。わたし／ぼくは＿＿＿＿＿＿＿といいます。

   ＿＿＿＿＿は ＿＿＿＿から ＿＿＿＿＿きました。

   ＿＿＿＿＿だいがくの＿＿＿＿＿ねんせいです。

   せんこうは ＿＿＿＿＿です。　どうぞよろしく。

ロールプレイ　Role Play
ろ　るぷれい

1. Approach and introduce yourself to the person who is sitting next to you, using the following dialogue as a model.

   You ：　あのう。

   Partner ：はい。

   You ：　おなまえは　なんですか。　ぼく／わたし、
   _zemer Patrick_って　いいます。どうぞ　よろしく。

   Partner ：こちらこそ。どうぞ　よろしく。ぼく／わたしの
   なまえは_Payne Dillon_です。

   You ：　ああ、そうですか。ぼく／わたしは_Norway_から
   きました。
   _Payne_さんは。

   Partner ：_Massachusetts_です。　ぼく／わたしは
   ハーバードだいがくの_よねん_せい
   です。

   You ：　そうですか。　ぼく／わたしも_よねん_せい
   です。せんこうは　なんですか。

   Partner ：_けいえいがく_です。

   You ：　そうですか。

2. Suppose that you are at an airport to pick up a Japanese person named Yamada whom you have never met. Approach someone and ask if he/she is the person you are looking for using the following dialogue as a starter. Then introduce yourself.

   You ：　　あのう、すみませんが。

   Partner ：　はい。

   You ：　　やまださんですか。

3. Suppose you have found a Japanese student on campus. Naturally, you want to practice Japanese with him/her. Introduce yourself and strike up a conversation.

カタカナ
Katakana

I. Introduction

In this section, you will learn how to read and write **katakana**. It is important to learn **katakana** because Japanese uses a large number of loan words, many of which are borrowed from English. The following chart shows both print and handwritten styles, with the reading of each **katakana** given in **hiragana**. Note that the use of small **tsu** ツ (つ) for double consonants, the two dots ゛ on the right shoulder to indicate voiced syllables, and the small **ya** ヤ (や), **yu** ユ (ゆ), and **yo** ヨ (よ) to indicate glides are exactly the same as **hiragana**. A dash ー indicates a long vowel, as explained in Chapter 1.

ン ん	ワ わ	ラ ら	ヤ や	マ ま	ハ は	ナ な	タ た	サ さ	カ か	ア あ
		リ り		ミ み	ヒ ひ	ニ に	チ ち	シ し	キ き	イ い
		ル る	ユ ゆ	ム む	フ ふ	ヌ ぬ	ツ つ	ス す	ク く	ウ う
		レ れ		メ め	ヘ へ	ネ ね	テ て	セ せ	ケ け	エ え
		ロ ろ	ヨ よ	モ も	ホ ほ	ノ の	ト と	ソ そ	コ こ	オ お

II. Katakana ア〜ソ
あ　そ

Study the first fifteen **katakana**. Using the mnemonic devices in the right-hand column, practice reading each character. Then practice writing them in your Student Activities Manual following the correct stroke order.

a	ア	ア	ア		I'd like an *ice*-cream cone.
i	イ	イ	イ		I need an *easel* to draw.
u	ウ	ウ	ウ		It's a *wick* of a candle.
e	エ	エ	エ		An *egg* is on an egg stand.
o	オ	オ	オ		*Oh*, what an odd way to walk.
ka	カ	カ	カ		*Karate* kick.
ki	キ	キ	キ		This is a *key*.
ku	ク	ク	ク		A baby is sleeping in a *cradle*.
ke	ケ	ケ	ケ		This is a *crooked* K
ko	コ	コ	コ		This letter has two *corners*.
sa	サ	サ	サ		This is a *saddle* on a horse.

shi	シ	シ	シ		*She* (the cat) is sleeping.
su	ス	ス	ス	ス	Here is a *swing set.*
se	セ	セ	セ	セ	Say, isn't that *Señor* García?
so	ソ	ソ	ソ	ソ	I'm *sewing* with a needle.

れんしゅう Practice

Read the following words in katakana and guess what they mean.

1. キス   2. ケーキ   3. サーカス   4. ケース   5. アイス
6. コース   7. エース   8. オアシス   9. シーソー

III. Katakana タ〜ホ
た   ほ

Study the following カタカナ . Using the mnemonic devices in the right-hand
か た か な
column, practice reading each character. Then practice writing them in your Student
Activities Manual following the correct stroke order.

ta	タ	タ	タ	タ	A crooked *tie.*
chi	チ	チ	チ	チ	A *chick* is trying to fly.
tsu	ツ	ツ	ツ	ツ	A cat *gets* up on her feet.
te	テ	テ	テ	テ	The cat's *tail* is wagging to the left.
to	ト	ト	ト	ト	An Indian *toma-hawk.*

na	ナ	ナ	ナ	ナ	A *knife*.
ni	二	二	二		A *neat* tennis court.
nu	ヌ	ヌ	ヌ		*Noodles* are difficult to eat with chopsticks.
ne	ネ	ネ	ネ		A *necker-chief* is around my neck.
no	ノ	ノ	ノ		Someone's *nose*.
ha	ハ	ハ	ハ		A *hat*.
hi	ヒ	ヒ	ヒ		A *heel*.
fu	フ	フ	フ		A child's *hood*.
he	ヘ	ヘ	ヘ		I have a bad *head-ache*.
ho	ホ	ホ	ホ		Two hands *hold* a cross.

れんしゅう Practice

Read the following words in katakana and try to guess what they mean. Remember that the small ッ indicates a double consonant.

1. カタカナ 2. ネット 3. セーター 4. カヌー 5. ノート

6. エチケット 7. テキスト 8. カッター 9. ホット 10. ニット 11. テスト

IV. Katakana マ〜ン
ま ん

Study the following カタカナ. Using the mnemonic devices in the right-hand column, practice reading each character. Then practice writing them in your Student Activities Manual following the correct stroke order.

ma	マ	マ	マ		A giant *mush-room*
mi	ミ	ミ	ミ		Who's three? *Me!*
mu	ム	ム	ム		The *moon* is sleeping.
me	メ	メ	メ		The knife is *melting*.
mo	モ	モ	モ		A *monster* appears in Tokyo.
ya	ヤ	ヤ	ヤ		A *yacht* in the ocean.
yu	ユ	ユ	ユ		It's a *U-boat!*
yo	ヨ	ヨ	ヨ		*Yoga* is fun.
ra	ラ	ラ	ラ		A *rabbit* with long ears.
ri	リ	リ	リ		This *ribbon* has long tails.
ru	ル	ル	ル		A tree with deep *roots*.

re	レ	レ	レ	*Let's*	*Let's* write a capital L.
ro	ロ	ロ	ロ		A *loaf* of bread.
wa	ワ	ワ	ワ		A *wine* glass.
n	ン	ン	シ	ン	A needle is sharp at the *end*.

れんしゅう Practice

Read the following words in katakana and try to guess what they mean.

1. ワシントン *Washington*
2. ユタ *Utah*
3. アイオワ *Iowa*
4. オハイオ *Ohio*
5. ノースカロライナ *North Carolina*
6. アメリカ *America*
7. イタリア *Italy*
8. ロシア *Russia*
9. テキサス *Texas*
10. オクラホマ *Oklahoma*
11. ミネソタ *Minnesota*
12. アーカンソー *Arkansas*
13. サウスカロライナ *South Carolina*
14. メキシコ *Mexico*
15. スイス *Swiss?*
16. インドネシア *Indonesia*
17. モンタナ *Montana*
18. ミシシッピー *Mississippi*
19. イリノイ *Illinois*
20. テネシー *Tennessee*
21. メイン *Maine*
22. オーストラリア *Australia*
23. フランス *France*

V. Transcribing katakana

A. Rules that apply to transcribing both hiragana and katakana

1. The diacritic marker [゛] indicates a voiced sound, as in ガ [ga] or ギ [gi]. A small circle [゜] indicates the [p] sound as in パ [pa].
2. Small ヤユヨ are used to form sounds such as キャ [kya], シュ [shu], and ミョ [myo].
3. A small ツ indicates a double consonant, as in ホットドッグ *hot dog*.

B. Conventions used in transcribing English words into katakana

1. The English sounds -er, -or, and -ar are heard as [aa] in Japanese. A dash represents the long vowels.

   カーター   Carter
   ハート   heart

When **katakana** is written vertically, the long vowel marker (ー) is also written vertically.

リ　サ　ハ
ー　ッ　ー
ダ　カ　ト
ー　ー

2. The English [v] is heard in Japanese as [b]. Accordingly, [va], [vi], [vu], [ve] and [vo] become [ba], [bi], [bu], [be] and [bo] in Japanese.

カバー	cover
バイオリン	violin

3. The English [l] and [r] are both heard as an [r] in Japanese.

ライト	right or light
リーダー	reader or leader
ロビー	lobby or Robby

4. The English [th] as in *think* and *third* is heard as [s] and the [th] as in *that* or *mother* is heard as [z].

サンクスギビング	Thanksgiving
マザーグース	Mother Goose
サードベース	third base
バスルーム	bathroom

5. If an English word ends in [k], [g], [m], [f], [v], [l], [s], [z], [th], [p], or [b], the vowel [u] is added in Japanese. The vowel [u] is also added when these sounds are followed immediately by consonants in English.

ミルク	milk
リング	ring
ホテル	hotel
ミス	Miss
ジャズ	jazz

6. If an English word contains [t] or [d], the vowel [o] is added in Japanese.

コスト	cost
スピード	speed
ラスト	last
ベッド	bed

7. The English vowel sounds in *bus* and *cut* or *bath* or *gas* are both heard as [a] in Japanese.

バス	bus or bath
カット	cut
バット	bat
ガス	gas

8. To approximate as much as possible the pronunciation of people's names and other borrowed sounds, the following combinations are commonly used. Note that these combinations are never used in **hiragana**.

ウィ [wi]	ウィンストン	Winston	ウィスコンシン	Wisconsin
ウェ [we]	ウェイン	Wayne	ハイウェイ	highway
ウォ [wo]	ウォルター	Walter	ウォッカ	vodka
シェ [she]	シェリル	Sheryl	シェーバー	shaver
ジェ [je]	ジェーン	Jane	ジェスチャー	gesture
チェ [che]	チェイス	Chase	チェロ	cello
ティ [ti]	カーティス	Curtis	アイスティー	iced tea
ディ [di]	ディーン	Dean	ディズニーランド	Disneyland
デュ [dju]	デューク	Duke	デュエット	duet
ファ [fa]	ジェニファー	Jennifer	ファッション	fashion
フィ [fi]	マーフィー	Murphy	フィンランド	Finland
フェ [fe]	フェイ	Fay	フェンシング	fencing
フォ [fo]	フォード	Ford	フォーク	fork

Try writing your name in katakana. Use the above conventions if your name contains any of the sounds listed.

れんしゅう **Practice**

A. The following words appeared in Chapter 1. Read them and write their meanings in English.

1. アジアけんきゅう _____

2. アメリカ _____

3. イギリス _____

4. オーストラリア _____

5. カナダ _____

6. スペイン _____

7. フランス _____

8. メキシコ _____

B. Guess what the following words are in English.

1. Food and drinks

1. ハンバーガー   2. ステーキ   3. ホットドッグ   4. カレー
5. スパゲティ   6. サンドイッチ 7. サラダ   8. トマト
9. レタス   10. オレンジ   11. レモン   12. フルーツ
13. バター   14. チーズ   15. ケーキ   16. アイスクリーム
17. チョコレート   18. クッキー   19. ジュース   20. ミルク
21. ポテトチップス 22. ビール   23. コーラ   24. ワイン

2. Sports

1. フットボール   2. バスケットボール 3. テニス   4. サッカー
5. ジョギング   6. スキー   7. スケート   8. バレーボール
9. ラケットボール 10. ゴルフ   11. サーフィン

3. Music

1. ピアノ   2. バイオリン   3. ギター   4. オーケストラ
5. トランペット   6. ジャズ   7. ロック   8. クラシック

4. Household items

1. キッチン   2. リビングルーム 3. ランプ   4. オーブン
5. トースター   6. ラジオ   7. レコード   8. ビデオ
9. カメラ   10. カレンダー

5. Countries

1. ブラジル   2. イギリス   3. ドイツ   4. オランダ
5. イタリア   6. スイス   7. イスラエル   8. ロシア
9. オーストラリア 10. インド   11. タイ   12. ベトナム
13. サウジアラビア

6. Cities

1. ニューヨーク   2. ボストン   3. シカゴ   4. ロサンゼルス
5. サンフランシスコ 6. トロント   7. モントリオール 8. ロンドン
9. パリ   10. ベルリン 11. モスクワ   12. カイロ
13. シドニー   14. バンコク 15. ホンコン

Chapter 3

だ
い
さ
ん
か

まいにちの　せいかつ
Daily Routines

Objectives	Describing daily routines
Vocabulary	Daily activities, numbers, minutes, relative time, days of the week
Japanese Culture	College life (1)
Dialogue	じゅぎょうが　あります。　*I have a class.*
Grammar	I. Talking about routines, future actions, or events using the polite present form of verbs and the particles に, へ, を, or で
	II. Presenting objects or events using 〜が あります
	III. Telling time using the particle に
	IV. Using adverbs to express frequency of actions
	V. Expressing past actions and events using the polite past form of verbs
Listening	Listening for general ideas
Communication	Using あいづち (2)
Reading	Scanning

たんご
Vocabulary

Nouns

あさ	朝	morning
あさごはん	朝御飯	breakfast
あさって	明後日	the day after tomorrow
あした	明日	tomorrow
うち	家	home
えいが	映画	movie
おととい	一昨日	the day before yesterday
おふろ	お風呂	bath
がっこう	学校	school
かようび	火曜日	Tuesday
きのう	昨日	yesterday
きょう	今日	today
きんようび	金曜日	Friday
クラス くらす		class
げつようび	月曜日	Monday
コーヒー こ　ひ		coffee
ごはん	御飯	meal, cooked rice
こんしゅう	今週	this week
こんばん	今晩	tonight
シャワー しゃわ		shower
しゅうまつ	週末	weekend
じゅぎょう	授業	class, course
しゅくだい	宿題	homework
すいようび	水曜日	Wednesday

せいかつ	生活	life, living
せんしゅう	先週	last week
つぎ	次	next
テレビ		television, TV
でんわばんごう	電話番号	telephone number
としょかん	図書館	library
どようび	土曜日	Saturday
にちようび	日曜日	Sunday
ばん	晩	night, evening
ばんごはん	晩御飯	supper, dinner
ひる	昼	afternoon
ひるごはん	昼御飯	lunch
べんきょう	勉強	study
ほん	本	book
まいあさ	毎朝	every morning
まいしゅう	毎週	every week
まいにち	毎日	every day
まいばん	毎晩	every night
もくようび	木曜日	Thursday

う -verbs

あります		(to) be held, (to) have; the dictionary form is ある.
いきます	行きます	(to) go; the dictionary form is いく .
かえります	帰ります	(to) return, (to) go home; the dictionary form is かえる.
のみます	飲みます	(to) drink; the dictionary form is のむ.
はいります	入ります	(to) take (a bath), (to) enter; the dictionary form is はいる. おふろに　はいります take a bath
よみます	読みます	(to) read; the dictionary form is よむ.

る -verbs

あびます	浴びます	(to) take (a shower) シャワーを あびます take a shower; the dictionary form is あびる.
おきます	起きます	(to) get up, (to) wake up; the dictionary form is おきる.
たべます	食べます	(to) eat; the dictionary form is たべる.
ねます	寝ます	(to) go to bed; the dictionary form is ねる.
みます	見ます	(to) see, (to) watch; the dictionary form is みる.

Irregular verbs

きます	来ます	(to) come; the dictionary form is くる.
します		(to) do; the dictionary form is する.
べんきょうします	勉強します	(to) study; the dictionary form is べんきょうする.

Question word

いつ	when

Numbers

ゼロ		zero
れい	零	zero
いち	一	one
に	二	two
さん	三	three
よん、 し	四	four
ご	五	five
ろく	六	six
なな、 しち	七	seven
はち	八	eight
きゅう、 く	九	nine
じゅう	十	ten

Counter

～ふん	～分	～ minute(s), (for) ～ minute(s)

Adverbs

いつも		always
ぜんぜん	全然	not at all (used with negative verb forms)
たいてい		usually
ときどき	時々	sometimes
よく		often; well

Particles

に		at; on; in (point in time) １０じに　ねます
に		to (goal, activity) クラスに　いきます〈くらす〉
で		at; in; on; etc. (location of action or event) としょかんで　べんきょうします
へ		to (direction) がっこうへ　いきます
を		direct object marker ほんを　よみます

Prefixes

こん～	今～	this こんしゅう、こんばん
まい～	毎～	every まいしゅう、まいあさ、まいばん、まいにち

Suffixes

～ようび	～曜日	day (of the week)
～ごろ	～頃	about ～ (used only with time expressions)

たんごの　れんしゅう　Vocabulary Practice

A. まいにちの　せいかつ　Daily activities

おきます

(to) wake up

ねます

(to) go to bed

あさごはんを
たべます

(to) eat breakfast

ひるごはん
を　たべます

(to) eat lunch

うちで　ばんごはんを
たべます

(to) eat dinner at home

べんきょうします／
べんきょうを　します

(to) study

としょかんで
べんきょうします。

(to) study at the library

しゅくだいを
します

(to) do homework

ほんを
よみます

(to) read a book

コーヒーを
のみます

(to) drink coffee

テレビを
みます

(to) watch TV

えいがを　みます

(to) watch a movie

シャワーを　あびます

(to) take a shower

おふろに　はいります

(to) take a bath

じゅぎょうが
あります

There is / I have a class.

がっこうに／がっこうへ
いきます

(to) go to school

クラスに／クラスへ
くらす　　くらす
きます

(to) come to the classroom

うちに／うちへ　かえります
(to) go home

Activity 1

Say what activities you do in the morning, in the afternoon, and at night.

Example: あさ　じゅぎょうが　あります (*I have class in the morning.*)

1. あさ (*morning*)
2. ひる (*afternoon*)
3. ばん (*night*)

Activity 2

Work with a partner. Put the activities you have just described in chronological order and tell your partner what your day is like.

B. Relative time expressions

Japanese has a set of words that indicate points in time with respect to the current time. Their English equivalents are words such as today, tomorrow, and yesterday. These words are categorized as relative time expressions because the day we call "yesterday" today will not be "yesterday" tomorrow. On the other hand, time expressions that are fixed, such as 1977, three o'clock, or Friday, are classified as absolute time expressions. Some relative time expressions follow.

いつ	when	きのう	yesterday
あさ	morning	おととい	the day before yesterday
ひる	afternoon		
ばん	night	まいにち	every day
こんばん	tonight	まいしゅう	every week
しゅうまつ	weekend	まいあさ	every morning
きょう	today	こんしゅう	this week
あした	tomorrow	まいばん	every night
あさって	the day after tomorrow	せんしゅう	last week

Activity 3

Answer the following questions.

1. いま、あさですか。ひるですか。ばんですか。
2. 「まいあさ」、「まいにち」、「まいばん」の「まい」って　なんですか。
3. 「まいしゅう」、「こんしゅう」、「せんしゅう」、「しゅうまつ」の「しゅう」って　なんですか。
4. 「こんばん」、「こんしゅう」の「こん」ってなんですか。

Activity 4

For each activity shown on pages 88-89, create a sentence using the time expressions that apply to your own daily routine. If you want to use きのう (yesterday) or せんしゅう (last week), change the verb form to 〜ました instead of 〜ます, as in みました (watched) instead of みます (watch).

Example:　おきます (to) wake up

　　　　　あさ、おきます。(*I wake up in the morning.*)

　　　　　せんしゅう、えいがを　みました。(*I watched a movie last week.*)

C. ～ようび　Days of the week

Note that each day of the week ends with ようび.

Which day of the week?	なんようび
Sunday	にちようび
Monday	げつようび
Tuesday	かようび
Wednesday	すいようび
Thursday	もくようび
Friday	きんようび
Saturday	どようび

Activity 5

Look at the calendar and give the day of the week for the following dates.

1. 10/16
2. 10/26
3. 10/31
4. 10/1
5. 10/21
6. 10/4
7. 10/27
8. 10/8
9. 10/5
10. 10/7
11. 10/17
12. 10/25

Activity 6

Answer the following questions in Japanese.

1. きょうは　なんようびですか。
2. あしたは　なんようびですか。
3. あさっては　なんようびですか。
4. きのうは　なんようびでしたか。(でした = *was*)
5. おとといは　なんようびでしたか。(でした = was)
6. つぎの　にほんごの　クラスは　なんようびですか。
　　　　　　　　　く ら す

D. すうじ　Numbers

Read the following numbers aloud.

0	ゼロ、れい	7	なな、しち	20	にじゅう
	ぜ ろ				
1	いち	8	はち	30	さんじゅう
2	に	9	きゅう、く	40	よんじゅう
3	さん	10	じゅう	70	ななじゅう、しちじゅう
4	よん、し	11	じゅういち	90	きゅうじゅう
5	ご	12	じゅうに	99	きゅうじゅうきゅう、
6	ろく	13	じゅうさん		きゅうじゅうく

NOTES

- Numbers between 11 and 19 are formed by using the number ten followed by the appropriate single digit.

  11 = 10 + 1　じゅういち＝じゅう＋いち

  12 = 10 + 2　じゅうに＝じゅう＋に

  13 = 10 + 3　じゅうさん＝じゅう＋さん

- The numbers 20, 30, 40, 50, 60, 70, 80, and 90 are formed by using the appropriate single digit followed by 10.

  20 = 2 X 10　にじゅう＝に X じゅう

  30 = 3 X 10　さんじゅう＝さん X じゅう

  40 = 4 X 10　よんじゅう＝よん X じゅう

- Numbers like 23 and 35 are formed by combining the tens digit and the ones digit.

  23 = 20 + 3　にじゅうさん ＝ にじゅう＋さん

  35 = 30 + 5　さんじゅうご ＝ さんじゅう＋ご

- The numbers 4, 7, and 9 have two possible pronunciations. The number *40* is usually pronounced よんじゅう. The number *70* can be pronounced either ななじゅう or しちじゅう, and the number *90* is always pronounced きゅうじゅう.

Activity 7

Say the following telephone numbers（でんわばんごう）in Japanese. Use の to indicate a dash.

Example:　123-4567　　いちにさんの　　よんごろくなな

1. 356-2891
2. 245-6689
3. 8217-0370
4. 03-3986-5772
5. 06-4463-5998
6. 0895-23-5005
7. 090-7244-1456
8. 080-4647-4176

Activity 8

Take turns asking classmates their telephone numbers（でんわばんごう）.

Example:　A:　あのう、でんわばんごうは　なんですか。

　　　　　B:　いちにさんの　よんごろくななです。

　　　　　A:　そうですか。どうもありがとう。

Activity 9

Read the following numbers aloud.

1.	2	6.	11	11.	75
2.	5	7.	17	12.	94
3.	6	8.	20	13.	81
4.	8	9.	49	14.	62
5.	10	10.	53	15.	99

Activity 10

Work in groups of three. One person writes five numbers in Arabic numerals on five separate slips of paper. As he or she shows the numbers, the other two members of the group compete to be the first to call out each number correctly.

E. 〜ふん　Minute(s)

Note: * indicates a sound change.

1	＊いっぷん	8	＊はっぷん／はちふん
2	にふん	9	きゅうふん
3	＊さんぷん	10	＊じゅっぷん／じっぷん
4	よんふん／よんぷん	11	＊じゅういっぷん
5	ごふん	12	じゅうにふん
6	＊ろっぷん	20	＊にじゅっぷん／にじっぷん
7	しちふん／ななふん	21	＊にじゅういっぷん

＊なんぷん *how many minutes?*

Activity 11

Say the following times in Japanese.

1.	4:10	5.	12:30	9.	4:17 p.m.	13.	6:55 a.m.
2.	2:25	6.	6:40	10.	9:18 a.m.	14.	9:03 p.m.
3.	7:37	7.	8:09	11.	7:11 p.m.	15.	3:53 p.m.
4.	1:44	8.	1:56	12.	9:02 a.m.	16.	8:30 a.m.

ダイアローグ
だいあろぐ
Dialogue

はじめに　Warm-up

Answer the following questions in Japanese.

1. まいにち　じゅぎょうが　ありますか。
2. なんじに　じゅぎゅうが　ありますか。
3. たいてい　どこで　ひるごはんを　たべますか。
4. たいてい　なんじごろ　うちに　かえりますか。
5. きのう　なんじごろ　うちに　かえりましたか。
6. せんしゅうの　しゅうまつ　なにを　しましたか。

じゅぎょうが　あります。 *I have a class.*

It is 9:45 a.m. Ueda is eating a sandwich in front of the foreign language building. Li passes by.

うえだ：　あ、リーさん、おはよう。

リー：　ああ、うえださん。おはよう。　いま、あさごはんですか。

うえだ：　ええ、きょうは　はちじに　じゅぎょうが　ありました。

リー：　そうですか。たいへんですね。

うえだ：　ええ。で、リーさんは？

リー：　ぼくは　としょかんへ　いきます。　あさは　たいてい
　　　　としょかんで　しゅくだいを　します。

うえだ：　そうですか。クラスは？

リー：　いちじはんに　にほんごの　じゅぎょうが　あります。
　　　　うえださんは？

うえだ：　じゅうじに　れきしの　クラスが　あります。

リー：　そうですか。

DIALOGUE PHRASE NOTES

- In the dialogue, the topic particle は follows the time expressions きょう and あさ. In Japanese, a topic does not necessarily have to be the subject of sentence, but it does introduce the item about which the speaker wishes to comment. In the dialogue above, Ueda wants to say something about "today," and Li wants to say the same thing about "mornings." For further discussion of topic particles, refer to the supplementary notes titled "More about the topic particle は" on p. 106 of this chapter.
- たいへんですね means *that's hard*, in which たいへん means *tough, hard, serious*. ね is an affective particle that commonly appears in conversation to express shared feelings or assumptions. In the dialogue, ね expresses Li's sympathy toward Ueda.
- The で in the phrase で、リーさんは？ is often used in conversation. It can be interpreted as well then, so, or by the way. It is not used in written Japanese.

ダイアローグの　あとで　　Comprehension

A. Read each statement below. Then circle はい if the statement is true and いいえ if it is false.

1. はい　いいえ　　リーさんは　きょうのごご　としょかんで べんきょうします。
2. はい　いいえ　　うえださんは　ごご　じゅぎょうが　あります。
3. はい　いいえ　　うえださんは　きょうのあさ　じゅぎょうが ありました。

B. Answer the following questions in Japanese.

1. うえださんは　なんじごろ　あさごはんを　たべましたか。
2. にほんごの　じゅぎょうは　なんじに　ありますか。
3. じゅうじに　なにが　ありますか。

にほんの　ぶんか
Japanese Culture

The academic year in Japan

Japanese colleges and universities usually begin the academic year in April. Summer vacation starts at the end of July. The fall semester, or session, runs from September or October through January or February. The winter break is usually short, from the end of December through the beginning of January.

College classes

The usual class period in Japanese colleges is 90 or 100 minutes. Apart from seminars and some science classes, most classes are straight lectures, and little interaction takes place between students and professors. Many classes meet once a week for a full academic year, resuming after summer vacation and winter break. Major examinations are usually held only once, at the end of the academic year, and the exam period lasts a couple of weeks.

College housing

The majority of Japanese colleges are commuter schools, and few have dormitories. Those dormitories that do exist are rarely found on campus. Most Japanese college students live at home or in an apartment. Their average commute is about an hour but may be as long as two hours in large cities.

Financial aid

Many parents pay for their children's college education in Japan. Although there are scholarships available from various sources, student loans do not exist.

According to a recent study by a student support organization (**Gakusei Engoka**) over 80 percent of students have part-time jobs or アルバイト／バイト (from the German "arbeiten," meaning *work*). Common jobs for students include convenience store or supermarket clerk, かていきょうし (private tutor for junior and senior high school students), and waiter or waitress.

ぶんぽう
Grammar

> ### I. Talking about routines, future actions, or events using the polite present form of verbs and the particles に, へ, を, or で

Chapter 2 (see p. 46) introduced the copula verb です and the topic particle は. This chapter deals with regular verbs and four additional particles.

A. Polite present form of verbs

Unlike English, all Japanese verbs have a polite form and a plain form. The polite form is used with acquaintances, people of different age groups, strangers in public places, on TV and radio broadcasts, and in letters. The plain form is used among family members, young children, close friends of the same age, and in newspapers and magazine articles. You will first learn the basics of Japanese verbs using the polite form in this book.

Verb tenses

Japanese verbs have only two tenses: past and non-past. The non-past tense indicates both present and future actions or states.

Question			
		Verb	
がっこう	に	いきます	か。

Answer	
	Verb
いいえ、	いきません。

Do you go to school? / Are you going to school?   *No, I don't. / No, I'm not.*

In the above example, いきます can indicate either the habitual action of going to school or future action. The meaning must be taken from the context.

Verb classes

There are three classes of Japanese verbs: う-verbs, る-verbs, and irregular verbs. Japanese has only two irregular verbs: きます and します. (します can be combined with certain nouns to produce irregular compound verbs, as noted below.) These verb classes will become more useful as you learn different forms of inflection in Chapter 7 (see pp. 267–68).

	Polite affirmative form	Polite negative form	Verb class
to go	いき<u>ます</u>	いき<u>ません</u>	う -verb
to go home	かえり<u>ます</u>	かえり<u>ません</u>	う -verb
to read	よみ<u>ます</u>	よみ<u>ません</u>	う -verb
to get up	おき<u>ます</u>	おき<u>ません</u>	る -verb
to go to bed	ね<u>ます</u>	ね<u>ません</u>	る -verb
to eat	たべ<u>ます</u>	たべ<u>ません</u>	る -verb
to come	き<u>ます</u>	き<u>ません</u>	Irregular
to do	し<u>ます</u>	し<u>ません</u>	Irregular
to study	べんきょうし<u>ます</u>	べんきょうし<u>ません</u>	Irregular

Note that べんきょうします is considered an irregular verb because it is a compound verb consisting of べんきょう and します. You will learn more compound verbs (noun +します) in later chapters.

B. Direct object particle, を

The particle を marks a direct object. The direct object receives the action of the verb. For example, in the sentence "John buys a car," car is the direct object. In English, the direct object is understood by its location (it generally appears immediately after the verb), but in Japanese it is followed by を, as in the following examples. The particle を was once pronounced *wo*, but is now pronounced *o*.

Topic	Direct object		Verb (action)
	Noun	Particle	
わたしは	ひるごはん	を	たべます。

I eat lunch. / I will eat lunch.

スミス： しゅうまつ、よく　なにを　しますか。
What do you often do on weekends?

たなか： テレビを　みます。
I watch TV.

スミス： そうですか。わたしも　よく　テレビを　みます。
Is that so? I often watch TV, too.

NOTES

- べんきょうします consists of the noun べんきょう, which means *study*, and the verb します. Thus, it can be paraphrased as べんきょうを　します, which literally means *do the study*. In the latter sentence, use の to indicate what is being studied.

  にほんごを　べんきょうします。
  I study Japanese.

  にほんごの　べんきょうを　します。
  I study Japanese. (literally, *I do the study of Japanese.*)

- を may be omitted when the meaning can easily be inferred from the context of the conversation. However, it is not easy to determine exactly when to delete を. In this textbook you will sometimes see instances in which particles have been omitted.

C. Destination or goal particles に and へ

The particle に indicates a goal, a destination, or a point of arrival or contact. It is similar to the English prepositions *to*, *into*, or *onto*. The particle へ indicates a direction toward which something or someone moves. When used as a particle, the pronuciation of へ is exactly the same as that of え [e]. When used in other contexts, it is pronounced like the English word *hay*. Like を, the particles に and へ may be omitted when the meaning can be inferred easily from the context.

Destination/Goal		Verb
Place noun	Particle	
うち	に／へ	かえります

I will go home. / I am going home.

スミス：　どこに　いきますか。　　*Where are you going?*
たなか：　がっこうへ　いきます。　*I am going to school.*

へ can replace に in verbs of motion such as いきます, きます, and かえります, but these particles are not interchangeable with other types of verbs.

がっこうに／へ　いきます。
I will go to school. / I go to school.

だいがくに／へ　きます。
I will come to the university. / I come to the university.

おふろに　はいります。
I will take a bath. / I take a bath.

かばん (*bag*) に　ほんを　いれます (*put*)。
I will put a book in the bag. / I put a book in the bag.

D. Place of action and event, で

The particle で indicates the place at which an action or event takes place. It is translated as *in*, *at*, or *on* in English.

Place of action		Verb phrase (action)
Noun	Particle	
としょかん	で	えいがを　みます。

I see a movie at the library. / I am going to see a movie at the library.

スミス：　どこで　べんきょうしますか。
すみす
Where do you (will you) study?

たなか：　としょかんで　します。
I study (will study) at the library.

はなして　みましょう　　Conversation Practice

Activity 1

Complete each sentence using the appropriate particles.

Example:　しゅくだい　／　します
　　　　　　しゅくだいを　します。

1. ほん　／　よみます
2. おふろ　／　はいります
3. うち　／　ねます
4. テレビ　／　みます
   てれび
5. クラス　／　きます
   くらす

6. としょかん　／　いきます
7. シャワー　／　あびます
   しゃわ
8. がっこう　／　ひるごはん　／　たべます
9. うち　／　かえります

Activity 2

Answer the following questions.

Example:　よく　としょかんに　いきますか。
　　　　　　ええ、いきます。　or いいえ、いきません。

1. あさごはんを　たべますか。
2. まいあさ　コーヒーを　のみますか。
   こ　ひ
3. よく　テレビを　みますか。
   てれび
4. よく　えいがに　いきますか。
5. こんばん　としょかんで　べんきょうしますか。

Activity 3

Work with a partner. In the column headed わたし below, write はい if you are thinking of doing the stated activity today, and いいえ if you are not. Then ask your partner whether he/she is planning to do these activities. Start your questions with the phrase あとで (later). Switch roles after you reach the bottom of the list.

Example:　A:　あとで、ほんを　よみますか。

　　　　　　B:　ええ、よみます。 or いいえ、よみません。

	わたし	パートナー
	はい／いいえ	はい／いいえ
ほん／よみます		
ほかの (another) じゅぎょう／いきます		
おふろ／はいります		
シャワー／あびます		
えいが／みます		
にほんごの　しゅくだい／します		
テレビ／みます		
ごはん／たべます		
うち／かえります		

II. Presenting objects or events using ～が あります

The phrase X が あります means *there is X*. This phrase is used to describe an object, event, or activity. Depending on the context, ～が あります can also be used to express possession.

ほんが あります。
There is a book. / I have a book.

えいがが あります。
There is a movie.

しゅくだいが あります。
There is homework. / I have homework.

スミス： しゅうまつ なにを しますか。
すみす *What are you going to do this weekend?*

たなか： がっこうに いきます。
I am going to school.

スミス： え、どうしてですか。
すみす *Really, why?*

たなか： としょかんで にほんの えいがが あります。
There is a Japanese movie (playing) at the library.

スミス： あ、そうですか。
すみす *Oh, I see.*

NOTES

- Use the particle で to describe where an event will take place, as in the dialogue above.

  としょかん<u>で</u> えいがが あります。
  There is a movie <u>at</u> the library.

- When ～が あります expresses possession, use ～は to indicate the possessor.

  <u>ぼくは</u> じゅぎょうが あります。
  <u>I</u> have a class.

  <u>やまださんは</u> テレビが ありません。
  　　　　　　てれび
  <u>Yamada-san</u> does not have a TV.

はなして みましょう   Conversation Practice

Activity 1

Work with a partner. You have the following event listing for Tokyo Disney Resort. Tell your friend about various shows and locations.

Example: ワールド・バザールで　ドローイング・クラスが　あります。
          わ る ど ば ざ る   ど ろ いん ぐ くら す

Tokyo Disney Resort Theme Park	Special Events
ワールド・バザール わ る ど ば ざ る	ドローイング・クラス ど ろ いん ぐ くら す
ファンタジー・ランド ふ ぁん たじ らん ど	アリスのティーパーティ あ り す てぃ ぱ てぃ
ウエスタン・ランド う え す たん らん ど	フロンティア・レビュー ふ ろん てぃ あ れ びゅ
アメリカン・ウォーターフロント あ め り かん う ぉ た ふ ろん と	ミュージカル「アンコール」 み ゅ じ かる あん こ る
メディテレーニアン・ハーバー め でぃ て れ にあん は ば	ウォーター・カーニバル う ぉ た か に ばる
マーメイド・ラグーン ま めい ど ら ぐん	ミュージカル「アンダー・ザ・シー」 み ゅ じ かる あん だ ざ し
アラビアン・コースト あ ら びあん こ す と	マジック・ショー ま じっ く しょ

Activity 2

Work with the class. Ask at least three classmates if they have a class after Japanese class, and if they do, find out what and where it is. Then fill in the chart with the classmate's name, class and location.

Example: A: このあと (*after this class*) じゅぎょうが ありますか。

B: ええ、<u>ぶんがくの　じゅぎょう</u>が　あります。

A: そうですか。<u>どこで</u> ありますか。

B: <u>スミス・ホール</u> (*Smith Hall*)で　あります。

or

A: このあと (*after this class*) じゅぎょうが　ありますか。

B: いいえ、ありません。～さんは？

A: わたしは <u>えいごの　じゅぎょう</u>が　あります。

なまえ	じゅぎょう	ばしょ (location)

III. Telling time using the particle に

The particle に with a time expression indicates a specific point in time. This use of に corresponds to the English prepositions at, in, or on. It may be used to express clock times, days of the week, months, or years. For example:

ごじ<u>に</u> <u>at</u> 5 o'clock		げつようび<u>に</u> <u>on</u> Monday
ごがつ<u>に</u> <u>in</u> May		１９９６ねん<u>に</u> <u>in</u> 1996

The particle に is never used with the words きょう, いま, あさ, ばん, いつ, まい〜 (every 〜), こん〜 (this 〜), らい〜 (next 〜).

Point in time		
Time	**Particle**	
ろくじはん	に	おきます。

スミス：   うえださんは　きょう　きますか。
Is Ms. Ueda coming today?

たなか：   ええ、ごじに　きますよ。
Yes, she is coming around 5 o'clock.

スミス：   リーさんも　きますか。
Is Mr. Li coming, too?

たなか：   いいえ、リーさんは　どようびに　きます。
No, he is coming on Saturday.

たなか：   すみません。いま　なんじですか。
Excuse me. What time is it now?

スミス：   じゅうじ　よんじゅうさんぷんです。
It's 10:43.

たなか：   どうも　ありがとう。
Thank you very much.

スミス：   いいえ。
Not at all.

NOTES

- For the pronunciation of numbers and number +ふん, refer to vocabulary sections D and E, pages 91-93.
- The pronunciation of some numbers may change, depending on the counters being used. For example:

よん　　→　よじ　　よんふん

いち　　→　いちじ　いっぷん

- We have seen the use of はん meaning "half past the hour." Another way to say this is the more literal さんじゅっぷん. For example: さんじさんじゅっぷん／さんじはん = 3:30.
- When two or more time expressions are used together, list them from the largest to the smallest unit (for example, day and time), and connect them with の. A few words like まいにち do not take の. For example,

どようびの　さんじに　きます。
I am coming at 3: 00 o'clock on Saturday.

まいにち　はちじに　おきます。
I wake up at 8 o'clock every day.

- Use ～ごろ or ごろ（に）　to express an approximate time. For example,

たなか：　きょう　なんじごろ（に）　かえりますか。
About what time are you going to go home today?

スミス：　よじごろ　かえります
すみす
I will go home around 4 o'clock.

はなして みましょう Conversation Practice

Activity 1

Work with a partner. A Japanese film festival is going on all week at the student union. Look at the following schedule and ask each other what time the various screenings begin.

Example: A: となりの トトロは いつ ありますか。
とととろ

B: げつようびの ごぜん じゅういちじに あります。

Movie titles	Date and Time
となりの トトロ と と ろ	Monday 11:00 A.M. Wednesday 5:35 P.M. Friday 8:30 P.M.
たんぽぽ	Tuesday 10:50 A.M. Thursday 12:05 P.M. Saturday 3:15 P.M.
フラガール ふ ら が る	Wednesday 10:00 A.M. Friday 10:55 A.M. Sunday 7:45 P.M.
ゴジラ ご じ ら	Monday 9:40 P.M. Thursday 10:20 A.M. Saturday 12:00 P.M.
リング り ん ぐ	Tuesday 4:25 P.M. Friday 6:08 P.M. Sunday 10:25 A.M.
シャル・ウイ・ダンス し ゃ る う い だ ん す	Wednesday 9:10 P.M. Thursday 12:00 P.M. Saturday 9:30 A.M.
手紙 (Letter) て が み	Monday 2:33 P.M. Tuesday 11:10 A.M. Sunday 11:44 A.M.

Activity 2

Combine the following phrases to form complete sentences. Use whatever particles are necessary.

Example: ごじ／かえります

ごじに かえります。

1. まいあさ／コーヒー／のみます
   こ ひ
2. あした／ばん／とうきょう／いきます
3. げつようび／じゅういちじごろ／かえります

4. らいしゅう／どようび／えいが／みます

5. まいにち／しちじごろ／おふろ／はいります

6. いま／クラス／あります
   くらす

Activity 3

Work with your classmates. Following the model in Box 1 of the chart below, fill in all the blanks with the appropriate particles. Use an X to indicate that no particle is required. Then ask your classmates はい／いいえ questions based on the statements in the chart. If someone answers はい, write his or her name in the box. Try to fill one row or column with different names.

Example: A: スミスさんは　まいにち　ほんを　よみますか。
          すみす

          B: はい、よみます。

          Write スミスさん in Box 1.
                すみす

①＿＿＿さん	②＿＿＿さん	③＿＿＿さん	④＿＿＿さん
まいにち＿X＿ ほん＿を＿ よみます。	がっこう＿＿＿ しゅくだい＿＿＿ します。	きょう＿＿＿ コーヒー＿＿＿ こ　ひ のみます。	まいしゅう＿＿＿ げつようび＿＿＿ としょかん＿＿ いきます。
⑤＿＿＿さん	⑥＿＿＿さん	⑦＿＿＿さん	⑧＿＿＿さん
もくようび＿＿＿ じゅぎょう＿＿＿ あります。	としょかん＿＿＿ べんきょう＿＿＿ します。	こんばん＿＿＿ しゅくだい＿＿＿ します。	うち＿＿＿ ひるごはん＿＿＿ たべます。
⑨＿＿＿さん	⑩＿＿＿さん	⑪＿＿＿さん	⑫＿＿＿さん
あさはちじごろ ＿＿＿ ごはん＿＿＿ たべます。	じゅうにじはん ＿＿＿ じゅぎょう＿＿＿ あります。	まいあさ＿＿＿ テレビ＿＿＿ て　れ　び みます。	にちようび＿＿＿ がっこう＿＿＿ きます。
⑬＿＿＿さん	⑭＿＿＿さん	⑮＿＿＿さん	⑯＿＿＿さん
まいばん＿＿＿ おふろ＿＿＿ はいります。	さんじごろ＿＿＿ うち＿＿＿ かえります。	こんばん＿＿＿ はちじ＿＿＿ テレビ＿＿＿ て　れ　び みます。	まいあさ＿＿＿ しちじ＿＿＿ シャワー＿＿＿ し　ゃ　わ あびます。

Activity 4

Ask a partner about his or her class schedule for the week to complete the following chart. Then switch roles.

Example: A: げつようびは　じゅぎょうが　ありますか。

B: ええ、ありますよ。

A: そうですか。　いつですか。

B: ごぜんはちじに　にほんごの　じゅぎょうが　あります。

　　そして、くじに　ぶんがくの　じゅぎょうが　あります。

〜ようび	じゅぎょう
げつようび	8 A.M.- にほんご　9 A.M.- ぶんがく
かようび	
すいようび	
もくようび	
きんようび	

IV. Using adverbs to express frequency of actions

Japanese has a variety of adverbs that express how often one does something, as shown in the following illustration.

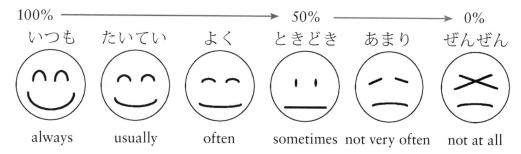

| 100% ——————————————→ 50% ——————→ 0% |

いつも　　　たいてい　　　よく　　ときどき　　あまり　　ぜんぜん

always　　usually　　often　　sometimes　not very often　not at all

Sentences containing いつも, たいてい, よく or ときどき end with an affirmative verb form.

わたしは　いつも　あさ　コーヒーを　のみます。
I _always_ drink coffee in the morning.

わたしは　たいてい　じゅういちじに　ねます。
I _usually_ go to bed at eleven o'clock.

わたしは　よく　としょかんに　いきます。
I _often_ go to the library.

わたしは　ときどき　じゅうじごろ　おきます。
I _sometimes_ get up about l0:00.

The adverbs あまり and ぜんぜん must always be used with the negative form of the verb.

わたしは　あまり　ほんを　よみません。
 I _don't_ read books _very much_.

わたしは　ぜんぜん　あさごはんを　たべません。
I _don't_ eat breakfast _at all_.

スミス：よく　あさごはんを　たべますか。
　　　　Do you always eat breakfast?

たなか：いいえ、ぜんぜん　たべません。
　　　　No, I never eat it.
　　　　スミスさんは？
　　　　How about you, Mr. Smith?

スミス：わたしは　たいてい　たべますよ。
　　　　I usually do.

たなか：そうですか。
　　　　I see.

NOTES

- とても may be used before よく in order to express very frequent actions.

  たなかさんは　とても　よく　としょかんに　いきます。
  Mr. Tanaka goes to the library very often.

- The position of an adverb of frequency in a sentence is relatively flexible. These adverbs usually appear immediately before the verb, but may appear before the direct object without any significant change in meaning.

  わたしは　としょかんに　あまり　いきません
  I don't go to the library very often.

  わたしは　あまり　としょかんに　いきません。
  I don't go to the library very often.

はなして　みましょう　Conversation Practice

Activity 1

Complete the sentences below with an adverb of frequency that best describes your own habits. Choose from いつも, たいてい, よく, ときどき, あまり, or ぜんぜん.

Example: うちで　あさごはんを　たべます。

うちで　あさごはんを　あまり　たべません。

1. りゅうがくせいセンター (*International Student Center*) に　いきます。
2. としょかんで　べんきょうします。
3. シャワーを　あびます。
4. うちで　しゅくだいを　します。
5. おふろに　はいります。
6. あさ　ほんを　よみます。

Activity 2

Ask a partner whether he or she does something often. Then fill in the chart with activities that he or she does and does not do frequently.

Example: A: 〜さんは　ほんを　よく　よみますか。

          B: いいえ、あまり　よみません。

	パートナー	わたし
いつも		
よく		
ときどき		
あまり		
ぜんぜん		

Activity 3

Work with members of your class. Write down what you do or don't do frequently in the chart in Activity 2. Tell individual classmates what you do and ask whether he or she has similar habits. Find a classmate who shares your interests.

Example: A: わたしは　ときどき　としょかんに　いきます。

              〜さんは　よく　としょかんに　いきますか。

         B: はい、　わたしも　ときどき　としょかんに　いきます。

        or はい、　よく　いきます。

        or いいえ、　わたしは　あまり　いきません。

        or いいえ、　わたしは　ぜんぜん　いきません。

V. Expressing past action and events using the polite past forms of verbs

Forming the polite past form of a verb is quite easy. All you need to do is to use
ました instead of ます for an affirmative sentence, and ませんでした instead of
ません for a negative sentence.

Question	
	Verb (past)
あさごはんを	たべましたか。

Did you eat breakfast?

Answer	
	Verb (past)
いいえ、	たべませんでした。

No, I didn't.

スミス：　きのう　しゅくだいが　ありましたか。
　　　　Was there an assignment yesterday?

たなか：　いいえ、ありませんでしたよ。
　　　　No, there wasn't.

スミス：　そうですか。どうも。
　　　　I see. Thank you.

	Polite affirmative form		Polite negative form		Verb class
	present	past	present	past	
	～ます	～ました	～ません	～ませんでした	
to go	いきます	いきました	いきません	いきませんでした	う -verb
to eat	たべます	たべました	たべません	たべませんでした	る -verb
to come	きます	きました	きません	きませんでした	Irregular
to do	します	しました	しません	しませんでした	Irregular

はなして みましょう   Conversation Practice

Activity 1

The chart below lists everything Mr. Smith did yesterday. Looking at the chart,
describe each of his activities.

Example:　スミスさんは　しちじに　おきました。

7:00 A.M.	Wake up	1:30 P.M.	English class
7:10 A.M.	Shower	2:30 P.M.	Study at the library
8:00 A.M.	Breakfast	4:30 P.M.	Go home
8:45 A.M.	Go to school	6:00 P.M.	Dinner
9:00 A.M.	Japanese class	7:30 P.M.	Watch TV
10:00 A.M.	Literature class	9:00 P.M.	Do homework
12:00 P.M.	Lunch at school	12:00 A.M.	Go to bed

Activity 2

Answer the following questions, based on Mr. Smith's chart in Activity 1.

Example: A: スミスさんは　きのう　はちじに　おきましたか。

B: いいえ、おきませんでした。

1. スミスさんは　きのう　おふろに　はいりましたか。
2. スミスさんは　きのう　がっこうで　ひるごはんを　たべましたか。
3. スミスさんは　きのう　れきしの　じゅぎょうが　ありましたか。
4. スミスさんは　きのうのばん　シャワーを　あびましたか。
5. スミスさんは　きのう　としょかんへ　いきましたか。
6. スミスさんは　うちで　しゅくだいを　しましたか。
7. スミスさんは　じゅういちじごろ　ねましたか。

Activity 3

Work with a partner. Fill in the table below with as much detail as possible describing what you did yesterday. Your partner will have a blank table and will ask you questions to figure out what you did. Compare the two tables when you are done.

Example: A: きのう　なんじに　おきましたか。

B: はちじごろ　おきました。〜さんは？

A: わたしは　しちじに　おきました。

B: そうですか。あさごはんは　たべましたか。

A: いいえ、たべませんでした。でも、コーヒーを　のみました。

5 A.M.		4 P.M.	
6 A.M.		5 P.M.	
7 A.M.		6 P.M.	
8 A.M.		7 P.M.	
9 A.M.		8 P.M.	
10 A.M.		9 P.M.	
11 A.M.		10 P.M.	
12 P.M.		11 P.M.	
1 P.M.		12 A.M.	
2 P.M.		1 A.M.	
3 P.M.			

MORE ABOUT THE TOPIC PARTICLE は

In Chapter 2 (see pages 46–47), the topic of the sentence was also the subject of the sentence as in わたしは　がくせいです (*I am a student*). As you learned in the Dialogue section of this chapter, the subject serves often as the topic, but not always. The function of the topic is to present something the speaker wishes to comment on, so topics can include time expressions, direct objects, goals, locations, and other words. Understanding how the topic works in Japanese conversation and learning how to use topics can be quite difficult, and more explanations follow later in this book. Do not be surprised if the topic particle は appears when you don't expect any particle, as in きょうは (*today*) or where you expect a different particle, as in しゅくだいは (*homework*) instead of しゅくだいを .

> しゅくだいは　あした　します。
> *I will do the homework tomorrow.*
> (literally, *Speaking of homework, I will do it tomorrow.*)

> あしたは　じゅぎょうが　あります。
> *There is a class tomorrow.*
> (literally, *Speaking of tomorrow, there is a class.*)

A:　よく　えいがを　みますか。
Do you watch movies often?

B:　ええ。
Yes.

A:　じゃあ、テレビは？
　　　て れ び
Well, how about TV?

B:　テレビは　みませんね。
　　て れ び
No, I don't watch TV.

A:　しゅうまつは　なにを　しますか。
What will you do this weekend?

B:　えいがを　みます。にほんの　えいがですよ。
I'm going to a movie. A Japanese film.

A:　そうですか。いいですね。
Is that so? That sounds good.

きく　れんしゅう
Listening

じょうずな　ききかた　　Listening Strategy

Listening for general ideas

Conversations are often full of redundancy and unimportant details, and it is not necessary to understand every single spoken word. It is more important to pick up a few key words and to get a general idea of what the conversation is about. If you need to know specific details or information, you can always ask questions about them for clarification.

みっつの　ライフスタイル　　Three different lifestyles
らいふすたいる

Think about your lifestyle and write down some of the words and phrases that describe it. Then listen to three people talking about their daily lives. Decide which person's life is most like yours. Try to explain the reasons for your choice. There will be some conversational fillers and unknown words in what you hear, but don't worry about them. Try to pick out a few words at a time, write them down, and get the gist of each monologue. Then, try to guess which one of the following people fits in each description.

1. _____

2. _____

3. _____

A　　　　　B　　　　　C　　　　　D　　　　　E

ききじょうず　はなしじょうず
Communication

Communication Strategy

Using あいづち　(attentive feedback) 2

In Chapter 2 (p. 66), you learned that the Japanese give feedback, or あいづち, in several ways during a conversation, and that はい and ええ do not necessarily indicate agreement. In addition to indicating that the listener is following the conversation, the use of はい and ええ can mean that the listener sympathizes with the speaker, or that the listener agrees with the speaker's opinion. It is not easy for people unfamiliar with this use of あいづち to interpret correctly which meaning of はい and ええ is intended in many cases. A classic example is that of an American businessperson who reports that a negotiation seemed to be going well because his or her Japanese counterpart appeared to be agreeing with what was being said, but that the deal ultimately fell through, leaving the American bewildered.

The words はい and いいえ are used between phrases as well as between sentences. In the following example, speaker B constantly interrupts speaker A so that A never finishes a sentence.

A: きのう えいがが あって ...	A: *There was a movie yesterday, and . . .*
B: ええ、	B: *Yeah/Yes.*
A: おもしろいって いうから いってみたんですが ...	A: *I went because I heard it would be interesting, but . . .*
B: ええ、ええ	B: *Yeah, yeah.*
A: ぜんぜん おもしろくなくて ...	A: *It was not interesting at all, and . . .*

Although this might appear rude according to Western standards, by Japanese standards B is not being rude, because A expects constant feedback from B. Indeed, A would feel uncomfortable if B waited for him or her to finish the sentence. In fact, this type of interruption can be seen in many types of conversational feedback in Japanese.

れんしゅう　Practice

Work with a partner. Imagine that both of you are in front of the library and your partner is pointing out different buildings on campus. Say はい or ええ between phrases and sentences to indicate that you understand what he or she is saying.

よむ　れんしゅう
Reading

じょうずな　よみかた　Reading Strategy

Scanning

There are many ways to read a text. Reading style depends on the reader's purpose. For example, if you are looking for certain information, such as the title of a movie, a date, or a topic, you may scan for a specific word or phrase. If you are looking for a reference article, you might skim the abstracts of papers. If you are writing a critique of an article, you will read it in detail. In this chapter, we will discuss the scanning process.

Scanning is a technique used to located specific information or facts quickly. People scan a text to look up a word in a dictionary or a name in the telephone directory, or to search for an answer to a comprehension question. In order to scan, a reader must know what he/she is looking for to be able to search for specific words or phrases.

Scanning is also an effective pre-reading tool when reading numerous texts. The reader may scan the text to assess its relevance, then skim it to get the gist, and if necessary, go back to the text yet again for more detailed reading. When scanning is used as a pre-reading tool, it is a good idea to look for items that signal text organization, such as numbers, steps, or words such as first and second. Also, words that appear in boldface, italics, a larger font size, or a different color may also indicate key information.

れんしゅう　Practice

A. Your friend asks you when you are available to go out for lunch next week. You check your appointment book, which is shown on the next page. Use the information there to answer the following:

  1. What kind of information you look for in an appointment book in cases like this.

  2. The day of the week and time that is most convenient for you. Use the phrase ～ようびの　～じは　どうですか (*How about ～?*).

  Example: げつようびの　じゅうにじは　どうですか。
  How about 12 o'clock Monday?

B. Another friend asks you to play tennis with him. Check your appointments in the table below to let him know the day of the week and time that you can play. Use the phrase ～ようびの　～じは　どうですか (*How about ～?*)

10/1 〜 10/7			
10/1 月 げつ	9時〜12時　クラス じ　　じ　　くらす 1時半〜2時　クラス じはん　じ　くらす 3時半〜10時　アルバイト じはん　じ　あるばいと	10/5 金 きん	9時〜12時　クラス じ　　じ　　くらす 1時半〜2時　クラス じはん　じ　くらす
10/2 火 か	9時〜10時　クラス じ　　じ　　くらす 10時半〜12時　クラス じはん　じ　くらす 1時〜2時　田中先生 じ　じ　たなかせんせい 4時〜6時　クラス じ　じ　くらす	10/6 土 ど	9時〜5時　アルバイト じ　じ　あるばいと
10/3 水 すい	9時〜12時　クラス じ　　じ　　くらす 1時半〜2時　クラス じはん　じ　くらす 4時半〜7時半　クラス じはん　じはん　くらす	10/7 日 にち	デート で　と
10/4 木 もく	9時〜10時　クラス じ　　じ　　くらす 10時半〜12時　クラス じはん　じ　くらす 4時〜6時　テスト じ　じ　てすと	NOTES	

ジョンソンさんの一日　Ms. Johnson's Daily Routine
じょんそん　　いちにち

よむ まえに　Pre-reading

A. Write five Japanese sentences about your daily routine.

B. Read the question below and identify the words or phrases to scan for in order to find out the answer quickly.

ジョンソンさんは　まいにち　じゅぎょうが　ありますか。
じょんそん

When you are done, scan the passage on the following page. Give your answer to the instructor as soon as you find it.

ことばの リスト　Vocabulary
りすと

そして	and, then
その後 あと	after that
ですから	so, therefore
でも	but
学生会館 がくせいかいかん	Student Union Building

私の一日
わたし　いちにち

キム・ジョンソン
きむ　じょんそん

私は毎日七時半に起きます。そして、シャワーを浴びます。た
わたし　まいにちしちじはん　お　　　　　　　しゃわ　　あ

いてい八時ごろ朝ご飯を食べます。そして、八時半ごろ大学
はちじ　あさ　はん　た　　　　　　　はちじはん　　だいがく

へ行きます。日本語の授業は毎朝九時にあります。その後、
い　　　にほんご　じゅぎょう　まいあさくじ　　　　　　　あと

よく図書館で勉強します。昨日も図書館でテストの勉強をしま
としょかん　べんきょう　　きのう　としょかん　てすと　べんきょう

した。

昼ご飯はたいてい学生会館で食べます。でも、昨日は食べま
ひる　はん　　　　がくせいかいかん　た　　　　　　きのう　た

せんでした。月曜日と水曜日と金曜日の午後は英語と文学の
げつようび　すいようび　きんようび　ごご　えいご　ぶんがく

授業があります。火曜日と木曜日の午後は授業がありませ
じゅぎょう　　　　　かようび　もくようび　ごご　じゅぎょう

ん。たいてい五時半ごろ家に帰ります。六時ごろ晩ご飯を食
ごじはん　　うち　かえ　　　ろくじ　　ばん　はん　た

べます。そして、宿題をします。テレビはあまり見ません。い
しゅくだい　　　　てれび　　　　み

つも十一時半に寝ます。
じゅういちじはん　ね

よんだ　あとで　Comprehension

Answer these questions in Japanese.

1. ジョンソンさんは　なんじごろ　おきますか。
じょんそん
2. ジョンソンさんは　いつ　ねますか。
じょんそん
3. げつようびは　なんの　じゅぎょうが　ありますか。
4. ジョンソンさんは　がくせいかいかんへ　よく　いきますか。
じょんそん
5. ジョンソンさんは　きのう　なにを　しましたか。
じょんそん
6. ジョンソンさんは　よく　テレビを　みますか。
じょんそん　　　　　てれび

そうごう　れんしゅう
Integration

すずきさんの　まいにち

Form a group of three people. There should be three types of groups: A, B, and C. Your instructor will tell you which group you are in. Listen to an interview with Suzuki-san, and take notes on the schedule sheet below. Discuss the interview with your partners and make sure that your information is correct. Then form a different group of three. All of the members in this group should come from different groups, one from Group A, another from Group B, and the other from Group C. Exchange information with the others to discover if there are discrepancies in your information.

〜ようび	なにを　しますか。
にちようび	
げつようび	
かようび	
すいようび	
もくようび	
きんようび	
どようび	

ロールプレイ   Role Play
ろ　　る　ぷ　れ　い

Imagine that you are talking to a Japanese friend. Explain to him or her how a typical American college student might spend a week.

Chapter 4

第
四
課
<ruby>だい<rt></rt></ruby><ruby>よん<rt></rt></ruby><ruby>か<rt></rt></ruby>

にほんの まち
Japanese Cities

Objectives	Asking about places and indicating location
Vocabulary	Buildings, landmarks, adjectives
Dialogue	このへんに　ぎんこうが　ありますか。 *Is there a bank around here?*
Japanese Culture	Geography and demographics of Japan
Grammar	I.　Referring to things using これ, それ, あれ, どれ
	II.　Asking for and giving locations using ～は　～に　あります／います and ここ, そこ, あそこ
	III.　Describing people and things using adjectives + noun, and polite present forms of adjectives
	IV.　Describing people, things, and their locations using ～に　～が　あります／います
	V.　Using よ and ね
Listening	Using redundancy in speech
Communication	Getting someone's attention (1)
Kanji	Introduction to **kanji** 大 学 校 先 生
Reading	Using script types as clues to word boundaries

単語
たん ご
Vocabulary

Nouns

アパート		apartment
えき	駅	station
えんぴつ	鉛筆	pencil
かばん	鞄	luggage, bag
カフェ		coffee shop, café (recent term)
きっさてん	喫茶店	coffee shop (traditional term)
きょうかしょ	教科書	textbook
ぎんこう	銀行	bank
けしゴム	消しゴム	eraser
こうえん	公園	park
こうばん	交番	police box
このへん	この辺	this area
コンビニ		convenience store
じしょ	辞書	dictionary
スーパー		supermarket
たてもの	建物	building, structure
テスト		test
デパート		department store
ノート		notebook
ビル		building
びょういん	病院	hospital
ペン		pen
ボールペン		ballpoint pen

ほんや	本屋	bookstore
まち	町	town
ゆうびんきょく	郵便局	post office
りょう	寮	dormitory
レストラン		restaurant

る -verbs

| います | | to be; to exist (used for an animate beings). |
| | | The dictionary form is いる. |

Demonstrative words

ここ		here, this place
これ		this object, this
そこ		there, that place (close to the listener or slightly removed from both speaker and listener)
それ		that object, that (close to the listener or slightly removed from both speaker and listener)
あそこ		over there, that place (far away from both speaker and listener)
あれ		that, that object over there

い -adjectives

あおい	青い	blue
あかい	赤い	red
あたらしい	新しい	new
いい		good
おおきい	大きい	big
きいろい	黄色い	yellow
くろい	黒い	black
しろい	白い	white
たかい	高い	tall, high
ちいさい	小さい	small

| ちゃいろい | 茶色い | brown |
| ふるい | 古い | old |

な -adjectives

きれい (な)		clean, pretty, neat
ゆうめい (な)	有名 (な)	famous
りっぱ (な)	立派 (な)	fine, splendid, nice

Question words

だれ		who
どれ		which one
どんな		what kind of

Adverbs

あまり		very (always used with a negative form)
とても		very (always used with an affirmative form)
どうも		very

どうも　ありがとう　Thank you very much
どうも　すみません　I'm very sorry

Suffix

| ～や | ～屋 | store (for example, ほんや   bookstore) |

単語の 練習 Vocabulary Practice
たんご れんしゅう

A. まち Towns

Activity 1

Complete the chart with the Japanese word for each symbol.

Location	Map Symbol	Japanese
station		
bank		
post office		
supermarket		
school		
hospital		
restaurant		
coffee shop		
police box		
department store		
convenience store		

Activity 2

Answer these questions in Japanese.

1. よく　カフェに　いきますか。
2. よく　コンビニに　いきますか。
3. なんじごろ　うちに　かえりますか。
4. 〜さんは　うちに　すんでいますか。アパートに　すんでいますか。
　 りょうに　すんでいますか。(すんでいます to live)
5. せんしゅう　スーパーに　いきましたか。
6. しゅうまつは　ときどき　デパートに　いきますか。
7. よく　どこで　べんきょうしますか。
8. レストランで　よく　なにを　たべますか。

B. Adjectives

あたらしい	new	あおい	blue
大きい おお	big	あかい	red
たかい	tall, high	きいろい	yellow
ちいさい	small	くろい	black
ふるい	old	しろい	white
きれい (な)	clean, pretty, neat	ちゃいろい	brown
ゆうめい (な)	famous		
りっぱ (な)	nice, fine, splendid		

Activity 3

Write an antonym for each of the following words. Follow the example.

Example: きたない (dirty) → きれい

大きい おお	
あたらしい	
しろい	
あかい	
むめい (unknown)	

Activity 4

Create as many sentences as you can using 〜は　adjectives です and the adjectives in the above list.

Example: わたしの　学校は　大きいです。
　　　　　　　　がっこう　　　おお

C. School supplies

えんぴつ　　けしゴム　　ペン　　ボールペン

ノート　　きょうかしょ　　じしょ　　かばん

Activity 5

Create sentences describing the color(s) and/or size for each of the items above that you own.

Example: わたしの　かばんは　ちゃいろいです。じしょは　しろいです。

ダイアローグ
Dialogue

はじめに   Warm-up

The Shibuya/Harajuku District is a popular hangout for young Japanese. Look at the map of Shibuya and Harajuku below and try to identify some of the landmarks in the area.

Shibuya and Harajuku

このへんに　ぎんこうが　ありますか。 *Is there a bank around here?*

Ueda is meeting a friend in Shibuya. She has just gotten off the train, and realizes that she needs to withdraw some cash. She approaches a passerby (つうこうにん) in front of Shibuya Station (しぶやえき).

うえだ：　　　　　あのう、すみませんが。

つうこうにんA：　はい。

うえだ：　　　　　このへんに　ぎんこうが　ありますか。

つうこうにんA：　ええ、ありますよ。あそこに　たかい　ビルが　ありますね。

うえだ：　　　　　ええ。

つうこうにんA：　あれですよ。

うえだ：　　　　　あ、そうですか。どうも　ありがとう　ございます。

つうこうにんA：　いいえ。

In the building:

うえだ：　　　　　あのう、すみません。

つうこうにんB：　はい。

うえだ：　　　　　ぎんこうは　どこに　ありますか。

つうこうにんB：　あ、ぎんこうは　それですよ。

うえだ：　　　　　ああ、どうも。

つうこうにんB：　いいえ。

At the entrance of the bank:

うえだ： あのう、すみませんが、ATM は　どこですか。

こういん (*clerk*)： そこに　ございます。

うえだ： ああ、どうも。

DIALOGUE PHRASE NOTES

- When someone thanks you, it is common to say いいえ. In this case, いいえ means *Don't mention it*, or *You're welcome*.
- Like English, Japanese uses a variety of expressions, such as あ (*Ah / Oh*), ああ (*Oh / OK*), へえ〜 (*Hmm / Oh*) to indicate understanding or surprise.
- どうも is an abbreviation of phrases such as どうも　ありがとう and どうも　すみません. It is very common to use only どうも in conversation.
- ございます is the polite form of あります. In this dialogue, the bank clerk uses it when speaking with Ueda.

ダイアローグの　後(あと)で　Comprehension

Answer the following questions in Japanese.

1. うえださんは　どこに　いきますか。
2. それは　しぶやえきに　ありますか。
3. どんな　たてものですか。

日本の文化
に ほん ぶん か
Japanese Culture

Geography and demographics of Japan

Japan is an island nation consisting of about 3,000 islands. Among them, Honshu, Hokkaido, Kyushu, and Shikoku are the four major islands. Japan lies east of

北海道
ほっかいどう

本州
ほんしゅう

九州
きゅうしゅう

四国
しこく

Korea, Russia, and China and is separated from continental Asia by the Sea of Japan. The country is comparable in size to the state of California, with a climate that varies from cool temperate in the north to subtropical in the south.

Mountains cover nearly three quarters of Japan. Since so little flat area exists, many hills and mountainsides are cultivated all the way to the top. There are many volcanoes in Japan because the country lies in an area where several continental plates meet. The most famous volcano is Mt. Fuji, which is the highest point of Japan, with an elevation of 3,776m (12,388 feet). Considered to be one of the most beautiful mountains in the world, Fuji-san, as the Japanese call it, is held sacred and can be seen from Tokyo when the weather is clear.

As Japan is situated in a volcanic zone along the Pacific deeps, frequent low-intensity earth tremors and occasional volcanic activity are felt throughout the islands. Destructive earthquakes occur several times a century. Hot springs are numerous and have been developed as resorts.

The population of Japan is about 125,000,000. While nearly the entire population is Japanese, more than half of the non-Japanese population is Korean. Several smaller minorities from other parts of Asia, India, Latin America, and the Mideast live mostly in Tokyo and other large cities.

Japanese neighborhoods

Japanese neighborhoods tend to develop around a train station. Surrounding a station are various stores, restaurants, banks, post offices, bus terminals, and other buildings. It is also common to find a police box (こうばん) in front of a station. A police box usually has a couple of officers on duty around the clock. People often ask officers for directions.

Police boxes in Tokyo are designed to match the atmosphere of the neighborhood. Many of them include artistic architectural detail, with "KOBAN" signs written in romanized text instead of the characters 交番, to appear more friendly and modern.

Map symbols

In Japan, streets are not usually laid out with a north-south or east-west orientation, and many are designated only by number, so being able to read a Japanese map and keeping one handy is essential to getting around in Japan. If you happen to be in a car, GPS navigation systems are common, and some cell phones have a feature to access maps online. For a chart of Japanese map symbols and their meanings, visit the Nakama 1 student website.

カフェ vs きっさてん

Around the turn of the last century, the term カフェ came into use in Japan. Until then きっさてん had been the only word for *coffee shop*. These words now refer to different types of coffee shops. A カフェ usually has a modern interior and hip urban feel, and serves food and coffee intended to appeal to women and younger consumers. (for example, Starbucks, or スタバ as the Japanese tend to call it.) The term きっさてん refers to a more traditional coffee shop and tends to imply a less sophisticated atmosphere. Many きっさてん allow smoking inside, so they are often considered resting spots for smokers, especially businessmen.

文法
ぶんぽう
Grammar

I. Referring to things, using これ, それ, あれ, どれ

In Chapter 1, you learned the Japanese words to ask about objects around you, using これ／それ／あれは　にほんごで　なんと　いいますか. This chapter introduces the general use of これ, それ, あれ and どれ. これ, それ, あれ and どれ are nouns that refer to things.

A. これ means *this* or *this thing*. It refers to something that is close to the speaker.

これは　わたしの　えんぴつです。
This is my pencil.

B. それ means *that* or *that thing*. It refers to something that is closer to the listener than the speaker or somewhat away from both of them.

それは　わたしの　えんぴつです。
That is my pencil.

C. あれ means *that* or *that thing over there*. **It refers to something away from both of them.**

あれは　わたしの　えんぴつです。
That one over there is my pencil.

D. どれ means *which* or *which thing*. **It is a question word that asks for a choice between two or more items.**

スミス：　たなかさん、それは　なんですか。
　　　　　Ms. Tanaka, what is that?

たなか：　これは　にほんごの　きょうかしょです。
　　　　　This is a Japanese textbook.

スミス：　あ、そうですか。じゃあ、あれも　にほんごの　きょうかしょ
　　　　　ですか。
　　　　　I see. Then, is that one over there a Japanese textbook, too?

たなか：　いいえ、あれは　にほんごの　じしょです。
　　　　　No, that's a Japanese dictionary.

スミス：　それは　たなかさんの　ほんですか。
　　　　　Is that one your book?

たなか：　いいえ、ちがいます。
　　　　　No, it isn't.

スミス：　じゃあ、たなかさんの　ほんは　どれですか。
　　　　　Which one is your book, Ms. Tanaka?

たなか：　あれです。
　　　　　That one over there.

スミス： あれは　だれの　ノートですか。
Whose notebook is that over there?

たなか： あれですか。キムさんの　ノートです。
That one over there? It's Ms. Kim's.

スミス： そうですか。
Is that so?

NOTES

- これ, それ, あれ and どれ are pronouns and cannot be followed by another noun.
- It is rude to refer to people using これ, それ, あれ, どれ because they refer to things. However, you can use them to refer to a person in a picture because he/she is not considered a person.
- Actual distances that these words indicate vary depending on context. それ would imply much greater distance when it is used to point out a building than when it is used to point to an item in a room. In the picture below, これ refers to the building in front of the speaker and the listener, あれ refers to the house far away from them, and それ refers to the one that is somewhat away from them but not quite far enough for them to call it あれ.
- だれ means *who*, but it also means *whose* if followed by the particle の.

  だれが　きますか。　　　　　*Who is coming?*
  これは　だれの　ほんですか。　*Whose book is this?*

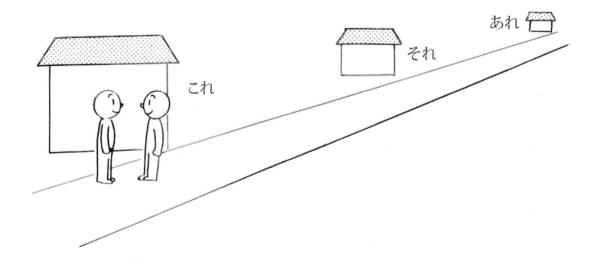

話して　みましょう　Conversation Practice
はな

Activity 1

Look at the following drawing of a room. Smith is asking Kimura the Japanese words for various objects in the room. Complete the following conversations using これ, それ and あれ.

Example:　スミス：　<u>これ</u>は　にほんごで　なんと　いいますか。
　　　　　　きむら：　けしゴムと　いいます。

1.　スミス：　＿＿＿＿＿＿は　にほんごで　なんと　いいますか。
　　きむら：　けしゴムと　いいます。

2.　スミス：　＿＿＿＿＿＿は　にほんごで　なんと　いいますか。
　　きむら：　じしょと　いいます。

3.　スミス：　＿＿＿＿＿＿は　にほんごで　なんと　いいますか。
　　きむら：　えんぴつと　いいます。

4.　スミス：　＿＿＿＿＿＿は　にほんごで　なんと　いいますか。
　　きむら：　ノートと　いいます。

5.　スミス：　＿＿＿＿＿＿は　にほんごで　なんと　いいますか。
　　きむら：　かばんと　いいます。

Activity 2

Work with a partner. Look at the following drawing. Pretend you are person A, and your partner is person B. Some erasers, pencils, books, and dictionaries are scattered around the room. First, let your partner decide who among the following people owns each item and mark it on the drawing.

たなか先生　きむらさん　アリスさん　キムさん　スミスさん
　せんせい
リンさん

Then ask who owns each item and write it under the owner's name. After you finish, have your partner check your answers.

Example:　A:　これ／それ／あれは　だれの　ほんですか。

　　　　　　B:　<u>きむらさんの　ほん</u>です。

Activity 3

Work with a partner. Looking at the map below, ask a classmate to locate certain buildings using これ, それ and あれ. Assume that both of you are standing in front of the police box.

Example:　A: これ／それ／あれは _____ですか。

　　　　　　B: はい、そうです。　or いいえ、そうじゃありません。

Activity 4

Work with a partner. Look at the following town maps. Imagine that your partner is a new student and you are showing him/her the campus. First, decide where you and your partner are among the locations numbered 1 through 4. Then, describe the buildings around you, using これ, それ, あれ, どれ.

Example:　A:　これ／それ／あれは＿＿＿＿＿＿＿＿＿です。

　　　　　　B:　そうですか。じゃあ、これ／それ／あれは　なんですか。

　　　　　　A:　＿＿＿＿＿＿＿です。

II. Asking for and giving locations using ～は ～に あります／います and ここ, そこ, あそこ

A. ここ、そこ、あそこ、どこ

The words これ, それ, あれ, どれ refer to objects. When these words are used to point out a building, the speaker is viewing the building as an object rather than as a location. However, buildings and facilities are also considered places or locations. In order to refer to the location, you need to use ここ, そこ, あそこ, どこ instead.

ここ means *here* or *this place*, and refers to the area close to the speaker.

そこ means *there* or *that place*, and refers to the area close to the listener but away from the speaker, or between, or some distance from both of them.

あそこ means *that place over there*, and refers to the area far away from both the speaker and the listener.

どこ means *where*.

B. ～は ～に あります

In Chapter 3 (p. 103), you learned that the verb あります (*there is X*) is used to describe the existence of an object or event. It is commonly used to ask or identify the location of objects such as pens, books, and buildings. To ask about location, use ～は どこに ありますか. Here に is a particle that indicates the location of an object.

じしょは どこに ありますか。　　*Where is the dictionary?*

りょうは どこに ありますか。　　*Where is the dormitory?*

The answer to these questions might be: Location に あります.

ここに あります　　*It's here.*

あそこに あります。　　*It's over there.*

The word あります is never used to indicate the location of animate objects such as people, pets, and other animals, because it is used only for lifeless objects. Use います to talk about the location of living beings.

キム： まもるさんは どこに います か。　*Where is Mamoru?*

スー：　　　　　ここに います。　　*He is here.*

スミス： あのう、すみませんが、ゆうびんきょくは どこに ありますか。
Um, excuse me, but where is the post office?

たなか： そこに あります。
It's there.

スミス： あ、そうですか。どうも。
I see. Thanks.

(The teacher is taking attendance, but he doesn't see Ms. Kim.)

先生：　キムさんは　どこに　いますか。
せんせい
Where is Ms. Kim?

ブラウン：　先生、いま　としょかんに　います。
せんせい
Professor, she is in the library now.

先生：　あ、そうですか。じゅぎょうに　きますか。
せんせい
I see. Is she coming to class?

ブラウン：　さあ、よくわかりません。
Well, I am not sure.

NOTES

- Location に　あります／います can be abbreviated as Location です.

  なかがわ：　スミスさんの　りょうは　<u>どこですか</u>。
  Where is Mr. Smith's dormitory?

  スミス：　<u>あそこです</u>。
  Over there.

  先生：　キムさんは　どこに　いますか。
  せんせい
  Where is Ms. Kim?

  ジョンソン：　としょかんです。
  In the library.

- You cannot use the particle で in this structure because で indicates a location at which an event or activity takes place. When you are merely asking or indicating the location of a building or object, no activity is implied.

  スミス：　どこ<u>で</u>　えいがが　ありますか。
  Where is the movie?

  なかがわ：　あそこ<u>で</u>　あります。
  It will be over there.

  キム：　こうえんは　どこ<u>に</u>　ありますか。
  Where is the park?

  やまだ：　あそこ<u>に</u>　あります。
  It's over there.

話してみましょう Conversation Practice
はな

Activity 1

Work with a partner. Look at the drawing of a room. One person asks questions about the location of the objects and people, 〜は どこに あります/いますか and the other person responds using ここ/そこ/あそこ and 〜に あります/います or 〜です. Follow the model.

Example: A: <u>ノート</u>は　どこに　ありますか。

B: <u>ここに　あります。／ここです。</u>

1. けしゴム
2. やまださん
3. にほんごの　じしょ
4. スミスさん
5. ボールペン
6. きょうかしょ

やまだ

スミス

Activity 2

Look at the following drawing of a street. Your partner will ask you where the following buildings are. Answer his/her questions based on the picture.

Example: A: あのう、としょかんは　どこに　ありますか。
B: そこに　あります。
A: ああ、そこですね。どうも。

1. こうえん
2. こうばん
3. ゆうびんきょく

4. ほんや
5. としょかん

III. Describing people and things using adjectives + noun, and polite present forms of adjectives

There are two types of adjectives in Japanese. Both of them modify nouns directly and can be used at the end of sentence to describe a noun. One is called an い -adjective because it ends in い before a noun, as in 大きい　うち (big house) and ちいさい　うち (small house). The other type is called a な -adjective, because the adjective takes な before a noun as in りっぱな　うち (fine house) and きれいな　うち (pretty house).

A. Describing people and things, using adjectives and adverbs + noun

りょうは　ふるい　たてものです。
The dormitory is in an old building.

えきビルは　ゆうめいな　たてものです。
The station building is a famous building.

The formation of adjective + noun is the following. Note that the dictionary form is the form in which dictionaries list adjectives and verbs.

い -adjectives

Dictionary form　大きい

大きい　＋　うち　→　大きい　うち

な -adjectives

Dictionary form:　きれい

きれいな　＋　うち　→　きれいな　うち

やまなか：　あれは　わたしの　うちです。
That one over there is my house.

スミス：　へえ、大きい　うちですね。
Wow, it's a large house, isn't it?

ジョンソン：　ゆうびんきょくは　どこに　ありますか。
Where is the post office?

ほんだ：　ゆうびんきょくですか。あそこです。
The post office? Over there.

ジョンソン：　ああ、りっぱな　たてものですね。
I see, it's a nice building.

B. Describing and commenting on places using adjectives (polite affirmative and negative forms), and とても and あまり.

Polite affirmative form

わたしの　かばんは　<u>あかいです</u>。
My bag is red.

おがわさんのりょうは　<u>とても</u>　<u>ちいさいです</u>。
Mr. Ogawa's dorm is very small.

びょういんは　<u>とても</u>　<u>きれいです</u>。
The hospital is very clean.

Polite negative form

わたしの　かばんは　<u>くろくありません</u>。
My bag is not black.

わたしの　かばんは　<u>くろくないです</u>。
My bag is not black.

びょういんは　<u>あまり</u>　<u>大きくありません</u>。
The hospital is not very big.

びょういんは　<u>あまり</u>　<u>大きくないです</u>。
The hospital is not very big.

すずきさんのりょうは　<u>あまり</u>　<u>りっぱじゃありません</u>。
Mr. Suzuki's dorm is not very nice.

すずきさんのりょうは　<u>あまり</u>　<u>りっぱじゃないです</u>。
Mr. Suzuki's dorm is not very nice.

The following charts show the formation of polite forms and adjective + noun for い- and な-adjectives.

い -adjectives

Dictionary form	Polite affirmative form	Polite negative form	adjective + noun
大きい (large)	大き<u>い</u>です	大き<u>く</u>ありません 大き<u>く</u>ないです	大き<u>い</u>うち
いい * (good)	<u>いい</u>です	<u>よく</u>ありません <u>よく</u>ないです	<u>いい</u>うち

* い -Adjective いい, meaning *good*, has an irregular negative form.

な -adjectives

Dictionary form	Polite affirmative form	Polite negative form	Adjective + noun
ゆうめい (famous)	ゆうめいです	ゆうめい<u>じゃ</u>ありません ゆうめい<u>じゃ</u>ないです	ゆうめい<u>な</u> うち

ジョンソン： ほんださんの　うちは　どこですか。
Where is your house, Mr. Honda?

ほんだ： それです。
It's there.

ジョンソン： ああ、とても　きれいな　うちですね。
Wow, it's a very nice house, isn't it.

ほんだ： ありがとう。でも、　あまり　大きくありませんよ。／
大きくないですよ。
Thank you, but it is not very big.

NOTES

- The alternative negative form, 〜ないです, is considered colloquial and only used in spoken language.

- Note that the negative form of a な-adjective is the same as that of a <u>noun + です</u>.

  Negative of <u>noun + です</u>　　大学生じゃありません。

  Negative of な -adjective　　きれいじゃありません。

  りょうは　<u>とても</u>　きれいです。
  The dormitory is <u>very</u> nice/clean.

  りょうは　<u>あまり</u>　きれいじゃありません。
  The domitory is <u>not very</u> nice /clean.

- The adverbs とても and あまり are often used with adjectives, and both may be translated as *very* in English. とても occurs with an affirmative form, and あまり occurs with a negative form. The combination of あまり　〜ません／ないです means *not very*.

- Use どんな (*what kind of* 〜) to ask about characteristics of people and objects.

  イー： どんな　たてものですか。
  What kind of building is it?

  ホン： くろい　たてものです。
  It is a black building

話してみましょう   Conversation Practice
はな

Activity 1

Describe buildings, objects, and people using the boxed adjectives and the phrases listed below.

Example: わたしの　りょう／たてもの

　　　　　　わたしの　りょうは　ふるい　たてものです。

大きい	ちいさい	あたらしい	ふるい	たかい
おお				
あかい	あおい	しろい	くろい	きいろい　いい
きれい	りっぱ	ゆうめい	ちゃいろい	

1. わたしの　大学／大学
　　　　　　だいがく　だいがく
2. わたしの　うち／たてもの
3. わたしの　かばん／かばん

4. にほんごの　先生／ひと (person)
　　　　　　　せんせい
5. びょういん／たてもの
6. 先生の　ペン／ペン
　　せんせい

Activity 2

Work with a partner. Ask your classmates what kinds of places they prefer for doing one of the following activities:

Example: うちを　かいます。 (to buy)

　　　　　　A:　どんな　うちが　いいですか。

　　　　　　B:　ふるい　うちが　いいですね。

1. 大学院に　はいります。
　だいがくいん
2. カフェで　べんきょうします。
3. びょういんに　いきます。
4. りょこうに　いきます。 (to go on a trip)
5. レストランで　ごはんを　たべます。

Activity 3

Look at the chart describing various buildings, and answer the following questions, paying attention to はい, いいえ, とても and あまり.

Examples:　A:　ゆうびんきょくは　大_{おお}きいですか。

　　　　　　B:　<u>いいえ、大_{おお}きくありません。</u>

　　　　or　<u>いいえ、大_{おお}きくないです。</u>

　　　　　　A:　ぎんこうは　大_{おお}きいですか。

　　　　　　B:　<u>はい、とても　大_{おお}きいです。</u>

	ゆうびんきょく	ぎんこう	スーパー	びょういん
大きい	いいえ	とても	あまり	はい
あたらしい	とても	いいえ	はい	あまり
いい	あまり	いいえ	とても	とても
きれい	はい	いいえ	はい	はい
ゆうめい	いいえ	あまり	いいえ	はい
りっぱ	あまり	とても	いいえ	はい

1. スーパーは　いいですか。
2. ゆうびんきょくは　あたらしいですか。
3. びょういんは　きれいですか。
4. びょういんは　あたらしいですか。
5. ゆうびんきょくは　いいですか。
6. ぎんこうは　りっぱですか。
7. ぎんこうは　ゆうめいですか。

Activity 4

Work with a partner. Using the adjectives you have just learned, tell your partner about your home and belongings. Then ask your partner whether his/her place and belongings also share these characteristics. Follow the model.

Example:　A:　わたしの　アパートは　あたらしいです。

　　　　　　　　～さんの　アパートも　あたらしいですか。

　　　　　　B:　ええ、とても　あたらしいです。／

　　　　　　　　いいえ、あまり　あたらしくありません。

IV. Describing people, things, and their locations using 〜に　〜が　あります／います

The phrase 〜に　〜が　あります／います *means there is a person/object in a certain location*. It uses the same verbs and the location particle に like 〜は　〜に あります／います, but their usage is different. Whereas 〜は　〜に　あります／ います is used to ask for or tell the location of something or someone, 〜に　〜が あります／います is used to describe a scene in which someone or something exists in a given location or to ask what is in that location.

あ、ここに		ねこが	います。	*Oh, there is a cat right here.*
ほら、あそこに	すずきさんが	います。	*Look! I see Mr. Suzuki over there.*
大学に だいがく	ほんやが	あります。	*There is a bookstore in the university.*
えきに	ゆうびんきょくが	あります。	*There is a post office in the station.*

ブラウン：　そこに　ほんが　ありますか。
Is there a book there (near you)?

おがわ：　ええ、ありますよ。ブラウンさんの　ほんですか。
Yes, there is. It that yours?

ブラウン：　ええ、そうです。ありがとう。
Yes, it is. Thank you.

たなか：　このへんに　なにが　ありますか。
What is in this area?

スミス：　とても　ゆうめいな　こうえんが　あります。
There is a very famous park.

うえだ：　すみません、このへんに　スーパーが
あります。
Excuse me. Is there a supermarket around here?

つうこうにん (passerby)：　ええ、ありますよ。
Yes, there is.

うえだ：　そうですか。どこに　ありますか。
I see. Where is it?

つうこうにん (passerby)：　あそこですよ。
It is over there.

NOTES

- The location may be marked by には instead of just に, if the location is the topic of a sentence.

  Example: にほんには　ふじさんが　あります。
  As for Japan, Mt. Fuji is there.

- ～に　～が　あります cannot be replaced with ～は　～です.

話してみましょう Conversation Practice
はな

Activity 1

The box below represents a room. You are at location A. Decide where to place the objects listed in the chart and fill in blanks 2 through 8 accordingly. Then, assuming you are talking with a person at location B, complete the chart with the location number and correct location noun (ここ, そこ or あそこ). Finally, create sentences describing the location of each object, following the example.

Example: ここに　くろい　ペンが　あります。

```
┌──────────────────────────────────────────────────────────┐
│                                                          │
│   1 くろい　ペン        A          B        2 _____   │
│                                                          │
│   6 _____                              7 _____   │
│                                                          │
│                                                          │
│                        3 _____                   │
│                                                          │
│   5 _____       8 _____          4 _____       │
│                                                          │
└──────────────────────────────────────────────────────────┘
```

Location 1–8	ここ／そこ／あそこ	Object
1	ここ	くろい　ペン
		あかい　ボールペン
		ふるい　かばん
		しろい　かばん
		きいろい　ノート
		ちゃいろい　えんぴつ
		ふるい　じしょ
		きれいな　きょうかしょ

Activity 2

Work with a partner. Ask your partner where the objects in Activity 1 are located on his/her map for the same exercise, and write in the name of the objects in the correct location below. Use the location number to specify the exact location.

Example: A:　1に　なにが　ありますか。

B:　くろい　ペンが　あります。

1 くろい　ペン　　　A　　　　B　　　2 ＿＿＿＿＿＿

6 ＿＿＿＿＿＿　　　　　　　　　7 ＿＿＿＿＿＿

3 ＿＿＿＿＿＿

5 ＿＿＿＿　　8 ＿＿＿＿＿　　4 ＿＿＿＿＿

Activity 3

Work with a new partner. Ask your partner about buildings in his/her neighborhood. Then write a description of the neighborhood using adjectives you have just learned.

Example: A: このへんに　どんな　たてものが　ありますか。

B: <u>ぎんこうが　あります。</u>

A: どんな　たてものですか。

B: <u>たかい　たてものです。でも、あまり</u>
<u>きれいじゃありません。</u>

Activity 4

Work in a group of four. One person will think of a famous city or a country. Try to guess the name of the city or the country by asking who lives there or what landmarks are found there. Use そこ to refer to the target city or country.

Examples: A: そこに　なにが　ありますか。

B: ビッグベン (Big Ben) が　あります。

A: ロンドンですか。

B: はい、そうです。

V. Using よ and ね

Japanese employs a variety of sentence final particles to indicate the speaker's assumption, intention, and other subtle nuances. Two of the most common particles used in conversation are ね and よ.

A. The particle ね

The particle ね can be translated as ~*isn't it?/right?/correct?* in English. It indicates that the speaker thinks the listener shares the same information, opinions, or feelings. ね is used when the speaker is seeking the listener's agreement, or confirming a fact, or to create a sense of togetherness between the speakers. For example, in the following exchange, Li is confirming that a **kanji** quiz is scheduled for today.

> リー： きょう　かんじの　テストが　ありますね。
> *We have a kanji test today, right?*

> キム： ええ。
> *Yes.*

In the following sentence, Li thinks that Yoyogi Park is pretty and assumes Kim thinks the same. So, he is seeking her agreement.

> リー： 代々木公園は　きれいですね。
> *Yoyogi Park is pretty, isn't it?*

> キム： ええ、ほんとうに　きれいですね。
> *Yes, it is indeed pretty.*

In the following sentence, John does not necessarily assume that Yamashita shares the same opinion about the park. Instead, he invites Yamashita to share his opinion by using ね. The speaker uses ね in this way to create a sense of togetherness or familiarity with the listener.

> やました： こうえんは　あそこです。
> *The park is over there.*

> ジョン： ああ、りっぱな　こうえんですね。
> *Wow, it is a nice park, isn't it?*

B. The particle よ

The particle よ can be translated as *I tell you* or *you know* in English. よ indicates the speaker's assumption that the listener does not share the speaker's opinion or information. Therefore, it is used when the speaker wishes to emphasize to the listener that he/she is imparting completely new information, and can sound authoritative. When overused or used improperly, よ sounds pushy and overly aggressive.

リー： 先生、あした　テストが　ありますか。
せんせい
Are we going to have a test tomorrow?

先生： いいえ。テストは　あさってですよ。
せんせい
No, it will be the day after tomorrow.

ブラウン： このへんに　ぎんこうが　ありますか。
Is there a bank around here?

つうこうにん (*passerby*)： ええ、そこに　ありますよ。
Yes, it is there.

ブラウン： あ、あかいたてものですね。
Ah, the red building, right?

つうこうにん (*passerby*)： ええ、そうです。
Yes, it is.

話してみましょう　**Conversation Practice**
はな

Activity 1

Complete the following conversations by choosing ね or よ.

Example: A: あのう、このへんに　コンビニが　ありますか。

B: ええ、 あります（ね／よ）。あそこです。

A: あ、あれです（ね／よ）。どうも　ありがとう　ございます。

1. A: すみません、いま　なんじですか。
   B: ３じはんです（ね／よ）。
   A: そうですか。どうも　ありがとう。

2. A: きょう　なんじに　かえりますか。
   B: ６じごろ　かえります。
   A: ６じごろです（ね／よ）。じゃあ、６じはんに　いきます。

3. A: あの、これは　スミスさんの　じしょですか。
   B: いいえ、それは、うえださんの　じしょです（ね／よ）。
   A: あ、そうですか。どうも。

4. A: あの、先生、テストは　あしたです（ね／よ）。
   せんせい
   B: ええ、そうです。

5. A: あの、先生、らいしゅうの　かようびは　やすみです（ね／よ）。
   せんせい
   B: いいえ、かようびは　じゅぎょうが　あります。
      やすみは　すいようびです（ね／よ）。

6: A: すみません。ゆうびんきょくは　どこですか。

B: あそこに　たかいビルが　あります（ね／よ）。

A: ええ。

B: ゆうびんきょくは　あそこに　あります。

A: ああ、そうですか。どうも。

B: いいえ。

Activity 2

Work with a partner. The following conversations sound slightly unnatural because they are missing the particle ね or よ. Revise the conversation using ね or よ where appropriate.

Example: A: あのう、すみませんが、やまだびょういんは　どこですか。

B: やまだびょういんですか。あそこです。

A: あ、あれですね。どうも　ありがとう　ございます。

B: いいえ。

1. A: あのう、このへんに　びょういんが　ありますか。

B: いいえ、ありません。びょういんは　とおい (*far away*) です。

A: そうですか。どうも。

2. A: そこに　しろい　たてものが　あります。

B: ええ。

A: それは　なんですか。

B: それは　ほんやです。

3. A: これは　なんですか。

B: なっとうです。

A: え、なっとう？　なっとうって　なんですか。

B: Fermented soy beans です。

4. A: あれは　デパートですか。

B: いいえ、スーパーです。

A: とても　りっぱな　スーパーです。

B: そうです。

聞く　練習
き　　　れんしゅう
Listening

上手な　聞き方　Listening Strategy
じょうず　　き　かた

Using redundancy in speech

In Chapters 2 and 3 (see p. 67 and p. 117), you learned that it is not necessary to understand every single word in order to understand a conversation, and that it is important to pick up only a few key words. In face-to-face conversations, there are many clues as to what a person is saying, such as facial expressions, gestures, and intonation. Context and general knowledge will also help you guess words you may have missed.

学生街　Campus Town
がくせいがい

聞く　前に　Warm-up
き　　まえ

Listen to the following conversations. They take place on a busy street that runs near Joto University. Since there is a lot of background noise, some of the words in the conversations cannot be heard. Try to guess the missing words and write them down.

1. _____

2. _____

3. _____

聞いた　後で　Comprehension
き　　あと

Based on the conversation you have just heard, complete the following sentences with the correct building names.

1. しろい　たてものは＿＿＿＿＿＿＿＿＿です。

2. ＿＿＿＿＿＿＿＿は　ほんやの　ちかくに　あります。

3. そのちゃいろい　たてものは＿＿＿＿＿＿＿＿＿です。

聞き上手　話し上手
き　　じょうず　　はな　　じょうず
Communication

Communication Strategy

Getting someone's attention (1)

In Chapter 1 (p. 18), you learned the phrase, あのう、すみません (*Excuse me*) as a way of getting someone's attention. In this chapter, you will learn more about すみません along with other phrases commonly used in this context.

In current Japanese, すみません has three separate functions: to apologize, to get someone's attention, or to thank. すみません is probably the phrase most commonly used to get someone's attention. It is often preceded by あのう (*ah . . .*) or ちょっと (*well . . .*) and followed by が (but), as in あのう　すみませんが, ちょっと　すみませんが, and あのう　ちょっと　すみませんが.

あのう by itself may also be used to get someone's attention. For example, if someone wants to initiate a conversation at a meeting or a party, the person can say あのう and wait for the listener to respond. あのう is also used as a conversation filler when one cannot think of the right word. If you want to ask someone a personal question, first say しつれいですが or あのう　しつれいですが (literally, *I am being rude, but . . .*). For instance, あのう　しつれいですが、にほんの　かたですか is a polite way of asking someone whether he/she is Japanese.

Finally, along with あのう or すみません,　おねがいします (literally, *I am requesting*) may also be used to get the attention of someone who provides a service, such as a store clerk.

練習　Practice
れんしゅう

A. Listen to three dialogues and identify the phrase used to approach the listener in each dialogue.

B. You are looking for a certain building or facility, and your classmates are all strangers. Ask for its location using the appropriate expression.

漢字
かん じ
Kanji

漢字   Introduction to Kanji
かん じ

In addition to **hiragana** and **katakana**, the Japanese writing system makes extensive use of **kanji**, which are characters borrowed from Chinese. When the Japanese adopted **kanji**, they also adopted the Chinese way of reading them. At the same time, the Japanese gave the Chinese characters Japanese readings for existing Japanese words. Consequently, a **kanji** character has two or sometimes more readings. The Chinese reading of a **kanji** is called the **on** reading, and the Japanese reading is called the **kun** reading. For example, the **on** reading for the kanji 大 (*big*) is だい as in 大学. Its **kun** reading is おお as in 大きい. Chinese words incorporated into
だいがく   おお
Japanese are usually given **on** readings, as in 大学, 学生 and 先生.
だいがく がくせい   せんせい

A **kanji** can be used only for its specific meaning. Thus, even if 五 (*five*) is read ご, one may not use it to replace the **hiragana** ご in おはようございます or あさごはん.

Kanji originated as pictographs and some of the characters still retain their pictorial qualities. For example, 川 (*river*) developed from the picture 川, 大 (*big*) from 大 (a man extending arms and legs), and 生 (*life*) from 生 (picture of a plant coming out). The exact number of existing **kanji** has never been clear, but it is estimated to be more than 40,000. Approximately 3,000 **kanji** are commonly used in Japan. The Japanese Ministry of Education has designated 1,945 for use in publications such as newspapers and magazines.

Learning **kanji** can be a laborious process. However, once a certain number of **kanji** have been learned, it becomes easier because **kanji** can be associated on the basis of their components. In dictionaries, **kanji** are classified according to 214 basic component shapes, or radicals, each of which has a unique meaning. The following **kanji**, which share the common radical 言, have something to do with language: 訳 (*translation*), 話 (*talk*), 語 (*language*), and 読 (*reading*).

A **kanji** is written according to a fixed stroke order. The general rule is to write from top to bottom, and left to right. Also, a horizontal line is usually drawn before a vertical one.

In Japanese, **kanji** are used mostly for nouns and stems of verbs, adjectives, and adverbs. Grammatical markers, such as particles and inflectional endings, are not written in **kanji**. For example, in the following sentence, the nouns わたし and さかな are written with the **kanji** 私 and 魚, and the verb stem た of たべます is written with the **kanji** 食. The particles は and を as well as the verb ending べます are written in **hiragana**.

私は魚を食べます。(わたしは　さかなを　たべます。*I eat fish.*)

Note the following format for the **kanji** charts used in this book The charts will contain the typeset version of the character, a handwritten version, and stroke order. The **on** readings are in **katakana** and the **kun** readings are in **hiragana**.

学 学	to study, learn	` ｀ ｀` `ﾞ` `ﾞﾞ` `ﾞﾞﾞ` `ﾞﾞﾞ` 学 学 学 学 学
	まな（ぶ）　ガク・ガッ　学校　大学	
	がっこう　だいがく	

How to write kanji: Stroke order

Stroke order is very important not only in writing but also in reading, especially when reading handwritten **kanji**. In the handwritten style, lines are often connected and some strokes are simplified. The following are the basic rules for writing **kanji**.

1. Write from left to right.

2. Write from top to bottom.

3. Write ⺆ as shown.

4. When enclosing a square, write the bottom line last.

    It is also important to distinguish the following three types of strokes:

    stop

    release

    hook

| 大大 | big, large
おお(きい)　ダイ | 一 ナ 大 大 大 大 大 大 大 大
大学生
だいがくせい |

| 学学 | to study, learn
まな(ぶ)　ガク・ガッ | 、 ゛ ゛゛ ゛゛ ⺍ 学 学 学 学 学
学校　　大学
がっこう　　だいがく |

| 校校 | school
コウ | 一 十 十 木 朴 朴 杧 杧 柼 校
学校
がっこう |

| 先先 | ahead; previous
さき　セン | ノ 丿 牛 生 牛 先 先 先 先 先
先生
せんせい |

| 生生 | life, to live
なま・う(まれる)　セイ | ノ 丿 牛 牛 生 生 生 生 生 生
学生　　先生
がくせい　　せんせい |

練習　Practice
れんしゅう

Read the following sentences.

1. スミスさんはニューヨーク大学の学生です。
2. ジョンソンさんは学校の先生です。
3. 学生：「やまだ先生、おはようございます。」
    先生：「あっ、きむらさん、おはよう。」

読む　練習
よ　　れんしゅう
Reading

上手な　読み方　Reading Strategy
じょうず　　よ　かた

Using script types as clues to word boundaries

Unlike English, Japanese words are not separated by spaces. However, there are certain ways of identifying word and phrase boundaries. For example, **katakana** and **kanji** are always used for content words such as nouns, verbs, and adjectives. If a series of **katakana** appears within a sentence, it usually indicates a word or name. **Hiragana** is always used for particles like は, が, の and に and for the endings of verbs and adjectives. Other content words are written in **hiragana** as well. When several **hiragana** appear in the middle of a sentence, you should read them carefully because they may contain more than one word.

練習　Practice
れんしゅう

Read the following sentences and try to identify word boundaries using script types as a clue. In this exercise, each noun should be grouped with its particle as one word. Then insert a slash between the words. Don't worry about understanding the meaning of the sentences completely, and don't be overwhelmed at the sight of **kanji** you don't know the readings for.

私はアメリカのウエストサイド大学の三年生です。
専攻は歴史とフランス語です。でも、日本語も勉強しています。

城東大学　Joto University
じょうとう

Scan the following reading and circle the words you don't know. Then read the passage and try to guess from context what the unknown words mean.

城東大学は東京にあります。学生は三万人ぐらいいますが、教授は
じょうとう　　とうきょう　　　　　　　　さんまんにん　　　　　　　　きょうじゅ
千人ぐらいです。とても古い大学です。キャンパスはあまり大きくあ
せんにん　　　　　　　　　　ふる
りませんが、きれいな建物がたくさんあります。公園もあります。そ
　　　　　　　　　　　　　　たてもの　　　　　　　　　　　こうえん
れから、大学の図書館はとても有名です。城東大学には経済学部
　　　　　　　　しょかん　　　　　　ゆうめい　　じょうとう　　　　けいざいがくぶ
と文学部と商学部と法学部があります。留学生センターもあります。
ぶんがくぶ　しょうがくぶ　ほうがくぶ　　　　　　　　りゅう
アメリカとオーストラリアからたくさん留学生が来ます。
　　　　　　　　　　　　　　　　　　　　りゅう　　き

読んだ　後で　Comprehension
よ　　　あと

Answer these questions in Japanese.

1. 城東大学は　どこに　ありますか。
じょうとう
2. 城東大学は　あたらしい　大学ですか。
じょうとう
3. 城東大学の　キャンパスは　どんな　キャンパスですか。
じょうとう
4. 城東大学には　ゆうめいな　たてものが　ありますか。
じょうとう
5. 城東大学には　どんな　学生が　たくさん　いますか。
じょうとう

総合練習
そうごうれんしゅう
Integration

学校しょうかい   School introductions

Form groups of three or four. Have each person create one or two sentences about your school such as its location, size, things you see on campus, famous buildings, etc. Then work together to write a brief paragraph describing your school to students in Japan who are interested in studying abroad.

ロールプレイ   Role Play

With a partner, act out each of the following scenarios, then switch roles.

1. You want to go to a hospital. You see a white building in the distance as you pass a police box. Ask the police officer if it is a hospital.
2. You are looking for a bank. Approach a passerby and ask if there is a bank in the neighborhood.
3. You have invited a Japanese friend to your neighborhood. Show your friend around your house.

Chapter 5

第五課
だいごか

日本の　うち
にほん
Japanese Homes

単語
<ruby>たん ご</ruby>
Vocabulary

Location nouns

うえ	上	on, above, over
うしろ	後ろ	behind, in back of
した	下	under, beneath
そと	外	outside
ちかく	近く	near, in the vicinity of
となり	隣	next to
なか	中	in, inside
ひだり	左	to the left, left side
まえ	前	in front of, in the front
みぎ	右	to the right
よこ	横	next to, at the side of

Nouns

いす	椅子	chair
いぬ	犬	dog
え	絵	picture
おしいれ	押し入れ	Japanese-style closet, storage space
がくしょく	学食	school cafeteria (a shortened form of 学生しょくどう)
がくせいかいかん	学生会館	student union
かわ	川	river
き	木	tree
きょうしつ	教室	classroom
くるま	車	car
こくばん	黒板	chalkboard
コンピュータ		computer
じてんしゃ	自転車	bicycle

しゃしん	写真	photograph
ソファ		sofa
たいいくかん	体育館	gym
たんす	箪笥	chest, drawers
つくえ	机	desk
テーブル		table
でんわ	電話	telephone
ドア		door
トイレ		toilet, restroom
とけい	時計	clock, watch
ところ	所	place
ねこ	猫	cat
バス		bus
ビデオ		video
ひと	人	person
ふとん	布団	futon
ベッド		bed
へや	部屋	room
ほんだな	本棚	bookshelf
まど	窓	window
もの	物	thing (tangible)
やま	山	mountain
ラボ		laboratory

う -verb

かかります	to take (time), it costs; the dictionary form is かかる .

Demonstrative words

この	this [+ noun]
その	that [+ noun]
あの	that [+ noun] over there
どの	which [+ noun]?

い -adjectives

あかるい	明るい	bright
くらい	暗い	dark
せまい	狭い	cramped, narrow
はやい	速い	fast, quick
ひろい	広い	spacious, wide

な -adjective

しずか (な)	静か (な)	quiet

Particles

から		from
で		by means of, by, with
まで		until, to

Suffixes

～ぐらい／くらい	about ～ (duration or quantity)
～じかん	～ hours

Expressions

あがってください	上がって下さい	Please come in.
あるいて	歩いて	on foot
いらっしゃい		Welcome! Come in.
おじゃまします	お邪魔します	Thank you. (literally, *I will intrude on you.*) (said before going inside someone's house or apartment)
ごめんください	御免下さい	Excuse me, Anyone home?

Question word

どのぐらい／どのくらい	how long, how much, how many

単語の練習   Vocabulary Practice
たんご れんしゅう

A. キャンパス   College campus

としょかん

たいいくかん

学生会館	student union	たいいくかん	gym
かいかん			
学食	school cafeteria	ラボ	laboratory
がくしょく			
きょうしつ	classroom	トイレ	restroom
メディアセンター	media center		

> **Activity 1**

しつもんに　こたえて下さい。　Answer these questions in Japanese.
くだ

1. ラボで　なにを　べんきょうしますか。
2. コンピュータのラボは　どこに　ありますか。
3. 学生会館に　どんなものが　ありますか。
   かいかん
4. たいいくかんは　どこに　ありますか。
5. 学生会館に　学食が　ありますか。
   かいかん　　がくしょく
6. よく　学食で　べんきょうしますか。
   がくしょく
7. 学生会館に　きょうしつが　ありますか。
   かいかん
8. トイレは　どこに　ありますか。

B. へやと きょうしつ   Rooms and classrooms

ドア	door	ふとん	futon
まど	window	たんす	chest, drawers
おしいれ	Japanese-style closet	ビデオ	video
いぬ	dog	コンピュータ	computer
ねこ	cat	でんわ	telephone
つくえ	desk	とけい	clock, watch
いす	chair	え	picture
ソファ	sofa	しゃしん	photograph
テーブル	table	こくばん	chalkboard
本棚 ほんだな	bookshelf	ベッド	bed

Activity 2

Look at the pictures on page 170 and name all the objects you see.

Example:　ドアが　あります。

Activity 3

しつもんに　こたえて下さい。Answer these questions in Japanese.

1. きょうしつに　どんな　ものが　ありますか。
2. ～さんの　へやに　どんな　ものが　ありますか。
3. としょかんに　どんな　ものが　ありますか。
4. ラボに　どんな　ものが　ありますか。

C. しぜん　Nature

山 *mountain*
やま

き　*tree*

川　*river*
かわ

Activity 4

しつもんに　こたえて下さい。Answer these questions in Japanese.

1. このへん (*this area*) に　山が　ありますか。
やま
2. このへん (*this area*) に　川が　ありますか。
かわ
3. 大学の　キャンパスに　川が　ありますか。山が　ありますか。
かわ　　　　　　やま
4. キャンパスに　大きい　きが　ありますか。どこに　ありますか。

D. のりもの   Transportation

くるま
car

じてんしゃ
bicycle

バス
bus

Activity 5

In small groups, guess who owns a car or a bicycle and write the number in the column, YOUR GUESS. Then ask each person in your group whether he/she has a car or a bicycle, and write the correct total in the ANSWER (こたえ) column.

Example:　A:　～さんは　くるまが　ありますか。

　　　　　B:　ええ、あります。～さんも　くるまが　ありますか。

　　　　or　いいえ、ありません。～さんは　くるまが　ありますか。

　　　　　A:　ええ、あります。

　　　　or　いいえ、ありません。

　　　　　B:　そうですか。

	YOUR GUESS	ANSWER (こたえ)
くるま		
じてんしゃ		

E. Describing buildings and rooms

あかるい	bright		ひろい	spacious, wide
くらい	dark		せまい	cramped, narrow
しずか	quiet			

Activity 6

Work with the entire class. Ask each other what kinds of rooms your classmates have.

Example:　A:　～さんの　アパートは　どんなところですか。

　　　　　B:　あまり　ひろくありません。でも、あかるいです。

ダイアローグ
Dialogue

はじめに　Warm-up

しつもんに　こたえて下さい。 Answer these questions in Japanese.

1. 今　どんなところに　すんでいます (*to live*) か。アパートですか。
   りょうですか。うちですか。（〜にすんでいます = *to reside in* 〜）

2. 〜さんのへやは　どんな　へやですか。

3. 〜さんのへやに　どんな　ものが　ありますか。

リーさんの　アパート　*Mr. Li's apartment*

Ueda pays a visit to Li's apartment.

上田： ごめん下さい。

リー： あ、上田さん。いらっしゃい。どうぞ　あがって下さい。

上田： おじゃまします。

上田： わあ、とても　あかるいですね。

リー： ええ。この　アパートは　たかい　ところに　ありますから。

上田： あそこに　りっぱな　たてものが　ありますね。あれは
大学ですか。

リー： ええ、あれは　じょうとう大学の　たいいくかんですよ。

上田： え、じゃあ、たいいくかんの　となりの　ちゃいろい　ビルは
うえ だ
　　　　なんですか。

リー： あれは　としょかんです。そして、その　まえのが　学生会館
かいかん
　　　　です。

上田： そうですか。ここから　大学まで　どのくらい　かかりますか。
うえ だ

リー： バスで　にじゅっぷんぐらい　かかります。

　　　　でも、ぼくは　たいてい　じてんしゃで　いきますよ。

上田： そうですか。じてんしゃでは　どのくらい　かかりますか。
うえ だ

リー： じゅうごふんぐらいです。

上田： へえ、はやいですね。
うえ だ

DIALOGUE PHRASE NOTES

- ごめん下さい means *Is anyone home?* It is used when you have
  くだ
  arrived at the entrance of someone's residence and need to get his
  or her attention.
- いらっしゃい means *welcome.* あがって下さい means *please*
  くだ
  enter. Both are common expressions to invite someone inside.
- おじゃまします means *thank you* and is used when you enter
  someone's house or room.
- Sentence + から means *It's because* ～.

  このアパートは　たかいところに　ありますから。
  It's because this apartment is high up (on a hill).

- へえ means, *Is that so?* or *Really?* へえ indicates the speaker's
  mild surprise about what has just been said. はやい means *fast.*
  Ueda expresses her surprise about how fast Li can get to school by
  saying へえ、はやいですね (*Really, that fast?*).

ダイアローグの後で　Comprehension

Answer the following questions in Japanese.

1. リーさんの　アパートは　どんな　ところですか。
2. リーさんの　アパートから　大学まで　じてんしゃで　どのくらい
　かかりますか。
3. たいいくかんは　どんな　たてものですか。
4. としょかんは　どこに　ありますか。

日本の文化
に ほん ぶん か
Japanese Culture

Japanese houses

A traditional Japanese house is made of wood with heavy ceramic tiles, or かわら. Although it is being replaced with more modern western-style houses or a combination of Japanese and western-style houses, the traditional Japanese house can still be found in many parts of Japan, especially in rural areas.

Some elements of traditional houses have been incorporated into western-styles houses as well.

For example, both traditional and contemporary houses have a mudroom, or げんかん, where you must take off your shoes inside the entrance. Typically, this area is lower than the main portion of the house.

After taking off your shoes, it is polite to put them down facing the door. A host or hostess of the house usually invites people in by saying あがって下さい
（くだ）
(*please come in*) or its polite form, おあがり下さい.
（くだ）
These phrases literally mean *please come up*, because the main portion of the house is above the area where the shoes are left.

Many contemporary homes contain one or more traditional Japanese rooms as well. These rooms are divided by a sliding door, ふすま, or by a paper screen, しょうじ. The flooring consists of straw mats called たたみ. The room may have an area (とこのま) where a flower arrangement is placed and a scroll is hung.

Traditional Japanese rooms also contain a large closet, called おしいれ, to store ふとん (Japanese bedding). ふとん are spread on the たたみ mats at bedtime, then folded and put away in the morning, so that the room can be used for multiple purposes. A futon sofa is an American invention.

Most contemporary rooms have wood floors. Carpet is not a popular choice because the high level of humidity in summer poses a potential hazard for bacteria and germs. The door to a room, whether Japanese or Western style, is almost always closed. A closed door doesn't necessarily mean *don't disturb*, so knock to find out if anyone is in the room. Still, don't be surprised if a Japanese person comes into your room without knocking. It happens often among family members.

Japanese bathrooms

Most Japanese people prefer to take a bath every night, instead of taking a shower in the morning. The Japanese bathroom, or おふろ, is a room only for bathing. The toilet is in a separate room. The bathroom has a tiled area for washing and rinsing prior to entering the tub. The water is usually very hot (about 110°F/41–42°C). Cold water may be added from the faucet if it is too hot, but overdoing it means that the water won't be warm for the rest of the family, who will use the same hot water. When finished, instead of draining the tub, the cover is replaced to retain the heat. Although Japanese-style toilets are still used in Japan, western-style toilets are now more common in private homes, and often come equipped with a cleansing device called a Washlet® (ウォシュレット). These operate similarly to bidets, but offer a range of high-tech features. Most models have seat-warming controls, and some even have sensors to raise and lower the toilet lid automatically.

A pair of slippers is usually placed inside the restroom. Be careful not to walk out with these slippers on! The door to a restroom, public or private, should be kept closed at all times. Always knock on the door to see if the room is occupied, and do not forget to close the door afterward.

Public restrooms are often marked W.C. (water closet) or with the Japanese term お手洗い / 御手洗い (literally, *handwashing*). The sign for the men's room is usually indicated by a male icon or the character for man (男). A female icon or the character for woman (女) indicates the women's room. In some women's restrooms, an electronic device called 音姫 ® conveniently provides the white noise of running water or air. While it's sometimes necessary to press a button, most 音姫 ® are sensor-activated.

文法
ぶんぽう
Grammar

I. Referring to people, places, and things using この, その, あの, どの

The words この, その, あの, どの constitute another series of demonstrative words that indicate the location of an object in relation to the speaker and listener, but they are adjectives that must modify nouns and cannot be used by themselves. In contrast, これ, それ, あれ, どれ and ここ, そこ, あそこ, どこ are nouns that must be used alone.

この + **Noun**　　this [Noun] (close to the speaker)

その + **Noun**　　that [Noun] (away from the speaker and close to the listener, or somewhat away from both the speaker or the listener.)

あの + **Noun**　　that [Noun] over there (far away from both the speaker and the listener.)

	Noun		
この	へや	は	あかるいですね。

This room is bright, isn't it?

	Noun		
その	人 ひと	は	田中さんですか。 た なか

Is that person Mr./Ms. Tanaka?

		Adjective	Noun	
すずきさんの　うちは		どの	たてもの	ですか。

Which building is your house, Ms. Suzuki?

	Noun	
あの	うち	です。

It's that house over there.

山中
やまなか：　本田さんの　うちは　どの　うちですか。
ほんだ
Which house is your house, Mr. Honda?

本田
ほんだ：　それです。
It's that one.

山中
やまなか：　りっぱな　うちですね。
Oh, it's splendid, isn't it!

本田
ほんだ：　いいえ。
Not at all.

NOTES

- これ,それ,あれ,どれ are not used to refer to people unless you are discussing people in a photo or drawing, but この, その, あの, どの can be used to refer to people without being impolite, such as この人, その人, あの人, どの人.
　　ひと　　　ひと　　　ひと　　　ひと

- A more polite way to refer to people is to say このかた, そのかた, あのかた, どのかた instead of この人, その人, あの人, どの人. Use かた to refer to someone you don't know
　ひと　　　ひと　　　ひと　　　ひと
well, whom you want to treat politely.

- その can be used to refer to something previously mentioned.

  山中
やまなか：　上田さんは　ウエストサイド大学の　学生です。
うえだ
Ms. Ueda is a student at Westside University.

  チョイ：　その　人は　日本人ですか。
　　　　　　ひと　　に ほんじん
Is she (literally, that person) a Japanese?

話してみましょう   Conversation Practice
<ruby>はな</ruby>

Activity 1

Look at the drawing of the bedroom. 上田さん is standing on the left side of the
<ruby>うえ だ</ruby>
room (A), and you are at location B. You are making comments about the room to
上田さん. Change the following sentences into your comments addressed to
<ruby>うえ だ</ruby>
上田さん, using この, その, あの, どの.
<ruby>うえ だ</ruby>

Example: いい　ベッドですね →   <u>その　ベッドは　いいですね。</u>

1. あかるい　へやですね。
2. 大きい　きですね。
3. ひろい　つくえですね。
4. りっぱな　テレビですね。
5. ふるい　とけいですね。
6. 大きい　いぬですね。

Activity 2

Work with a partner. Look at the drawing of the living room. You are sitting on the sofa (location A) and your partner is at location B. Your partner will name some items. Create statements about each item using この, その, あの.

Example: Your partner: ソファ

　　　　　　You: <u>この</u>　ソファは　きれいですね。

II. Using location nouns: 中, そと, となり, よこ, ちかく, うしろ, まえ, 上, 下, みぎ, ひだり

Location nouns such as まえ (*front*) and うしろ (*back*) are used to describe the location of an object relative to another object, such as *X is in front of Y* and *Z is behind Y*.

つくえの	まえ	in front of	the desk
つくえの	うしろ	behind	the desk
つくえの	上	on/above	the desk
つくえの	下	below/under	the desk
つくえの	みぎ	to the right of	the desk
つくえの	ひだり	to the left of	the desk
つくえの	ちかく	close to	the desk

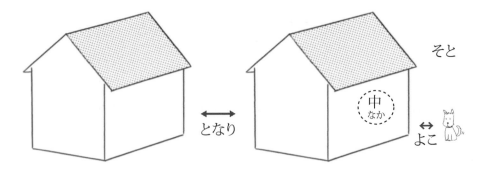

うちの	中	inside	the house
うちの	そと	outside	the house
うちの	となり	next to	the house
うちの	よこ	next to/adjacent to	the house

Both となり and よこ mean *next to*. Use となり if two things next to each other are of the same type, such as two houses or two desks. Use よこ if two things belong to different categories such as a dog next to a house.

わたしは　こくばんの　まえに／へ　いきました。
I went to the chalkboard. (literally, I went to the front of the chalkboard)

ドアの　まえまで　きました。
I came to the door. (literally, I came to the front of the door)

チョイ：　どこで　ひるごはんを　たべますか。
　　　　　Where do you eat lunch?

高田：　わたしは　よく　その　きの　下で　たべます。
　　　　I usually eat it under that tree.

ブラウン：　山田さんは　どこですか。
　　　　　　Where is Mr. Yamada?

大川：　たいいくかんの　ちかくで　みましたよ。
　　　　I saw him near the gym.

中山：　そこに　いぬが　いますか。
　　　　Is there a dog there?

ジョンソン：　ええ、つくえの　下に　いますよ。
　　　　　　　Yes, it is under the desk.

アリソン：　学食は　どこですか。
　　　　　　Where is the school cafeteria?

山本：　学生会館の　中です。
　　　　It's inside the student union.

NOTES

- Expression with location nouns can be used with any place particles, such as に, へ, で.
- Location nouns can be used with the Noun の Noun construction. For example:

うちの　うしろの　山　　*the mountain behind my house*
うちの　まえの　川　　*the river in front of my house*
となりの　うち　　*the house next door*
となりの　人　　*a person next to me, my next-door neighbor*
上の　アパート　　*the apartment above my floor*

話してみましょう Conversation Practice
はな

Activity 1

Look at the drawing of a classroom. Answer the following questions, using location nouns and 〜は 〜に　あります／います.

Example:　こくばんは　どこに　ありますか。／こくばんは　どこですか。
　　　　　　<u>先生の　うしろに　あります。／先生の　うしろです。</u>

1. コンピュータは　どこに　ありますか。つくえの上に あります
2. いぬは　どこに　いますか。そと に います
3. 先生の　かばんは　どこに　ありますか。先生の ひだり
4. ノートは　どこに　ありますか。
5. まどは　どこに　ありますか。へやの ひだりに あります
6. テレビは　どこに　ありますか。
7. えんぴつは　どこに　ありますか。つくえの上 に あります
8. けしゴムは　どこに　ありますか。

Activity 2

Look at the drawing of the room. Some objects are missing and their locations are indicated with question marks. Ask your partner what is in each location, then write in the names of the objects in the appropriate locations. Your partner will answer the questions using the drawing on page 180.

Example: A: つくえの　上に　なにが　ありますか。
　　　　　　　　　　　うえ
　　　　　　 B: でんわが　あります。

Activity 3

Work with a partner. Have your partner draw the following objects in the picture. As you ask your partner about their locations, write the items in your own copy of the house. When you are done, check your drawing with your partner's.

Example: A: じてんしゃは　どこに　ありますか。／じてんしゃは
どこですか。

B: ドアの　みぎに　あります。

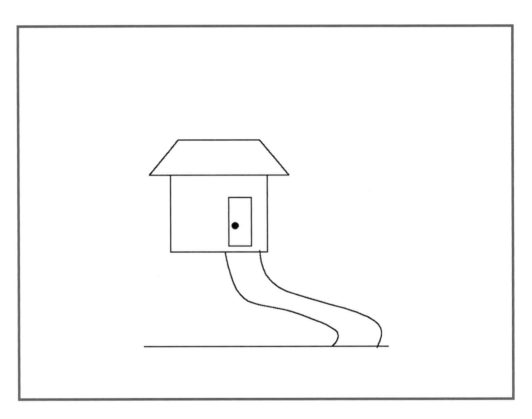

1.　まど

2.　ドア

3.　山
　　やま

4.　川
　　かわ

5.　き

6.　くるま

7.　いぬ

8.　ねこ

9.　じてんしゃ

Activity 4

Look at the drawing of the campus. Your partner will ask you where the following buildings are. Answer his/her questions based on the picture.

Example:　A:　あのう、すみません。学生会館は　どこですか。
　　　　　　　　　　　　　　　　かいかん

　　　　　　B:　その　大きい　きの　うしろに　あります。

　　　　　　A:　そうですか。どうも　ありがとう　ございます。

1. 留学生センター
　　りゅう
2. たいいくかん
3. コンピュータのラボ
4. 学食
　　がくしょく
5. としょかん

Activity 5

Ask a partner about the location of various buildings on your campus. Take notes, then check your partner's answers against a campus map.

Example:　A:　あのう、すみません。

　　　　　　　　ラボは　どこに　ありますか。／ラボは　どこですか。

　　　　　　B:　この　ビルの　中に　あります。／この　ビルの　中です。
　　　　　　　　　　　　　　　　なか　　　　　　　　　　　　　　　　　　なか

　　　　　　A:　あ、そうですか。どうも　ありがとう　ございます。

III. Referring to things mentioned immediately before, using noun/adjective + の (pronoun)

The pronoun の means *one* or *ones* in English, as in "red one" and "big one." の usually refers for things and is rarely used for people. It must be directly preceded by an adjective or a noun.

い -adjective +	の	ちゃいろいの	*brown one*
な -adjective +	の	きれいなの	*pretty one*
Noun +	の	スミスさんの	*Mr. Smith's*

イアン： この　りっぱな　かばんは　だれ<u>の</u>ですか。
Whose is this nice bag?

中本： その　大きい<u>の</u>ですか。
なかもと *That big one?*

それは　田中さんの　かばんですよ。
た なか
It's Mr. Tanaka's.

石川： この　あかい　ソファは　きれいですね。
いしかわ *This red sofa is pretty.*

中田： ええ、でも、あのくろいのも　いいですよ。
なか だ *Yes, but that black one over there is nice, too.*

石川： あの　大きいのですか。
いしかわ *Do you mean, that big one over there?*

中田： ええ。
なか だ *Yes.*

石川： ああ、あれも　いいですね。
いしかわ *Oh, that one is nice, too.*

Note that the pronoun の cannot be used with the particle の or with この, その, あの or どの.

話してみましょう   Conversation Practice
はな

Activity 1

Use の to state what belongs to whom. Follow the model. Start your sentences with この or あの .

Example: スミスさんの　りっぱな　かばん／わたしの　小さい　かばん
ちい
　　　　　　<u>この　　りっぱな　　かばんは　　スミスさんのです。</u>
　　　　　　<u>あの　　小さいのは　　わたしのです。</u>
　　　　　　　　　ちい

1. スミスさんの　ふるい　つくえ　／　田中さんの　あたらしい
　　　　　　　　　　　　　　　　　　　た なか
　　　　　　　　　　　　　　　　　　　　　つくえ
2. わたしの　あおい　ボールペン　／　先生の　あかい
　　　　　　　　　　　　　　　　　　　　ボールペン
3. すずきさんの　ひろい　へや　／　わたしの　せまい　へや
4. 上田さんの　しろい　とけい　／　キムさんの　くろい　とけい
　　うえ だ
5. リーさんの　あかるい　へや／　スミスさんの　くらい　へや

Activity 2

Work with the class. Look around at various belongings in the classroom. Ask who owns what to complete the chart below.

Example: A:　あのう、すみません、この　　あかい　　ボールペンは
　　　　　　　　だれのですか。

　　　　　　B:　先生のですよ。

　　　　　　A:　あ、そうですか。どうも。

Item	Owner
あかい　ボールペン	先生

IV. Expressing distance and duration using the particles から, まで and で and the suffix 〜ぐらい／くらい

The particles から (*from*) and まで (*until, to*) express starting and end points in time and space. The particle で specifies a tool or means such as transportation, craft tools, and kitchen utensils. The suffix ぐらい／くらい (*about, approximately*) indicates approximate distance, duration of time, or amount. These expressions are often used to talk about how long someone does something or how long it takes to get from one place to another. Note that くらい and ぐらい are interchangeable.

A. 〜から (*from*),　〜まで (*to, until*)

アパートから	学生会館まで	いきました。	*I went from the apartment to the student union.*
ここから	あの川まで	１０ぷん かかります。	*It will take ten minutes from here to the river.*
月曜日から	金曜日まで	じゅぎょうが あります。	*I have a class from Monday through Friday.*
5じから	6じまで	やすみです。	*I have a break from 5 o'clock to 6 o'clock.*

B. で (*by means of, with, by*)

なんで	きましたか。	*How (literally, by what means) did you come?*
バスで	かえります。	*I go home by bus.*
テレビで	みました。	*I saw it on TV.*
えんぴつで	かきます。	*I write with a pencil.*

Note that the particle で cannot be used to express *on foot*. Use あるいて instead.

あるいて　いきます。	*I go on foot. / I walk.*

C. 〜ぐらい (*about, approximately*)

8じかんぐらい／くらい	ねました。	*I slept about eight hours.*
どのぐらい／くらい	かかりますか。	*How long does it take?*
３０ぷんぐらい／くらい	かかります。	*It will take about 30 minutes.*

山本：　ここから　小川さんの　うちまで　どのぐらい　かかりますか。
　　　How long does it take from here to your house, Mr. Ogawa?

小川：　じてんしゃで　5ふんぐらい　かかります。
　　　It's about five minutes by bicycle.

山本：　そうですか。はやいですね。
　　　I see. That's fast.

NOTES

- 〜じ as in いちじ, にじ means *o'clock*. To indicate duration, use 〜じかん.

  いちじかん (*for one hour*) にじかん (*for two hours*) にじかんはん (*for two and a half hours*)

- 〜ふん can be used to indicate both a specific time as in いちじ じゅっぷん (*1:10*) and duration, as in じゅっぷん (*for ten minutes*).

- Omit ぐらい／くらい if you want to talk about precise duration of time:

  大学から　えきまで　バスで　２３ぷん　かかります。
  It takes 23 minutes by bus from the university to the station.

  たいいくかんまで　あるいて　５ふん　かかります。
  It takes five minutes to get to the gym on foot.

話してみましょう   Conversation Practice
<small>はな</small>

Activity 1

State how long it takes to get to each destination in the chart below. Follow the model.

Example:　うち　学校　じてんしゃ　about 5 minutes

　　　　　うちから　学校まで　じてんしゃで　ごふんぐらいかかります。

Starting point	Destination	Transportation	Time
うち	学校	じてんしゃ	5 minutes
ここ	としょかん	あるいて	About 10 minutes
としょかん	びょういん	くるま	15 min
ボストン	ニューヨーク	バス	4.5 hours
ボストン	ニューヨーク	くるま	About 4 hours

Activity 2

Working with a partner, ask how long it takes to get from location A to B and fill out the information.

Example: A: うちから　学校まで　あるいて　どのぐらい／くらい
　　　　　　　　かかりますか。

　　　　　　B: 20 ぷんぐらい／くらい　かかります。

　　　　　　A: そうですか。

Location A	Location B	あるいて	じてんしゃ	バス	くるま
うち	学校				
としょかん	たいいくかん				
うち	びょういん				
このまち	となりのまち				

Activity 3

Ask your partner what he/she is planning to do after class today. Use から～まで～ as well as the time expressions and daily routine vocabulary that you have learned in earlier chapters.

Example: A: 今日は　これから　なにを　しますか。
　　　　　きょう

　　　　　　B: そうですね。3じから　4じまで　じゅぎょうが
　　　　　　　　あります。そして、　5じごろ　かえります。

　　　　　　A: そうですか。

　　　　　　B: ～さんは？

　　　　　　A: わたしは　うちに　かえります。

　　　　　　　　そして、ばんごはんまで　べんきょうします。

V. More about the topic marker は and the similarity marker も (double particles and は vs. が)

As explained in the supplementary note in Chapter 2, the particle は specifies the topic. Because it is the part of a sentence about which the speaker wishes to make some statement, it usually appears at the beginning of the sentence. The particle は can be used to mark any type of noun as the topic of a sentence, including the subject or direct object, a location, or a time expression.

This section introduces more uses of は in relation to particles that have some related characteristics, such as the similarity marker も and the subject marker が.

A. Double particles with the topic marker は and the similarity marker も

Both は and も may replace を (direct object) or が (subject) but they must follow after other particles.

Subject	わたしは　学生です。 上田さんも　学生です。 うえだ	I am a student. Ms. Ueda is a student, too.
Direct Object	コーヒーは　あさ　のみます。 ジュースも　あさ　のみます。	I drink coffee in the morning. I drink juice in the morning, too.
Place of action で	としょかんでは　べんきょうしました。 ラボでも　べんきょうしました。	I studied in the library I studied in the lab, too.
Place of existence に	いすの　下には　ねこが　います。 した いすの　上にも　います。 うえ	There is a cat under the chair. There is one on the chair, too.
Starting point から	先生からは　でんわが　ありました。 ともだちからも　でんわが　ありました。	I got a phone call from the teacher. I got one from my friend, too.

Occasionally, some particles such as に (point in time) and に／へ (goal) may be deleted if they are easily recoverable from the context. For example, the time particle に is often deleted when the noun indicates a day of the week.

Time に	火曜日（に）は　クラスが　あります。 かようび 木曜日（に）も　あります。 もくようび	I have a class on Tuesday. I have one on Thursday, too.
Goal に／へ	びょういん（に／へ）は　明日　いきます。 あした ぎんこう（に／へ）も　いきます。	I will go to the hospital tomorrow. I will go to the bank, too.

ペギー： しゅうまつは　なにを　しましたか。
What did you do on the weekend?

下田： 山に／へ　いきました。
しも だ　　やま
I went to the mountains.

ペギー： いいですね。山（に／へ）は　よく　いきますか。
　　　　　　　　　　やま
That's nice. Do you go to the mountains often?

下田： ええ、らいしゅうの　土曜日（に）も　いきます。
しも だ　　　　　　　　　　どようび
Yes, I am going there next Saturday, too.

アリソン： 大学までは　あるいて　どのぐらい　かかりますか。
How long does it take to get to school on foot?

川中： 1じかんぐらい　かかります。
かわなか
It takes about an hour.

アリソン： え、そうなんですか。毎日　あるいて　きますか。
　　　　　　　　　　　　　　まいにち
Is that so? Do you walk to school every day?

川中： いいえ、バスで　きます。
かわなか
No, I come to school by bus.

Note: Relative time expressions such as 今日 and 明日 do not take a particle. は and
　　　　　　　　　　　　　　　きょう　　あした
も follow the noun directly.

今日は　びょういんに　いきます。　明日も　いきます。
きょう　　　　　　　　　　　　　あした
I will go to the hospital today. I will go tomorrow as well.

B. は vs. が

The particle は cannot be used with a question word, because は specifies the topic
of a sentence, which is information already known to the speaker. Use は when there
is a question word in the comment (the part of the sentence that follows the topic).

学生会館は　どこですか　　　　　　　*Where is the student union?*
　　かいかん

山田さんは　どの人ですか。　　　　　　*Which person is Mr. Yamada?*
やま だ　　　　ひと

たいいくかんは　どこに　ありますか。　*Where is the gym?*

チョイさんは　どこへ　いきましたか。　*Where did Ms. Choi go?*

The particle が marks the grammatical subject of a sentence. Always use が when the subject is, or contains, a question word.

どの人が 先生ですか。	*Which person is the teacher?*
そこに なにが ありますか。	*What is there?*
だれが いきますか。	*Who will go?*

Also use が when information about a subject is important or situationally new to the listener and/or the speaker. This use of が generally occurs when the speaker introduces a situation or scene he/she has just noticed.

あ、あそこに ねこが いますよ。	*Look, there is a cat over there!*
あ、中本さんが きました。	*Ah, Ms. Nakamoto has just arrived.*

Once a subject noun has been mentioned, は is often used when referring to the same subject in subsequent sentences. For example:

本田： あそこに いぬが いますね。
There is a dog over there.

小川： ええ、あれは わたしの いぬです。
Yes, that's my dog.

Note: それ can also be used to refer to something mentioned previously. In this usage, それ means *it* in English. Likewise, その〜 and そこ can be used in the same way.

あそこに かばんが あります。
There is a bag over there.

それ／そのかばんは 田中さんのです。
It is Mr./Ms. Tanaka's.

学生会館に 学食が あります。
There is a cafeteria in the student union.

そこは とても きれいです。
It (that place) is very clean/nice.

話してみましょう Conversation Practice
はな

Activity 1

First circle the question words, then complete the following sentences with が or は .

Example: (だれ)　が　学生ですか。

1. リーさん＿＿は＿＿どの　人ですか。
ひと
2. どれ＿＿が＿＿びょういんですか。
3. どの　コンピュータ＿＿が＿＿あたらしいですか。
4. 学食＿＿は＿＿どこですか。
がくしょく
5. アリスさん＿＿は＿＿どんな　人ですか。
ひと
6. だれ＿＿が＿＿いますか。
7. デパート＿＿は＿＿どこに　ありますか。
8. すずきさん＿＿は＿＿どちらから　きましたか。
9. あの　きれいな　たてもの＿＿は＿＿なんですか。

Activity 2

Create two sentences based on each sentence below. One should express a similarity with the first sentence; the other should contrast with the first sentence.

Example: あさごはんを　たべます。

ばんごはんも　たべます。でも、ひるごはんは　たべません。

1. バスは　じゅうじに　きました。
2. 留学生は　日本から　きます。
りゅう　　　　にほん
3. バスで　大学に　いきます。
4. 昨日　おふろに　はいりました。
きのう
5. 昨日の　ばん　シャワーを　あびました。
きのう

Activity 3

Work with a partner. Ask your partner a question using the words supplied in column A. Your partner will answer the question using the words in column B to create a topic from the subject of the question (underlined in the example).

Example:　　　　　　　A　　　　　　　　　　　　　B

　　　　いつ／コーヒーを　のみます。　　　　　あさ

　　　　A:　いつ　コーヒーを　のみますか。

　　　　B:　コーヒーですか。コーヒーは　あさ　のみますね。

　　　　　　　　　A　　　　　　　　　　　　　　B

1. どこ／その　本を　みました。　　　　　　大学の　本や
2. なに／びょういんに　いきました。　　　　くるま
3. いつ／その　えいがを　みました。　　　　昨日
4. どこ／ジョンソンさんと　いきました。　　きっさてん
5. なに／えきから　いきました。　　　　　　バス
6. だれ／いました。　　　　　　　　　　　　先生
7. いつ／しゅくだいを　します。　　　　　　しゅうまつ
8. どんな　くるま／きました。　　　　　　　トヨタ

Activity 4

Work with a partner. Choose two cities with which you're both familiar and write their names in the following chart. First discuss, then list, the aspects they share in common. Think of as many things as you can.

Example:　とうきょう, シカゴ

　　　　A:　とうきょうには　いい　レストランが　ありますよ。

　　　　B:　そうですか。シカゴにも　たくさん　ありますよ。

　　　　A:　そうですか。日本の　レストランも　ありますか。

　　　　B:　ええ、たくさん　ありますよ。

Similarity	City 1:_____	City 2:_____

Interrogative Expressions

You have learned a lot of question words. Here is a summary of Japanese interrogative expressions.

だれ	who	だれの　へやですか。 *Whose room is it?*
なに／なん	what	おなまえは　なんですか。 *What is your name?* なんねんせいですか。 *What year are you in school?* いま　なんじですか。 *What time is it now?*
いつ	when	山田さんは　いつ　きますか。 *When will Mr. Yamada come?*
どこ	where	山田さんは　どこに　いますか。 *Where is Mr. Yamada?*
どの + noun	which	山田さんは　どの　人ですか。 *Which person is Mr. Yamada?* 山田さんの　りょうは　どの　たてもの ですか。 *Which building is Mr. Yamada's dormitory?*
どれ	which one	山田さんのりょうは　どれですか。 *Which one is Mr. Yamada's dormitory?*
どんな + noun	what kind of	山田さんの　へやは　どんな　ところ ですか。 *What kind of place is your room, Mr. Yamada?*

聞く 練習
き   れんしゅう
Listening

上手な聞き方   Listening Strategy
じょうず き かた

Distinguishing sounds in words and phrases

Listening to conversations in Japanese can seem like reading long sentences without **kanji** or other clues to distinguish word boundaries. It takes practice to be able to distinguish words and phrases from a succession of sounds. Listening for repeated words, familiar words, intonation, and pauses can help you to identify word boundaries. If you are listening to an announcement, anticipate what to expect and try to listen for important information.

ひっこしを　てつだう (Helping a friend move into a new apartment)

Useful Expressions

おきます	to place
おいて下さい	please place/put
くだ	

聞く 前に   Warm-up
き   まえ

When you're moving into a new place, what kinds of words do you expect to use? Circle the terms you are most likely to use.

き　　まえ　　ベッド　　山　　バス　　よこ　　テレビ
　　　　　　　　　　　　やま

たいいくかん　　ぎんこう　　いす　　みぎ　　ひだり　　ちかく

Now listen to the conversation and write down words you hear repeatedly.

1. _____
2. _____
3. _____
4. _____
5. _____
6. _____

聞いた後で   Comprehension
き   あと

Listen to the conversation again. Then verify the layout of the apartment. Are all the objects in the room properly described?

Describe each object in the room as thoroughly as you can, using different location nouns.

Now describe the place where you live in a few sentences.

聞き上手　話し上手
き　　じょうず　はな　　じょうず

Communication

Communication Strategy

Getting someone's attention (2)

Talking to someone in your non-native language can be a strain, especially if the person is a stranger. This is certainly true in Japan as well, where people tend to be less open with strangers. One explanation for this is that Japan was isolated from the Western world for over 250 years under the government's seclusion policy, from the seventeenth to the mid-nineteenth century. During that period Japan virtually remained a relatively homogeneous nation. Moreover, under the feudal order, a strong sense of hierarchy was developed. The sense of hierarchy and distinction between in-group and out-group remains strong in modern Japan. In-group refers to one's family, people at one's place of work, classmates, etc. The Japanese are very aware of the difference in intimacy that should be maintained between those in the in-group and out-group, and act accordingly. Any non-Japanese by definition belongs to the out-group, and thus, along with the fear of not being able to communicate, a Japanese person might deliberately avoid contact with a non-Japanese, even at the risk of appearing indifferent. This of course is a generalization, and there is a great deal of variation in individual behavior. It is important, however, to understand this background, and to use the appropriate phrases in approaching a stranger or someone you don't know well. The following is a summary of some useful expressions and other strategies you can employ.

Approaching people:

あのう（ちょっと）

すみませんが／しつれいですが。

あのう　すみませんが／しつれいですが。

ちょっと　すみませんが／しつれいですが。

あのう　ちょっと　すみませんが／しつれいですが。

おねがいします。　　(used to get the attention of someone who provides services, such as a store clerk)

Thanking someone:

すみません。
ありがとう　ございます。

Giving feedback as a listener:

Nodding
Avoiding prolonged eye contact
ええ／いいえ

練習　Practice
れんしゅう

A. Imagine that you are in Japan and want to ask someone the time. Approach the person to get attention. Ask the time. Thank him/her. Try to act out the scene with a partner.

B. Imagine that you are at a party on a college campus and want to meet someone from Japan. There are many Asian students at the party, but you are not sure if they are Japanese. Approach someone and find out if he/she is Japanese. If the person is from Japan, introduce yourself.

漢字
かんじ
Kanji

Kanji derived from pictures and symbols (1)

Kanji derived from pictures

The number of **kanji** derived from pictures and symbols totals to only about 200, but these characters tend to represent basic or core meanings. Many of them also appear in more complex characters. Therefore, it is important to become familiar with their shapes and meaning.

山   mountain

日   sun, day

川   river

田   rice paddy

人   person

学   study, learn (A child in a school)

生   life, to live

Some **kanji** that represent abstract ideas have been created from symbols.

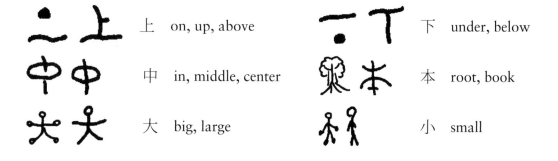

上   on, up, above

下   under, below

中   in, middle, center

本   root, book

大   big, large

小   small

山 山	mountain やま　サン・ザン	山川さん　富士山　山の上 やまかわ　　ふじさん　やま　うえ	丨 山 山 山 山 山 山 山 山
川 川	river かわ・がわ　セン	小川さん　川中さん　ミシシッピー川 おがわ　　かわなか　　　　　　がわ	ノ 川 川 川 川 川 川 川 川
田 田	rice paddy た　デン	上田さん　田中さん うえだ　　た なか	丨 冂 冂 田 田
人 人	person ひと　ジン・ニン	日本人 にほんじん	ノ 人 人 人 人 人 人 人 人
上 上	on, up, above うえ　ジョウ・カミ	テーブルの上 うえ	丨 卜 上 上 上 上 上 上 上
中 中	in, middle, center なか　チュウ	へやの中　中国 なか　　ちゅうごく	丨 冂 口 中 中 中 中 中 中
下 下	under, below した　くだ(さい)　カ・ゲ	まどの下　いって下さい した　　　　くだ	一 丅 下 下 下 下 下 下 下
小 小	small ちい(さい)　ショウ	小さいへや ちい	亅 小 小
日 日	sun, day ひ・び　ニチ・ニ・ジツ・カ	日本　昨日＊　今日＊　明日＊ にほん　きのう　きょう　あした	丨 冂 月 日
本 本	root, book もと　ホン・ボン・ポン	山田さんの本　日本 やまだ　　　ほん　にほん	一 十 才 木 本

An asterisk (*) indicates an irregular reading.

よめるようになったかんじ (**kanji** and compounds you can now read)

山　川　田中　日本人　上　下　中　小さい　日本　本　本棚　本屋

毎日　中国　今日　明日　明後日　昨日　一昨日　日曜日　上がって下さい
まい　　ごく　きょう　あした　あさって　きのう　おととい　　よう　　あ　　　　くだ

日本人のなまえ (Japanese family names): 山川　田中　中田　川中　山中
　　　　　　　　　　　　　　　　　　　やまかわ　たなか　なかだ　かわなか　やまなか

上田　本田　小川　大川　中川　下田　中本　山本
うえだ　ほんだ　おがわ　おおかわ　なかがわ　しもだ　なかもと　やまもと

練習　Practice
れんしゅう

Read the following sentences.

1. 山田先生は日本大学の先生です。
2. 「上田」は日本語のなまえですが、上田さんはアメリカ人です。
3. きょうしつの中に小さいとけいがあります。
4. ふとんの下にねこがいます。
5. 日本にはきれいな山と川がたくさんあります。
6. なまえをかいて下さい。

読む　練習
よ　　　れんしゅう
Reading

上手な読み方　Reading Strategy
じょうず　よ　かた

Using visual clues

Photos, illustrations, and graphs can often help you understand what you read. For example, it's much easier to understand a description of a room or a house while looking at a floor plan. Such visuals not only help create context for a text, but they may also provide additional information not included in the text.

読む　前に　　Pre-reading
よ　　まえ

Look at the picture of an office, and determine what kinds of information it conveys.

田中先生の研究室　Professor Tanaka's Office
けんきゅうしつ

Vocabulary

奥（おく）	the inner part of a building, room, etc.
手前（てまえ）	this side (side closer to the speaker)
鉢植（はちうえ）	potted plant
たくさん	many, a lot

田中先生の研究室はとても広いです。部屋の右には大きい本棚
があります。本棚には本がたくさんあります。本棚の横には窓
があります。窓は部屋の右にあります。窓の外には小さい鉢植
があります。そして、窓の近くには先生の机があります。机の上
には本がたくさんあります。机は部屋の左側にあります。机の
上にはコンピュータと電話があります。部屋の手前には小さい
ソファがあります。ソファの上にも本がたくさんあります。ソフ
ァの横に小さい椅子があります。ソファの下にねこがいます。

読んだ後で　Comprehension
よ　あと

Identify four discrepancies between the text and the drawing, and write them on the lines below.

1. _Plant is outside_
2. _There's a cat_
3. _Lots of books on the desk_
4. _____

総合練習
そうごうれんしゅう
Integration

アパートさがし   Looking for an apartment

1. You are a Tokyo real estate agent. Bring to class or draw a floor plan of an apartment indicating the location of the door, windows, bedrooms, kitchen (キッチン), bathroom, and any other rooms. Then complete the information below.

Number of bedrooms_____

Apartment location _____

Distance from campus_____

Facilities near the apartment _____

2. Your instructor will divide the class into two groups. Half of the class will act as real estate agents, and the other half will try to rent an apartment. Prospective tenants should talk to as many agents as possible, take notes on each rental property, and decide which apartment to rent.

ロールプレイ   Role Play

1. You are showing around a visitor from Japan who doesn't speak English. Tell the visitor about your campus as he/she asks you questions.

2. Your host family asks you what kind of place you live in. Describe your dorm or apartment.

Chapter 6

第六課
だいろっか

休みの 日
やす
Leisure Time

Objectives	Describing routine and leisure activities
Vocabulary	Routine activities (2), leisure activities, adjectives of emotion and condition
Dialogue	週末は どうでしたか。*What did you do over the weekend?* しゅうまつ
Japanese Culture	Japanese colleges and college life
Grammar	I. Using the particles と and に
	II. Commenting about the past, using polite past adjectives and the copula verb です
	III. Connecting verb and adjective phrases and sentences using the て-form of verbs; making requests using the て-form
	IV. Connecting phrases, using the て-forms of verbs and adjectives
	V. Extending an invitation using ませんか
Listening	Making sense of missing pronouns
Communication	Using そうですか and そうですね
Kanji	**Kanji** derived from pictures and symbols (2) 今 私 月 火 水 木 金 土 曜 何 週 末 休
Reading	Identifying missing nouns

単語
たん ご
Vocabulary

Nouns

アルバイト		part-time job
うんどう	運動	exercises うんどう　（を）　します to exercise （を is commonly deleted)
おんがく	音楽	music
かいもの	買い物	shopping
ゲーム		game
コンサート		concert
こんど	今度	next time
ざっし	雑誌	magazine
さんぽ	散歩	walk, stroll さんぽ　（を）　します to take a walk
しごと	仕事	job
しつもん	質問	question しつもん　（を）　します (to) ask a question
ジョギング		jogging
しんぶん	新聞	newspaper
せんたく	洗濯	laundry
そうじ	掃除	cleaning
てがみ	手紙	letter
テニス		tennis テニスを　します to play tennis
ともだち	友達	friend
パーティ		party
ピクニック		picnic

プール		pool
メール		e-mail
やすみ	休み	rest, absence, a day off
やすみのひ	休みの日	a day off, holiday
りょうしん	両親	parents
りょうり	料理	cooking, cuisine
		りょうり （を） します to fix a meal

う -verbs

あいます	会います	(to) meet; the dictionary form is あう .
あそびます	遊びます	(to) play; the dictionary form is あそぶ .
あるきます	歩きます	(to) walk、〜まで　あるきます (to) walk (up) towards; the dictionary form is あるく .
いいます	言います	(to) say; the dictionary form is いう .
およぎます	泳ぎます	(to) swim; the dictionary form is およぐ .
かきます	書きます	(to) write; the dictionary form is かく .
ききます	聞きます / 聴きます	(to) ask （聞きます, (to) listen to(聴きます); the dictionary form is きく .
はなします	話します	(to) talk; the dictionary form is はなす.
まちます	待ちます	(to) wait; the dictionary form is まつ .
よびます	呼びます	(to) call (someone), (to) invite; the dictionary form is よぶ .

る -verbs

かけます		(to) make (a phone call); the dictionary for is かける. でんわを　かけます
でかけます	出かけます	(to) go out; the dictionary form is でかける .

い -adjectives

いそがしい	忙しい	busy
うれしい	嬉しい	happy
おもしろい	面白い	interesting

かなしい	悲しい	sad
さびしい	寂しい	lonely
たのしい	楽しい	fun
つまらない		boring
むずかしい	難しい	difficult
やさしい	易しい、優しい	easy（易しい）, kind（優しい）

さびしい (handwritten in margin)

な -adjectives

げんき（な）	元気（な）	healthy, cheerful, lively (person)
ざんねん（な）	残念（な）	sorry, regrettable
だいじょうぶ（な）	大丈夫（な）	all right, no problem
たいへん（な）	大変（な）	tough
にぎやか（な）	賑やか（な）	lively (place or event)
ひま（な）	暇（な）	free, idle, unscheduled

にぎやか / *ひま* (handwritten in margin)

Adverbs

いっしょに	一緒に	together
ぜひ	是非	By all means. / I'd love to.
ゆっくり		slowly, ゆっくりします, to relax, to take it easy

Particles

と		with, together with (association)
と		and (exhaustive listing)
に		in order to, for (purpose)
に		to (goal, receiver)

Expressions

| ちょっと つごうが わるくて | ちょっと都合が悪くて | I'm a little busy. (*literally*, Sorry, it's a little inconvenient.) |
| ちょっと ようじが あって | ちょっと用事があって | Sorry, I have some errands/ business to attend to. |

単語の練習 Vocabulary Practice
たんご　れんしゅう

A. 毎週すること Household chores and other activities
まいしゅう

りょうりを します
(to) fix a meal

せんたくを します
(to) do laundry

そうじを します
(to) clean /dust a room

アルバイトを します
(to) have a part-time job

しごとを します
(to) work

しんぶんを よみます
(to) read a newspaper

かいものに いきます
(to) go shopping

メールを かきます
(to) write e-mail

先生に ききます
to ask the teacher

しつもんします

(to) ask a question

日本語で はなします
ご
(to) talk in Japanese

でんわを
します／かけます
(to) make a phone call

Activity 1

Charades. Work in groups of three or four. Take turns performing an action from the list below while the rest of the group try to guess the expression.

ごはんを　たべます	アルバイトを　します
りょうりを　します	しんぶんを　よみます
せんたくを　します	かいものに　いきます
そうじを　します	メールを　かきます
シャワーを　あびます	日本語で　はなします
おふろに　はいります	テレビを　みます
しゅくだいを　します	ともだちに　でんわを　かけます
コーヒーを　のみます	先生に　しつもん　します

Activity 2

Work in pairs. Ask each other what things you do every day, sometimes, not very often, and never. List each of your partner's activities in the appropriate box.

Example:　A:　〜さんは　毎日
まいにち　あさごはんを　たべますか。

　　　　　　B:　いいえ、たべません。

　　　　　　A:　そうですか。じゃあ、ひるごはんは　たべますか。

	パートナーの　こたえ
毎日 まいにち　します。	
ときどきします。	
あまりしません。	
ぜんぜんしません。	

B. 休みの日に すること　**Things to do on a day off**
やす

おんがくを ききます

(to) listen to music

コンサートに いきます

(to) go to a concert

ピクニックに
いきます

(to) go on a picnic

うんどうします
(to) exercise

テニスを します
(to) play tennis

ジョギングを します
(to) go jogging

プールで およぎます

(to) swim in the pool

でかけます

(to) go out

ともだちに／と
あいます
(to) meet a friend

ともだちを まちます
(to) wait for a friend

さんぽを します
(to) take a walk

あそびます
(to) play, (to) have fun

ゲームを します
(to) play a game

うちで ゆっくりします
(to) relax at home

てがみを かきます
(to) write a letter

ざっしを よみます   パーティを します   ともだちを
                                                  うちに よびます

(to) read a magazine   (to) have a party   (to) invite / call a friend over

C. きもちや ようすを あらわす ことば   Adjectives of emotion
and condition

いそがしい	busy	つまらない	boring
うれしい	happy	やさしい	easy, kind
おもしろい	interesting	むずかしい	difficult
かなしい	sad	たのしい	fun
ざんねん（な）	sorry, regrettable	大変（な） たいへん	tough
ひま（な）	free, idle, with nothing to do		
だいじょうぶ（な）	all right, no problem		

VOCABULARY NOTES

- （お）げんきですか
  げんきですか and its polite version おげんきですか can be
  translated as *How are you?*, but this expression is not used in the
  same way as in English. げんきですか／おげんきですか is used
  when you have not seen someone you know for an extended period
  of time. In function, its sense is closer to *How have you been?* For
  daily greetings, use おはよう（ございます）, こんにちは,
  こんばんは.

- ざんねん vs. すみません
  Both ざんねん and すみません may be translated as *sorry*, but
  their usage is very different. すみません is used for apologizing,
  but ざんねん merely expresses regret, disappointment, or sympathy (and may also function as an adjective). For example, if you are
  not able to finish your homework by the due date, you might say
  すみません to your teacher. The teacher might then reply
  ざんねんですね, to express his/her disappointment. すみません
  can also be used to approach someone (meaning *Excuse me. /
  Pardon me.*), or to express thanks. ざんねん cannot be substi-
  tuted in these instances.

ダイアローグ
Dialogue

はじめに   Warm-up

しつもんに　こたえて下さい。Answer these questions in Japanese.

1. 週末は　うちで　よく　何を　しますか。
　　しゅうまつ　　　　　　　なに
2. 週末は　よく　どこに　あそびに　いきますか。
　　しゅうまつ
3. 休みの日に　よく　でかけますか。どこへ　いきますか。
　　やす
4. 休みの日に　よく　何を　しますか。
　　やす　　　　　　　　なに

週末は　どうでしたか。   *What did you do over the weekend?*
　　しゅうまつ

Ueda and Li meet in class on Monday.

上田：　リーさん、おはようございます。

リー：　あ、上田さん、おはようございます。週末は
　　　　　　　　　　　　　　　　　　　　　　しゅうまつ
　　　　どうでしたか。

上田：　とても　たのしかったです。

リー：　それは　よかったですね。

上田：　ええ、みちこさんと　しぶやに　かいものに　いって、

リー：　ええ、

上田：　コンサートへ　いきました。

5

リー：　そうですか。

上田：　リーさんの　週末は　どうでしたか。　　　　　10
　　　　　しゅうまつ

リー：　いそがしくて　あまり　おもしろくなかったです。

　　　　先週は　しゅくだいが　たくさんあって、大変でした。
　　　　せんしゅう　　　　　　　　　　　　　　　　　　たいへん

上田：　そうですか。じゃあ、週末は　うちに　いましたか。
　　　　　　　　　　　　　　　しゅうまつ

リー：　ええ、うちで　ずっと　べんきょうしました。

上田：　それは　大変でしたね。　　　　　　　　　　15
　　　　　　　　たいへん

リー：　ええ。

上田：　じゃあ、来週の　週末も　いそがしいですか。
　　　　　　　　らいしゅう　しゅうまつ

リー：　いいえ、来週は　あまり　いそがしくありません。
　　　　　　　　　らいしゅう

上田：　じゃあ、うちに　あそびに　きませんか。

リー：　ありがとう。ほんとうに　いいんですか。　　　20

上田：　ええ。土曜日は　どうですか。
　　　　　どようび

リー：　ええ、土曜日は　大丈夫です。
　　　　　　どようび　　だいじょうぶ

上田；　じゃあ、土曜日の　あさ、でんわしてくれませんか。
　　　　　　　　どようび

リー：　わかりました。じゃあ、でんわします。　　　24

DIALOGUE PHRASE NOTES

- The それ in それは　よかったですね in line 5 refers to Ueda's statement that she had fun. It does not refer to any physical object in the scene. Similarly, the それ in それは　大変でしたね in
  　　　　　　　　　　　　　　　　　　　　　　　　　　たいへん
  line 15 refers to Li's having studied all weekend.
- Li interjects ええ while Ueda is talking in line 7. This ええ is the あいづち you learned about in Chapters 2 and 3. In this case, he is signaling to Ueda that he is following her story and wants her to continue. Similarly, Ueda says ええ in line 21 after Li's utterance. あいづち are generally used at phrase boundaries, for example, immediately after the て-form of verbs as shown in this dialogue, or after the conjunction が.
- ずっと means *for a long time*. In this context, it suggests *all day long*.
- ほんとうに　いいんですか means *Are you sure?*
- あとで means *later*.
- In Japanese, あそびに　きませんか is often used to invite a friend to get together or hang out, as in Ueda's invitation in line 23.

ダイアローグの後で　Comprehension

A. Read each statement and circle はい if the statement is true or いいえ if it is false.

1. はい　　いいえ　　　リーさんは 日曜日に べんきょうしました。
2. はい　　いいえ　　　リーさんは 土曜日に でかけました。
3. はい　　いいえ　　　リーさんは おもしろい えいがを みました。
4. はい　　いいえ　　　上田さんは キムさんと コンサートに いきました。
5. はい　　いいえ　　　上田さんは 先週の 週末に かいものを しました。

B. しつもんに こたえて下さい。　Answer these questions.

1. 上田さんは 先週 何を しましたか。
2. リーさんは 何を しましたか。
3. リーさんは 来週の 週末 いそがしいですか。
4. リーさんは 来週 何を しますか。

日本の文化
ぶん か
Japanese Culture

Japanese Colleges and College Life

According to a 2005 government survey, nearly all Japanese students (97.6%) attend high school after completing junior high, and about a half of them (51.5%) will continue on to college or junior college. Most of those who do enroll in college attend school full-time, spending four to five days a week in class, and depend financially on their parents.

Japanese college class sizes tend to be large. As there are few graduate teaching assistants, professors themselves do most of the teaching. Undergraduates usually spend four years at college. Though most liberal arts students earn the necessary credit hours to graduate by the end of their junior year, they usually continue their course work through senior year. Job hunting starts junior year, and most students enter the workforce immediately upon graduation.

Traditionally, graduate schools in Japan have been regarded as institutions dedicated to producing academicians and researchers. Since Japanese law and medical schools accept students directly from high schools, in contrast with the

U.S. system, these are not considered graduate programs. Professional degrees were not available in Japan before 2002. Due to a series of educational reforms, however, over 120 institutions now offer MBAs as well as master's degrees and PhDs in a range of other fields. As a result, the number of graduate students in Japan is on the rise—currently, about 15% of college graduates. Over 80% of graduate students do not take a break from their studies after earning an undergraduate degree.

Another factor that has shaped college life in Japan today is the economic depression that began in the early 1990s and lasted through 2005. A decade-long job shortage caused many students to prioritize their studies much higher than their social lives at school. (**Zenkoku Daigaku Seikatsu Kyoodoo Kumiai 2005**). Still, most Japanese college students engage in a variety of extra-curricular activities, such as participating in college clubs, doing volunteer work, hanging out with friends, and traveling domestically and internationally. Over three-quarters of students work part-time during the school year as well as on spring break and summer vacation. The average student has a weekly budget of approximately 37,000 yen (about US$320 in 2006) that is put toward dining out, clothing purchases, online communications, and savings. (**Tokyo FM, 2005**).

文法
ぶんぽう
Grammar

I. Using the particles と and に

A. Particle と

The particle と has two separate usages that are conceptually related.

1. と , *together with, with*

The first usage indicates association between two items and is translated as *with* or *together with*. For example:

私は わたし	チョイさんと	べんきょうしました。	*I studied with Ms. Choi.*
リーさんは	田中さんと	えいがを みました。	*Mr. Li watched a movie with Mr. Tanaka.*
私は わたし	ペギーさんと	でんわで はなします。	*I talk with Peggy on the phone.*
中山さんは	ともだちと	かいものに いきます。	*Mr. Nakayama goes shopping with a friend.*

2. と , *and*

The second usage is to connect two or more nouns.

スミスさんと	私は わたし	学生です。	*Mr. Smith and I are students.*
そうじと	せんたくを	しました。	*I did cleaning and laundry.*
しんぶんと	ざっしを	よみました。	*I read a newspaper and a magazine.*
金曜日と きんよう び	土曜日に ど よう び	ここへ きます。	*I will come here on Friday and Saturday.*
ナイフと	フォークで	たべます。	*(I) eat with a knife and a fork.*

All of the above examples show that the particle と connects nouns only. It cannot be used to connect two or more sentences, or verb or adjective phrases.

Use the て-form of verbs (see p. 230, Grammar III) or the conjunction そして to connect sentences and verb phrases.

そうじを <u>して</u>、 せんたくも しました。
I did the cleaning and the laundry.

そうじをしました。 <u>そして</u>、 せんたくも しました。
I cleaned the house. Then I did the laundry.

B. The particle に

So far, you have learned three functions of the particle に : に for time as in
土曜日に (*on Saturday*) and いちじに (*at one o'clock*); に for goals/destinations,
as in 学校に いきます (*go to school*) ; and に for the location of a person or
object, as in うちに あります／います (*It/Someone is in my house.*) This chapter
introduces two more usages of the particle に , but they are related to に used for goals.

1. に to (recipient, target, goal, destination)

に can indicate the recipient or the target person to which an action is directed.

	Noun	**Particle**	
私は	ともだち	に	てがみを かきます。

I will write a letter to a friend.

ともだちに	でんわを かけます。	*I make a phone call to a friend.*
りょうしんに	メールを かきます。	*I write e-mail to my parents.*
先生に	ききます。	*I ask my teacher.*
先生に	しつもんします。	*I ask my teacher a question.*
先生に	はなします。	*I talk to/tell my teacher.*
ともだちに	あいます。	*I meet my friends.*

NOTES

- に in this usage indicates the endpoint of an action, so it is
  conceptually related to the goal 〜に／へ いきます／きます／
  かえります. However, unlike the above usage, 〜に／へ
  いきます／きます／かえります cannot take a person as a goal.
- In some cases, the particle と association (with) is used instead of
  に with verbs like あいます and はなします. Although the
  English translation does not differentiate between に or と, the
  meaning is very different in Japanese. When に is used, the action
  is uni-directional, so 先生に はなします indicates that the
  speaker is telling something or speaking to the teacher, but not
  having a conversation. Conversely, と indicates bi-directional
  orientation, so 先生と はなします indicates that the speaker
  and the teacher collaboratively engage in conversation.

先生に はなします	*I speak to/tell something to the teacher.*
先生と はなします	*I converse with the teacher.*

  Similarly, ともだちに あいますis used when the speaker goes to
  the friend to talk or bumps into the friend on the street, but
  ともだちと あいます suggests that the speaker and the friend
  have made a prior arrangement before meeting each other.

2. Purpose に いきます／きます／かえります／でかけます

に can also indicate the purpose for going somewhere. It is used with the verbs いきます, きます, かえります and でかけます. The purpose may be a noun indicating an activity such as かいもの and コンサート.

アリソンさんは　かいものに　でかけました。　　*Alison went shopping.*

リーさんは　コンサートに　いきます。　　*Mr. Li is going to a concert.*

When purpose is represented by a verbal expression such as テニスを　します or ごはんを　たべます に should be attached to the verb stem (the part of verb that comes before ます).

	Verb stem	Particle	Verb of movement
ごはんを	たべ	に	でかけます。

I'm going out to eat.

Note いきます, きます, かえります and でかけますare commonly used with an expression of a desination such as としょかんに／へ　いきます. When combined with the purpose, the sentence can have more than one に, such as としょかんに　べんきょうしに　いきます (*go to the library to study*).

うちに ねに　かえります。　　*I am going home to take a nap.*

上田さんに あいに　きました。　　*I came to see Ms. Ueda.*

上田さんに あいに　ここに　きました。　*I came here to see Ms. Ueda.*

キム：　あ、どこへ　いきますか。
Where are you going?

田中：　たいいくかんに　およぎに　いきます。
I am going to the gym to swim.

キム：　そうですか。
I see.

話してみましょう　Conversation Practice
_{はな}

Activity 1

The pictures below show what Mr. Suzuki did last week. Complete the following statements using the appropriate particles.

Example:

鈴木さん／ともだち／でんわ／かけました。
_{すず き}
鈴木さんは　ともだちに　でんわを　かけました。
_{すず き}

1. 鈴木さん／ともだち／としょかん／べんきょうしました。
_{すず き}
2. 鈴木さん／ともだち／デパート／かいもの／いきました。
_{すず き}
3. 鈴木さん／かのじょ (*girlfriend*) ／でんわ／はなしました。
_{すず き}
4. 鈴木さんの　かのじょ／鈴木さんの　うち／あそび／きました。
_{すず き}　　　　　　　_{すず き}
5. 鈴木さんの　かのじょ／鈴木さん／りょうり／しました。
_{すず き}　　　　　　　_{すず き}
6. 鈴木さんの　かのじょ／鈴木さん／ゲーム／しました。
_{すず き}　　　　　　　_{すず き}
7. 鈴木さん／かのじょ／メール／かきました。
_{すず き}

Activity 2

Based on each situation, create a sentence stating a purpose, using a verb stem +
に　いきます／きます／かえります．

Example:　昨日　スーパーへ　いきました。そして、アルバイトを　しました。
きのう
　　　　　昨日　スーパーへ　アルバイトを　しに　いきました。
きのう

1. たいいくかんへ　いきました。およぎました。
2. アパートに　かえります。そして、ゆっくり　します。
3. ここに　きました。そして、りょうりを　しました。
4. としょかんへ　いきました。そして、しんぶんを　よみました。
5. 先生の　けんきゅうしつ (office) に　いきます。そして、しつもんします。
6. このカフェに　よく　きます。そして、ともだちに　あいます。

Activity 3

Work in groups of three. One person chooses a place in the box but does not tell
anyone. The other two ask questions about the purpose of going there and try to
figure out which place it is. The person who has chosen the place will answer
はい or いいえ. Take turns.

としょかん	たいいくかん	ラボ	きょうしつ	本屋や	こうえん
ぎんこう	ゆうびんきょく	カフェ	コンビニ	びょういん	こうばん
デパート	ともだちのうち	日本	中国ごく	かんこく	フランス
スペイン	オーストラリア	カナダ	メキシコ	アメリカ	イギリス

Example:　B chooses としょかん

　　　　　A:　うんどうしに　いきますか。
　　　　　B:　いいえ。
　　　　　C:　本を　よみに　いきますか
　　　　　B:　はい。
　　　　　C:　としょかんですか。
　　　　　B:　はい、そうです。

Activity 4

Based on the sentences you completed in Activity 1, narrate Mr. Suzuki's day. Try
to use transition words like そして, when you can. To make the story sound more
natural, try to fill in some information such as when Mr. Suzuki went out and
came back, and when his girlfriend visited him and went home.

II. Commenting about the past, using polite past adjectives and the copula verb です

In Chapter 4, adjectives were introduced to describe the physical characteristics of an object. Another common use of adjectives is to comment on objects and events in the present and the past. This chapter introduces the past tense forms of adjectives and the copula verb です. Like the present forms, the formation of past tense forms differs depending on the adjective type.

A. い -adjectives

The past affirmative form of い-adjectives is formed by replacing い with かったです. The past negative form is formed by replacing い with くありませんでした or くなかったです. いい becomes よかったです in the affirmative form and よくありませんでした or よくなかったです in the negative form.

Dictionary form	Polite affirmative forms		Polite negative forms	
	Present	Past	Present	Past
あかい (red)	あかいです (It is red.)	あかかったです (It was red.)	あかくありません あかくないです (It is not red.)	あかくありませんでした あかくなかったです (It was not red.)
いい (good)	いいです (It is good.)	よかったです (It was good.)	よくありません よくないです (It is not good.)	よくありませんでした よくなかったです (It was not good.)

B. な -adjectives and the copula verb です

The ending of the な-adjectives and the copula verb are very similar. In both cases, you will change です to でした for the past affirmative form, じゃありません／じゃないです to じゃありませんでした／じゃなかったです for the past negative form.

Dictionary form	Polite affirmative forms		Polite negative forms	
	Present	Past	Present	Past
きれい (pretty)	きれいです (It is pretty.)	きれいでした (It was pretty.)	きれいじゃありません きれいじゃないです (It is not pretty.)	きれいじゃありませんでした きれいじゃなかったです (It was not pretty.)
ゲーム (game)	ゲームです (It is a game.)	ゲームでした (It was a game.)	ゲームじゃありません ゲームじゃないです (It is not a game.)	ゲームじゃありませんでした ゲームじゃなかったです (It was not a game.)

スミス：　週末は　どうでしたか。
　　　　しゅうまつ
How was your weekend?

山下：　とても　たのしかったです。
It was really fun.

スミス：　そうですか。よかったですね。
I see. I'm glad to hear that. (literally, that was good.)

上田：　パーティは　どうでしたか。
How was the party?

リー：　とても　にぎやかでした。
It was very lively.

上田：　山田先生と　はなしましたか。
Did you talk with Professor Yamada?

リー：　いいえ、先生は　いませんでした。
No, he wasn't there.

上田：　そうですか。ざんねんでしたね。
I see. That's too bad.

チョイ：　今日、いそがしいですか。
　　　　きょう
Are you busy today?

本田：　ええ、テストが　あります。
Yes, I have a test.

チョイ：　そうですか。大変ですね。
　　　　　　　　　たいへん
I see. That's tough!

話してみましょう　Conversation Practice
　はな

Activity 1

Change the adjectives into both the past tense affirmative form and the past tense negative form. Pay attention to the two kinds of adjectives, い -adjectives and な -adjectives. Use とても with the affirmative form and あまり with the negative form.

Example:　大きい

　　　　とても　大きかったです。　あまり　大きくありませんでした。

1. おもしろい	4. いい	7. ざんねん	10. げんき
2. きれい	5. たのしい	8. 大変	11. にぎやか
3. うれしい	6. かなしい	9. ひま	12. むずかしい

たいへん

Activity 2

Chat with a partner about events and occasions listed in the chart below. Discuss which ones were interesting, easy, difficult, etc., and complete the chart.

Examples: 1. A: 日本語の テストは どうでしたか。

          B: とても <u>やさしかったです。</u>

          A: そうですか。<u>よかったですね。</u>

    2. A: 日本語の テストは どうでしたか。

          B: あまり <u>よくなかったです。</u> ／
            とても <u>むずかしかったです。</u>

          A: そうですか。<u>ざんねんでしたね。</u>／<u>大変でしたね。</u>

	私	パートナー
日本語の テスト		
日本語の じゅぎょう		
週末		
パーティ		

Activity 3

With your partner, take turns asking about life in high school (高校生活) as well as about your high school classes and teachers. Fill in the chart as you ask and answer questions.

Example: A: 高校生活 は どうでしたか。

        B: とても たのしかったです。

        A: そうですか。よかったですね。

        B: ～さんの 高校生活は どうでしたか。

        A: わたしの 高校生活も とても よかったです。

	私	パートナー
高校生活		
じゅぎょう		
先生		

> ## III. Connecting verb and adjective phrases and sentences using the て -form of verbs; making requests using the て -form

Chapter 1 introduced request forms such as きいて下さい and みて下さい, in which 下さい roughly means *please*. The forms きいて and みて are the て-forms of the verbs ききます and みます, respectively. Also, Chapter 5 introduced the phrase あるいて　いきます, in which あるいて is the て-form of あるきます (*to walk*) and indicates how the speaker goes from one place to another. You may have also noticed headings such as はなして　みましょう (*Let's try speaking*) and きいて　みましょう (*Let's try listening*) in the chapters of this textbook. The form みましょう means *let's try*, and the preceding て-forms indicate what to try out. These are only a few uses of the て-form. As you continue to study Japanese, you will learn a variety of structures that use this form. This section explains the formation of the て-form of verbs and three request forms using the て-form and 下さい／下さいませんか／くれませんか.

A. Verb て-forms

The て-form of る-verbs and irregular verbs is easy to form. All you have to do is to replace ます with て.

Verb class		Polite affirmative form	て -form
る -verbs	to eat	たべ<u>ます</u>	たべ<u>て</u>
	to watch	み<u>ます</u>	み<u>て</u>
	to make a phone call	かけ<u>ます</u>	かけ<u>て</u>
Irregular verbs	to come	き<u>ます</u>	き<u>て</u>
	to do	し<u>ます</u>	し<u>て</u>
	to study	べんきょうし<u>ます</u>	べんきょうし<u>て</u>

The て-form of う-verbs is more complicated. There are five basic patterns and they are determined by the sound before ます, as shown in the chart below. The て-form of the verb いきます is いって though it is an う-verb. This is considered an exception.

Verb class		Polite affirmative form	て -form	Formation Patterns
う -verbs	to talk	はな<u>し</u>ます	はな<u>して</u>	し→して
	to listen	き<u>き</u>ます	き<u>いて</u>	き→いて
	to swim	およ<u>ぎ</u>ます	およ<u>いで</u>	ぎ→いで
	to take (a bath), enter	はい<u>り</u>ます	はい<u>って</u>	り、い、ち→って
	to say	い<u>い</u>ます	い<u>って</u>	
	to wait	ま<u>ち</u>ます	ま<u>って</u>	
	to read	よ<u>み</u>ます	よ<u>んで</u>	み、び、に→んで
	to call	よ<u>び</u>ます	よ<u>んで</u>	
	to die	し<u>に</u>ます	し<u>んで</u>	
	to go	い<u>き</u>ます	い<u>って</u>	Exception

B. 〜て下さい／〜て下さいませんか／〜てくれませんか

〜て下さい, 〜て下さいませんか and 〜てくれませんか are all used to make a request. Each expression generally indicates a polite request, but 〜て下さい is the most forceful form among the three forms because it is a command form. While a social superior such as your teacher or someone much older than you may use 〜て下さい to ask you to do something, it would be rude for you to say 〜て下さい to your social superior. Instead, use 〜て下さいませんか, a more polite request form commonly used for a social superior. 〜てくれませんか is less formal than 〜て下さいませんか, so it can be used with someone of equal social status or similar age.

To a social inferior:

CD を	きいて下さい。	*Please listen to the CD.*
こくばんを	みて下さい。	*Please look at the chalkboard.*
本を	よんで下さい。	*Please read the book.*

To a social superior:

先生、 かんじを かいて下さいませんか。
Could you write the kanji?

先生、もういちど いって下さいませんか。
Could you say it again?

先生、あしたまで まって下さいませんか。
Could you wait until tomorrow?

To a peer:

上田さん、あした　メールしてくれませんか。
Could you e-mail me tomorrow?

上田さん、としょかんへ　いってくれませんか。
Could you go to the library?

上田さん、この　てがみを　よんでくれませんか。
Could you read this letter?

話してみましょう　Conversation Practice
はな

Activity 1

Your teacher gives you one of the following commands in Japanese. Act out the command.

Example:　Your teacher says ここに　きて下さい.
You walk toward the teacher.

1. Come here.
2. Go to the back of the room.
3. Read the textbook.
4. Look at the chalkboard.
5. Write your name in Japanese.
6. Speak Japanese to a classmate next to you.
7. Turn in your work.　(しゅくだいを　だします。)
8. Make a phone call.

Activity 2

Working with a partner, make the requests in Activity 1, using 〜てくれませんか. Your partner will act out. You can create your own request if you like.

Example:　You say ここに　きてくれませんか.
Your partner walks toward you.

Activity 3

Use the table below to make a request to the addressee. Pay attention to the relationship between you and your addressee and choose 〜て下さい or 〜て下さいませんか or 〜てくれませんか.

Example: 先生   wants students to speak Japanese.

日本語で　はなして下さい。
ご

	You	**Your addressee**	**Request**
Example	先生	学生	Speak Japanese
1	学生	学生	Invite/call Tanaka-san
2	学生	先生	Write e-mail to you
3	学生	先生	Read this letter
4	先生	学生	Turn in the homework
5	学生	学生	Clean up the room
6	いしゃ (doctor)	かんじゃ (patient)	Walk every day
7	いしゃ (doctor)	かんじゃ (patient)	Relax at home
8	大学院生 いんせい	大学の先生	Meet me next week
9	学校１の先生 (teacher at a school)	学校２の先生 (teacher at another school)	Write a letter to school

(handwritten notes in the right margin:) よんでくれませんか。 このがみをよんが下さい） おんせいか

Activity 4

Work with a partner. Create dialogues in which you make requests in each of the following situations, using 〜て下さい or 〜てくれませんか.

Example: You are a teacher, and you are taking our students on a field trip tomorrow. So you want them to come to school at 7 a.m.

明日のあさ　7じに　学校へきて下さい。
あした

1. You are sick and can't go to school. You want your roommate to call your teacher.
2. You want to use **kanji** to write your name. Ask your teacher to write your name in **kanji**.
3. You are a teacher. Your students performed very poorly on the test and you want them to study.
4. You have a visitor, who looks younger than you. But you are busy with work so you want him/her to wait for you here.
5. Your neighbor comes to your house to discuss a neighborhood dispute with you. She/he is at the door. Invite him/her in.

IV. Connecting phrases, using the て -forms of verbs and adjectives

A. The て-form of verbs indicating "and"

Another basic usage of the て-form is to connect phrases. As was mentioned in Grammar I, A-2 (p. 223), the particle と cannot be used to connect two or more sentences or phrases. The て-form is used instead. Note that the て-form by itself does not express when the action takes place or has taken place. The timing of the action is determined by the phrase at the end of the sentence. For example, テレビを <u>みて</u>、ねます indicates that the speaker goes or will go to bed after watching TV, but テレビを <u>みて</u>、ねました indicates that he/she went to bed after watching TV.

しんぶんを <u>よんで、</u> 学校に いきます	I read the newspaper and go to school.
おんがくを <u>きいて、</u> ねます。	I listen to the music and go to bed.
うちに <u>かえって、</u> ゆっくりしました。	I went home and relaxed.
ともだちを <u>よんで、</u> ゲームを しました。	I called my friend and played a game.
いぬの さんぽを <u>して、</u> でかけました。	I walked my dog and went out.
アルバイトが <u>あって、</u> いそがしかったです。	I had to work part-time and was busy.
田中さんが <u>いて、</u> にぎやかでした。	Mr. Tanaka was there, and/so it was lively.

Phrases connected by the て-form may indicate a chronological relationship or a cause-effect relationship, because the て-form loosely connects phrases without specifying how they should be related.

B. The て-form of adjectives indicating "and"

The て-form of adjectives and the copula verbs can connect phrases as well: The formation of the adjective て-form is relatively simple. い（です）is replaced by くて for い-adjectives, です is replaced by で for な-adjective and the copula verb. The て-form of いい is よくて.

い -adjectives	な -adjectives	Copula verb
たのし<u>いです</u> (it is fun.)	にぎやかです (it is lively.)	休みです (It is a day off.)
たのし<u>くて</u> (it is fun, and)	にぎやか<u>で</u> (it is lively, and)	休み<u>で</u> (It is a day off, and)

上田さんは やさし<u>くて、</u> きれいです。
Ms. Ueda is kind and pretty.

リーさんは　げんき<u>で、</u>　おもしろいです。
Mr. Li is cheerful and interesting.

かんじは　むずか<u>しくて、</u>　大変です。
たいへん
Kanji is difficult and tough.

パーティは　にぎやか<u>で、</u>　たのしかったです。
The party was lively and fun.

ひま<u>で、</u>　うちに　います。
I have nothing to do and stay at home.

しごと<u>で、</u>　フランスへ　いきます。
I am going to France for work.

さび<u>しくて、</u>　ともだちに　でんわしました。
I was lonely, and/so I called my friend.

話してみましょう Conversation Practice
はな

Activity 1

The following illustrations show what Ms. Yamamoto did last Sunday. Describe her activities using the て -form of verbs.

Example:　あさ　8じに　<u>おきて</u>、うんどうを　しました。

8:00 A.M.

8:30 A.M.

About 9:00 A.M.

9:30 A.M.

About 10:00 A.M.

11:00 A.M.

About 11:30 A.M.

12:00 P.M.

12:15 P.M.

12:30 P.M.   ABOUT 4:00 P.M.   6:00 P.M.

7:00 P.M.   8:00 P.M.   ABOUT 11:00 P.M.

Activity 2

Comment on the following things using the て -form of adjectives.

Example:　えいごのじゅぎょう

　　　　　えいごのじゅぎょうは　やさしくて、おもしろいです。

1. 日本語
2. そうじ
3. せんたく
4. アルバイト
5. おんがく
6. うんどう
7. コンピュータ・ゲーム

Activity 3

With a partner, discuss a movie, a TV program (テレビばんぐみ) you've seen, a concert you've attended, or some music you have listened to recently. Comment on the experiences using the て -form. Then complete the chart.

Example:　A:　さいきん (*recently*) どんな　えいがを　みましたか。

　　　　　B:　ハリー・ポッターを　みました。

　　　　　A:　どうでしたか。

　　　　　B:　とても　おもしろくて、よかったですよ。

Category	Type/Title	How was it?
えいが		
コンサート		
テレビばんぐみ		
おんがく		

V. Extending an invitation using ～ませんか

The negative question form of a verb ～ませんか is often used to extend an invitation. It conveys the idea in English of *won't you* ～, or *why don't we* ～. ～ませんか is often used with the phrase いっしょに (*together*) when the speaker wants to invite someone for an activity.

いっしょに ジョギングを しませんか。
Why don't we go jogging together?

今度の 休みに いっしょに ピクニックに いきませんか。
Why don't we go to a picnic on the next day off?

私と いっしょに べんきょうしませんか。
Won't you study with me?

NOTES

- Before extending an invitation, the speaker often checks the listener's availability or interest, or willingness. Because an overt rejection can often strain a relationship, Japanese people tend to avoid creating a situation in which a person may have to reject an offer or an invitation.

  ジョンソン： 今度の 休みは いそがしいですか。
  Are you busy during the next holiday?

  木村： いいえ、いそがしくありません。
  No, not really.

  ジョンソン： じゃあ、およぎに いきませんか。
  Then, why don't we go swimming?

  山田： テニスは よく しますか。
  Do you play tennis often?

  上田： ええ、しますよ。
  Yes, I do.

  山田： じゃあ、土曜日に テニスを しませんか。
  Well, why don't we play tennis on Saturday?

- Japanese people often avoid saying no explicitly to an invitation in order not to hurt other people's feelings. When you cannot accept an invitation, it's customary to apologize for not being able to accept it, and then give a reason. If you don't want to give a specific reason, use the following phrases.

  すみません、ちょっと つごうが わるくて。
  Sorry, I'm a little busy. (literally, *Sorry, it's a little inconvenient.*)

すみません、ちょっと ようじが あって。
Sorry, I have some errands/business to attend to.

- Some common expressions for accepting an invitation are:

いいですね。　　　　*That sounds great.*

ええ、ぜひ。　　　　*Yes, I'd love to.* (literally, *Yes by all means.*)

ええ、いいですよ。　*Yes, that would be fine.*

話してみましょう　Conversation Practice
はな

Activity 1

Work with a partner. Look at the following drawings and extend an invitation to each activity. Your partner will accept your invitation by saying ええ、いいですよ, いいですね or ええ、ぜひ.

Example:　A:　〜さん、いっしょに かいものに いきませんか。

B:　ええ、いいですよ。

Activity 2

Work with the class. In the chart below, write three activities that you want to do with someone on each day of this weekend. Invite at least one person for each activity. If someone invites you to do an activity, either accept using one of the phrases you've just learned, or decline the invitation politely if you're not interested.

Example: You have written えいがを みる for 金曜日.

A: 金曜日に えいがを みませんか。
きんようび

B: ええ、いいですよ。

or すみません、ちょっと つごうが わるくて。

ちょっと ようじが あって。

〜曜日 ようび	すること (Activities to invite for)	なまえ (Person who has agreed)
金曜日 きんようび		
土曜日 どようび		
日曜日 にちようび		

Activity 3

Invite a partner to do the following activities together. Before extending your invitation, ask about his/her availability and/or interest.

Example: A: 今週の 金曜日は いそがしいですか。
こんしゅう きんようび

B: いいえ、いそがしくないですよ。

A: じゃあ、いっしょに パーティに いきませんか。

B: いいですね。

1. いっしょに かいものに いきます。
2. いっしょに おんがくを ききます。
3. いっしょに しゅくだいを します。
4. いっしょに えいがを みます。
5. いっしょに こうえんの そうじを します。

SUPPLEMENTARY NOTE

In Japanese, verbal expressions can be abbreviated using です when the meaning can be guessed from context. This use of です appears often in response to a wh-question.

田中：　だれを　よびましたか。
Who did you invite?

ペギー：　上田さんと　アリソンさんです。
Ms. Ueda and Alison.

木村：　いつ　かえりますか。
（き むら）
When will you come back?

リー：　来週の　火曜日です。
（らい しゅう）（か よう び）
Next Tuesday.

山中：　だれと　はなしましたか。
Who did you talk to?

チョイ：　スミスさんです。
Mr. Smith.

In English, you can simply use nouns such as people's names without a verb, but in Japanese it sounds abrupt and can be rude to omit the verb, especially in formal conversations. In cases like this, です can be used instead of more specific verbal expressions.

　　This is true in the classroom where the instructor asks many questions. You should try to respond to your teacher with the verb from the question or with です when it is appropriate to do so. (But be careful not to overuse です because excessive repetition may be interpreted as a lack of interest in class!)

聞く練習
き　　　れんしゅう
Listening

上手な聞き方 Listening Strategy
じょうず　　き　　かた

Making sense of missing pronouns

Just as in writing, pronouns are often omitted in a conversation when they can be inferred from the context. Imagine that two people are talking with each other. If one person asks a question without an overt subject pronoun, the missing subject is likely to be *you*. If that person then makes a statement without a subject, the subject is most likely to be the speaker himself/herself. As you become more proficient with the language, you will understand who is mentioned without having to listen for subject pronouns.

A. だれの はなし? **Whose story is it?**

Listen to the following short dialogues. In each of the conversations, the subject in the man's speech is either *I* or *you*, but it's missing. Identify the missing subjects.

1. I	you	**4.** I	you
2. I	you	**5.** I	you
3. I	you		

B. 私の 生活
わたし　せいかつ

Listen to the following conversations, then the statements about them. Circle はい if a statement is true, or いいえ if it is false.

1. a. はい　　いいえ　　**d.** はい　　いいえ　　**g.** はい　　いいえ

　　b. はい　　いいえ　　**e.** はい　　いいえ　　**h.** はい　　いいえ

　　c. はい　　いいえ　　**f.** はい　　いいえ

2. a. はい　　いいえ　　**d.** はい　　いいえ

　　b. はい　　いいえ　　**e.** はい　　いいえ

　　c. はい　　いいえ　　**f.** はい　　いいえ

<h1 style="text-align:center">聞き上手　話し上手</h1>

き　　じょうず　はな　　じょうず

<h2 style="text-align:center">Communication</h2>

Communication Strategy

Using そうですか and そうですね

The expressions そうですか and そうですね are used often in conversation. These expressions are instrumental in making a conversation go smoothly. However, it is sometimes difficult to know which one to use. There are two そうですか: one with a falling intonation and one with a rising intonation. そうですか with a falling intonation means "I see" (*and I didn't know that*). It is used when you have just received new information. It is often preceded by ああ. そうですか with a rising intonation means "Is that so?" It is used to question what you have just heard, and is commonly preceded by えっ (*What!?*).

　　そうですね is usually spoken with a falling intonation. It means "That's right" so it would not be appropriate to say そうですね when you have just heard something new. そうですね is often preceded by ええ or はい.

練習　Practice
れんしゅう

1. Listen to the six short conversations. After each one, put a check mark in the box that corresponds to the correct meaning of そうですか／そうですね in the context of the conversation.

	1	2	3	4	5	6
I see.		◯				◯
Is that so?			◯		◯	
That's right.	◯			◯		

2. Working with a partner, read the sentences below one at a time, and choose one of these three phrases as your reply. More than one answer may be correct, as long as you know why you have chosen it.

ああ、そうですか。　えっ、そうですか。　ええ、そうですね。

1. 山田先生は　いい　先生です。
2. 山田先生は　れきしの　先生です。
3. ブラウンさんは　日本人のともだちと　でかけました。
4. このしゅくだいは　むずかしかったですね。
5. 昨日は　いそがしかったですね。
きのう
6. 明日　日本に　いきます。
あした

漢字
かんじ
Kanji

Kanji derived from pictures and symbols (2)

月 (moon)　　　　火 (fire)

水 (water)　　　　木 (tree)

金 (gold)　　　　土 (earth)

末 (end; tree with a focal point at the top)

| 今 | 今 | now
いま　コン | ノ 人 今 今 | | | | |
| | | | 今、何時ですか。
いま なんじ　　今週
こんしゅう　　今日
きょう | | | | |

| 私 | 私 | I; private
わたし・わたくし　シ | ′ ニ 千 禾 禾 私 私　私 私 私 私 |
| | | | 私 は日本人です。
わたし |

| 月 | 月 | moon, month
つき　ゲツ・ガツ | ノ 门 月 月　月 月 月 月 月 月　月 月 月 |
| | | | 月曜日
げつようび |

| 火 | 火 | fire
ひ　カ | ヽ ゛ 少 火　火 火 火 火 火 火　火 火 火　火 火 火 |
| | | | 火曜日
かようび |

| 水 | 水 | water
みず　スイ | 」 刁 水 水　水 水 水 水 水 水 |
| | | | 水曜日
すいようび |

| 木 | 木 | tree
き　モク | 一 十 オ 木　木 木 木 木 木 木 |
| | | | 木曜日
もくようび |

| 金 | 金 | gold, money, metal
かね　キン | ノ 人 ハ 今 牟 令 金　金 金 金　金 金 金 |
| | | | 金曜日
きんようび |

土 土	earth, soil, ground つち　ト・ド	一 十 土
	土曜日 どようび	

曜 曜	day of the week ヨウ	日 日ヨ 日ヨヨ 日ヨ 時ヨ 時ヨ 暗 曜 曜
	月曜日　火曜日　水曜日　木曜日　金曜日　土曜日 げつようび　かようび　すいようび　もくようび　きんようび　どようび	

何 何	what なに・なん	ノ イ イ 仁 何 何 何 何 何
	何曜日　何ですか。　何時ですか。 なんようび　なん　　　なんじ	

週 週	week シュウ	ノ 刀 月 冉 用 周 周 週 週
	今週の週末　先週 こんしゅう　しゅうまつ　せんしゅう	

末 末	end すえ　マツ	一 一 十 末 末
	週末に何をしますか。 しゅうまつ　なに	

休 休	to rest やす(む)　キュウ	ノ イ 仁 什 付 休
	休みの日に何をしますか。 やす	

読めるようになった漢字 (Kanji and compounds you can now read).
よ　　　　　　　　　　かんじ

今　今日　今日は　今晩　今週　来週　先週　私　月曜日　火曜日　水曜日　木
きょう　こんにち　ばん　　　らい

曜日　木　金曜日　土曜日　日曜日　何をしますか。　何ですか。何曜日　何時
じ

週末　今度　大変な　大丈夫です　毎週　休みの日
こんど　たいへん　だいじょうぶ　　まい

日本人の名前：金田　鈴木
なまえ　かねだ　すずき

練習　**Practice**
れんしゅう

Read the following.

1. 日曜日　月曜日　火曜日　水曜日　木曜日　金曜日　土曜日
2. 大川：「中田さんは今週の週末に何をしますか。」
　　本田：「土曜日に山にいきます。」
3. 先週の月曜日は休みでした。
4. 上田：「本田さんは何年生ですか」。
　　本田：「私は日本大学の３年生です。」
5. 中川：「今日のごご、何をしますか。」
　　山中：「アルバイトがあります。」

読む練習
よ　　れんしゅう
Reading

上手な読み方 Reading Strategy
じょうず　よ　　かた

Identifying missing nouns

In Japanese, it is not necessary to repeat nouns or pronouns in writing if they can be inferred from context. These omitted nouns are most likely to be either the subject or the topic, although they can be any other type of noun such as an object, place, or time. For example, in the sentences, 私は 学生です。三年生です。, the topic of the second sentence, 私は is missing because it is mentioned in the first sentence and can be inferred. This type of deletion makes a paragraph more cohesive. As you become more proficient with the language, this will become second nature to you.

読む前に   Pre-reading
よ　まえ

A. Identify any missing nouns in the following sentences.

1. 先週の日曜日は　はちじに　おきました。そして、くじごろ
   でかけました。
2. キムさんは　昨日　しゅくだいを　しませんでした。でも、今日
   　　　　　　きのう
   しました。
3. アリスさんに　でんわを　かけました。てがみも　かきました。
4. パーティには　鈴木さんを　よびました。でも、田中さんは
   　　　　　　すずき
   よびませんでした。

B. In Japanese, jot down five activities that you do often on weekends.

大川さんの週末

ことばの　リスト　　(Vocabulary)

[Sentence +] から	Because [+ sentence]
汚い（きたな）	dirty
ですから	so
はやく	early

> 　　先週の土曜日に両親（りょうしん）が私に会（あ）いに来（き）ました。とてもうれしかったですが、忙（いそが）しくて大変（たいへん）でした。木曜日と金曜日にテストがあって時間（じかん）がなかったから、アパートはとても汚（きたな）かったです。ですから、土曜日の朝早（あさはや）く起（お）きて、掃除（そうじ）と洗濯（せんたく）をしました。それから、スーパーに買い物（か もの）に行（い）きました。
>
> 　　12時（じ）ごろに両親（りょうしん）が私のアパートに来（き）ました。少（すこ）し話（はなし）をして、アパートの近（ちか）くのショッピング・センターに行（い）って、昼ご飯（ひる はん）を食（た）べました。その後（あと）、買い物（か もの）をして、キャンパスに行きました。図書館（としょかん）で上田さんに会（あ）いましたから、いっしょに図書館（としょかん）のカフェに行（い）って、コーヒーを飲（の）んで話（はなし）をしました。両親（りょうしん）は5時（じ）ごろ帰（かえ）りました。

読んだ後で（よ あと） Comprehension

A. しつもんに　こたえて下さい。Answer these questions in Japanese.

1. 大川さんの　週末は　どうでしたか。
2. 大川さんは　金曜日に　何を　しましたか。
3. 大川さんは　土曜日の　あさ　何を　しましたか。
4. 大川さんは　だれと　昼ご飯を　食べましたか。
5. どこで　食べましたか。
6. 土曜日の（た）　ごご、何を　しましたか。

B. Identify any missing nouns for each sentence of the reading.

C. Write a letter to a friend in Japan describing your weekend activities.

総合練習
そうごうれんしゅう
Integration

山田さんとさとうさんの一日　A Day in the Lives of Ms. Yamada and Mr. Sato

The illustration below shows a typical day for two Japanese college students, Ms. Yamada and Mr. Sato. Ms. Yamada lives with her parents. Mr. Sato lives in an apartment because he is from another area of Japan. In groups of four or five, complete the following tasks.

1. Describe what each student does in a day.
2. Compare and contrast Ms. Yamada's and Mr. Sato's routines.
3. Discuss simlarities and differences between their daily routines and your own.

ロールプレイ　Role Play

You are conducting a telephone survey of people's daily routines. With a partner, come up with five questions that you would like to ask. Then, pretend to make a phone call. Ask to speak with someone (your partner) politely. Once he/she comes to the phone, say すみません。アンケートちょうさなんですが、いいですか。 (*Excuse me. I am doing a survey. May I . . . ?*) Ask the five questions and take notes. Once the call is complete, reverse roles with your partner. Compare notes with several people in the class to see if your routines share anything in common.

Chapter 7

好きなものと　好きなこと
す　　　　　　　　す

Favorite Things and Activities

Objectives	Describing likes, dislikes, and preferences
Vocabulary	Food, beverages, sports, music, leisure activities
Dialogue	上田さんと　リーさんのしゅみ　*Ms. Ueda's and Mr. Li's Hobbies*
Japanese Culture	Popular leisure activities and consumer goods in Japan
Grammar	I.　Expressing likes or dislikes using 好き or きらい and the particle や す
	II.　Forming noun phrases using の and plain present affirmative verbs (dictionary form)
	III.　Making contrasts using the particle は, and expressing *but* using が
	IV.　Making comparisons using 一番 and ～（の）方が ～より, and いちばん ほう ～も～も and expressing lack of preference
	V.　Giving reasons using the plain form + ので
Listening	Identifying conversation fillers
Communication	Giving positive feedback with も; making contrasts with は
Kanji	時　間　分　半　毎　年　好　語　高　番　方　新　古　安　友
Reading	Understanding word formation

単語
たんご
Vocabulary

Nouns

うた	歌	song
エアロビクス		aerobics
おちゃ	お茶	tea, green tea
オレンジ		orange
カラオケ		Karaoke, sing-along
くだもの	果物	fruit
クラシック		classical music
こうちゃ	紅茶	black tea
コーラ		cola
こと		thing (intangible)
ゴルフ		golf
さかな	魚	fish
ジャズ		jazz
ジュース		juice
しゅみ	趣味	hobby
しょくじ	食事	dining しょくじする dine
スキー		skiing
スポーツ		sports
たべもの	食べ物	food
たまご	卵／玉子	egg
つり	釣り	fishing
トマト		tomato
ドライブ		driving (for pleasure)
にく	肉	meat

にんじん		carrot
のみもの	飲み物	beverage, drink
ハイキング		hiking
バスケットボール		basketball (abbreviated as バスケット or バスケ)
バナナ		banana
ヒップホップ		hip-hop music
ビール		beer
フットボール		(American) football (アメフト)
ポップス		pop music
みず	水	water
ミルク		milk
やきゅう	野球	baseball
やさい	野菜	vegetable
ラップ		rap music
りょこう	旅行	traveling りょこうする to travel
りんご		apple
レタス		lettuce
ロック		rock and roll
ワイン		wine

う -verbs

うたう	歌う	to sing
おわる	終わる	(for something) to end えいがが　おわる the movie is over.
つくる	作る	to make
とる	撮る	to take (a photograph) しゃしんを　とる
はじまる	始まる	(for something) to begin じゅぎょうが　はじまる the class begins

い -adjectives

おいしい		delicious, good, tasty
たかい	高い	expensive (Chapter 4: high, tall)
やすい	安い	inexpensive

な -adjectives

| きらい (な) | 嫌い (な) | dislike, hate |
| すき (な) | 好き (な) | like |

Question words

| どうして | why |

Adverbs

| もっと | more |

Particles

| や | and (when listing examples) |
| | おちゃや　コーヒー tea, coffee, and so on |

Prefixes

| だい | 大 | very much, 大すき like very much |

Conjunctions

それから		and, in addition, then
たとえば	例えば	for example
でも		but

Expressions

| すきでもきらいでもありません | 好きでも嫌いでもありません | I neither like nor dislike it. |
| 〜 (は) どうですか | | How about 〜 ? |

単語の練習　Vocabulary Practice
たんご　　れんしゅう

A. たべもの　　Food

Name each item in the picture.

1. さかな　　　fish
2. にく　　　　meat
3. たまご　　　egg
4. やさい　　　vegetable
5. くだもの　　fruit
6. レタス　　　lettuce
7. にんじん　　carrots
8. トマト　　　tomato
9. バナナ　　　banana
10. オレンジ　　orange
11. りんご　　　apple

◆ Activity 1

しつもんに　日本語で　こたえて下さい。　Answer these questions in Japanese.
　　　　　　　ご

1. にくを　よく　たべますか。さかなは　どうですか。
2. スーパーで　よく　何を　かいますか。　（かいます *to buy*)
3. 何を　あまり　たべませんか。
4. 今　どんなものが　高いですか。
　　　　　　　　　たか

★ Ask your instructor the word for any other food that you want to know how to say in Japanese.

Supplementary Vocabulary: Food

えび	海老	shrimp
キャベツ		cabbage
ぎゅうにく	牛肉	beef
きゅうり		cucumber
たまねぎ	玉ねぎ	onion
とりにく	鳥肉	chicken
ねぎ		green onion
ぶたにく	豚肉	pork
ほうれんそう		spinach
ピーマン		green pepper
みかん		tangerine
メロン		melon
いちご	苺	strawberry
ぶどう		grape

B. のみもの   Beverages

Look at the pictures below and read each word in Japanese.

おちゃ
tea, green tea

ジュース
juice

ミルク
milk

（お）さけ
rice wine / alcoholic beverage

コーヒー
coffee

こうちゃ
black tea

コーラ
cola

ワイン
wine

ビール
beer

水
みず
water

NOTES

- お in おちゃ is a polite prefix for the noun ちゃ, but it is rather rare to use ちゃ alone. Most people say おちゃ to refer either to green tea or tea as a general category of beverages.
- お in おさけ is also a polite prefix for the noun さけ. Although people say both おさけ and さけ, the latter tends to sound more masculine. （お）さけ can mean either Japanese rice wine or alcoholic beverages in general.

Activity 2

しつもんに　日本語で　こたえて下さい。Answer these questions in Japanese.

1. おさけを　のみますか。のみませんか。
2. どんなおさけを　のみますか。
3. よく　おちゃを　のみますか。のみませんか。
4. どんなおちゃを　のみますか。
5. どんなのみものを　よく　のみますか。どんなのみものは　あまり　のみませんか。
6. 学食には　どんなのみものが　ありますか。
7. スーパーには　どんなのみものが　ありますか。

C. スポーツ　　Sports

テニス　　　　　バスケットボール　　　フットボール
　　　　　　　　　　　　　　　　　　（アメフト）

ゴルフ　　　　　　つり　　　　　　　スキー

ハイキング　　　　やきゅう　　　　ジョギング

Activity 3

Match the Japanese words with their English equivalents in the above list.

_____1. エアロビクス   a. golf

_____2. バスケットボール   b. football

_____3. フットボール   c. jogging

_____4. ゴルフ   d. fishing

_____5. つり   e. hiking

_____6. スキー   f. skiing

_____7. ハイキング   g. aerobics

_____8. やきゅう   h. basketball

_____9. ジョギング   i. baseball

Activity 4

しつもんに 日本語で こたえて下さい。   Answer these questions in Japanese.

1. どのスポーツを よく しますか。

2. どのスポーツを よく みますか。

3. ～さんの友達は どのスポーツを よくみますか。

Supplementary Vocabulary: Sports

からて	空手	karate
サッカー		soccer
じゅうどう	柔道	judo
すいえい	水泳	swimming
スケート		skating
ソフトボール		softball
たいそう	体操	calisthenics, gymnastics
バレーボール		volleyball
ボーリング		bowling

D. おんがく Music

クラシック   ジャズ   ―ロック

classical   jazz   rock and roll

ポップス
pop music

ラップ、ヒップホップ
rap, hip-hop

Activity 5

Find the above words in the grid and circle them.

ク	ラ	シ	ラ	ク	ズ	ロ	ッ	プ
ジ	ク	ッ	ギ	タ	シ	ポ	ラ	ク
ポ	プ	ラ	ピ	ャ	ア	ッ	ジ	ズ
ッ	ズ	ッ	シ	ポ	ャ	プ	ポ	ロ
ノ	ノ	プ	ア	ッ	ズ	ス	ッ	ッ
シ	ラ	プ	ジ	ノ	ク	ラ	ク	ズ
ズ	ロ	ッ	ク	ス	ッ	ジ	ャ	ク
ク	ギ	シ	ッ	ク	ポ	ジ	ラ	プ
ジ	ロ	プ	ス	ラ	ッ	ス	ズ	ク

E. レジャーと　しゅみ　　Hobbies and leisure activities

Starting with this chapter, verbs are presented in dictionary form (plain present affirmative form).

りょこうする／
りょこうに　いく
to travel

ドライブに　いく／
ドライブを　する
to go for a drive

うたを　うたう
to sing songs

えを　かく
to draw

りょうりを　する／つくる
to cook

カラオケに　いく
to go sing karaoke

しゃしんを　とる
to take pictures

そとで　しょくじする
to dine out

Activity 6

Charades. Work in groups of three or four. Take turns acting out one of the activities listed above while the rest of the group tries to guess what it is in Japanese.

Activity 7

Say as many leisure activities as you can, using the following review expressions.

コンサート、おんがく、レストラン、かいもの、ビデオ、でんわ、テレビ、ゲーム、パーティ、およぐ（およぎます）、さんぽ、こうえん、あそびます（あそぶ）、メール

Supplementary Vocabulary: Hobbies and Leisure activities

いけばなを　する	生け花をする	to do **ikebana** (Japanese flower arrangement)
おどりに　いく	踊りに行く	(to) go dancing
ギターを　ひく	ギターを弾く	(to) play guitar
きってを　あつめる	切手を集める	(to) collect stamps
サイクリングに　いく	サイクリングに行く	(to) cycle, bike
せいじについて　はなす	政治について話す	(to) talk about politics
ガーデニングを　たのしむ	ガーデニングを楽しむ	(to) enjoy gardening
ピクニックに　いく	ピクニックに行く	(to) go on a picnic
ブログを　かく	ブログを書く	(to) write a blog
ペットと　あそぶ	ペットと遊ぶ	(to) play with a pet
ボランティアかつどうに　さんかする	ボランティア活動に　参加する	(to) participate in a volunteer activity

ダイアローグ
Dialogue

はじめに　Warm-up

しつもんに　日本語で　こたえて下さい。　Answer these questions in Japanese.

1. しゅみは　何ですか。
2. よく　スポーツを　しますか。
3. よく　スポーツばんぐみ (program) を　みますか。
4. どんなおんがくを　ききますか。

上田さんと　リーさんのしゅみ　*Ms. Ueda's and Mr. Li's Hobbies*

上田：　リーさんのしゅみは　何ですか。

リー：　そうですね。スポーツと　おんがくが　好きですね。

上田：　そうですか。どんなスポーツが　好きですか。

リー：　やきゅうや　バスケットボールが　好きですね。上田さんは？

上田：　私は　すいえいが　一番　好きです。でも、バスケットも
　　　　好きですよ。

リー：　そうですか。バスケットは　よく　しますか。

上田：　いいえ、バスケットは　するより　みる方が　好きですね。
　　　　リーさんは　バスケットを　よく　しますか。

リー： えe、バスケットは　みるのも　するのも　大好きです。

上田： そうですか。いいですね。

リー： ところで、上田さんは　おんがくが　好きですか。

上田： ええ、好きですよ。

リー： そうですか。どんなおんがくが　好きですか。

上田： しずかなおんがくが　好きなので、ジャズを　よく　ききます。

リー： そうですか。ぼくも　ジャズが　大好きです。

上田： そうですか。じゃあ、クラシックは　どうですか。

リー： ざんねんですが、　クラシックは　あまり。ぼくには　ちょっと
　　　 むずかしくて。

Dialogue Phrase Notes

- ところで means *by the way*.
- ぼくには means *to me*.
- When used before 好き, 大 does not mean *big*, but *very*.
- すいえい means *swimming* and it is used to indicate a catagory of sport rather than the act of swimming.

ダイアローグの後で   Comprehension

A.   Circle はい if the following statement is true, and circle いいえ if it is false.

1. はい　　いいえ　　　リーさんは　やきゅうが　好きです。

2. はい　　いいえ　　　上田さんと　リーさんは　バスケットが
　　　　　　　　　　　　好きです。

3. はい　　いいえ　　　上田さんは　バスケットを　するのが
　　　　　　　　　　　　好きです。

4. はい　　いいえ　　　上田さんは　ジャズが　好きです。

5. はい　　いいえ　　　リーさんは　クラシックの方が　ジャズより
　　　　　　　　　　　　好きです。

B.   Complete the following passage by filling in an appropriate word in each blank.

リーさんは　よく＿＿＿＿＿＿＿＿＿＿＿＿＿＿します。

上田さんは＿＿＿＿＿が　好きです。＿＿＿＿＿も　好きです。

日本の文化
ぶん か

Japanese Culture

Popular leisure actvities

A recent survey indicates that the following are the most popular leisure activities among Japanese between 18 and 30. The ranking of activities is based on the number of people who participated in the activities, not on frequency of participation.

<u>おとこの人</u>

1. ドライブに　いく
2. おさけを　のみに　いく
3. インターネットを　する
4. カラオケで　うたう
5. そとで　しょくじを　する

<u>おんなの人</u>

1. ドライブに　いく
2. そとで　しょくじを　する
3. おんがくを　きく
4. カラオケで　うたう
5. ビデオを　みる

Japanese ideas about sports have evolved in recent years. Where people once saw sports as a leisure activity they now see them as a lifestyle. Sports are no longer only to watch, but are for participation. A survey conducted by Hakouhodo, Inc., in 2006 found that 76.9 percent of the people surveyed had participated in some sort of sport over the past year, and that 65.7 percent hope to participate in the future.

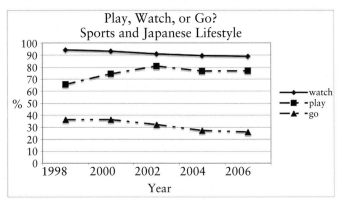

The same survey found that yoga and aerobics are the most popular sports, followed by jogging and track.

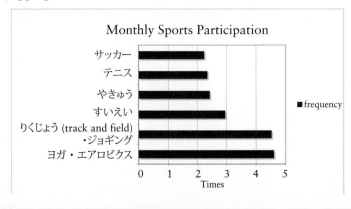

Traditional arts such as いけばな (flower arrangement), さどう (tea ceremony), and しょどう (calligraphy) ranked very low in terms of the number of participants.

Popular Consumer Goods

Cellular phones are extremely popular among Japanese. Young Japanese frequently use them to exchange e-mail, photos, and video clips. Cell phones are also used to download music, surf the Internet, play games, watch TV, and read books. Some phones can even be used like a debit card to make purchases in retail stores. As a result of such widespread cell-phone use, the number of public phones has greatly diminished, and it can be difficult to travel in Japan without a cell phone. Both Japanese travel agencies and phone companies with airport locations in Japan offer cell phone rentals to visitors.

Another well-known obsession of the Japanese, particularly among women, is their love of luxury goods by such designers as Gucci, Chanel, and Prada. Most major Japanese department stores have designer goods sections. Wherever you walk in Japan, you will see women carrying designer handbags and wearing expensive scarves and belts.

This popularity has continued for more than three decades and does not seem to be affected by economic conditions in Japan. For example, in the middle of

an economic depression in 2002, Louis Vuitton sold over one billion dollars' worth of merchandise in Japan—a 15% increase in profit over the previous year, and about half of the company's total sales for that year.

Why do the Japanese love brand-name items so much? One explanation is that Japanese people traditionally place a high value on quality. After the Meiji Restoration (1868–1912), many expensive foreign goods were imported from Europe, creating the association between quality and European luxury items. Today, brand names imply high quality, impeccable service, luxury, and status. Unlike a house or even furniture, these items are still within reach of the average consumer. Owning them gives some people the satisfaction of possessing something valuable and unique. At the same time, many others consider a preoccupation with brand names to be shallow.

文法
ぶんぽう
Grammar

I.   Expressing likes or dislikes using 好き or きらい and the particle や
す

In Japanese, 好き (like) and きらい (*dislike*, *hate*) are used to express one's likes and
す
dislikes. In English, *like*, *dislike*, and *hate* are verbs, but in Japanese 好き and
きらい are な - adjectives. Therefore, the negative form is じゃありません or
じゃないです. The object of 好き and きらい cannot be indicated by を because
す
they are not verbs. Instead, use が to mark the object.

Topic (person, animal)		Noun (thing that s/he likes)	Particle	
私の友達 ともだち	は	テニス	が	好きです。 す

My friend likes tennis.

To list two or more items you like or dislike, use the particle と (and) as introduced
in Chapter 5. However, と indicates that you like only the specific items you
mentioned. For more items that you like or dislike, and for which you wish to show
an example, use the particle や.

私は りんごと オレンジが 好きです。
す
I like apples and oranges (but nothing else).

私は りんごや オレンジが 好きです。
す
I like apples and oranges (and other food).

スミスさんは にんじんと たまごが きらいです。
Mr. Smith dislikes carrots and eggs.

スミスさんは にんじんや たまごが きらいです。
Mr. Smith dislikes carrots and eggs (and other things).

キム：   はやしさんは どんなのみものが 好きですか。
す
What kinds of drinks do you like, Ms. Hayashi?

はやし：   そうですね。私は こうちゃや 日本のおちゃが
大好きですね。
だいす
Well, I love black tea and Japanese tea (and so on).

キム：   じゃあ、おさけは どうですか。
How about alcoholic beverages?

はやし：   おさけは ちょっと。
Alcohol is a bit . . . (= I don't like alcoholic beverages very much.)

NOTES

- 好き and きらい can also be used before nouns. In this case, 好き means *favorite* and きらいな is the opposite of favorite.

  <u>私の好きな くだもの</u>は りんごです。
  My favorite fruit is the apple.

  <u>私のきらいな くだもの</u>は バナナです。
  The fruit that I don't like is the banana.

- You might want to avoid using きらい in an answer to a question because it has a strong negative connotation. You can use expressions such as 〜は ちょっと (〜 is a bit) and あまり.

- In Chapters 2 through 5, 〜は どうですか meant "How is 〜?" Another meaning of 〜は どうですか is "How about 〜?"

  大木： 私は ワインが 好きです。
  I like wine.

  水田： じゃあ、 ビールは どうですか。
  Well, how about beer?

  大木： ビールも 好きですよ。
  I like beer, too.

- The prefix 大 is commonly used with 好き and きらい. 大好き means *love* or *really like*, and 大きらい means *hate* or *really don't like*. 大好き and 大きらい are more commonly used than とても 好き or とても きらい.

- If you don't like or dislike something, use 好きでも きらいでも ありません or 好きでも きらいでも ないです. (*I neither like nor dislike it.*)

話してみましょう   Conversation Practice

Activity 1

The following chart indicates what Mr. Yamada and Ms. Brown like and dislike. Express what they like or dislike, using 好き, きらい. Use the particles と or や wherever appropriate.

Example: 山田さんは りんごが 好きです。

	山田さん		ブラウンさん	
	好き	きらい	好き	きらい
たべもの	apples	carrots and eggs	meat, fish, etc.	vegetables, fruit, etc.
のみもの	juice and coffee	milk	wine, beer, etc.	juice, black tea, etc.
スポーツ	golf, tennis, etc.	football	football	golf, jogging, etc.
おんがく	pop, jazz, etc.	classical music	rap and rock	classical music

Activity 2

Ask a partner what types of food, drinks, sports, and music he/she likes and dislikes. Your partner will give you examples using や.

Example: A: 〜さんは　どんなたべものが　好きですか。
　　　　　 B: りんごや　オレンジが　好きです。
　　　　　 A: そうですか。

	私	パートナー
たべもの		
のみもの		
スポーツ		
おんがく		

Activity 3

Now work with the class. Ask your classmates what kinds of food, drinks, sports, and music they like and dislike. See if you can determine the most popular item in each category.

Example: A: 〜さんは　どんなたべものが　好きですか。
　　　　　 B: 〜が　好きです。
　　　　　 A: そうですか。じゃあ、どんなたべものが　きらいですか。
　　　　　 B: 〜は　あまり　好きじゃありません。

	好き	きらい
たべもの		
のみもの		
スポーツ		
おんがく		

II. Forming noun phrases using の and plain present affirmative verbs (dictionary form)

The plain present affirmative form of a verb is also called the dictionary form because this is the form used for dictionary entries. This form also appears in time expressions, relative clauses, gerunds, and other structures. It is used in casual conversation, newspapers, expository writing, and other contexts. Learning when to use it appropriately can take some time.

In this section, you will learn to use the plain present affirmative form with の to convert verb phrases into noun phrases. This use of の is different from the pronoun の (one) and from the particle の in the structure Noun の Noun.

A. Plain present affirmative verbs (dictionary form)

The charts below show how to create the dictionary forms of verbs from their polite forms.

う -verbs

Remove ます from the polite verb form and change the vowel sound of the last letter to **u**.

ます -form	Plain present affirmative (dictionary) form		
よみます (*read*)	yomi + masu →	yomu	よむ
かきます (*write*)	kaki + masu →	kaku	かく
あいます (*meet*)	ai + masu →	au	あう
はなします (*talk*)	hanashi + masu →	hanasu	はなす
のみます (*drink*)	nomi + masu →	nomu	のむ

る -verbs

Change ます to る.

ます -form	Plain present affirmative (dictionary) form
たべます (*eat*)	→ たべる
ねます (*sleep*)	→ ねる
います (*be, exist*)	→ いる
おきます (*get up*)	→ おきる

Irregular verbs

ます -form	Plain present affirmative (dictionary) form
します (*do*)	→ する
きます (*come*)	→ くる

Once you know the plain affirmative form, it is relatively easy to identify the group to which it belongs (う-verb, る-verb, or irregular verb) by using the following three steps:

1. Remember that する and くる are the only irregular verbs.
2. If a dictionary form ends in -**Xiru** or -**Xeru** (X represents any consonant here), it is a る-verb. For example, since たべる ends in **beru** and おきる ends in **kiru**, they are る-verbs. However, つくる, おわる, and はじまる are not る-verbs, because they end in -**Kuru**, -**Waru**, and -**Maru**, and not -**Xiru** or -**Xeru**.
3. The rest are all う-verbs. There are some exceptions to this rule. Among them, the ones you have learned are かえる (*return*) and はいる (*enter*). These are う-verbs.

B. The plain present affirmative form + のが　好きです・きらいです (like/dislike doing ～)

The plain present affirmative form (dictionary form) + のが　好きです／きらいです is used to express one's likes or dislikes in terms of doing something. In English, the gerund (-*ing*) form of a verb and the infinitive (*to* + verb) may be used as nouns, as in examples such as *seeing is believing* or *to play a musical instrument is fun*. In a similar manner, Japanese adds の to the plain present affirmative form to create a noun phrase.

		Noun phrase			
		Verb (dictionary form)		Particle	
私は	本を	よむ	の	が	好きです。

I like reading books.

Here are some more examples.

私は えいがを みるのが 好きです。
I like watching movies.

えいがを みるのは おもしろいです。
Watching movies is fun.

スミス：田中さんは 何を するのが 好きですか。
　　　　What do you like to do, Ms. Tanaka?

田中：そうですね。私は インターネットで あそぶのが 好きですね。スミスさんは どうですか。
　　　Let's see. I like to surf the Internet. How about you, Mr. Smith?

スミス：ぼくは クラシックおんがくを きくのが 好きです。
　　　　I like to listen to classical music.

話してみましょう　Conversation Practice
<ruby>話<rt>はな</rt></ruby>

Activity 1

Create questions using the following expressions and　〜のが　好きですか.
<ruby>好<rt>す</rt></ruby>

Example:　てがみを　かきます

　　　　　てがみを　かくのが　好きですか。
<ruby>好<rt>す</rt></ruby>

1. 友達のしゃしんを　とります
<ruby>友達<rt>ともだち</rt></ruby>
2. そとで　しょくじを　します
3. ジョギングを　します
4. カラオケに　いきます
5. うたを　うたいます
6. ごはんを　つくります
7. えを　かきます
8. 日本語を　はなします
<ruby>語<rt>ご</rt></ruby>
9. おふろに　はいります
10. およぎます

Activity 2

Work with a partner. Using the questions you created in Activity 1, ask your partner which activities he/she likes to do.

Example:　たべます

　　　　A:　たべるのが　好きですか。
<ruby>好<rt>す</rt></ruby>

　　　　B:　ええ、大好きです。
<ruby>大好<rt>だいす</rt></ruby>

　　or　いいえ、あまり　好きじゃないです／好きじゃありません。
<ruby>好<rt>す</rt></ruby>　<ruby>好<rt>す</rt></ruby>

Activity 3

The following pictures illustrate activities that Kimura-san likes to do. Describe them using 〜のが　好きです.

Example: 木村さんは　テニスを　するのが　好きです。

Activity 4

Ask a partner what he/she likes to do during school breaks.

Example: A: 〜さんは　やすみの日に　何を　するのが　好きですか。
          B: そうですね。ねるのが　好きですね。

III. Making contrasts using the particle は, and expressing *but* using が

A. Using は for contrast

Besides indicating a topic, は can indicate a contrast between two items. In both of the following sentences, the second は in the example puts りょうり and そうじ in contrast.

私は よく りょうりを します。でも、そうじは あまり
しません。
I cook often but I don't do the cleaning very often.

キムさんは りょうりが 好きです。でも、そうじは 好きじゃ
ありません。
Mr. Kim likes cooking but he does not like cleaning.

The particle は for contrast is often used in sentences ending with negative forms. Often, there is no explicit item of contrast in this case.

田中： 明日も きますか。   *Are you coming tomorrow?*

スミス： いいえ、明日は きません。 *No, I am not coming tomorrow.*
                                      (but I may come some other time).

The use of は for contrast may appear in more than one sentence or clause to make the contrast explicit. In the following example sentences, the topic of the first sentence is 私, so it is marked with the topic marker は. And although this first sentence does not end in a negative form, コーヒー also takes は, because it is in contrast with コーラ in the second sentence.

私は コーヒーは 好きです。 でも、コーラは あまり 好き
じゃありません。
I like coffee. But I don't like cola very much.

は for contrast can be used with any type of noun as well. Like は for topic, and も for similarity, は replaces を (direct object) or が (subject), but it is usually added to another particle, as in the examples below. Some particles, such as に (point of time) and に・へ (goal) may be deleted if they can be easily understood from context.

よく としょかんで べんきょうします。でも、学生会館では
しません。
I often study in the library. But, I don't (study) in the student union.

ここに ねこが います。 あそこには いません。
There is a cat here. It's not over there.

山田さんは 今日は きません。でも、土曜日 (に) は きます。
Mr. Yamada does not come today. But, he will come tomorrow.

B. Expressing *but* using が

The particle が can be used to connect two sentences or clauses that oppose each other. が is attached at the end of the first sentence.

Clause	Particle (but)	Clause
こうちゃは　好きです	が、	おちゃは　あまり　好きじゃないです。

I like black tea but I don't like green tea very much.

Since が often connects two clauses in a contrasting or negative relationship, the contrast marker は is often used with が as well. For example:

ゴルフを　するのは　好きですが、みるのは　あまり　好きじゃありません。
I like playing golf but I don't like watching it.

あさは　ごはんを　たべませんでしたが、ひるは　たべました。
I did not eat breakfast but I did eat lunch.

そうじは　しましたが、せんたくは　しませんでした。
I did the cleaning but I didn't do laundry.

友達と　えいがは　みませんでしたが、テレビは　みましたよ。
I didn't watch a movie with my friends, but we did watch TV.

ゆうびんきょくには　いきませんでしたが、ぎんこうには　いきました。
I didn't go to the post office, but I did go to the bank.

NOTE

- が can also be used to open a conversation, or to introduce a topic of conversation. This is called a "weak but." It does not introduce a strong negative relation, and it is similar to the use of *but* in English as in: "Excuse me, <u>but</u> could you turn on the TV?"

  あのう　すみませんが、今　何時ですか。
  Excuse me, but what time is it?

  私のうちは　あれですが、田中さんのは　どれですか。
  My house is that one over there, but which one is Ms. Tanaka's?

話してみましょう　Conversation Practice
はな

Activity 1

Look at the drawings below and describe what Yamada-san likes, doesn't like very much, and positively dislikes. Use は to contrast his likes and dislikes.

Example:　山田さんは　りんごが　好きですが、トマトは　あまり
　　　　　　好きじゃありません。
すきじゃありません。

好きです	あまり	きらいです
	好きじゃありません	

Activity 2

Work with a partner. Referring to the items in the table below, ask questions to determine your partner's preferences. Try to use both particles も and は correctly in your follow-up questions.

Example:　A:　〜さんは　どんなたべものが　好きですか。
　　　　　　　　　　　　　　　　　　　　　　すき
　　　　　　B:　レタスが　好きです。
　　　　　　　　　　　　すき
　　　　　　Follow-up questions:
　　　　　　A:　そうですか。にんじんも　好きですか。
　　　　　　　　　　　　　　　　　　　　すき
　　　　　　B:　いいえ、にんじんは　あまり　好きじゃありません。
　　　　　　　　　　　　　　　　　　　　　　　　すき
　　　　　　A:　じゃあ、トマトは　どうですか。
　　　　　　B:　はい、トマトは　好きです。
　　　　　　　　　　　　　　　すき

Categories	Items
たべもの	トマト　にんじん　レタス　バナナ　オレンジ
どうぶつ	いぬ　ねこ　さかな　くま (bear)　とり (bird) さる (monkey)
のみもの	ビール　ワイン　コーラ　こうちゃ　コーヒー　ミルク ジュース　水_{みず}
スポーツ	エアロビクス　ハイキング　テニス　フットボール ゴルフ
おんがく	クラシック　ジャズ　ポップス　ロック　ラップ　ヒップホップ

Activity 3

For each statement below, create two sentences. One should express a similarity with the statement; the other should express a contrast.

Example: 私は　あさごはんを　たべます。

　　　　　ばんごはんも　たべます。でも、ひるごはんは　たべません。

1. 私は　よく　テレビを　みます。
2. 月曜日に　アルバイトを　します。
3. 昨日_{きのう}　山本さんに　メールを　かきました。
4. スミスさんは　先生に　しつもんしました。
5. 山本さんの友達_{ともだち}は　週末　よく　おんがくを　ききます。
6. 毎日_{まい}　りょうりを　します。

Activity 4

Describe what each person likes and does not like to do.

Example: 山田さんは　パーティに　いくのが　好_すきですが、

　　　　　パーティを　するのは　あまり　好_すきじゃありません。

	😀	😖
山田	パーティに　いきます	パーティを　します
小川_{おがわ}	あそびます	べんきょうします
山本	そとで　しょくじを　します	うちで　たべます
大川	えいがを　みます	ゲームを　します
金田_{かねだ}	コンサートに　いきます	うたを　うたいます
田中	しゃしんを　とります	えを　かきます

> ## IV. Making comparisons using 一番 and 〜（の）方が
> ## 〜より, and 〜も〜も and expressing lack of preference

In English, preference can be expressed by changing the form of an adjective into a superlative (e.g., the best, the prettiest, the nicest, the most wonderful) or a comparative (e.g., better, prettier, nicer, more wonderful). Japanese has a similar set of expressions, but the adjective forms do not change. Instead, preference is expressed in other parts of the sentence. This chapter introduces the superlative with the adverb 一番, the comparative with 〜の方が　〜より, and lack of preference using 〜も〜も.

A. Superlatives using 一番

一番 means *number one* or *first*, and it is used to form a superlative, such as the *nicest person, prettiest house, the best movie,* and *I like X the best.* 一番 must be followed by an adjective or adverb. For example, *the best movie* should be expressed as 一番 いい えいが. 一番 えいが is a common mistake that native English speakers make.

としょかんは　一番　大きい　たてものです。
The library is the <u>biggest building</u>.

このたまごが　一番　安いです。
These eggs are the <u>cheapest</u>.

ジャズが　一番　好きです。
I <u>like</u> jazz <u>the best</u>.

山本さんが　一番　よく　べんきょうします。
Ms. Yamamoto studies <u>the hardest</u>.

私の一番　好きな　たべものは　バナナです。
My <u>most favorite</u> food is bananas.

To indicate the scope of a preference, use the phrase 〜の中で.

スポーツの中で　何が　一番　おもしろいですか。
Which sport is the most interesting among sports?

くだものの中で　何を　一番　よく　たべますか。
Which fruits do you eat most?

のみものの中で　コーヒーが　一番　好きです。
Coffee is the beverage I like best.

If the preceding noun is a place noun, 中 is omitted:

<u>このクラスで</u> 山田さんが 一番 よく べんきょうします。
いちばん

Mr. Yamada studies the hardest in this class.

富士山は <u>日本で</u> 一番 高い 山です。
ふ じ さん   いちばん たか

Mt. Fuji is the highest mountain in Japan.

田中： このクラスで どの人が 一番 よくべんきょうしますか。
いちばん

Which person studies the most in this class?

石田： 山田さんが 一番 よく べんきょうします。
いし   いちばん

／山田さんです。

Mr. Yamada studies the hardest. / It's Mr. Yamada.

スミス： たべものの 中で 何が 一番 好きですか。
いちばん す

Which type of food do you like best?

大田： さかなが 一番 好きです。
いちばん す

I like fish the best.

B. Comparatives using 〜（の）方が 〜より
ほう

The expression 〜（の）方が 〜より is used to compare two items. The item
ほう
preceding 〜（の）方が is emphasized or preferred over the item that precedes
ほう
〜より. These items can be either noun phrases or verb phrases ending in the
dictionary form.

Noun (Preferred)	Particle	Noun	Particle	Noun (Less preferred)	Particle	
きょうと	の	方 ほう	が	（とうきょう	より）	きれいです。

Kyoto is prettier than Tokyo.

とうきょう の方が ニューヨークより 大きいです。
ほう

Tokyo is larger than New York.

このさかな の方が にくより 安いです。
ほう   やす

This fish is cheaper than meat.

りょうりは つくる 方が たべるより 好きです。
ほう   す

I like cooking more than eating.

やきゅうは みるより する方が たのしいです。
ほう

Playing baseball is more fun than watching it.

comparison → と

Loth / Neither A + B　└も

In order to ask one's preference between two items, use 〜と〜と どちらの方が.

Noun (Choice A)	Particle	Noun (Choice B)	Particle	Question word	Particle	Noun	Particle	
とうきょう	と	きょうと	と	どちら	の	方 ほう	が	きれいですか。

Which is prettier, Tokyo or Kyoto?

> とうきょうと ニューヨークと どちらの方が 大きいですか。
> ほう
> *Which is larger, Tokyo or New York?*

> さかなと にくと どちらの方が 安いですか。
> ほう　　　　　　　　やす
> *Which is cheaper, fish or meat?*

To ask about two actions, use the dictionary form + の. This の is the same one used in 〜のが 好きです.
　　　　　　　　　　　　　　　　　　　　す

> テニスを みるのと するのと どちらの方が 好きですか。
> ほう　　　す
> *Which do you like better, watching tennis or playing it?*

> ここに いるのと でかけるのと どちらの方が いいですか。
> ほう
> *Which is better, staying here or going out?*

> リー： 大川さんと 山本さんと どちらの方が よく りょうりを
> ほう
> 　　　します。
> *Who cooks more often, Mr. Okawa or Ms. Yamamoto?*

> 上田： 山本さんの方が よく りょうりを します。
> ほう
> *Ms. Yamamoto cooks more often.*

> リー： 上田さんは どうですか。
> *How about you, Ms. Ueda?*

> 上田： そうですね。私は りょうりを するより たべる方が
> ほう
> 　　　いいですね。
> *Well, eating is better than cooking in my case.*

When you want to compare the preference between two actions, use the dictionary form of verb + 方が.
　　　　　　　　　　　　　　　　　　　　　　　　　　　　ほう

NOTES

- If 〜より is obvious from the context, then it can be omitted, as in the above example conversation between Mr. Li and Ms. Ueda.
- The adverb もっと is used with adjectives or verbs, and it means *more* or *even more*.

> もっと たべませんか。　　　　　*Why don't you eat more?*
> 私のいぬは もっと 大きいです。　*My dog is bigger.*

C. Expressing lack of preference (comparisons of equality)

If you do not have preference for one item over another, use 〜も 〜も. Items can be two noun phrases or two verb phases ending with の.

Noun A	Particle	Noun B	Particle	
とうきょう	も	きょうと	も	好きです。

I like both Tokyo and Kyoto.

Noun A	Particle	Noun B	Particle	
とうきょう	も	きょうと	も	好きじゃありません。／ 好きじゃないです。

I don't like either Tokyo or Kyoto.

田中：　ペプシと　コカコーラと　どちらの方が　おいしいですか。
Which is more delicious, Pepsi or Coca-Cola?

中山：　ペプシも　コカコーラも　おいしいです。
Both Pepsi and Coca-Cola are delicious.

でも、私は　ペプシの方が　好きです。
But I like Pepsi better.

ペギー：　うちで　たべるのと　そとで　しょくじするのと
どちらの方が　好きですか。
Which do you like better, eating at home or dining out?

あやか：　そうですね。うちで　たべるのも　そとで
しょくじするのも　好きですが、
Well, I like both eating at home and dining out.

たいてい　うちで　たべます。
But I usually eat at home.

NOTE

- 〜も 〜も can be used in either a positive or negative statement. A も B も + affirmative statement means *both A and B*. A も B も + negative statement (or in a negative statement) means *neither A nor B*.

やきゅうも　バスケットも　好きです。
I like both baseball and basketball.

ロックも　ジャズも　好きじゃありません。
I don't like either rock or jazz very much.

話してみましょう   Conversation Practice
はな

Activity 1

Answer the questions.

Example: おんがくの中で　何が　一番　好きですか。
　　　　　　　　　　　　いちばん　す
　　　　　ジャズが　一番　好きです。
　　　　　　　　　いちばん　す

1. スポーツの中で　何が　一番　好きですか。
　　　　　　　　　　　いちばん　す
2. たべものの中で　何が　一番　きらいですか。
　　　　　　　　　　　いちばん
3. のみものの中で　何を　一番　よく　のみますか。
　　　　　　　　　　　いちばん
4. どんなおんがくを　一番　よく　ききますか。
　　　　　　　　いちばん
5. このクラスで　だれが　一番　よく　日本語を　はなしますか。
　　　　　　　　　　　　いちばん　　　　　ご

Activity 2

Ask a partner about places and things that have the most in some attribute, using the nouns and adjectives provided. Follow the example.

Example: アメリカ／川／大きい
　　　　　A: アメリカでは　どの川が　一番　大きいですか。
　　　　　　　　　　　　　　　　いちばん
　　　　　B: ミシシッピー川が　一番　大きいです。
　　　　　　　　　　　　がわ　　いちばん

1. アメリカ／まち／古い　　　　4. キャンパス／たてもの／新しい
　　　　　　　　ふる　　　　　　　　　　　　　　　あたら
2. 日本／山／高い　　　　　　　5. アメリカ／しゅう (state) ／小さい
　　　　　たか
3. せかい (world) ／まち／きれい　6. アメリカ／たべもの／おいしい

Activity 3

First determine the order of the two items in parentheses using the adjectives provided. Then form a comparative sentence.

Examples: 好き　（ こうちゃ／コーヒー ）
　　　　　す
　　　　　こうちゃの方が　コーヒーより　好きです。
　　　　　　　　　ほう　　　　　　　　す

　　　　　むずかしい（日本語で　かく／はなす）
　　　　　　　　　　　　ご
　　　　　日本語で　かく方が　はなすより　むずかしいです。
　　　　　　ご　　　ほう

1. いい（いぬ／ねこ）   5. 大きい（ニューヨーク／とうきょう）

2. しずか（としょかん／ラボ）   6. むずかしい（日本語／スペイン語）

3. いそがしい（先生／学生）   7. きらい
                               （りょうりをする／そうじを する）

4. 好き（たべる／ねる）   8. 大変
                               （べんきょうする／しごとを する）

Activity 4

Work with a partner. Using the items in Activity 3, taking turns asking each other three comparative questions.

Example: 好き （ こうちゃ／コーヒー ）

A: こうちゃと コーヒーと どちらの方が 好きですか。

B: コーヒーの方が 好きです。

A: 日本語で かくのと はなすのと どちらの方が
むずかしいですか。

B: かく方が はなすより むずかしいです。

Activity 5

Work with a partner. Ask your partner about at least two things he/she likes, and then ask him/her to rank them. If he/she likes both equally, write both words in Column 1.

Example: A: どんなくだものが 好きですか。

B: りんごや オレンジが 好きです。

A: じゃあ、りんごと オレンジと どちらの方が 好きですか。

B: そうですね。オレンジの方が 好きです。

or りんごも オレンジも 好きです。

Category	1	2
くだもの	りんご	オレンジ
のみもの		
スポーツ		
おんがく		

V. Giving reasons using the plain form + ので

The conjunction ので indicates a reason, and it is attached to the end of the clause that expresses the reason. If a sentence contains both a reason and result, the clause for the reason must come before the clause indicating the result. For example, in the sentence 来週から テストが はじまるので、今週はよく べんきょうします。 (*I will study hard this week because exams begin next week.*), the reason is stated at the beginning of the sentence and it ends with ので ; the cause is mentioned in the latter half of the sentence.

Clause (reason)	Particle (reason)	Clause (result)
いちごが 好きな	ので、	よく かいます。

I like strawberries, so I often buy some.

しごとが もうすぐ おわるので、ここで まって下さい。
My job will be finished soon, so please wait here.

J－ポップが 好きなので、よく J－ポップのうたを うたいます。
I like J-pop (Japanese pop music), so I often sing J-pop songs.

The 〜ので construction is preceded by a clause ending with the plain form of a verb or adjective. The following charts show the plain affirmative and negative forms of verbs and adjectives. In these charts, *I, it, he,* and *she* are given as subjects in English, but these forms can also be used to indicate *you, we,* and *they,* depending on context.

Plain form + ので / noun or な-adjective + な + ので

な -adjectives

In the case of な-adjectives, the affirmative is expressed by using the stem + ので.

Dictionary form	Prenominal form	Plain negative	〜ので (because 〜)	
			Affirmative (Plain)	Negative (Plain)
きれい pretty	きれいな（もの） pretty thing	きれいじゃない（もの） not pretty thing	きれいなので because it is pretty	きれいじゃないので because it is not pretty

Noun + です (copula verb)

Noun + な expresses the affirmative.

Dictionary form	Noun + な	Plain negative form	〜ので (because 〜)	
			Affirmative (Plain)	Negative (Plain)
日本人 *Japanese*	日本人<u>な</u> *be Japanese*	日本人<u>じゃない</u> *not Japanese*	日本人<u>な</u>ので *because he/she is Japanese*	日本人<u>じゃない</u>ので *because he/she is not Japanese*

い -adjectives

The plain affirmative form of an い-adjective is the same as its dictionary form. The plain negative form is created by deleting です from the polite version.

Dictionary form / Plain affirmative form	Plain negative form	〜ので (because 〜)	
		Affirmative (Plain)	Negative (Plain)
うれしい *happy, be happy*	うれし<u>くない</u> *not happy*	うれしいので *because he/she is happy*	うれし<u>くない</u>ので *because he/she is not happy*

う -verbs

To form the negative of a う-verb, delete ます from the ます-form, change the vowel sound of the last letter [i] to [a], and add ない.

ます -form	Dictionary form / Plain affirmative form	Plain negative form	〜ので	
			Affirmative (Plain)	Negative (Plain)
よみます /yom/+/<u>i</u>/+/masu/ *read*	よむ /yom/+/<u>u</u>/ *read*	よ<u>ま</u>ない /yom/+/<u>a</u>/+/nai/ *not read*	よむので *because he/she reads*	よまないので *because he/she does not read*
かきます /kak/+/<u>i</u>/+/masu/ *write*	かく /kak/+/<u>u</u>/ *write*	か<u>か</u>ない /kak/+/<u>a</u>/+/nai/ *not write*	かくので *because he/she writes*	かかないので *because he/she does not write*
はなします /hanash/+/<u>i</u>+ /masu/ *talk*	はなす /hanas/+/u/ *talk*	はな<u>さ</u>ない /hanas/ +/<u>a</u>+ /nai/ *not talk*	はなすので *because he/she talks*	はなさない ので *because he/she does not talk*
おわります /owar/+/<u>i</u>/+/masu/ *end*	おわる /owar/+/<u>u</u>/ *end*	おわ<u>ら</u>ない /owar/+/a/+/nai/ *not end*	おわるので *because it ends*	おわらない ので *because it does not end*

If there is no consonant before the [i] sound of the ます-form, as in あいます, change [i] to [wa] instead of [a]. The plain present negative form of あります is <u>ない</u>.

ます -form	Dictionary form/ Plain affirmative form	Plain negative form	〜ので	
			Affirmative (Plain)	Negative (Plain)
あいます /a<u>i</u> /+ /masu/ *meet*	あ<u>う</u> *meet*	あ<u>わ</u>ない /a<u>wa</u> +/nai/ *not meet*	あうので *because he/she meets*	あわないので *because he/she does not meet*
あります /a<u>ri</u>/+ /masu/ *be, exist**	ある *be, exist*	<u>ない</u> /nai/ *not be, exist*	あるので *because there is* 〜	ないので *because there isn't* 〜

*Remember that あります is used only for inanimate objects or events.

る -verbs

Change ます to ない to form the plain negative form.

ます -form	Dictionary form/ Plain affirmative form	Plain negative form	〜ので	
			Affirmative (Plain)	Negative (Plain)
たべます *eat*	たべる *eat*	たべ<u>ない</u> *not eat*	たべるので *because he/she eats*	たべないので *because he/she does not eat*
ねます *sleep*	ねる *sleep*	ね<u>ない</u> *not sleep*	ねるので *because he/she sleeps*	ねないので *because he/she does not sleep*
います *be, exist**	いる *be, exist*	い<u>ない</u> *not be, exist*	いるので *because there is* 〜	いないので *because there isn't* 〜

*Remember that います is used only for live beings such as people and animals.

Irregular verbs

ます -form	Dictionary form/ Plain affirmative form	Plain negative form	〜ので	
			Affirmative (Plain)	Negative (Plain)
します *do*	する *do*	<u>し</u>ない *not do*	するので *because he/she does*	しないので *because he/she does not do*
きます *come*	くる *come*	<u>こ</u>ない *not come*	くるので *because he/she comes*	こないので *because he/she does not come*

話してみましょう   Conversation Practice
_{はな}

Activity 1

Combine the following pairs of sentences using 〜ので . Make sure to start with the sentence that expresses a reason and is followed by ので.

Example:　にくを　たべます。さかなは　きらいです。

　　　　　さかなは　きらいなので、にくを　たべます。

1. 毎日　しごとを　します。いそがしいです。
_{まい}
2. よく　デパートに　いきます。かいものが　好きです。
_す
3. 七時に　おきます。八時に　じゅぎょうが　はじまります。
_{しち じ}　　　　　_{はち じ}
4. トマトが　たくさん　あります。トマトで　りょうりを　します。
5. うちで　ゆっくりします。今日は　いそがしくありません。
6. 今日は　じゅぎょうが　ありません。ひるまで　ねます。

Activity 2

Work with a partner. The following table shows what Mr. Tanaka dislikes and why. Create a conversation using the table and the dialogue model below. Note that もの refers to a tangible object such as food, drinks, and places and こと refers to an intangible thing like an activity and event.

Example:　A: 私の　きらいな　ものは　さかなです。

　　　　　B: え、どうしてですか。

　　　　　A: ほね (bone) が　あるので、きらいです。

　　　　　B: そうですか。

きらいなもの・きらいなこと		りゆう (reason)
Example:	さかな	ほね (bone) が　あります
1	レストランに　いきます。	高いです _{たか}
2	パーティ	人と　はなすのが　好きじゃありません。 _す
3	大きいまち	しずかな　ところが　好きです。 _す
4	カラオケに　いきます。	うたを　うたうのが　きらいです。
5	ハイキングを　します。	あるくのが　好きじゃありません。 _す

Activity 3

Work with a partner. Invite your partner to do an activity together. He/She will refuse the invitation and give a reason using ので.

Example: A: 来週の水曜日に　コンサートに　いきませんか。

　　　　　　　らい

B: ありがとうございます。でも、水曜日は、りょうしんが
あいに　くるので。

A: あ、そうですか。ざんねんですね。

B: すみません。あの、また　さそってくれませんか。
(さそう *to invite*)

A: いいですよ。じゃあ、また、今度。

　　　　　　　　　　　　　　ど

聞く練習
きく れんしゅう
Listening

上手な聞き方   Listening Strategy
じょうず きかた

Identifying conversation fillers

In conversations in English, you hear many empty words and expressions such as *hmm*, *uh*, and *well*. Their approximate equivalents in Japanese are えーと, あのう, and そうですね. These words are referred to as conversation fillers. While the words themselves have little meaning, they are used to keep the conversation flowing when the person speaking does not know what to say.

練習   Practice
れんしゅう

Listen to the following statements and short conversations. Circle the fillers you hear.

1. あのう　　えーと　　そうですね
2. あのう　　えーと　　そうですね
3. あのう　　えーと　　そうですね
4. あのう　　えーと　　そうですね

日本人学生に　きく　　Interviews with Japanese students

Listen to the interviews between a reporter for a student newspaper and four Japanese students who are visiting the college campus. Fill in the chart with their names and what each one likes to do.

	なまえ	好き す
Interview 1		
Interview 2		
Interview 3		
Interview 4		

聞き上手 話し上手
き　　じょうず　はな　　じょうず
Communication

上手な話し方 Communication Strategy
じょうず　はな　かた

Giving positive feedback with も; making contrasts with は

Like そうですか and そうですね, the particles も (similarity) and は (contrast) can be used to carry on a conversation more smoothly. If a person mentions something that you have in common, use も to give that person positive feedback.

中田：　大川さんは　どんなスポーツが　好きですか。
　　　　　　　　　　　　　　　　　　　　　　　す

大川：　やきゅうが　好きですね。
　　　　　　　　　　す

中田：　ああ、そうですか。私も　やきゅうが　大好きですよ。
　　　　　　　　　　　　す　　　　　　　　　だい す

By establishing that you both like baseball, the conversation can now progress to subtopics, such as which teams you do like. In cases where you do not share common interests, you can use は to mark a contrast.

スミス：　高山さんは　どんなスポーツが　好きですか。
　　　　　たかやま　　　　　　　　　　　　　　　す

高山：　そうですね。やきゅうが　好きですね。
たかやま　　　　　　　　　　　　　す

スミス：　ああ、そうですか。私は　テニスが　大好きです。
　　　　　　　　　　　す　　　　　　　　だい す

Be careful not to focus too much on your differences, however, since this may become disruptive or seem unfriendly. Instead, you might want to follow up with other questions to find something you do have in common.

上田：　リーさんは　どんなスポーツが　好きですか。
　　　　　　　　　　　　　　　　　　　　す

リー：　そうですね。やきゅうや　ゴルフが　好きですね。
　　　　　　　　　　　　　　　　　　　　す

上田：　そうですか。じゃあ、サッカーも　好きですか。
　　　　　　　　　　　　　　　　　　　　す

or　　　　サッカーは　どうですか。

リー：　ええ、サッカーも　よく　みますよ。

or　　　　そうですね、サッカーは　ちょっと。

Carrying on a conversation in any language is like playing catch. You must take turns speaking and listening while sustaining common topics. It is especially important to be aware of these strategies while trying to speak a second language. Being a good listener is key to participating successfully in a conversation.

練習　Practice
れんしゅう

With a partner, choose a topic below or one of your own. Discuss your individual preferences, incorporating the communicative strategies you have learned.

1. leisure activities
2. music
3. sports
4. movies
5. food
6. books

漢字
かんじ
Kanji

History of the Japanese Writing System

Historically Chinese characters are classified into the following six categories called 六書 . The first four categories are based on structural composition and the last two りくしょ are based on usage. The distinction among them is not clear-cut because some belong to more than one category and the definitions are not always clear.

象形文字 (Pictographs) are based on pictures of objects they represent, as しょうけい も じ explained in Chapter 5. For example, 大 in Chapter 4, 人 , 山 , 川 , 田 in chapter 5, and 月 , 火 , 水 , 木 , 金 , 土 , and 日 are all in this category. Some of them are very different from the original illustration, and are often hard to see the origin. The number of **kanji** in this category is only a few hundreds.

指事文字 (Logograms or ideographs) are originated from simple graphic し じ も じ representation of an abstract concept. The number of **kanji** in this category is extremely limited as they are primarily used for direction 上 and 下 and numbers 一 , 二 , 三 , 四 , 八 , 十 , and 百 . Others include 本 and 末 .

会意文字 (compound ideographs or ideographs) are a combination of かい い も じ pictographs and logograms to repent an overall meaning. For example, the combination of 人 (*person*) and 木 (*tree*), becomes 休 (*to rest*), and the combination of 日 and 月 becomes 明 (*bright*). Other examples are 学 and 先 .

形声文字 (semantic-phonetic characters, phonetic-ideographic characters) are けいせい も じ by far the largest **kanji** category, including kanji such common as 曜 , 時 , and 週 . The proportion of kanji varies depending on the total number of **kanji** considered, but it is usually estimated as between 80 to 90 percent of characters. They usually consist of phonetic component, which indicates on-reading of the **kanji**, and the semantic component, which indicates the categorical meaning of the **kanji**. For example, the left side of 語 , 言 means *to say*, indicating 語 has something to do with speech or language. The right side 吾 provides pronunciation /go/ for this **kanji**. The combination of the two indicates that 語 refers to language and it is pronounced as ご . Other semantically related words such as 話 (/wa/ story, talking) 読 (/doku/ reading), 訳 (/yaku/ translation) and 説 (/setsu/ explanation) all have 言 but have different pronunciation.

転注文字 (delivative characters) is not a well-defined category and thus is rather てんちゅう も じ problematic. It refers refer to **kanji** where the original meaning has become extended from its original usage. For example, 楽 (*music, comfort, ease*) is thought by some to have began as a picture of a drum, and by others to have represented bells on a plank of wood. The number of **kanji** in this category is extremely limited.

仮借文字 (phonetic loan characters) are characters from pronunciation in か しゃ も じ Chinese is imported into Japanese but not the meaning. For example, 来 was a pictograph that meant *wheat* in the ancient Chinese. When this **kanji** was imported, its pronunciation /rai/ was adopted but the meaning was not. Since one of the meanings of /rai/ is *to come* in Japanese, 来 is used to indicated to come and has the **on**-reading /rai/. Other common characters in its category are 今 , 五 , 六 , and 七 but the number in this category is also very limited.

時	time, hour とき　ジ	丨 冂 日 日 日 日 時 時	一時 いちじ　　二時半　　五時間べんきょうします。　その時 　　　　に じ はん　ご じ かん　　　　　　　　　　とき
間	interval, duration あいだ　カン	丨 冂 冂 冂 門 門 門 門 間 間	時間がありません。 じ かん
分	to divide, to understand, minute わ（ける）・わ（かる）　フン・ブン・プン	ノ 八 分 分	二十分　　分かりました。 にじゅっぷん　わ
半	half ハン	丶 丷 二 半 半	毎日六時半におきます。 まいにちろくじ はん
毎	every マイ	ノ 仁 乞 句 句 毎	毎週シカゴにいきます。　毎日　毎月 まいしゅう　　　　　まいにち　まいつき
年	year とし　ネン	ノ 仁 二 午 年 年	三年生　毎年 さんねんせい　まいとし
好	to like す（き）　コウ	く タ 女 女 妤 好	テニスが好きです。 す
語	language, word かた（る）　ゴ	二 言 言 言 言 訂 訝 語 語	日本語　フランス語ではなします。 に ほんご　　　　ご
高	high, expensive たか（い）　コウ	丶 二 古 古 古 高 高 高	古い高校　高い山 ふる　こうこう　たか
番	number, order, turn バン	ノ 丷 丵 平 釆 釆 番 番 番	やさいが一番好きです。 いちばんす

方	方	direction, person (polite) かた　ホウ	丶　一　方　方
			サッカーの方がフットボールより好きです。 ほう　　　　　　　　　　　　　　　　　す

新	新	new あたら(しい)　シン	亠　立　立　辛　亲　亲′　新　新　新
			新しいレストラン あたら

古	古	old ふる(い)　コ	一　十　古　古　古
			カラオケで古いうたをうたいます。 ふる

安	安	inexpensive, cheap やす(い)　アン	丶　丶　宀　安　安　安
			今日はやさいが安いです。 やす

友	友	friend とも　ユウ	一　ナ　方　友
			友達とかいものにいくのが好きです。 ともだち　　　　　　　　　　　　　　す

読めるようになった漢字 (Kanji and compounds you can now read)
よ　　　　　　　　　　　　　　かん　じ

一時　八時半　時々　時計　三時間　二週間　三十分　分かりました
　　　はち　　　　ときどき　とけい　さん　　　　に　　　　さんじゅっ

毎日毎朝　毎晩　毎週　毎年　毎月　来年　好き　大好き　日本語
　　　あさ　　ばん　　　　　　　　　　　　らい

英語中国語　高い　高校　一番　新しい　新聞　古い　安い　友達　水
えい　ちゅうごく　　　　　　　いち　　　　　　しんぶん　　　　　　　　だち　みず

日本人のなまえ：高山　古山　大木　大田　金田　中山　水田　石田
　　　　　　　　たかやま　ふるやま　おおき　おおた　かねだ　なかやま　みずた　いしだ

練習　Practice
れんしゅう

Read the following sentences written in **hiragana**, **katakana**, and **kanji**.

1. 私の友達は毎日5時半におきます。
　　　だち
2. 小川さんは古いきっさてんも新しいカフェも大好きです。
3. 大川さんは毎週テニスを二時間します。
　　　　　　　　　　　　　　　　　に
4. 本田：「安いワインと高いワインとどちらの方が好きですか。」
　　金田：「安いワインや高いワインより、おいしいワインが一番
　　　　　　　　　　　　　　　　　　　　　　　　　　　　いち
　　　　　好きです。」
5. スミスさんは日本の高校で一年間べんきょうしました。その時、
　　　　　　　　　　　　　　　いち
　　日本語もべんきょうしました。
6. 古山：「今、何時ですか。」
　　高田：「8時15分です。」

読む練習
（よ　れんしゅう）
Reading

上手な読み方　Reading Strategy
（じょうず　よ　かた）

Understanding word formation

Many words are made up of one or more words as well as prefixes and suffixes. It is important to examine the components of a word to guess its meaning and increase your vocabulary. For example, the suffix 〜や indicates a *store* or a *shop* in Japanese, and さかな means *fish*. So what does さかなや mean? How about にくや and くだものや?

読む前に　Pre-reading
（よ　まえ）

Take apart the following words and give their meanings. Follow the example.

Example:　大学院生
　　　　　　（いんせい）
　　　　　大学院 and 生, graduate school + student = graduate student
　　　　　（いん）

1. フランス人
2. しょくじする
3. そうじする
4. 大学生
5. 三年生
6. 毎日
7. のみもの
8. 大好き

本田さんのしゅみ

言葉のリスト
（ことば）

おそい	slow
モーツァルト	Mozart
ベートーベン	Beethoven
時間がかかる	to take time

私の趣味はスポーツと音楽です。スポーツの中ではテニスが一番好きです。それから、エアロビクスとスキーも大好きです。でも、野球やゴルフは時間がかかるので、あまり好きじゃないのです。バスケットボールは見るのは好きですが、するのはあまり好きじゃありません。

音楽はにぎやかな音楽の方が好きなので、クラシックよりポップスやロックをよく聞きます。クラシックは好きなのもありますが、きらいなのもあります。たとえば、モーツァルトはよく聞きますが、ベートーベンはあまり好きじゃないので、聞きません。

読んだ後で　Comprehension

A. しつもんに　日本語で　こたえて下さい。Answer these questions in Japanese.

1. 本田さんのしゅみは　何ですか。
2. 本田さんは　スキーと　バスケットと　どちらの方が　好きですか。
3. 本田さんは　どんなスポーツが　きらいですか。
4. 本田さんは　どんなおんがくを　よく　ききますか。
5. 本田さんは　だれのおんがくを　ききますか。

B. Underline the following transitional words in the text, and observe how they help indicate relationships between sentences.

それから　in addition, also, and
でも　　　but
たとえば　for example

C. Write a short paragraph about your hobbies. Describe at least two hobbies and provide details such as where, when, how often, and with whom you do them.

総合練習
そうごうれんしゅう
Integration

A. Work with a partner. You need to pick out a birthday present for your partner from a mail-order catalogue. In order to do so, you want to find out his/her hobbies, favorite things, and things that he/she wants. Ask your partner questions to come up with as many options as you can.

Example:　A:　～さんの しゅみは　何ですか。

　　　　　B:　そうですね。私は　しゃしんを　とるのが　好きですね。

　　　　　A:　そうですか。しゃしんですか。いいですね。

　　　　　　　ほかにも (*In addition*)　しゅみが　ありますか。

　　　　　B:　ええ、スポーツが　好きですよ。

　　　　　A:　どんなスポーツが　好きなんですか

　　　　　B:　ハイキングや　ゴルフが　好きですね。

　　　　　A:　そうですか。たべものは　どうですか。

　　　　　B:　たべものですか。ケーキ (*cake*)や　くだものが　好きですね。

B. Work with a new partner. Look at the following items in a mail-order catalogue. Ask each other about each person's previous partner's hobbies and favorite things. Then discuss and decide on what to buy for the previous partner. Compare at least two items.

Example:　A:　～さん (*previous partner*)は　何が　好きですか。

　　　　　B:　そうですね。しゃしんを　とるのが　好きです。そして、
　　　　　　　ゴルフと　ハイキングも　好きです。

　　　　　A:　たべものは　どうですか。

　　　　　B:　ケーキ (*cake*)や　くだものが　好きです。

　　　　　A:　そうですか。じゃあ、誕生日 (*birthday*)には
　　　　　　　たんじょう び
　　　　　　　どんなものが　いいですか。

　　　　　B:　そうですね。このフォトフレーム (*photo frame*)は　どうですか。

　　　　　A:　いいですね。でも、新しいデジカメも　ありますよ。

　　　　　B:　そうですね、でも、フォトフレームの方が　デジカメより
　　　　　　　安いので、フォトフレームの方が　いいです。

　　　　　A:　じゃあ、このフォトフレームは　どうですか。
　　　　　　　一番安いですよ。

　　　　　B:　そうですね。いいですね。

ピクチャーカラー
フォトフレームS
定価 700 円

パーカー クラシック
GT ボールペン
定価 4,000 円

ミラックス デジタル
カメラ
ウルトラミニ 50 万画素
定価 25,000 円

マグカップ 200
定価 750 円

おまかせフラワー
アレンジ
定価 4,000 円

トラベル キャリーケース
定価 3,000 円

ロールプレイ

1. Work with a partner. Using the dialogue as a model conversation, create a new conversation in which you ask your partner about his/her favorite things and hobbies.
2. You are at a party. Introduce yourself to someone and start a conversation. Find out whether he/she shares some of your interests.
3. You are planning a blind date for a friend. Find out what kind of person she/he likes.
4. You are looking for an apartment. Tell your real estate agent what kind of place you'd like. Mention your preferences for size, rooms, location, and other details that are important to you.

Chapter 8

第八課
だいはちか

買い物
か　　もの
Shopping

Objectives	Making requests, expressing quantities and numbers, talking about prices, shopping
Vocabulary	Clothing, accessories and departments; numbers 100 and above, expressions related to merchandise, prices, and activities in a store
Dialogue	デパートで　*At a department store*
Japanese Culture	Shopping in Japan, Japanese department stores, payment practices
Grammar	I.　Requesting and giving explanations or additional information, and creating harmony and shared atmosphere using 〜んです
	II.　Expressing desire using ほしい・ほしがっている and 〜たい・〜たがっている
	III.　Expressing quantities with numbers and the counters まい, 本, ひき, and さつ
	IV.　Expressing quantities using Japanese-origin numbers
	V.　Talking about prices using 円; indicating floor levels with かい えん
Listening	Recognizing the characteristics of speech
Communication	Asking for paraphrases and repetition
Kanji	Using **kanji** for numbers
	一　二　三　四　五　六　七　八　九　十　百　千　万　円　店
Reading	Scanning

単語
たん
Vocabulary

Nouns

アクセサリー		accessories
アクセサリーうりば	アクセサリー売り場	accessory department
イヤリング		earring
うでどけい	腕時計	wristwatch
うりば	売り場	department, section (of a store)
CD/DVD うりば	CD/DVD 売り場	CD/DVD section
かさ	傘	umbrella
くつ	靴	shoes
くつした	靴下	socks
コート		coat
ジーンズ		jeans
ジャケット		jacket
シャツ		shirt
しょくひん	食品	food
しょくひんうりば	食品売り場	food department
しんしふく	紳士服	menswear
しんしふくうりば	紳士服売り場	menswear department
スーツ		suit
スカート		skirt
ストッキング		stockings, pantyhose
ズボン		(primarily men's) trousers
セーター		sweater
セール		sale
たんじょうび	誕生日	birthday

ちか	地下	basement	ちかいっかい	B 1
Tシャツ		T-shirt		
ドレス		dress		
ネクタイ		tie		
ネックレス		necklace		
はこ	箱	box		
パンツ		(primarily women's) trousers, shorts		
ハンドバッグ		handbag		
ふく	服	clothing		
ふじんふく	婦人服	woman's clothing		
ふじんふくうりば	婦人服売り場	women's clothing section		
ブラウス		blouse		
ぶんぼうぐ	文房具	stationery		
ぶんぼうぐうりば	文房具売り場	stationery section		
ベルト		belt		
ぼうし	帽子	hat, cap		
みせ	店	store, shop		
ゆびわ	指輪	ring		

う -verbs

かう	買う	to buy
とる	取る	to take

取る is a general equivalent for *to take*, but 撮る is used when one takes a picture, records a video, or makes a copy.

る -verbs

いれる	入れる	to put はこに　いれる to put in a box
みせる	見せる	to show

Adverbs

すこし	少し	a little, a few
たくさん		a lot, many, much

ちょっと		a little, a few (more casual than すこし)
もう		〜 more, another 〜
もう　すこし	もう少し	a little more
もう　ちょっと		a little more

Counters

〜えん	〜円	counter for Japanese currency
〜かい	〜階	counter for floors of a building
〜つ		general counter (Japanese origin number)
〜ひき	〜匹	counter for fish and small four-legged animals
〜ほん	〜本	counter for long, cylindrical objects (e.g., bottles, films, pens, pencils)
〜まい	〜枚	counter for thin objects (e.g., film, paper, plates, shirts)
〜さつ	〜冊	counter for bound objects (e.g., books, magazines)

Question words

いかが		how (polite form of どう)
いくつ		how many
いくら		how much (money)

Expressions

いらっしゃいませ		Welcome
ぜんぶで	全部で	all together
〜は　ありませんか		Do you have 〜? Do you carry 〜? (literally, *Isn't there 〜?*)
〜を　ください	〜を下さい	Please give me 〜
やさしい　ことばで　いってください	やさしい言葉で言って下さい	Please say it in easier words

単語の練習 Vocabulary Practice
たん　　　れんしゅう

A. ふくとアクセサリー　Clothing and accessories

シャツ
shirt

T-シャツ
T-shirt

セーター
sweater

ブラウス
blouse

ジャケット
jacket

ドレス
dress

コート
coat

パンツ・ズボン
pants

ジーンズ
jeans

スカート
skirt

スーツ
suit

ネクタイ
tie

ベルト
belt

靴下
くつした
sock

ストッキング
stockings, pantyhose

くつ
shoes

かばん
bag, luggage

ハンドバッグ
handbag

ぼうし
hat/cap

腕時計
うで どけい
wristwatch

ネックレス
necklace

イヤリング
earrings

ゆびわ
ring

かさ
umbrella

Activity 1

Name the clothing that the following people are wearing.

チェイス	ジョーダン	山田	ブラウン
大木	リー	キム	フォード

Activity 2

Work with a partner. Name the clothing and accessories that your partner is wearing and list them.

Activity 3

しつもんに　日本語で　こたえて下さい。　Answer the questions in Japanese.

1. さいきん (recently) どんなふくを　かいましたか。
2. さいきん (recently) どんなアクセサリーを　かいましたか。
3. アクセサリーの中で　何が　一番好きですか。
4. ふくの中で　何が　一番好きですか。

Supplementary Vocabulary: clothing

あさ	麻	linen
ウール		wool
きもの	着物	kimono (traditional Japanese clothing)
サンダル		sandal
したぎ	下着	underwear
スーツ		suit
シルク		silk
スカーフ		scarf
スニーカー		sneaker(s)
ブーツ		boot(s)
ブレスレット		bracelets
コットン		cotton

B. うりば   Store Departments

ふじんふくうりば	women's clothing section
しんしふくうりば	mensw016 section
かばんうりば	luggage section
アクセサリーうりば	accessory section
しょくひんうりば	food section
ぶんぼうぐうりば	stationery section
CD ／ DVD うりば	CD/DVD section

Activity 4

Imagine where various sections of a large department store in your country might be located in the store. Then jot down a few items that you would find in each section.

Example: A: 一かいに　何が　ありますか。
　　　　　　　　 いっ

B: アクセサリーうりばが　あります。

A: そうですか。アクセサリーうりばには　どんなものが
　　あCRますか。

B: ハンドバッグやネックレスが　あります。

Floor	うりば	Items
ろっかい　(6F)		
ごかい　(5F)		
よんかい　(4F)		
さんがい　(3F)		
にかい　(2F)		
いっかい　(1F)		

C. 100 から上の数字   Numbers above 100
　　　　　　 すう じ

100	ひゃく	1,000	せん	10,000	いちまん
200	にひゃく	2,000	にせん	20,000	にまん
300	さんびゃく	3,000	さんぜん	30,000	さんまん
400	よんひゃく	4,000	よんせん	40,000	よんまん
500	ごひゃく	5,000	ごせん	50,000	ごまん
600	ろっぴゃく	6,000	ろくせん	60,000	ろくまん
700	ななひゃく	7,000	ななせん	70,000	ななまん
800	はっぴゃく	8,000	はっせん	80,000	はちまん
900	きゅうひゃく	9,000	きゅうせん	90,000	きゅうまん

NOTES

- Like ふん (*minute*), ひゃく (*hundred*) and せん (*thousand*) change their pronunciation with some numbers.
- Numbers like 346, 995, and 6,126 are formed by combining the thousands digit, hundreds digit, tens digit, and ones digit.

346	さんびゃくよんじゅうろく
995	きゅうひゃくきゅうじゅうご
6,126	ろくせんひゃくにじゅうろく

- For numbers 10,000 or larger, まん becomes the base unit.

10,000	いちまん
100,000	じゅうまん
1,000,000	ひゃくまん
20,000	にまん
200,000	にじゅうまん
2,000,000	にひゃくまん
35,000	さんまんごせん
350,000	さんじゅうごまん
3,500,000	さんびゃくごじゅうまん

Activity 5

Say the following numbers in Japanese.

Example: 100 ひゃく

1. 200	5. 600	9. 1,000	13. 88,666
2. 300	6. 700	10. 2,100	14. 142,918
3. 400	7. 800	11. 3,333	15. 153,000
4. 500	8. 900	12. 20,600	

Activity 6

Write the following mathematical problems in Japanese. The plus sign (+) is pronounced たす, and the minus sign (-) is pronounced ひく. The topic marker は is used for the equal sign (=).

Example: 100+200=300   ひゃく　たす　にひゃくは　さんびゃくです。

1. 300 + 9,500 =
2. 660 - 40 =
3. 12,350 + 45 =
4. 3,900 + 700 =
5. 45,000 - 870 =
6. 3,210 + 28 =
7. 7,600 - 283 =

Activity 7

Work with a partner. Your partner will write a three-digit number on your back. Say the number.

Example: Your partner writes 100 on your back. You say: ひゃく.

Activity 8

Work in groups of three or four. Each member writes five-digit numbers on two different cards. Show one card to the other members of the group, and have them read it aloud as quickly as they can. Give the card to the winner.

Activity 9

Work in groups of three or four. One person writes a number between 100 and 90,000 on a sheet of paper. The rest of the group guess the number using comparative expressions.

Example: A: そのすうじ (number) は 百より 大きいですか。小さいですか。

B: 大きいです。

C: じゃあ、二百より 大きいですか。小さいですか。

B: 小さいです。

D: 百五十より 大きいですか。小さいですか。

E: 大きいです。

D. 店で つかう ことば   Useful expressions in a store

〜を みせて下さい	Please show me 〜 (みせる to show)
〜を とって下さい	Please get, pick up 〜 (とる to pick up)
〜を はこに いれて下さい	Please put 〜 in a box (いれる to put)
〜は ありませんか	Do you have 〜 ?
〜を 下さい	Please give me 〜
セール	sale
Money/time します	It costs/takes 〜 (する *to cost/to take*)

Activity 10

Work with a partner. Take turns asking questions or making requests using one of the expressions from the table. Your partner either acts out or responds to the question.

かさを とる	本を かばんに いれる	シャツを みせる
セールが ある	ジャケットを みせる	腕時計を とる
10 ドル する	ネックレスを はこに いれる	靴下を みせる

Activity 11

Work with a partner. Take turns playing the roles of customer and store clerk. Each of you should make at least two requests.

Example:　あのコートを　とって下さい。
Your partner pretends to get a coat for you.

E. サイズ、りょう、ねだん Size, quantity, and price

たくさん	a lot
もっと たくさん	more quantity
もっと 高い	more expensive
もっと 安い	less expensive
もっと 大きい	larger
もっと 小さい	smaller
すこし／ちょっと	a little, less （すこし and ちょっと are interchangeable.）

もう すこし／もう ちょっと	a little more
もう すこし 大きい／もう ちょっと 大きい	a little bigger
もう すこし 小さい／もう ちょっと 小さい	a little smaller

Activity 12

Work with a partner. Complete the following conversation using the appropriate quantity and size expressions. There may be more than one possible answer.

Example:　A: コーヒーを　のみますか。
　　　　　B: ええ、大好きなので、<u>たくさん</u>　のみます。

1. A: このセーターは　いかがですか。
   B: 小さいですね。　_____のは　ありませんか。
2. A: このシャツは　いかがですか。
   B: すこし 高いですね。_____のは　ありませんか。
3. A: このくつは　いかがですか。
   B: ちょっと 大きいです。_____のを　みせて下さい。
4. A: このストッキングは　あまり　よく　ありませんね。
   B: じゃあ、_____ですが、こちらは　いかがですか。

ダイアローグ

はじめに　Warm-up

しつもんに日本語でこたえて下さい。Answer these questions in Japanese.
1. よく　デパートに　いきますか。
2. デパートで　何を　よく　かいますか。
3. アメリカのデパートには　どんなものが　ありますか。
4. よく　どんな店に　かいものに　いきますか。

デパートで　*At a department store*

今日は　石田さんの誕生日 (birthday) です。上田さんは　デパートに
いきました。

あんないがかり (*information assistant*)：　いらっしゃいませ。

　　　　上田：　すみません。しょくひんうりばは　どこに　ありますか。

あんないがかり：　しょくひんうりばは　地下一かいで　ございます。
(Clerk at information desk)

　　　　上田：　そうですか。じゃあ、しんしふくうりばは　何かい
　　　　　　　　ですか。

あんないがかり：　しんしふくうりばは　三かいで　ございます。

上田さんは　しょくひんうりばに　いきました。

店の人 (*sales clerk*)：　いらっしゃいませ。

　　　　上田：　あのう、このりんごを　三つ　下さい。それから
　　　　　　　　そのオレンジを　五つ　下さい。

　　　　店の人：　はい。　りんごを　三つと　オレンジ　五つですね。
　　　　　　　　　ぜんぶで 863 円に　なります。

上田さんは　しんしふくうりばに　います。

　　　　店の人：　いらっしゃいませ。

　　　　　　上田：　あのう、　そのネクタイを　みせて下さい。

　　　　店の人：　これですか。　どうぞ。

　　　　　　上田：　いくらですか。

　　　　店の人：　一万円です。

　　　　　　上田：　そうですか。もうすこし　安いのは　ありませんか。

　　　　店の人：　じゃ、こちらは　いかがでしょうか。

　　　　　　上田：　これは　いくらですか。

　　　　店の人：　四千円です。

　　　　　　上田：　いいですね。じゃあ、これ　下さい。

　　　　店の人：　かしこまりました。では、一万円　おあずかりします。
　　　　　　　　　おくりもので　ございますか。

　　　　　　上田：　はい、そうです。

店の人は　ネクタイを　はこに　いれました。

　　　　店の人：　六千円の　おかえしで　ございます。どうも
　　　　　　　　　ありがとうございました。

DIALOGUE PHRASE NOTES

- ～で　ございますis a polite form of ～です.
- ～に　なります is commonly used by store clerks instead of です.
- いかがでしょうか。is a polite expression for どうですか.
- おあずかりしますis a polite expression for あずかる, which means *to keep* or *to hold temporarily*.
- おくりもの means *present* or *gift*.
- おかえし is a polite expression for *change* (money returned).

ダイアローグの後で　Comprehension

A.　Fill in the blanks with the appropriate words.

上田さんは＿＿＿＿＿＿＿に　いきました。＿＿＿＿＿＿＿＿で
りんごと＿＿＿＿＿を　かって、＿＿＿＿＿＿で＿＿＿＿＿を
かいました。ぜんぶで＿＿＿＿＿＿＿＿＿円でした。

B. Circle はい if the a statement is true and いいえ if it is false.

1. はい　いいえ　　上田さんは　オレンジを　三つ　かいました。
2. はい　いいえ　　しんしふくうりばは　三かいに　あります。
3. はい　いいえ　　上田さんは　一万円の　ネクタイを　かいました。
4. はい　いいえ　　しょくひんうりばは　地下に　あります。

日本の文化
ぶん か
Japanese Culture

買い物　Shopping
か　もの

In addition to high-tech goods and high-fashion apparel, Japan is famous for its sheer silks, top-quality pearls, fine ceramics, lacquerware, colorful and historic

woodblock prints, handcrafted bamboo ware, and other crafts. Although the cost of living in Japan is high, there are many places to shop inexpensively. The Akihabara District in Tokyo, for example, is full of discount stores specializing in electronics, household appliances, CDs, DVDs, and anime merchandise. There are also many 百円ショップ
ひゃくえん
(100-yen shops) around

Japan, where you can purchase inexpensive household gadgets. Shopping hours in Japan are usually from 10 or 11 a.m. to 7 or 8 p.m., and most retail stores are open on weekends and holidays.

デパート　Department Stores

Japanese department stores are fun places to shop. They carry the latest fashions, traditional Japanese goods, gourmet foods, books, CDs, DVDs, and other merchandise. Some of the large department stores contain restaurants, spas, beauty salons, and amusements for children. Semiannual store sales are usually held in July and August, and December and January.

　To ask where something is sold, simply add the word うりば to the item you are looking for. For example, *food* is しょくひん in Japanese, so the *food section* would be しょくひんうりば.

Visit the *Nakama 1* student website to learn more about Japanese department stores.

Customer Service

As in other countries, customer service is very important in Japan. Some department stores even have uniformed elevator operators who announce each floor as well as sales and special events. Salespeople are trained to use very polite Japanese when speaking to customers. Here are some commonly used phrases :

いらっしゃいませ。	*Welcome, good of you to come.*
何か おさがしでしょうか。	*May I help you? (literally, Are you looking for something?)*
何〜／いくつ さしあげましょうか。	*How many 〜 do you need? (literally, Shall I give you?)*
〜は いかがですか。	*How about/is 〜? (polite form of 〜は どうですか)*
このセーターは いかがですか。	*How about this sweater?*
〜で ございます。	a polite form of 〜です
このコートは 一万円で ございます。 いちまんえん	*This coat is 10,000 yen.*
はい、かしこまりました。	*Yes, I shall do as you say.*
しょうしょう おまち下さい。	*Please wait a moment.*

Methods of payment

For retail transactions, cash is still the most common method of payment, although many stores do accept credit cards. A 5% consumption tax is applied throughout Japan. Some stores give discounts for cash payments. Personal checks are not used. There are also prepaid rechargeable contact-less smart cards, which are similar to debit cards and can be used at participating stores, vending machines, and websites. Payment by smart card works just like cash.

Some cell phones can be used just like a smart card. Charges to smart-card accounts can also be made online using a cell phone.

文法
ぶんぽう
Grammar

I.   Requesting and giving explanations or additional information, and creating harmony and shared atmosphere using 〜んです

The structure 〜んです is frequently used in conversation instead of 〜ます. The use of 〜んです helps to establish or maintain rapport with the listener. By using 〜んです the speaker treats the addressee as a member of his/her own social group rather than as an outsider. On the other hand, 〜ます merely conveys a fact as it is observed, so statements with 〜ます sound more neutral or impersonal in tone. Japanese people often use 〜んです to sound friendly and show concern for each other, as a way to be polite. The charts below show how 〜んです can be used.

Comment

	Verb (plain form)	
あまり	たべない	んですね。

You don't eat much.

Response

Topic		Adjective (plain form)	
にくは	あまり	好きじゃない	んですよ。

I don't like meat very much.

Although 〜んです is used in many different situations, there are a few situations where 〜んです is most commonly used. First, 〜んです is used to invite additional information or explanations beyond the simple answer. For example, おんがくが 好きなんですか indicates that the speaker not only wants to know whether the addressee likes music but also wants to learn more about it. On the other hand, おんがくが 好きですか merely asks the listener's likes and dislikes about music. This use of 〜んです can express the speaker's interest to the addressee and friendliness. If overused, however, it sounds nosy or imposing.

水本： あのシャツ いいですね。
みずもと
That shirt's nice.

田中： ええ、とても 好きなんですが、ちょっと 高いんですよ。
I really like it, but it's a bit expensive.

水本： そうですか。いくらぐらいですか。
みずもと
Really? How much is it?

田中： セールで 二万円です。
に まんえん
It's 20,000 yen on sale.

水本：　二万円！　それは　高いですね。
みずもと　　にまんえん
20,000 yen! That's really expensive.

NOTES

- ～んです can be also used to make an excuse or to explain the reasons for a situation without indicating it explicitly. In the following example, Mr. Kim gives a vague excuse when Ms. Smith approaches him.

  スミス：　あのう、すみませんが。
  Excuse me.

  キム：　すみません。今　ちょっと　いそがしいんです。
  Sorry, I'm tied up now.

- The ～んです structure is also used for confirming the speaker's assumption, or giving and requesting an explanation or reason. For example, if the speaker assumes that the listener is going home, he/she would likely use かえるんですか instead of かえりますか.

- In addition, ～んです can a imply surprise or irritation. In the following example, Ms. Lopez expresses her surprise by using ～んですか in her second utterance.

  ロペス：　どこに　いくんですか。
  Where are you going?

  山田：　びょういんです。
  To the hospital.

  ロペス：　えっ、びょういんへ　いくんですか。
  What? Are you going to the hospital?

- The structure ～のです・のだ is used in writing instead of ～んです. In casual speech, ～んです becomes の in a question or statement. A male speaker may use ～んだ・のだ in a statement as well.

  ロペス：　どこに　いくの？
  Where are you going?

  山田：　びょういんに　いくの。
  　　　　びょういんに　いくんだ。
  To the hospital.

- The question word どうして (*why*) is frequently used with ～んです, implying that an explanation is being asked for. The answer to such a question will also be given with ～んです as well as ので indicating that the explanation is being given. どうしてですか means *why is that?* どうして tends to imply surprise about someone's response or behavior and the demand for an explanation, so it can sound rather aggressive or accusatory.

話してみましょう   Conversation Practice
(はな)

Activity 1

You have heard various things about different people. Ask questions to confirm whether your understanding is correct.

Example: 大田さんは　新しいかれし (*boyfriend*) が　います。

　　　　　　<u>えっ、かれしが　いるんですか。</u>

1. 高山さんは　やさいを　たべません。
2. 古田さんの店は　山の中に　あります。
   (ふる た)　　(みせ)
3. 山本さんは　パンツ／ズボンが　好きです。
4. 友田さんは　ぜんぜん　りょうりをしません。
   (とも だ)
5. 大川さんのジーンズは　五万円します。([money] +する　means *to cost*.)
   　　　　　　　　　　　(ご まんえん)
6. 高田さんのジーンズは　古いです。
7. 上田さんは　スカートが　好きじゃありません。

Activity 2

Work with a classmate. Extend an invitation for this weekend. Your partner will refuse the invitation. Follow up by asking 何か　あるんですか。 (*Do you have something to do?*) Find out why your invitation was refused.

Example: A: 今週の週末に　あそびに　きませんか。

　　　　　　B: ありがとう。でも、ちょっと　つごうがわるくて。

　　　　　　A: そうなんですか。何か (*something*) 　あるんですか。

　　　　　　B: ええ、月曜日に　テストが　あるんですよ。

　　　　　　A: そうですか。それは　大変ですね。
　　　　　　　　　　　　　　　　　(たいへん)

Activity 3

Work with a partner. You bump into each other on the street. Both of you are going shopping today. First decide the place, the item, and/or your reason for shopping. Then ask each other about your plans.

Example: A: おでかけですか (*Are you going out?*)

　　　　　　B: ええ、ちょっと　友達と　デパートまで。
　　　　　　　　　　　　　　(だち)

　　　　　　A: そうですか。　おかいものですか。
　　　　　　　（おかいもの is a polite form of かいもの）

　　　　　　B: ええ、今日は　セールが　あるんですよ。

II. Expressing desire using ほしい・ほしがっている and 〜たい・〜たがっている

Japanese has two ways to indicate desire. ほしい means *I want* something, and たい means *I want to do* something. ほしい and たい express only what you (the speaker) want. To talk about what someone else wants, ほしい and たい are attached to other expressions such as 〜がっている (*showing a sign that* 〜), 〜んです (*it is the case that* 〜), and 〜そうです (*I heard that* 〜).

A. ほしい   I want (something)

ほしい is an adjective that indicates the speaker wants something (a physical object). The subject of ほしい must be the speaker in a statement and either the speaker or the listener in a question. The object of ほしい takes the particle が.

Question

Topic (subject)		Noun (object)	Particle	い -adjective	
スミスさん	は	何	が	ほしいです	か。

What do you want, Ms. Smith?

Answer

Noun (object)	Particle	い -adjective
ジャケット	が	ほしいです。

I want a jacket.

おきゃくさん (customer)： あのう、しろいブラウスが ほしいんですが。
Excuse me, I want a white blouse.

店の人： はい、こちらに ございますが。
みせ
Yes, here it is.

As shown in the chart, ほしい is an い-adjective and takes が to mark the object, though が is often replaced by the contrastive marker は in negative form.

くろいきれいな ストッキング<u>が</u> ほしいです。
I want pretty black pantyhose.

ストッキングは　ほしくありません。／ほしくないです。
I don't want pantyhose.

B. ほしがっている   Someone else wants (something)

To express what someone else wants, ほしい is often followed by the suffix ～がっている (*he/she is showing signs of ～*). When the suffix ～がっている is used, the object is marked by the particle を.

Topic (subject)		Noun (object)	Particle	い -adjective (stem)	Auxiliary verb
スミスさん	は	ジャケット	を	ほし	がっています。

Ms. Smith wants a jacket.

私の友達は 誕生日に 腕時計を ほしがっている。
My friend wants a wristwatch for his birthday.

This ～がっている form is used because the Japanese language considers that one's emotional state is known only by that person. Others can only guess about another person's feelings. For this reason, expressions of emotive states, such as ～ほしい and ～たい, are reserved for the speaker. To talk about other people's emotions, always use expressions that imply an understanding or a guess on the part of the speaker, such as ～がっている (*showing a sign of*), ～んです (*it is the case that ～*), and そうです(*I heard*) (see chapter 12, grammar IV, for a detailed explanation). Note that with ～んです and そうです, the direct object particle remains が, because the phrase ～が ほしい is part of a clause embedded in the main clause with ～んです and そうです.

山本さんは しろいドレスが ほしいそうです。

I heard that Ms. Yamamoto wants a white dress.

鈴木さんは くろいコートが ほしいんですよ。

It is the case that Mr. Suzuki wants a black coat.

C. ～たい   I want (to do something)

Unlike ほしい, ～たい indicates the speaker's wish to do something (an action). This is conveyed using verb-masu stem + たい. Compare these two examples.

このケーキが ほしい。
I want this cake .

このケーキが／を たべたい。
I want to eat this cake.

Topic (subject)		Direct object	Particle	Verb (stem)	Auxiliary (い -adjective)
私	は	コーヒー	が／を	のみ	たいです。

I want to drink some coffee.

山田：　日本で　何が　したいですか。
What do you want to do in Japan?

トム：　そうですね、富士山が　みたいですね。
　　　　　　ふ じ さん
Well, I want to see Mt. Fuji.

それから、きょうとにも　いきたいですね。
I want to go to Kyoto, too.

NOTES

- With たいです, the direct object marker を can be replaced with が. The first two sentences below are identical in meaning. Other particle usages remain unchanged.

  私は　そのくつを　かいたいです。
  I want to buy those shoes .

  私は　そのくつが　かいたいです。
  I want to buy those shoes.

  私は　おふろに　はいりたいです。
  I want to take a bath.

  私は　ここで　まちたいです。
  I want to wait here.

- It is impolite to use ～たいですか to your superior when asking if a superior wants to do something. Use ～ますか or ～いかが ですか instead.

  ごはんを　たべますか。
  Would you like to eat (rice/a meal)?

  ケーキは　いかがですか。
  Would you like some cake?

As with ほしい, add ～たがっている to express what someone else wants to do, and use を for the direct object marker.

Topic (subject)		Direct object	Particle	Verb (stem)	たがっている (る -verb)
山田さん	は	スーツ	を	かい	たがっています。

Mr. Yamada wants to buy a suit.

キム：　ジョンソンさんは　四月に　日本に　いくんですか。
　　　　　　　　　　　　　　し がつ
Is Ms. Johnson going to Japan in April?

高子：　ええ、日本で　日本語を　べんきょうしたがっているので。
たか こ
Yes, because she wants to study Japanese in Japan.

You can also use ～たいんです and ～たいそうです. The direct object particle can be が or を.

田中さんは その本が／を かいたいんです。
It is that Mr. Tanaka wants to buy the book.

田中さんは その本が／を かいたいそうです。
I heard that Mr. Tanaka wants to buy the book.

話してみましょう   Conversation Practice
はな

Activity 1

Each of the following people wants certain gifts for certain occasions. Assume the identity of each person to tell others what you would like. Use ほしい.

Example: Assume you are Mr./Ms. Smith.

私は 誕生日に いぬが ほしいです。
たんじょう び

	スミス	リー	ジョーンズ	キム
誕生日 たんじょうび	いぬ	腕時計 うでどけい	じてんしゃ	ジャケット
クリスマス／ ハヌカ (Hanukkah)	ハンドバック	ネックレス	ぼうし	スーツ
バレンタインデー	イヤリング	ベルト	ネクタイ	ゆびわ

Activity 2

Now look at the chart again and use ほしがっている and/or ほしいんです to say what each person wants for the various occasions.

Example: スミスさんは 誕生日に いぬを ほしがっています。
たんじょう び

スミスさんは 誕生日に いぬが ほしいんです。
たんじょう び

Activity 3

Work with a partner. You are a customer and your partner is a salesperson in a clothing department in a department store. First think about a few clothing items you want. Then ask for his/her assistance.

Example: おきゃくさん： あのう、すみません。ジャケットが ほしいんですが。

店の人： ジャケットですか。じゃあ、こちらは いかがですか。

おきゃくさん： ああ、いいですね。

Or ちょっと 小さいですね。もっと 大きいのが ほしいんですが。

店の人： じゃあ、こちらは いかがですか。

おきゃくさん： ああ、いいですね。

Activity 4

Conjugate the verbs using the phrases 私は ～たいです and スミスさんは ～たがっています.

Example: うちに かえる

<u>私は うちに かえりたいです。スミスさんは うちに かえりたがっています。</u>

1. りょこうに いく
2. 新しいふくを かう
3. おちゃを のむ
4. 日本で べんきょうする
5. ゲームを する
6. おふろに はいる

Activity 5

In pairs, say what you want to do in each of the following situations. Note that だったら means if ～ is ～.

Example: A: お金持ち (rich person) だったら、何が したいですか。

B: <u>そうですね。大きい うちを かいたいですね。</u>

1. 大学の先生だったら、何が したいですか。
2. おとこ (male) だったら／おんな (female) だったら、何が したいですか。
3. 日本人だったら、何が したいですか。
4. 有名人 (celebrity) だったら、何が したいですか。
5. 明日 休みだったら、何が したいですか。

Activity 6

Work with the class. Ask your classmates what they want and what activities they want to do on their birthdays. Then decide which items or activities are most popular and which is the most unusual.

Example:　A: ～さんは 誕生日に どんなことが したいですか。

　　　　　B: そうですね。うちで パーティが したいですね。

　　　　　A: そうですか。いいですね。

　　　　　　 じゃあ、プレゼントは どんなものが いいですか。

　　　　　B: そうですね。新しいくつが ほしいですね。

なまえ	したいこと	ほしいもの

III. Expressing quantities with numbers and the counters まい, 本, ひき, and さつ

You have already learned some expressions with numbers such as 〜時, 〜時間, and 〜分. These are called counter expressions. In this chapter, you will learn more of them and how they work. In counting things, and even people, a counter must be attached to the number. Some English equivalents of Japanese counters are expressions such as "two *cups* of coffee" or "three *sheets* of paper." Japanese uses a number of different counters. The type, shape, and size of an object determines which counter should be used.

Counter	Object Type	Examples
〜まい	thin objects	paper, plates, T-shirts, CDs, DVDs
〜ひき	fish, small four-legged animals	dogs, cats, mice
〜本	long cylindrical objects	pencils, pens, bottles, cans, belts, ties, trousers, movies/films
〜さつ	bound objects	books, dictionaries, magazines

The following chart illustrates how to combine numbers with counters. As you have seen in 分, 百, and 千, combining counters with numbers sometimes changes the pronunciation of both the numbers and the counters themselves. The underlined expressions in the chart are examples of these changes. Pronunciation changes for 本 and ひき follow the same pattern.

		Thin, flat objects 〜まい	Cylindrical objects 〜ほん（本）	Fish, animals 〜ひき	Bound objects 〜さつ
?	何	なんまい	※なんぼん	※なんびき	なんさつ
1	一	いちまい	※いっぽん	※いっぴき	※いっさつ
2	二	にまい	にほん	にひき	にさつ
3	三	さんまい	※さんぼん	※さんびき	さんさつ
4	四	よんまい	よんほん	よんひき	よんさつ
5	五	ごまい	ごほん	ごひき	ごさつ
6	六	ろくまい	※ろっぽん	※ろっぴき	ろくさつ
7	七	ななまい	ななほん	ななひき	ななさつ
8	八	はちまい	※はっぽん	※はっぴき	※はっさつ
9	九	きゅうまい	きゅうほん	きゅうひき	きゅうさつ
10	十	じゅうまい	※じゅっぽん	※じゅっぴき	※じゅっさつ

The counter expressions come immediately after the object and its particle.

Noun + Particle	Number + Counter	Verb	
セーターを	一まい いち	かいました。	*I bought one sweater.*
水を	四本 よんほん	のみました。	*I drank four bottles of water.*
ねこが	十ぴき じゅっ	います。	*There are ten cats.*
そのざっしを	二さつ に	下さい。	*Give me two magazines.*
ベルトを	何本 ぼん	かいますか。	*How many belts will you buy?*
本は	何さつ	ありますか。	*How many books are there?*

山田： このTシャツを 三まい 下さい。
　　　　　　　　　　　さん
Please give me these three T-shirts.

店の人： 三まいですね。かしこまりました。
みせ　　 さん
Three of them. Certainly, sir.

田中： そこに えんぴつが 何本 ありますか。
　　　　　　　　　　　　　　ぼん
How many pencils are there?

スミス： 六本 あります。
　　　　　ろっぽん
There are six.

山田： ねこを 何びき みましたか。
How many cats did you see?

山本： 二ひき みました。
　　　　　に
I saw two.

上田： としょかんには 日本語の本が たくさん ありますか。
Are there a lot of Japanese books in the library?

川口： ええ。四千さつぐらい ありますよ。
　　　　　　よんせん
Yes, there are about four thousand.

When talking about multiple items in a single sentence, the particle と comes after the counter expression.

大きいノートを 三さつと、小さいのを 二さつ 下さい。
　　　　　　　　さん　　　　　　　　　　に
Please give me three large notebooks and two small ones.

そのシャツ 二まいと、ベルトを はこに いれて下さい。
　　　　　　　に
Please put two shirts and a belt in the box.

話してみましょう　Conversation Practice
はな

Activity 1

Describe each picture using an appropriate counter expression.

Example:　ネクタイが　一本　あります。
　　　　　　　　　　　　いっぽん

1.　　　　　2.　　　　　3.　　　　　4.　　　　　5.

6.　　　　　7.　　　　　8.　　　　　9.　　　　　10.

Activity 2

Work in groups of three or four. Ask your classmates how many of the following items they own. Find out who owns the most of each item. Then write down the name of the person and the quantity.

Example:　A:　～さんは　セーターが　何まい　ありますか。

　　　　　　B:　そうですね。十まいぐらい　ありますね。
　　　　　　　　　　　　　　じゅう

なまえ	私（　　　）			
セーター				
日本語の本				
ペット (いぬ／ねこ／ other)				
ベルト				

Activity 3

Work with a partner. Ask what kind of clothing and how many items your partner would have if he/she were a famous movie star. Note that おもちですか is a polite expression that means *to own*. Take turns.

Example:　A:　あのう、どんなふくを　おもちですか 。

　　　　　　B:　そうですね。パンツ／ズボンが　六十本と　シャツが
　　　　　　　　　　　　　　　　　　　　　　　ろくじゅっぽん
　　　　　　　　百まいぐらい　ありますね。
　　　　　　　　ひゃく

　　　　　　A:　すごいですね。(*Wow!*).

IV. Expressing quantities using Japanese-origin numbers

Numbers such as いち, に, and さん are Chinese-origin numbers. There is another series of numbers called *Japanese-origin numbers*. These numbers do not require counter expressions and are usually used for round, discrete objects, such as apples, oranges, or pebbles, or for objects that do not fit any specific category. Japanese-origin numbers only go up to ten. For numbers larger than ten, Chinese-origin numbers are used. The corresponding question word is いくつ.

		Japanese-origin numbers			Chinese-origin numbers			Chinese-origin numbers
1	一	ひとつ	11	十一	じゅういち	30	三十	さんじゅう
2	二	ふたつ	12	十二	じゅうに	45	四十五	よんじゅうご
3	三	みっつ	13	十三	じゅうさん	100	百	ひゃく
4	四	よっつ	•	•	•			
5	五	いつつ	•	•	•			
6	六	むっつ	•	•	•			
7	七	ななつ	•	•	•			
8	八	やっつ	•	•	•			
9	九	ここのつ	•	•	•			
10	十	とお	20	二十	にじゅう			

タン：　ぼうしは　いくつ　ありますか。
How many hats are there?

モリル：　十二 あります。
　　　　じゅうに
There are twelve.

店の人：　いらっしゃいませ。
みせ
Welcome.

リー：　あのう　りんごを　五つと　バナナを　五本 下さい。
　　　　　　　　　いつ　　　　　　　　ごほん
Could you give me five apples and five bananas.

店の人：　りんごを　五つと　バナナを　五本ですね。はい。
みせ　　　　　　いつ　　　　　　　ごほん
Five apples and five bananas. Here they are.

話してみましょう Conversation Practice
はな

Activity 1

Describe the following pictures using the appropriate counter expression.

Example: ゆびわが 一つ あります。
ひと

1.

2.

3.

4.

5.

6.

7.

8.

9.

10.

11.

12.

Activity 2

Classify the following words using the appropriate counter. Then make a sentence for each item with the counter.

えんぴつ、かばん、CD、きょうかしょ、けしゴム、じしょ、ノート、ペン、ボールペン、本、木、ねこ、いぬ、ざっし、コーラ、さかな、たまご、トマト、にんじん、セーター、バナナ、ビール、りんご、レタス、ワイン

Example: えんぴつ　　えんぴつを 十本 下さい。
じゅっぽん

Counter	Item
まい	
さつ	
本	えんぴつ
ひき	
Japanese-origin numbers	

Activity 3

Work with a partner. You are going shopping and your partner is the clerk at each of the stores in the table below. First make out a shopping list. Then go to each store and ask for the items on your list. Your partner will ask how many you need of each item and write down your purchases.

Example: A: いらっしゃいませ。

B: あのう、りんごを 下さい。

A: いくつ さしあげましょうか。

B: 一つ 下さい。
ひと

スーパー	デパート	コンビニ

Activity 4

Work with a different partner. Say what you have bought in Activity 3, and compare your purchases. Follow the example.

Example: 私は スーパーで りんごを 二つ かいました。
ふた
　　　　〜さんは りんごを 二つ かいました。
ふた

V. Talking about prices using 円; indicating floor levels with かい

A. Asking about and stating prices with 円

You are probably familiar with the ¥ symbol for Japanese currency. *Yen* can also be written as 円. Numbers that precede 円 are pronounced in the same way as with the counter まい, except that four yen becomes よえん. The question word for price is いくら.

1（一）	いちえん	6（六）	ろくえん
2（二）	にえん	7（七）	ななえん
3（三）	さんえん	8（八）	はちえん
4（四）	*よえん	9（九）	きゅうえん
5（五）	ごえん	10（十）	じゅうえん

上田： これは いくらですか。
How much is this?

店の人： 百五十円です。
It is 150 yen.

スミス： きれいなイヤリングですね。
You have pretty earrings on.

田中： ありがとう。でも 安かったんですよ。
Thanks, but they were inexpensive.

スミス： そうですか。いくらだったんですか。
Really? How much were they?

田中： 二千円です。
2000 yen.

スミス： それは いい かいものですね。
That's a good buy!

B. Indicating floor levels with かい

Numbers before the counter かい are pronounced in the same way as with the counter 本. Both さんかい (*third floor*) and なんかい (*what floor?*) can be pronounced as さんがい and なんがい, respectively. Use 地下〜 (*underground*) to indicate a basement floor. (地下いっかい = B1)

？	なんかい なんがい		
1（一）	いっかい	6（六）	ろっかい
2（二）	にかい	7（七）	ななかい
3（三）	さんかい さんがい	8（八）	はちかい
4（四）	よんかい	9（九）	きゅうかい
5（五）	ごかい	10（十）	じゅっかい

Because floor levels indicate location, かい is used with a variety of location particles, such as に (*place of existence*), に (*goal*), で (*place of action*) , まで (*to*), and から (*from*).

リー：　アクセサリーうりばは　何かいに　ありますか。
Which floor is the accessory department on?

店の人：　一かいに　ございます。
みせ　　　いっ
It's on the first floor.

山本：　すみません。ぶんぼうぐうりばは　どこですか。
Excuse me. Where is the stationery section?

店の人：　六かいに　ございます。
みせ　　　ろっ
It's on the sixth floor.

二かいまで　あるいていきます。
に
I will walk up to the second floor.

三がいで　あいませんか。
さん
Why don't we meet on the third floor?

話してみましょう　Conversation Practice
はな

 Activity 1

Look at the following pictures of Japanese currency and say how many yen each one is worth.

Example: 一円
いちえん

1. 　　2. 　　3. 　　4.　　5.

6. 　　7.

8.

Activity 2

Look at the following items and say how much each one costs.

Example: 25円

えんぴつは　二十五円です。
にじゅうごえん

1. 750円　　2. 50円　　3. 3400円

4. 8700円　　5. 19800円　　6. 4600円

7. 1290円　　8. 2800円

Activity 3

Work with a partner. You want to buy items in the chart and your budget is 20,000 yen. Your partner is a salesperson, and he/she decides on the price of each item. Ask your partner how much each item costs and say whether you will buy it. Make sure to stay within your budget!

Example:　A:　すみません、この靴下は　いくらですか。
　　　　　　　　　　　くつした

　　　　　　 B:　〜円です。
　　　　　　　　　　えん

　　　　　　 A:　じゃ、これを　下さい。(*if buying*)

　　　　 or　そうですか。じゃ、また　きます。(*if not buying*)

	〜円 えん	かう？
靴下 くつした		
シャツ		
ジーンズ		
ジャケット		
ベルト		

Activity 4

Look at the floor directory below, and answer the following questions using 〜かい.

Example:　くつうりばは　何がいに　ありますか。
　　　　　　一かいに　あります。
　　　　　　　いっ

おくじょう (R)	ゆうえんち (*amusement center*)
8F	レストラン
7F	ぶんぼうぐ 本 CD ／ DVD おもちゃ (*toys*)
6F	でんきせいひん　(*electrical appliances*)
5F	かぐ (*furniture*) しょっき (*tableware*) だいどころようひん (*kitchenware*)
4F	こうげいひん (*traditional Japanese crafts and giftware*) きもの (*kimonos*)
3F	ふじんふく
2F	しんしふく
1F	ハンドバッグ (*handbags*) くつ ネクタイ かばん アクセサリー けしょうひん (*cosmetics*)
B1	しょくひん

1. レストランは　何がいに　ありますか。
2. どこで　つくえを　かいますか。
3. どこで　パンツ／ズボンを　かいますか。
4. ぶんぼうぐうりばは　どこに　ありますか。
5. どこで　スカートを　かいますか。
6. 何がいで　にくを　かいますか。

Activity 5

Work with a partner. You are the customer and your partner works at the information desk on the first floor of a department store. Your partner will make a floor directory. Ask where the following sections or facilities are and write the information in the chart below.

Example:　A:　いらっしゃいませ。

　　　　　　B:　すみませんが、かばんうりばは　どこですか。

　　　　　　A:　かばんうりばは　一かいに　ございます。
　　　　　　　　　いっ

　　　　　　A:　一かいですね。どうも　ありがとう。
　　　　　　　　いっ

1. かばんうりば
2. トイレ
3. CD うりば
4. レストラン
5. ふじんふくうりば
6. しんしふくうりば
7. しょくひんうりば
8. アクセサリーうりば

8F	
7F	
6F	
5F	
4F	
3F	
2F	
1F	
B1F	

聞く練習
き　　　れんしゅう
Listening Practice

上手な聞き方　Listening Strategy
じょうず　き　かた

Recognizing the characteristics of speech

Being aware of the characteristics of spoken language will help you to understand it better. Spoken language is highly redundant; that is, it repeats the same information more than once. It also contains hesitations, false starts, incomplete sentences, interruptions, and over-talk. These are all integral parts of authentic speech.

練習
れんしゅう

A. Listen to two conversations. For each one, write in English whether the customer is willing to buy the items. Then try to identify which characteristics of speech indicate the customer's intent.

1. _____

2. _____

B. 何を　かいましたか。

You will hear three conversations. Listen to each one and list in Japanese the items the customer bought and the quantity of each item. Then write the total amount the customer paid.

	何	ねだん (price per item)	いくつ	ぜんぶで いくら
1				
2				
3				

聞き上手 話し上手
<ruby>聞<rt>き</rt></ruby> <ruby>じょうず<rt></rt></ruby> <ruby>はな<rt></rt></ruby> <ruby>じょうず<rt></rt></ruby>
Communication

上手な話し方   Communication Strategy
じょうず　はな　かた

Asking for paraphrase and repetition

So far, you have learned some strategies for providing feedback to indicate that you are listening to the speaker and understanding what is being said. For example, you nod your head and say はい or ええ. There will be times when you find yourself in situations where you don't understand what the speaker is saying and can't respond, because you don't know the words used or you didn't hear what was said. In these cases it is important to know how to ask for repetition or paraphrasing, and how to ask someone to speak more loudly or more slowly. Chapter 1 introduced these phrases using おねがいします, but you can also use ～てくれませんか (Chapter 6) to articulate your request even more clearly. The following is a list of some useful expressions to employ in these situations.

Asking for repetition:	もう一度 いってくれませんか。 *Please say it again.*
Asking for paraphrasing:	やさしいことばで いってくれませんか。 *Please say it in easier words.*
Asking someone to speak slowly:	ゆっくり いってくれませんか。 ゆっくり はなしてくれませんか。 *Please say it / speak slowly.*
Asking someone to speak more loudly:	大きいこえで いってくれませんか。 大きいこえで はなしてくれませんか。 *Please say it / speak more loudly.*

Also remember that it is a good strategy to add conversation fillers and phrases like あのう and すみませんが before making a request. These phrases not only soften a request—an essential part of communicating in Japanese—but give you time to think of your next phrases.

練習
れんしゅう

Work with a partner. Imagine that you are a store clerk. Find polite expressions used by sales staff in this chapter. Say those expressions to your partner and have your partner respond with the expressions above.

漢字
かん じ
Kanji

Using kanji for numbers

Although you can write any number in **kanji**, you don't normally see numbers written in a long string of kanji, such as 六万三千五百二十二円 (¥63,522). In general, relatively simple numerical expressions are written in **kanji**, while long expressions are written in Arabic numerals.

The following are some common examples:

Prices with simple numbers such as 100, 100, 2000, etc.: 百円　千円　二千円
ひゃくえん　せんえん　に せんえん

Counter expressions with single- or double-digit numbers: 三本　四　八階
さんぼん　よん　はっかい

Dates: 六月二十五日　　十二月三十日
ろくがつ に じゅう ご にち　じゅう に がつさんじゅうにち

Times: 一時　三時二十分
いち じ　さん じ　に じゅっぷん

Pronunciation changes for kanji with numbers

Pronunciations of **kanji** sometimes change slightly. For example, 一 (いち) is pronounced いっ when it is used in the word 一本. 本 (ほん) in this example is
いっぽん
pronounced ぽん.

えんぴつを 一本 下さい。
　　　　　いっぽん
えんぴつを 二本 下さい。
　　　　　に ほん

When you read a sentence, you don't see any markings indicating such changes, because the reader makes the adjustment automatically. By the same token, you don't add any markings when you write them. (Note that the **furigana** accompanying new **kanji** is intended as a learning aid here.)

		one	一						
一	ひと(つ) イチ	一つ 一本 いぬが一匹います。 ひと いっぽん いっぴき							

		two	一 二						
二	ふた(つ) ニ	りんごが二つあります。 二さつ 二本 ふた に に ほん							

		three	一 二 三						
三	みっ(つ) サン	けしゴムを三つかいました。 三本 みっ さんぼん							

四	四	four よ・よん・よっ(つ) シ	一 冂 冂 四 四					
			四つ　四時　ビールが四本あります。 よっ　よじ　　　　よんほん					

五	五	five いつ(つ) ゴ	一 丁 五 五					
			五つ　ベルトが五本あります。 いつ　　　　ごほん					

六	六	six むっ(つ) ロク・ロッ	゛ 一 ナ 六					
			六つ　六時　えんぴつが六本あります。 むっ　ろくじ　　　　ろっぽん					

七	七	seven なな(つ) シチ	一 七					
			七時　七本　オレンジが七つあります。 しちじ　ななほん　　　　なな					

八	八	eight やっ(つ) ハチ・ハツ	ノ 八					
			八つ　八時　ペンが八本あります。 やっ　はちじ　　　　はっぽん					

九	九	nine ここの(つ) キュウ・ク	ノ 九					
			九つ　九時　バナナが九本あります。 ここの　くじ　　　　きゅうほん					

十	十	ten とお ジュウ・ジュッ	一 十					
			靴下が十あります。　十本　十時 くつした　とお　　じゅっぽん　じゅうじ					

百	百	hundred ヒャク・ビャク・ピャク	一 丁 丆 百 百 百					
			二百　三百　六百 にひゃく　さんびゃく　ろっぴゃく					

千	千	thousand セン・ゼン	ノ 二 千					
			二千　三千　八千　千円 にせん　さんぜん　はっせん　せんえん					

万	万	ten thousand マン	一 フ 万					
			一万円　百万円 いちまんえん　ひゃくまんえん					

円	円	yen (Japanese currency) エン	一 冂 冂 円					
			五十円　このセーターは、七千八百円です。 ごじゅうえん　　　　ななせん はっぴゃくえん					

店	店	store, shop みせ テン	゛ 一 广 庁 庁 店 店					
			大きい店　店の人 みせ　みせ					

読めるようになった漢字 (Kanji and compounds you can now read)

一時　一本　一つ　一緒に　もう一度　二時　二本　二つ　三時

三本　三つ　四時　四本　四つ　五時　五本　五つ　六時　六本

六つ　七時　七本　七つ　八時　八本　八つ　九時　九本　九つ

十時　十本　十　百円　千円　一万円　店の人　喫茶店　腕時計

靴下　誕生日　地下　婦人服

日本人のなまえ：川口　友田　古田　水本

練習

Read the following sentences with numerical kanji.

1. 田中さんは十一時三十分に学生会館にきます。
2. としょかんには日本の本が四千五百さつぐらいあります。
3. 山川さんのつくえの上に二万八千円あります。
4. 私は六時にごはんをたべます。そして、七時に大学にいきます。
5. そこに小さい店があります。

読む練習
Reading Practice

上手な読み方　Reading Strategy

Scanning

It is not always necessary to read an entire text when you are looking for specific information. For example, when you want to find out which floor of a department store sells food, you do not read the entire floor directory. You would look for a specific character such as the kanji 食 (eat). By employing this strategy, you will be able to find the information you need more quickly.

The same is true when you read a text looking for particular information. You can skip through the passage to find the specific information you need. This method of reading is called scanning.

練習

Read the following advertisements and find out what is being sold in each ad.

1.

2.

3.

4.

きんじょのスーパー   Neighborhood supermarket

言葉の　リスト
ことば

タオル	towel
スリッパ	slippers
洗剤 せんざい	soap

(handwritten note: 日ようひん daily products)

私の家の近くに大きいスーパーがあります。そのスーパーの地下
うち　ちか　　　　　　　　　　　　　　　　　　　　　　　　　　　　ち
一階には食品売り場があります。高いものはありませんが、私
かい　しょくひんう　ば
はそこでよく野菜や魚を買います。二階は日用品売り場です。
やさい　さかな　か　　　かい　にちようひんう　ば
タオルやスリッパやシャンプーや洗剤があります。　三階には本や
せんざい　　　　　　　かい
文房具があります。昨日、私はこのスーパーでノートを三冊と
ぶんぼうぐ　　　　きのう　　　　　　　　　　　　　　　　　さつ
ボールペンを五本買いました。
か

読んだ後で　　Comprehension
あと

A. しつもんに　日本語で　こたえて下さい。Answer these questions in Japanese.

1. この人は　このスーパーで　何を　よく　かいますか。 *(handwritten: やさいゃ 魚)*
2. このスーパーの　三階に　何が　ありますか。
   　　　　　　　　　　かい
3. 三階に　何が　ありますか。*(handwritten: 本や て 文)*
   かい
4. 魚は　何階に　ありますか。*(handwritten: とか いかい)*
   さかな　かい
5. 日用品って　何ですか。
   にちようひん
6. 昨日　この人は　何を　かいましたか。それは　どこに　ありましたか。
   きのう

B. Write a short passage about a department store you know. Use the following questions as a guide for what information to include.

1. デパートは　どこに　ありますか。
2. デパートは　大きいですか。小さいですか。
3. いいデパートですか。
4. デパートに　どんなうりばが　ありますか。
6. いりぐち (entrance) のちかくに　何が　ありますか。
7. そのデパートで　何を　よく　かいますか。どうしてですか。

総合練習
そうごうれんしゅう
Integration

A. デパートのうりば   Department Store Sections

The following is the floor directory of a full-scale department store in Tokyo. Work with a partner to describe the types of items available on different floors. Try to guess the meanings of the words written in **katakana**. Next, your instructor will give you a list of specific items to purchase. Figure out where each item would be located.

東館(ひがしかん)	西館(にしかん)
R/8 学生服(がくせいふく)/商品券(しょうひんけん) サービス/介護用品(かいごようひん)	屋上遊園(おくじょうゆうえん) 金魚(きんぎょ)・熱帯魚(ねったいぎょ) **R**
7 呉服（ごふく）/宝飾品(ほうしょくひん) 時計(とけい)・メガネ・文具(ぶんぐ) レストラン	レストラン/催事場(さいじじょう) **7**
6 催事場(さいじじょう)/婦人服(ふじんふく) [Lサイズ]	こども服(ふく)・ベビー用品 (ようひん)/おもちゃ **6**
5 婦人服(ふじんふく) [プレタポルテ＆エレガンス]	リビング用品(ようひん)/タオル/ 寝具（しんぐ）/家具(かぐ) インテリア/美術画廊(びじゅつがろう) **5**
4 婦人服(ふじんふく) [デザイナーズブティック＆カジュアル] 婦人肌着(ふじんはだぎ)	リビング/和洋食器(わようしょっき)/ 調理(ちょうり)・日用品(ようひん)/ ギフトサロン **4**
3 婦人服(ふじんふく) [インポートブティック]	紳士服(しんしふく)/紳士用品(しんし ようひん)/紳士靴(しんしぐつ) **3**
2 婦人服(ふじんふく) [キャリアブティック]	紳士服(しんしふく)/紳士用品(しんし ようひん)/ゴルフウェア/カバン **2**
1 ハンドバッグ/婦人靴(ふじんぐつ) 婦人小物(ふじんこもの)/アクセサリー/ 化粧品(けしょうひん)	ファッション雑貨(ざっか) **1**
B1 食品(しょくひん) [和洋菓子(わようがし)/のり/茶(ちゃ)/ 和洋酒(わようしゅ)・缶詰(かんづめ)] 地下鉄連絡口(ちかてつれんらくぐち)	食品(しょくひん)[鮮魚(せんぎょ) 精肉(せいにく)・野菜(やさい) 和洋中華惣菜(わようちゅうかそうざい)] **B1**
	レストラン/喫茶(きっさ) 書籍(しょせき) **B2**

ロールプレイ

1. Work in a group of six. You and one other person are customers in a department store with 50,000 yen each to spend. The other classmates of the group are salesclerks in different departments, and your instructor will give them a price list of items for their department. Go to as many departments as you can, and make one or more purchases. Before leaving each department, note what you have bought and how much you paid. You must buy at least four different items. Try to spend all your money. Whoever is left with the smallest amount of change wins.

Examples:

店の人：	いらっしゃいませ。
おきゃくさん (*Customer*)：	あのう、あかいハンドバッグが ほしいんですが。
Or	そのあかいハンドバッグを みせて下さい。
店の人：	はい、どうぞ。
おきゃくさん：	ちょっと小さいですね。もっと大きいのは ありますか。
店の人：	じゃあ、こちらはいかがですか。
おきゃくさん：	ああ、いいですね。いくらですか。
店の人：	四万円です。
おきゃくさん：	ああ、ちょっと高いですね。

店の人：	いらっしゃいませ。
おきゃくさん：	しろいシャツが ほしいんですが。
店の人：	こちらは いかがですか。
おきゃくさん：	いいですね。
Or	ちょっと高いですね。もうすこし 安いのは ありますか。

2. You have run out of fruits and vegetables. Go to a market and buy the following items.

Item	Amount
レタス	1
トマト	3
にんじん	5
たまご	12
バナナ	6

Chapter 9

第<ruby>九<rt>く</rt></ruby><ruby>課<rt>か</rt></ruby>
<ruby>第<rt>だい</rt></ruby>

レストランとしょうたい
Restaurants and Invitations

Objectives	Extending invitations, ordering at a restaurant
Vocabulary	Dishes, types of cuisine, food expressions
Dialogue	レストランで　*At a restaurant*
Japanese Culture	Eating habits in Japan, Japanese restaurants
Grammar	I.　Indicating choices using 〜にします; making requests using 〜をおねがいします
	II.　Eliciting and making proposals using 〜ましょうか and 〜ましょう
	III.　Using question word + か + (particle) + affirmative and question word + (particle) +も + negative
	IV.　Giving reasons using から; expressing opposition or hesitation using けど
	V.　Making inferences based on direct observation using verb and adjective stems + そうだ
Listening	Using context
Communication	Introducing a new topic
Kanji	Creating inflectional endings with **okurigana**
	行 来 帰 食 飲 見 聞 読 書 話 出 会 買 起 寝 作 入
Reading	Understanding Japanese e-mail formats

単語
たん

Nouns

アイスクリーム		ice cream
あぶら	油 (oil) ／脂 (fat)	oil あぶらが おおい fatty, oily
イタリア		Italy
		イタリアりょうり Italian cuisine
うどん		Japanese wheat noodles
ランチ		lunch, lunch set A ランチ Lunch A
カレーライス		Japanese curry and rice dish
		(abbreviation: カレー)
カロリー		calorie
クッキー		cookie
ケーキ		cake
(お) さしみ	御刺身	sashimi (fillet of fresh raw fish,
		usually preceded by お)
サラダ		salad
サンドイッチ		sandwich
スープ		soup
(お) すし	御寿司／鮨	sushi (usually preceded by お)
ステーキ		steak
スパゲティ		spaghetti
セット		a Western-style fixed menu,
		ハンバーガーセット hamburger set
そば	蕎麦	Japanese buckwheat noodles
チーズ		cheese
チキン		chicken
チャーハン		Chinese-style fried rice
ちゅうかりょうり	中華料理	Chinese cuisine
ちゅうもん	注文	order ちゅうもんする to order

チョコレート		chocolate
ていしょく	定食	a Japanese or Asian-style dish set, さしみていしょく sashimi set
デザート		dessert
てんぷら	天ぷら / 天麩羅	tempura (fish, shrimp, and vegetables battered and deep-fried)
トースト		toast
ハンバーガー		hamburger
パン		bread
ビーフ		beef
ピザ		pizza
フライドチキン		fried chicken
ポーク		pork
ようしょく	洋食	Western-style cuisine
ライス		rice ライス is served on a plate, not in a bowl. ごはん is a generic term for cooked rice.
ラーメン		ramen (Chinese-style noodles in broth)
ランチ		lunch A ランチ lunch set A
わしょく	和食	Japanese cuisine (also 日本りょうり)

う -verbs

| いる | 要る | to need something ソースがいる (It needs sauce.) |

い -adjectives

あたたかい	温かい	warm
あつい	熱い	hot
あまい	甘い	sweet
おおい	多い	a lot, much
かたい	固い	hard, tough

からい	辛い	spicy
しょっぱい		salty
すくない	少ない	little (in number), few
すっぱい	酸っぱい	sour
つめたい	冷たい	cold
にがい	苦い	bitter
ひくい	低い	low, カロリーがひくい low in calories
やわらかい	柔らかい	soft

Prefixes

| ご〜 | 御〜 | polite prefix　ごちゅうもん |

Expressions

| 〜に　します | | to decide on 〜 |
| 〜を　おねがいします | 〜をお願いします | I would like to have 〜 |

単語の練習
たん　　　れんしゅう

A. りょうり Types of food

(お) すし
sushi

(お) さしみ
sashimi

てんぷら
tempura

うどん
udon noodles

そば
buckwheat noodles

ラーメン
Chinese noodles

チャーハン
Chinese fried rice

カレーライス
Japanese curry and rice

スパゲティ
spaghetti

ステーキ
steak

サラダ
salad

フライドチキン
fried chicken

ハンバーガー
hamburger

サンドイッチ
sandwich

スープ
soup

チーズ
cheese

A ランチ
Lunch A (Western-style)

さしみ定食
ていしょく
sashimi set (Japanese or Asian style)

デザート
dessert

アイスクリーム
ice cream

クッキー
cookies

ケーキ
cake

おぼえていますか　　**Do you remember these words?**

さかな、にく、たまご、やさい、くだもの、レタス、トマト、にんじん、バナナ、オレンジ、りんご、おちゃ、ジュース、ミルク、（お）さけ、コーヒー、こうちゃ、ワイン、ビール、水、コーラ

Activity 1

しつもんに日本語でこたえて下さい。

1. レストランでよく何をちゅうもんしますか。

2. あさは、よく何を食<small>た</small>べますか。よく何を飲<small>の</small>みますか。

3. おひるごはんには、よく何を食<small>た</small>べますか。よく何を飲<small>の</small>みますか。

4. ばんごはんはどうですか。

5. どんなりょうりを よく作<small>つく</small>りますか。

6. 今何が食<small>た</small>べたいですか。

7. あなたのくにには (*in your country*) どんなランチセットや定食<small>ていしょく</small>がありますか。

B. りょうりのタイプ　　**Types of cuisine**

Country names are often, but not always, used to identify types of dishes, as shown in the table below. スペインりょうり、メキシコりょうり、かんこくりょうり、インド (Indian) りょうり are commonly used terms in Japanese, but Japanese has no specific terms for "American" or "Canadian" cuisine.

Activity 2

In the table below, write the names of some dishes that belong to each category and say them aloud.

タイプ	りょうり
和食<small>わしょく</small>／日本りょうり　*Japanese cuisine*	
中華<small>ちゅうか</small>りょうり　*Chinese cuisine*	
イタリアりょうり　*Italian cuisine*	
フランスりょうり　*French cuisine*	
そのほかの (*other*)　　洋食<small>ようしょく</small>	

Activity 3

しつもんに日本語でこたえて下さい。

Example: A: おさしみは何りょうりですか。

B: 和食です。
わしょく

1. どのくに (country) のりょうりが好きですか。
2. 何りょうりのレストランによく行きますか。
3. どのくに (country) のりょうりは好きじゃないですか。
い
4. ちかくにどんなレストランがありますか。

C. 食べ物をせつめいすることば   Food expressions
た　もの

あまい	sweet	あつい	hot (temperature)
からい	spicy	つめたい	cold
しょっぱい	salty	あたたかい	(comfortably) warm
すっぱい	sour	かたい	hard, tough
にがい	bitter	やわらかい	soft
あぶらがおおい	oily, fatty	あぶらがすくない	not oily
カロリーが高い	high-calorie	カロリーがひくい	low-calorie

おぼえていますか。　　おいしい

Activity 4

Work in groups of four. Discuss the dishes of the countries listed in the table, then fill in the right-hand column with the adjectives or expressions that you feel best describe the cuisine of each one.

〜のりょうり	どんなりょうりですか。
日本	
中国
ごく	
かんこく	
イギリス	
フランス	
メキシコ	
アメリカ	
イタリア	

Activity 5

Ask a partner about his/her food preferences.

Example:　あまい／からい

        A:　あまいものとからいものと、どちらの方が好きですか。

        B:　あまいものの方が好きです。

1. あまいもの／からいもの
2. あぶらが　おおいもの／あぶらが　すくないもの
3. つめたいスープ／あたたかいスープ
4. あついコーヒー／つめたいコーヒー
5. かたいりんご／やわらかいりんご
6. からいカレー／あまいカレー
7. すっぱいもの／からいもの
8. すこししょっぱいチップス (chips)/ すこしにがいチョコレート
9. カロリーが高いもの／カロリーがひくいもの

ダイアローグ

はじめに   Warm-up

A. しつもんに日本語でこたえて下さい。

1. 週末に友達と何をよくしますか。

2. 和食のレストランにはどんなものがありますか。

3. 中華りょうりのレストランにはどんなものがありますか。

4. どんな洋食が好きですか。

B. Make a phone call inviting a partner out to eat somewhere. Remember to use 〜ませんか and the expressions you've learned to identify yourself when calling and responding to a caller.

レストランで   *At a restaurant*

今日は土曜日です。石田さんと上田さんと山本さんはしぶやにあそびに来ました。

　　　石田： あのう、上田さん、山本さん。

上田と山本： はい。

　　　石田： そろそろ十二時ですから、何か食べませんか。

　　　山本： いいですね。じゃあ、あそこはどうですか。

　　　上田： イタリアりょうりですね。いいですよ。

石田：　じゃあ、あそこへ行きましょう。

石田さんと上田さんと山本さんはレストランでメニューを見ています。

上田：　何にしましょうか。

石田：　そうですね。このピザはどうですか。

山本：　おいしそうですね。上田さん、どうですか。

上田：　ええ。私もピザは大好きです。

山本：　じゃあ、そうしましょう。ほかに何がいいですか。

上田：　フライドチキンはどうですか。

石田：　いいですね。じゃあ、飲み物は？

山本：　のどが かわきましたから、ビールにしませんか。

石田：　いいですね。じゃあ、ぼくもそうします。上田さんはどう

　　　　しますか。

上田：　私は水でいいです。

ウェイターが来ました。

　ウェイター：　いらっしゃいませ。ごちゅうもんは。

　　　　石田：　このピザとフライドチキンとビールをおねがいします。

　ウェイター：　ピザを一まいとフライドチキンをお一つですね。

　　　　　　　　ビールは何本にしましょうか。

　　　　石田：　一本おねがいします。

　ウェイター：　一本ですね。かしこまりました。

　　　　上田：　あ、それから、私はお水を下さい。

　ウェイター：　はい、かしこまりました。

Dialogue Phrase Notes

- そろそろ十二時です means *it's about 12 o'clock.*
- ほかに means *in addition.*
- のどがかわきました means *I am thirsty.*
- ごちゅうもんは? means *What would you like to order?"*
- かしこまりました *(Yes, I shall do as you say)* was introduced in the Japanese Culture section for Chapter 8. This phrase is used in restaurants as well as in shops.

ダイアローグの後（あと）で

A. Circle はい if the statement is true, or いいえ if it is false.

1. (はい) いいえ　上田さんは何か食べ（た）たがっています。
2. (はい) いいえ　石田（いし）さんは山本さんとレストランに行きました。
3. (はい) いいえ　石田（いし）さんと山本さんはレストランでビールを飲（の）みました。
4. はい (いいえ)　山本さんはピザとフライドチキンをちゅうもんしました。
5. はい (いいえ)　上田さんは何も飲（の）みませんでした。

B. Complete the following passage by filling in the appropriate particle for each blank.

石田（いし）さん＿と＿上田さん＿と＿山本さんは、土曜日＿に＿しぶや＿に＿
あそび＿に＿行（い）きました。おなかがすきましたから、イタリアりょうりの
レストラン＿に＿行（い）って、ピザ＿と＿フライドチキン＿を＿食（た）べました。
石田（いし）さん＿と＿山本さん＿は＿ビール＿を＿飲（の）みました。

日本の文化
ぶん か

日本の食生活   Eating habits in Japan
しょくせいかつ

For many Japanese, not a day goes by without eating some rice. A traditional Japanese breakfast consists of a bowl of rice, miso soup, a raw egg with some soy sauce, seaweed, pickles, and a small piece of fish. Western-style breakfasts consisting of buttered toast, an egg, green salad, and coffee or tea are also very popular. Many restaurants and cafes offer special breakfast sets for commuters. These are called モーニングサービス or モーニングセット, and the breakfast may be either Japanese- or Western-style.

At lunchtime, some people bring a box lunch (おべんとう), go to the company or university cafeteria, or eat at restaurants and cafes that offer a choice of special lunch sets of the day (日替りランチ). Popular lunches
ひ がわ
include noodles, Italian pasta, curried rice, fried rice, or bowls of rice topped with stewed beef, pork cutlet, and eggs, or tempura. Local eateries, convenience stores, supermarkets, and department stores also sell a variety of おべんとう. Most primary schools provide lunch for the children, while students at secondary schools usually bring their own.

For most Japanese, dinner is the largest meal of the day, and is eaten around 6 or 7 p.m. A wide range of dishes (tempura, sashimi, grilled fish, sukiyaki

[stewed pork]) as well as other foreign dishes are cooked at home. Many local food shops offer a variety of prepared dishes for working mothers and businesspeople. Small local restaurants usually offer free delivery, so sushi, noodles, and Chinese dishes, can be ordered by phone as well.

The most popular international dishes are Chinese, Italian, and French. Some Korean and Indian dishes, such as grilled beef and curry, are also popular. American franchise stores like McDonald's have Western fast food. Hamburgers, pizza, and fried chicken are popular, particularly among young people. Mexican cuisine is still not well known in Japan.

Before a meal, the Japanese say いただきます (literally, *I humbly receive this*). After the meal, they say ごちそうさまでした (literally, *It was a feast*). Both are expressions of gratitude to those who made the meal possible (farmers, fishermen, cooks), as well as for natural phenomena, like rain.

日本のレストラン

Restaurants in Japan range from the very inexpensive to outrageously expensive places. Many restaurants display realistic-looking models of food in the front

window to give an idea of the dishes they serve and their prices. Moderately priced restaurants tend to have free seating, that is, you don't have to wait to be seated. As soon as you are seated, a waiter or waitress often brings a steaming hot towel called おしぼり to wipe your hands and face. Since the service charge is included in the bill, it is customary not to tip.

Dining out or going for drinks is very common among Japanese business people and students. Instead of hosting parties at home, Japanese people prefer to hold parties in restaurants, pubs, and hotels. The organizer often sets the menu and collects cash from the guests ahead of time. At the beginning of a party, it is customary to have a toast, or かんぱい. Pouring a drink into your own glass or drinking directly from a bottle is not polite. Instead, you should fill other people's glasses and let them fill yours.

If you are treated to a restaurant meal, thank the person after the meal (ごちそうさまでした), and again the next time you meet. You might say 昨日／先日はどうもごちそうさまでした . (Thank you for the feast yesterday/the other day.) And remember that the reciprocation of invitations and other favors plays a vital role in relationships among the Japanese.

文法
ぶんぽう

> ## I. Indicating choices using 〜にします; making requests using 〜をおねがいします

When ordering something in a restaurant, you may say 〜にします or 〜をおねがいします as well as 〜を下さい, as you learned in Chapter 8. します in the 〜にします construction does not mean *do* but something like *decide on* 〜. It may also be used in other contexts, as in トヨタにします (*decide on a Toyota when you buy a car*).

ウェイター： お飲みものは、何に します か。
の
> *What would you like to drink?* (literally, *As for drinks, what will you decide on?*)

きゃく (*customer*)： オレンジジュースに します。
> *I will have orange juice.* (literally, *I decide on juice.*)

オレンジジュースを おねがいします。
> *I will have orange juice.* (literally, *I request orange juice.*)

オレンジジュースを 下さい。
> *Please give me orange juice.*

With 〜をおねがいします and 〜を下さい (but not with 〜にします), you can use a number of quantity expressions depending on what it is you are asking. Use 〜つ (Japanese origin number) to order dishes and drinks and 〜本 for bottles. The quantity expression directly follows the particle を. When two or more items are listed, the sentence takes the form of "X を Quantity Expression と Y を Quantity Expression . . ." おねがいします.

コーヒーを一つ下さい。
> *Please bring one coffee.*

ビールを二本おねがいします。
> *Please bring two bottles of beer.*

こうちゃを一つとコーヒーを一つおねがいします。
> *Please bring one tea and one coffee.*

鈴木： 何、飲みますか。
すず　　　　　の
> *What would you like to drink?*

リン： そうですね。鈴木さんは？
すず
> *Let's see. How about you, Mr. Suzuki?*

鈴木： ぼくはコーラにします。
すず
> *I will have some cola.*

リン： そうですか。じゃあ、私もコーラにします。
Well then, I will have cola, too.

鈴木： (to the waiter) すみません。コーラを二つおねがいします。
すず
Excuse me. We will have two colas.

話してみましょう
はな

Activity 1

Place an order using 〜を おねがいします. Use すみません to get the server's attention.

Example: そば／ 1

すみません。そばを一つおねがいします。

1. コーラ／ 1   5. ラーメン／ 5
2. サンドイッチ／ 2   6. A ランチ／ 1
3. こうちゃ／ 1   7. おさしみ／ 4
4. ハンバーガー／ 3   8. うどん／ 2

Activity 2

Work with a partner. You are going to a restaurant with your partner. Think about a dish that you would like to order. Discuss with your partner and decide on the restaurant.

Example: A: 今、何が食べたいですか.
た

B: そうですね。スパゲティが食べたいですね。
た

A: そうですか。じゃあ、イタリアりょうりのレストランにしませんか。

B: あ、いいですね。

Activity 3

Work with a new partner. You are a customer and your partner is the waiter or waitress. Circle one item that you would like to have from each category in the table below. The waiter/waitress will ask for your order by saying ごちゅうもんは？(Your order?). Place your order.

Example:　　ウェイター：　ごちゅうもんは？

おきゃくさん (*customer*)：　こうちゃとサンドイッチとケーキを
おねがいします。

ウェイター：　こうちゃとサンドイッチとケーキですね。
かしこまりました。

飲み物 _の_{もの}	ミルク　オレンジジュース　おちゃ　水　ワイン　ビール コーヒー　こうちゃ
食べ物 _た_{もの}	スープ　サンドイッチ　ハンバーガー　サラダ　スパゲティ ピザ　(お)すし　(お)さしみ　てんぷら　チャーハン カレーライス　ステーキ
デザート	ケーキ　アイスクリーム　クッキー

Activity 4

Work in groups of three. One person is the waiter/waitress at a restaurant. The other two are customers. Look at the menu to decide what you are going to order. The waiter/waitress will ask ごちゅうもんは？, then write down your orders and confirm them by saying X と Y ですね。かしこまりました. Change roles and repeat the role play until everyone has had a turn taking orders.

Example:　　ウェイター：　ごちゅうもんは？

A：　飲み物はどうしますか。
_の_{もの}

B：　ぼくはビールにします。

A：　私はオレンジジュースにします。じゃあ、
ビールを一本とオレンジジュースを一つ
おねがいします。

ウェイター：　ビールを一本とジュース一つですね。
かしこまりました。

1 spaghetti
1 curry rice
2 cola

メニュー

オードブル

オードブル取り合わせ	¥800
スモークサーモン	¥1,000
シュリンプ・カクテル	¥900

スパゲティ

スパゲティ・ナポリタン	¥900
スパゲティ・ミートソース	¥1,000

スープ

コンソメスープ	¥400
オニオングラタンスープ	¥600

サラダ

グリーンサラダ	¥500
ミックスサラダ	¥500
チキンサラダ	¥700

魚料理

ebi furai
ebi guratan
kanikorokke

エビフライ	¥1,200
エビグラタン	¥1,200
カニコロッケ	¥1,000

米飯料理

カレーライス	¥800
オムライス	¥900
エビピラフ	¥800

ebipiraf

肉料理

サーロインステーキ	¥3,500
ビーフシチュー	¥3,000
ハンバーグステーキ	¥1,000
ポークソテー	¥1,200
チキンコロッケ	¥1,000

サンドイッチ

ハムサンド	¥600
タマゴサンド	¥500
やさいサンド	¥500
ミックスサンド	¥600

飲み物

ビール	¥400
オレンジジュース	¥500

II. Eliciting and making proposals using 〜ましょうか and 〜ましょう

In Chapter 6, the negative question form of a verb 〜ませんか is used for extending an invitation or making a suggestion. 〜ましょうか (*shall we*) and 〜ましょう (*let's 〜*) are used to elicit or make proposals.

Eliciting proposal	Making proposals
どこへ行きましょうか。 *Where shall we go?*	きょうとへ行きませんか。 *Why don't we go to Kyoto?* きょうとへ行きましょう。 *Let's go to Kyoto.*
何を食べましょうか。 *What shall we eat?*	和食にしませんか。 *Why don't we have Japanese food?* 和食にしましょう。 *Let's have Japanese food.*
どこで会いましょうか。 *Where shall we meet?*	えきで会いませんか。 *Why don't we meet at the station?* えきで会いましょう。 *Let's meet at the station.*

リー：　上田さん、今週の金曜日にコンサートに行きませんか。
　　　　　Ms. Ueda, why don't we go to a concert together this Friday?

上田：　ええ、ぜひ。何時にどこで会いましょうか。
　　　　　Yes I would love to. Well, what time and where shall we meet?

リー：　そうですね。三時十五分ごろに学生会館のまえはどうですか。
　　　　　Let's see, how about around three fifteen in front of the student union?

上田：　いいですね。じゃあ、三時十五分に学生会館のまえで。
　　　　　That would be fine. Okay then, in front of the union at three fifteen.

話してみましょう
はな

Activity 1

Work with a partner. Extend an invitation by rephrasing the following sentences with the ～ませんか form. Your partner will accept your invitation saying ええ、～ましょう. Then switch roles.

Example:　A: ～さん、明日こうえんに行って、テニスをしませんか。
　　　　　　　　あした　　　　　　　　　　　　い
　　　　　　B: ええ、しましょう。

1. 木曜日に一緒にえいがを見る
　　　　　　しょ　　　　　み
2. アイスクリームを食べに行く
　　　　　　　　　　た　　い
3. 明日一緒にべんきょうする
　あした　しょ
4. うちに来て、コーヒーを飲む
　　　　き　　　　　　　　の
5. あのカフェに入る
　　　　　　はい
6. 今日ばんごはんを一緒に食べる
　　　　　　　　　しょ　た
7. 一緒に帰る
　しょ　かえ

Activity 2

Invite a new partner to do the following activities. Then decide on the time and place together.

Example:　A: 一緒に買い物に行きませんか。
　　　　　　　しょ　か　もの　い
　　　　　　B: ええ、いいですね。いつ行きましょうか。
　　　　　　　　　　　　　　　　　　い
　　　　　　A: 明日はどうですか。
　　　　　　　あした
　　　　　　B: いいですよ。どこに行きましょうか。
　　　　　　　　　　　　　　　い
　　　　　　A: ～に行きませんか。
　　　　　　　　い
　　　　　　B: ええ、いいですよ。　じゃあ、～に行きましょう。
　　　　　　　　　　　　　　　　　　　　い

	いつ	どこ
一緒に買い物に行く しょ　か　もの　い		
コンサートに行く い		
一緒にしゅくだいをする しょ		
一緒にばんごはんを作る しょ　　　　　　　つく		
おちゃを飲む の		

Activity 3

Work in small groups. You want to go on a trip for vacation. Think about a fun place to go, then invite a few people to come along, and negotiate the details of when to meet, where to go, what to do, etc. 今度の休みに means the next vacation.

Example:
　鈴木：　木村さん、スミスさん、今度の休みにハワイにあそびに行きませんか。

　木村：　ハワイですか。いいですね。

　スミス：　そうですね。私も、ぜひ行きたいです。

　鈴木：　じゃあ、そうしましょう。

　木村：　いつ行きましょうか。

　　　　　どんなホテルにしましょうか。

　　　　　何をしましょうか。

III. Using question word + か + (particle) + affirmative and question word + (particle) + も + negative

Question words can be combined with other words to form new expressions in Japanese. This chapter introduces both indefinite and negative expressions using question words.

A. Using question word + か + (particle) ~ affirmative statement or question.

Indefinite expressions are formed by adding か to a question word.

なに ＋ か ＝ なにか　　something
どこ ＋ か ＝ どこか　　somewhere
だれ ＋ か ＝ だれか　　someone
いつ ＋ か ＝ いつか　　sometime

Question word ＋ か is used with affirmative sentences and in questions.

何か　食べます。　　*(I) eat something.*

あそこに　だれか　います<u>か</u>。　　*Is there someone over there?*

Question word ＋ か can also be used with 〜ませんか, as in the following examples. Although the verbs here are in the negative form, their meanings are not negative.

何か　食べませんか。　*Why don't we eat something?*

どこか　行きませんか。　*Why don't we go somewhere?*

The particles は, も, or に (of time) are not used with indefinite expressions. The particles が and を are usually omitted with indefinite expressions, and the particles へ／に (of direction) are optional. Other particles are added after か.

だれか	来ました。	*someone came*
何か	食べます。	*eat something*
いつか	帰ります。	*come/go back sometime*
どこか (へ／に)	行きました。	*went somewhere*
どこかで	会いました。	*met somewhere*
だれかと	話します。	*talk with someone*

山本：	何か飲みませんか。	*Why don't we drink something?*
中川：	ええ、いいですよ。	*Sure. (literally, Yes, that would be fine.)*
山本：	何にしましょうか。	*What will you have?*
中川：	私はジュースにします。	*I'll have some juice.*

山田：	どこかに今日の新聞はありませんか。
	Is today's paper somewhere?

中山：　そこにありますよ
It's right there.

NOTES

- Questions that employ question word + か + (particle) are はい／
いいえ questions, even though they appear to be information
questions:

    友田：　何か飲みますか。
    Are you going to drink something?

    中本：　いいえ、どうぞ　おかまいなく。
    No, please don't bother.

    友田：　何を飲みますか。
    What are you going to drink?

    中本：　コーヒーを飲みます。
    I will drink coffee.

- To decline an offer of food or drinks, use the following phrases.

    いいえ、どうぞおかまいなく。　*No, please don't bother.*
    いいえ、けっこうです。　　　　*No, thank you.*

- To form indefinite expressions such as *something delicious*, add
adjective + noun after question + か

    何かおいしいものを作ります。
    I will make something good.
    だれか好きな人がいるんですか。
    Is there someone you like?
    どこかしずかなところへ行きましょう。
    Let's go somewhere quiet.

- Notice that in Japanese, unlike the equivalent English expressions,
you must include a noun (もの, 人, ところ) after the modifying
adjective.

B. Using question word + (particle) + も〜 negative statement.

Question word + (particle) + も〜 followed by a negative statement means "not 〜
any" or "no 〜." The expression must be used with a negative statement.

何も　　食べませんでした。　*I did not eat anything.*
だれも　いません。　　　　　*There isn't anyone/There is no one.*
どこも　よくありません。　　*There isn't any good place.*
　　　　　　　　　　　　　　(literally, *None of the places is good.*)

The particles は, も, が, and を are not used with question word + (particle) + も. Other particles are added before も.

だれも	来ませんでした。	*No one came.*
何も	買いません。	*I am not going to buy anything.*
いつも	来ません。	*(He) never comes.*
どこ (へ／に) も	行きませんでした。	*I didn't go anywhere.*
だれとも	話しませんでした。	*I didn't talk to anyone.*

山本： 昨日、どこかへ出かけましたか。
Did you go somewhere yesterday?

中川： いいえ、どこへも行きませんでした。
No, I didn't go anywhere.

石田： 何か飲みますか。
Would you like to drink something?

ペギー： いいえ、今はいいです。何もいりません。
No, thanks. I don't need anything.

NOTES

- いつも in an affirmative sentence means always, as introduced in Chapter 3.

  いつも 来ます。　　*(He) always comes.*

  いつも 来ません。　*(He) never comes.*

- どこでも (どこ + で + も) is an exception to this pattern. It means everywhere and is always used with a positive statement.

話してみましょう

Activity 1

しつもんに日本語でこたえて下さい。

Examples: 今日何か食べましたか。

　　　　ええ、食べました。 or いいえ、食べませんでした。

　　　　今日何を食べましたか。

　　　　サンドイッチを食べました。

1. いつか日本に行きたいですか。
2. よくどこで食事をしますか。
3. いつうちに帰りますか。
4. 今日だれかに会いますか。
5. 週末どこかへ出かけますか。
6. よくだれと話しますか。

Activity 2

Create questions that correspond to each of the following answers.

Example: ええ、コーヒーをおねがいします。

　　　　　何か飲みませんか。

1. ええ、食べました。　レストランに行って、おいしいフランスりょうりを食べました。
2. 十一時に寝ました。
3. ざっしを買いましょう。
4. いいえ、うちにいました。
5. ええ。田中さんに会って、話しました。
6. 六時ごろ起きます。
7. ええ、図書館に行って、日本語の本を読みました。

Activity 3

Fill in the chart below, then extend invitations to a partner for food, drinks, places to go, and things to do.

Example: A: 何か飲みませんか。

　　　　　B: いいですね。／ええ、いいですよ。

　　　　　A: 何を飲みましょうか。

　　　　　B: こうちゃはどうですか。／こうちゃにしませんか。

	Items / Places / Things
飲み物	
食べ物	
行くところ (*place to go*)	
すること (*thing to do*)	

Activity 4

Answer the following questions using いいえ、question word + (particle) + も ～ negative.

Example:　(in a dark place) そこに　だれか　いますか。

　　　　　<u>いいえ、　だれも　いません。</u>

1. (At a party, your friend is going to a bar counter and says) ～さん、何か いりますか。
2. うちのねこをどこかで見ましたか。
3. そのことについて (about that matter)、だれかと話しましたか。
4. 昨日だれかにメールを書きましたか。
5. しゅくだいについて (about homework)、何か聞きましたか。

Activity 5

You are conducting a survey on breakfast habits. Ask your classmates if they have eaten or drunk anything today. If they have, find out what they had. Then determine how many people in all didn't have anything in the morning and what the most popular breakfast was for the class.

Example:　A: スミスさん、今日のあさ、何か食べましたか。

　　　　　B: いいえ、何も食べませんでした。

　　　　　A: 何か飲みましたか。

　　　　　B: ええ、カフェに行って、コーヒーを飲みました。

なまえ	食べ物	飲み物
スミス	-------	コーヒー

IV. Giving reasons using から; expressing opposition or hesitation using けど

In Chapter 7, you learned that the conjunction ので expresses a reason and が expresses a contrast or opposition. This chapter introduces an additional set of conjunctions that are commonly used in conversational Japanese.

A. The conjunction から (because)

The conjunction から indicates a reason, and it is attached to the end of the clause that expresses the reason. If a sentence contains both a reason and a result, the clause containing the reason precedes the clause indicating the result. から tends to reflect the speaker's personal opinion or judgment more than ので. Reasons expressed with から may sound a little stronger and those using ので. ので, thus, may sound softer and more polite, especially in formal speech.

Clause with から (reason)	Clause (result)
日本のおちゃが好きですから、	よく買_かいます。

I like Japanese tea, so I often buy some.

～から can be used with both polite and plain forms. The plain form that precedes から is similar to the forms preceding ～ので and ～んです except that だ is used instead of な for the copula verb and な-adjectives.

Verbs	よく<u>食べます</u>／<u>食べる</u>から、げんきです。	*He is healthy because he eats a lot.*
	あまり<u>寝ません</u>／<u>寝ない</u>から、ねむい (sleepy) です。	*He is sleepy because he doesn't sleep much.*
い-adjectives	これ、<u>あまいです</u>／<u>あまい</u>から、食べませんか。	*Why don't you eat this because it's sweet?*
	これ、<u>あたたかくありません</u>／<u>あたたかくない</u>から、いりません。	*I don't want it because it isn't warm.*
な-adjectives	ねこが<u>好きです</u>／<u>好きだ</u>から、ほしいです。（ねこが好き<u>な</u>ので、ほしいです。）	*I want it because I like cats.*
	いぬは<u>好きじゃありません</u>／<u>好きじゃない</u>から、いりません。	*I don't want it because I don't like dogs.*
Copula verbs	<u>じゅぎょうです</u>／<u>じゅぎょうだ</u>から、行きます。（じゅぎょう<u>な</u>ので、行きます。）	*I am going because my class is starting.*
	<u>水じゃありません</u>から／<u>水じゃない</u>から、いりません。	*I don't want it because it is not water.*

NOTES

- ～から can be used without a main clause expressing results.

    A: デザートはいりませんか。
    You don't want any dessert?

    B: ええ、カロリーが高いですから。
    That's right, because they're high in calories.

- Plain form + からです is also commonly used for reasons.

    石田さんと田中さんは、今、学校にいます。スミスさんは
    今日はやく帰りました。

    石田： スミスさん、今日ははやく帰りましたね。
    Mr. Smith went home early today, didn't he?

    田中： 明日のあさ、日本に行くからですよ。
    It's because he is going to Japan tomorrow morning.

    石田： ああ、そうなんですか。
    Oh, I see.

B. The conjunction けど *(but, although)*

Like が, the conjunction けど is used to connect two sentences or clauses that oppose each other, and is attached to the end of the first sentence. けど tends to sound more colloquial than が and is often used in casual conversation.

Clause with けど (reason)	Clause (result)
ちょっとにがいです／にがいけど、	日本のおちゃが好きです。

I like Japanese tea although it is slightly bitter.

～けど can be used with both polite and plain forms. The plain form that precedes けど is the same as that used with から.

Verbs	その人にはよく<u>会います</u>／<u>会う</u>けど、なまえはわかりません。	*Although I meet him often, I don't know his name.*
	あまり<u>寝ません</u>／<u>寝ない</u>けど、げんきです。	*He is energetic although he doesn't sleep much.*
い-adjectives	このステーキは<u>やわらかいです</u>／<u>やわらかい</u>けど、ちょっとあぶらがおおいですね。	*This steak is tender but it's a bit fatty.*
	あまり<u>ほしくありません</u>／<u>ほしくない</u>けど、<u>買い</u>ました。	*I bought it though I did not really want it.*
な-adjectives	図書館は<u>きれいだ</u>けど、あまりあかるくありません。	*The library is not very bright but it is pretty.*
	キムチは<u>好きじゃありません</u>／<u>好きじゃない</u>けど、かんこくは<u>好き</u>です。	*I don't like Korean pickles but I like Korea.*
Copula verbs	<u>休みです</u>／<u>休みだ</u>けど、学校へ行きます。	*I am going to school even though it's a holiday.*
	<u>水じゃありません</u>／<u>水じゃない</u>けど、飲みました。	*I drank it even though it wasn't water.*

NOTES

- 〜けど can be also used without a main clause expressing results.

  A: よくテレビを見ますか。
    Do you watch TV often?

  B: ええ、いそがしいですけど。
    Yes, though I am busy.

- Like が, 〜けど can be used to open a conversation, or to introduce a topic of conversation as well. It does not introduce a strong negative relation, and it is similar to the use of *but* in English as in: *Excuse me, but could you turn on the TV?*

  あのう、すみませんけど、今何時ですか。
  Excuse me, but what time is it?

  明日食事に行くんですけど、田中さんも来ませんか。
  We are going to eat out tomorrow, so why don't you join us?

話してみましょう
はな

Activity 1

Combine the following pairs of sentences using 〜から. Make sure to start with a sentence containing a reason and followed by から.

Example: 明日テストがあります。今日べんきょうします。
あした
明日テストがあるから、今日べんきょうします。
あした
明日テストがありますから、今日べんきょうします。
あした

1. このワインは古いです。すっぱいです。
2. 水がいります。このスープはしょっぱいです。
3. 七時に起きます。八時にじゅぎょうがあります。
　　　　お
4. 水にします。今日はくるまで帰ります。
　　　　　　　　　　　　　かえ
5. 週末はどこにも行きませんでした。まだ (yet) 友達がいません。
　　　　　　　い　　　　　　　　　　　　　ともだち
6. トマトがたくさんあります。イタリアりょうりを作ります。
　　　　　　　　　　　　　　　　　　　　　つく
7. あぶらがおおいりょうりは好きじゃありません。さかなをちゅうもん
します。

Activity 2

Invite your partner to do one of the activities in the chart below. Your partner will refuse using the corresponding reason and だめなんです。(*I can't*). Create a conversation using the table and the dialogue model in the example, then switch roles.

Example: A: 明日あそびに来ませんか。
　　　　　あした　　　き
B: すみません、明日は友達がうちに来るから、だめなんです。
　　　　　　　　あした　ともだち　　　　き
A: そうですか。それは、ざんねんですね。
B: すみません。今度またよんで下さい。
　　　　　　　こんど

Invitation	Reason for refusal
明日あそびに来る。 あした　　　く	友達がうちに来ます。 ともだち　　　き
金曜日にえいがを見に行く。 　　　　　　み　い	びょういんへ行きます。 い
今晩一緒にしゅくだいをする。 ばん　しょ	アルバイトがあります。
一緒にテニスをする。 しょ	今日はとてもいそがしいです。
今からひるごはんを食べる。 た	今からじゅぎょうです。
ビールを飲みに行く。 の　い	おさけはあまり好きじゃありません。

Activity 3

Draw lines between the expressions in Column A and Column B that you feel are in opposition to each other. Then create a sentence for each set using けど.

Example: にくはきらいだけど、やさいは好きですよ。

にくはきらいですけど、やさいは好きですよ。

Column A	Column B
1 さかなはきらいです。	カロリーが高いから、食べません。
2 高いです。	てんぷらはあぶらがおおいです。
3 あまりからいものは食べません。	おすしはよく食べます。
4 和食はカロリーがひくいです。	カレーは大好きです。
5 コーヒーはにがいです。	よくフランスりょうりのレストランに行きます。
6 バター (butter) クッキーをよく作ります。	ブラック (black) で飲みます。

Activity 4

Work with a partner. Using the same situation in Activity 2, invite your partner for an activity. Your partner will refuse the invitation but provide an alternative using けど and the example. Make a conversation and take turns.

Example: A: 明日あそびに来ませんか。

B: すみません。

明日はいそがしいんですけど、明後日はどうでしょうか。

A: じゃあ、明後日にしましょうか。

B: いいですか。ありがとうございます。

Invitation	Solution
明日あそびに来る。	
金曜日にえいがを見に行く。	
今晩一緒にしゅくだいをする。	
一緒にテニスをする。	
今からひるごはんを食べる。	
ビールを飲みに行く。	

V. Making inferences based on direct observation using verb and adjective stems + そうだ

Verb/adjective stem + そうだ expresses an impression or an inference based on what the speaker has seen or felt. The degree of certainty in such statements is fairly low. In some cases, information is visual, but it can be auditory as well. Its meaning is similar to the expressions *to look (like)* or *to appear*. そうだ cannot be used with adjectives of shape, color, and other exressions that show the result direct visual observation, not inferences. That is, anyone can tell if something is pretty, red, or round by just looking at it, so you cannot say きれいそうです, あかそうです, or まるそうです (looks round).

わあ、このステーキおいしそうですね！
Wow, this steak looks delicious!

この水、つめたそうですね。
This water looks cold.

あの人、もうすぐ寝そうです。
It looks like that person might fall asleep at any time.

あかちゃんが起きそうです。
The baby appears to be waking up.

	Plain affirmative form	Affirmative そう (look like 〜)	Plain negative form	Negative そう (doesn't look like 〜)
Verbs	いる (to be)	<u>い</u>そう	いない	<u>い</u>なさそう いそうにない
な - Adjectives	しずかな (quite)	<u>しずか</u>そう	しずかじゃない	しずかじゃ<u>なさ</u>そう しずか<u>そう</u>じゃない
い - Adjectives	からい (spicy)	<u>から</u>そう	からくない	からく<u>なさ</u>そう から<u>そう</u>じゃない
	いい (good)	<u>よさ</u>そう	よくない	<u>よさ</u>なさそうだ <u>よさ</u>そうじゃない

大田： カレーがありますけど、食べますか。
　　　There is curry. Would you like to have some?

リー： わあ、おいしそうですね。いいんですか。
　　　Wow, it looks delicious. Are you sure?

大田： もちろん、はい、どうぞ。
　　　Of course, here you are.

リー： いただきます！
　　　Thank you (literally, *I humbly receive*)

NOTES

- To negate a phrase with そう, you can either negate そう itself or negate the verb or adjective before そう. Because そう is a な-adjective, its negative form is そうじゃない, except that そうにない should be used for verbs. To negate the verb or adjective, change the negative ending ない to なさ before そう. For example, "*It does not look fun,*" using the adjective たのしい (*fun*), could be stated as either たのしそうじゃない or たのしくなさそう. The verb 来る becomes 来そうにない／来なさそう (*He/She does not appear to come*).
- The affirmative form of the adjective いい becomes よさ before そう.
- Since そう is a な- adjective, it can be used to describe nouns.

あまそうなアイスクリーム	*ice cream that looks sweet*
たのしそうなアルバイト	*a part-time job that looks fun*
むずかしそうなテスト	*a test that looks difficult*

話してみましょう
はな

Activity 1

Look at the following pictures and state what appears to be taking place.

Example: このアイスクリーム、おいしそうですね。
　　　　　　おいしそうなアイスクリームですね。

1

2

3

4

5

6

7

8

9

10

11

Activity 2

Work with a partner. Choose an adjective from the box below and act it out.
Have your partner guess the adjective and comment on your condition using
～そうですね. Then create a dialogue to explain why you feel the way you do.

たのしい　うれしい　かなしい　つまらない　ひま　いそがしい
さびしい　たいへん

Example:　B is singing and smiling while cooking.

　　　　A:　たのしそうですね。

　　　　B:　ええ、今日は私の誕生日だから、今晩パーティが
　　　　　　あるんですよ。

　　　　A:　そうですか。それはいいですね。

Activity 3

Work with a partner. Based on the above pictures, create as many short
conversations as you can using から or けど.

Example:　A:　おいしそうなアイスクリームですね。

　　　　B:　ほんとに (really) おいしいですよ。すこし食べませんか。

　　　　A:　ありがとうございます。食べたいけど、今ダイエット中
　　　　　　なんです。

　　　　B:　そうですか。

聞く練習
き　　　れんしゅう

上手な聞き方
じょうず　　き　　かた

Using context

It is not necessary to understand every single word of a conversation to be able to comprehend what is going on. If you can get the gist or pick up key words, you will probably be able to guess the words you miss. Context provides many clues that help you to figure out the words you don't completely understand.

練習
れんしゅう

You are on the phone with Mr. Li, who is telling you about his vacation in Florida, but the connection isn't very good. Each time you hear static, indicating that the line has cut out, write the word or part of the word you miss by guessing from the context.

言葉のリスト
こ と ば

オーランド	Orlando
マイアミ	Miami
ディズニーワールド	Disneyworld

1.＿＿＿＿＿＿＿＿＿＿＿＿＿＿

2.＿＿＿＿＿＿＿＿＿＿＿＿＿＿

3.＿＿＿＿＿＿＿＿＿＿＿＿＿＿

レストランの会話　Restaurant conversations
かい わ

Listen to each conversation and fill in the blanks to complete the sentences below.

1. このレストランは ＿italia＿ りょうりのレストランです。
   この人は ＿Spaghetti＿ を食べます。
   　　　　　　　　　　た

2. このレストランは ＿中国＿ りょうりのレストランです。
   男の人 おとこの人は今日 ＿Chahan＿ を食べます。
   おんなの人は ＿raymen＿ をちゅうもんしました。
   　　　　　　　　　　　た

3. このレストランは ＿japanese＿ りょうりのレストランです。
   おんなの人は ＿Sashimi teishoku＿ をちゅうもんしました。
   さしみていしょくは ＿1200＿ 円です。
   おとこの人は ＿A lunch＿ をちゅうもんしました。

聞き上手話し上手
きじょうずはなじょうず

上手な話し方
じょうずはなかた

Introducing a new topic

After greeting someone or getting their attention（あのう、（すみません）），the next step is to introduce a topic of conversation. An unfinished sentence ending with a conjunctive particle such as けど and が as well as んです is often used to introduce a topic. For example, the following phrases may be used as introductory remarks to extend an offer or invitation.

おいしいケーキがあるんですけど、食べませんか。
た
I have a delicious cake, so would you like to have some?

土曜日は山田さんの誕生日なんですが、何かしませんか。
たんじょう
Saturday is Mr. Yamada's birthday, so why don't we do something?

This function of けど and が is different from their original meaning (*but*) because what follows these words does not contrast with the preceding statement. Phrases such as 〜のことなんですけど／が and 〜についてなんですけど／が are also commonly used to introduce conversational topics. For example:

日本語のプロジェクトのことなんですけど、一緒にしませんか。
しょ
About the Japanese project, would you like to do it with me?

クラスのパーティについてなんですが、来週の金曜日はどうですか。
らい
As for the class party, how does next Friday sound?

In some cases けど and が are used to end an utterance without finishing the sentence:

山田：　あのう、スミスさん。
Well, Mr. Smith.

スミス：　はい。
Yes?

山田：　明日のミーティングなんですけど、
あした
About tomorrow's meeting.

スミス：　ええ。
Yeah?

山田：　すみませんが、キャンセルしたいんです。
I'm sorry but I want to cancel it.

スミス：　え、どうして？
Why?

山田：　明後日、大変なテストがあるんです。
あさって　　たいへん
I have a difficult exam the day after tomorrow.

Following these steps and allowing your listener to respond is considered polite speech in Japanese.

練習
れんしゅう

A. Work with a partner. Think of a fun event. Then initiate a conversation with some small talk and invite your partner to the event by introducing your topic as shown in the examples above.

B. Work with a new partner, who will pretend to be your Japanese instructor. Think of some requests that you can make. Role-play a situation where you approach the instructor, introduce a topic, and make a request. Then switch roles.

漢字
<ruby>かんじ</ruby>

Creating inflectional endings with okurigana

Okurigana are the **hiragana** that follow verbs and adjectives written in **kanji**. For example, the きい in 大きい and the く in 行く are **okurigana**. One of the main functions of **okurigana** is to indicate inflectional endings of verbs and adjectives, as shown below.

う - verbs:	行<u>く</u>、 行<u>かない</u>、 行<u>きます</u>、 行<u>って</u>
	買<u>う</u>、 買<u>わない</u>、 買<u>います</u>、 買<u>って</u>
る - verbs:	見<u>る</u>、 見<u>ない</u>、 見<u>ます</u>、 見<u>て</u>
	寝<u>る</u>、 寝<u>ない</u>、 寝<u>ます</u>、 寝<u>て</u>
い - adjectives:	古<u>い</u>、 古<u>くない</u>、 古<u>かったです</u>
	安<u>い</u>、 安<u>くない</u>、 安<u>かったです</u>
な - adjectives:	大変<u>な</u>、 大変<u>じゃない</u>、 大変<u>でした</u>

Cases in which **okurigana** are used for more than just the final verb and adjective endings need to be learned individually.

食<u>べる</u>、 食<u>べない</u>、 食<u>べます</u>、 食<u>べて</u>
大<u>きい</u>、 大<u>きくない</u>、 大<u>きかったです</u>
新<u>しい</u>、 新<u>しくない</u>、 新<u>しかったです</u>

(All い -adjectives ending in しい follow this pattern.)

好<u>きな</u>、 好<u>きじゃない</u>、 好<u>きでした</u>

All of the **kanji** presented in this chapter are used in verbs with **okurigana**.

行 行	to go い(く)　コウ	ノ　ノ　彳　彳　行　行
		来年日本に行きます。 <ruby>らいねん</ruby>　　　　<ruby>い</ruby>

来 来	to come, coming く(る)　ライ	一　一　一　一　平　来　来　来　来
		いつアメリカに来ますか。　来週は来ない。 　　　　　　　<ruby>き</ruby>　　　<ruby>らいしゅう</ruby>　<ruby>こ</ruby>

帰 帰	to return, to go home かえ(る)　キ	ﾉ　リ　リ　リﾖ　リﾖ　リﾖ　リﾖ　リ帚　帰　帰
		たいてい七時にうちに帰ります。 　　　　　　　　　　<ruby>かえ</ruby>

食 食	to eat た(べる)　ショク	ノ　へ　へ　今　今　今　食　食　食
		あさごはんを食べてください。　学食 　　　　　　　<ruby>た</ruby>　　　　　　<ruby>がくしょく</ruby>

Kanji		Meaning / Readings	Stroke order	Example
飲	飲	to drink の(む)　イン	𠂉 今 今 食 食 食 飲 飲 飲	ビールを二本飲みました。 の
見	見	to look at, to watch み(る)　ケン	丨 冂 冂 月 目 貝 見	えいがを見に行きませんか。 み　い
聞	聞	to listen, to ask, inquire き(く)　ブン	冂 尸 門 門 門 門 聞 聞 聞	インターネットでラジオを聞く　　新聞 き　　　　　　　　しんぶん
読	読	to read よ(む)　ドク	丶 言 言 計 計 計 読 読 読	本を読むのが好きです。 よ
書	書	to write, writing か(く)　ショ	𠃌 ⊐ ヨ ヨ 聿 聿 書 書 書	てがみをあまり書きません。 か
話	話	to talk, to speak はな(す)　ワ	丶 言 言 訂 訂 訂 訂 話 話	友達と日本語で話すのが好きです。 だち　　　　　　はな
出	出	to come out, to leave, to mail, to turn in で(る)・で(かける)・だ(す)　シュッ	丶 丨 屮 出 出	出かけます。 で
会	会	to meet, to see あ(う)　カイ	丿 𠆢 𠆢 会 会 会	人と会って、カフェで話をします。 あ　　　　　　　　はなし
買	買	to buy か(う)　バイ	丶 冂 罒 罒 罒 買 買 買	買い物が好きです。 か　もの
起	起	to get up お(きる)　キ	十 土 キ キ 走 走 起 起 起	毎朝六時に起きます。 あさ　　　　お
寝	寝	to go to bed, to lie down ね(る)　シン	丶 宀 宀 宀 宀 宀 寝 寝 寝	十二時ごろ寝ます。 ね
作	作	to make つく(る)　サク	丿 亻 亻 作 作 作 作	ばんごはんはカレーを作りましょう。 つく

| 入 | 入 | to enter
はい(る)・い(れる)　ニュウ | ノ　入 | | | | | はこに入れます。　店に入ります。
い　　　　　　　はい |

読めるようになった漢字
かんじ

行く　銀行　旅行　来る　来週　来年　帰る　食べる　食べ物　食事
　　　ぎんこう　りょこう　　　　　　　　　　　　　　　　もの　しょくじ

和食　洋食　定食　食品　飲む　飲み物　見る　聞く　新聞　読む
わしょく　ようしょく　ていしょく　しょくひん　　　　もの　　　　　　しんぶん

書く　図書館　教科書　辞書　話す　電話　出る　出かける　会う
　　　としょかん　きょうかしょ　じしょ　　　　でんわ

学生会館　会話　買う　買い物　起きる　寝る　作る　入る
かいかん　かいわ　　　　もの

押し入れ　中華
お　　い　　ちゅうか

練習
れんしゅう

1. 昨日、日本食のレストランで、ビールをすこし飲んで、ばんごはんを
　食べました。

2. カフェでフランス人の友達と日本語で話しました。
　　　　　　　　　　　だち

3. 先週インド人の友達が来たので、カレーを作って、インドの
　　　　　　　　だち
　おんがくを聞きました。

4. 新宿に出かけて、買いものをしました。そして、友達と会って、
　しんじゅく　　　　　　　　　　　　　　　　　　　　だち
　えいがを見に行きました。

5. （私の一日）私は毎日六時半に起きて、新聞を読みます。八時に
　大学に行って、たいてい五時ごろ帰ります。よるはテレビを見て、
　メールを書いて、十時ごろおふろに入ります。たいてい十一時に
　寝ます。

読む練習
れんしゅう

上手な読み方
じょうず　　かた

Understanding Japanese e-mail formats

The format of Japanese e-mail programs for the PC is very similar to their counterparts in English, except that all of the English words are written in Japanese. However, Roman letters in parentheses such as (F) and (E) remain part of the menu commands, which will give you some clue as to what a menu is about. For example, (F) often represents File option and (E) usually stands for Editing options. So you can guess the contents of some of the fields using your knowledge of English e-mail.

練習
れんしゅう

Look at the e-mail screen above and try to guess the meaning of the following words.

挿入 (そうにゅう)
書式 (しょしき)
メッセージ
ツール
送信者 (そうしんしゃ)
宛先 (あてさき)
件名 (けんめい)

E - メールが来ました

ファイル(F)　編集(E)　書式(O)　送受信(S)　ヘルプ(H)

送信者： 大木　高子　takako@westside.ac.jp
宛先： Sara Jones sjones@hotmail.com
Cc：
件名： パーティのこと

サラさん、

こんにちは。高子です。

来週の木曜日に山本さんの誕生日パーティがあるんですが、よかったら来ませんか。６時から、ぎんざのマルスというフランス料理のレストランでします。会費は一人５０００円です。

カードを買いましたから、あとで何か書いてくれませんか。

じゃあ、おへんじまっています。

読んだ後で Comprehension

A. しつもんに日本語でこたえて下さい。

1. このメールはだれが書きましたか。
2. このメールはだれに書きましたか。
3. どうしてメールを書きましたか。
4. だれのパーティがありますか。
5. パーティはいつどこでありますか。
6. 一人 (per person) いくらかかりますか。

B. Imagine that you are the recipient of this e-mail and write a response.

総合練習
そうごうれんしゅう

Your instructor will give you a card with a day of the week written on it to indicate which day you have off from class. On the card, write in Japanese an activity you'd like to do with someone. Your instructor will then divide the class into two groups. Everyone in the first group must find someone in the second group with a matching card and extend an invitation to do the activity. Together, negotiate the details, such as where to go, what time to meet, and where. Remember to use the expressions and strategies you have learned in this chapter to introduce a topic and extend an invitation.

Example: You are free on: 水曜日

Activity: えいがを見る

ロールプレイ

1. You are with a friend at a Japanese department store and want to have lunch. You go up to the eighth floor, where there are a variety of restaurants (めいてんがい). Discuss your options (和食、洋食、中華りょうり わしょく   ようしょく   ちゅうか etc.) and decide where to eat.

2. You have gone out to eat with your friend. Place your orders and find out how long they will take. If any one of the dishes require more than 15 minutes to prepare, order something else.

Chapter 10

第十課
だいか

私の家族
か ぞく
My family

Objectives	Describing people, addressing family members
Vocabulary	Kinship, parts of the body, physical appearance, personality, verbs of resultant states, age, number of people, and order in a family
Dialogue	私の家族は五人家族です。*There are five people in my family.* か ぞく　ご にん か ぞく
Japanese Culture	The Japanese family
Grammar	I. Stating the order within a family using 番 (目) め
	II. Describing a resultant state using verb て- form + いる
	III. Describing physical appearance and skills using ～は ～が
	IV. Describing people and things using nouns and modifying clauses
	V. Expressing opinions using ～とおもう
Listening	Using one's background knowledge about a person
Communication	Being modest about yourself and your family
Kanji	**Kanji** derived from pictures; **kanji** for kinship terms and parts of the body 男 女 目 口 耳 足 手 父 母 姉 兄 妹 弟 家 族 両 親 子
Reading	Creating charts and figures

単語
たん

Nouns

あし	足	leg, foot
あたま	頭	head, あたまがいい smart, intelligent
あに	兄	older brother (the speaker's)
あね	姉	older sister (the speaker's)
いもうと	妹	younger sister (the speaker's)
いもうとさん	妹さん	younger sister (someone else's)
おかあさん	お母さん	mother (someone else's)
おくさん	奥さん	wife (someone else's)
おこさん	お子さん	child (someone else's)
おじいさん	お祖父さん	grandfather (someone else's)
おとうさん	お父さん	father (someone else's)
おとうと	弟	younger brother (the speaker's)
おとうとさん	弟さん	younger brother (someone else's)
おとこ	男	male, おとこの人 man
おにいさん	お兄さん	older brother (someone else's)
おねえさん	お姉さん	older sister (someone else's)
おばあさん	お祖母さん	grandmother (someone else's)
おんな	女	female, おんなの人 woman
かいしゃいん	会社員	businessperson
かお	顔	face
かぞく	家族	family, speaker's family
かみ	髪	hair
きょうだい	兄弟	sibling(s)
くち	口	mouth
けっこん	結婚	marriage, 〜とけっこんする to marry 〜, けっこんしている to be married

こ	子	child, おとこのこ boy, おんなのこ girl
ごかぞく	ご家族	family (someone else's)
ごきょうだい	ご兄弟	siblings (someone else's)
ごしゅじん	ご主人	husband (someone else's)
こども	子供	child
しゅじん	主人	husband (the speaker's)
せ	背	back (part of the body), height (of a person)
そふ	祖父	grandfather (the speaker's)
そぼ	祖母	grandmother (the speaker's)
ちち	父	father (the speaker's)
つま	妻	wife (the speaker's)
て	手	hand
とし	年	age　としうえ elder, older　としした younger
はな	鼻	nose
はは	母	mother (the speaker's)
ひとりっこ	一人っ子	only child
ブロンド		blond
まんなか	真ん中	center, middle, middle child
みみ	耳	ear
め	目	eye
めがね	眼鏡	glasses

う -verbs

かぶる		to put on (a hat or cap)
すむ	住む	to reside, 〜にすんでいる to live in 〜
はく		to put on (skirt, pants, socks, shoes)
ふとる	太る	to gain weight, ふとっている to be fat
わかる	分かる	to understand, 〜がわかる

る -verbs

| かける | | to put on (glasses) |

きる	着る	to put on (sweater, shirt, jacket)
つとめる	勤める	to become employed
		〜につとめている to be employed at, work for
やせる		to lose weight, やせている to be thin

Irregular verbs

| する | | to put on (accessories) |

Auxiliary verbs

| 〜ている | | resultant state |

い -adjectives

あかるい	明るい	cheerful (Chapter 4, bright)
かっこいい		good-looking, cool, neat
かわいい	可愛い	cute, adorable
しかくい	四角い	square
ながい	長い	long
ほそながい	細長い	long/elongated
まるい	丸い	round
みじかい	短い	short (length)

な -adjectives

| じょうず（な） | 上手（な） | good at, skillful |
| しんせつ（な） | 親切（な） | kind |

Question words

| いくつ | | How old 〜? おいくつ (polite form) |

Prefixes

しょう〜	小〜	elementary, 小学生 elementary school student,
		小学校 elementary school
ちゅう〜	中〜	middle, 中学生 middle school student,
		中学校 middle school, junior high school

Suffixes

～さい	～歳／才	～ years old
～にん	～人	～ people
～ばん（め）	～番（目）	～ th (ordinal suffix)
～かた	～方	person (polite form of 人)
		いいかた (nice person)

Expressions

いいえ、そんなことはありません。	No, that's not the case.
いいえ、まだまだです。	No, I still have a long way to go.

単語の練習
たん　　れんしゅう

A. 家族　Kinship terms
かぞく

Japanese has two sets of kinship terms. One is used to refer to one's own family and the other is used to refer to someone else's.

	Your own family member (humble form)	Someone else's family member (polite form)
family	家族 (かぞく)	ご家族 (かぞく)
father	父 (ちち)	お父さん (とう)
mother	母 (はは)	お母さん (かあ)
parents	両親 (りょうしん)	ご両親 (りょうしん)
older brother	兄 (あに)	お兄さん (にい)
older sister	姉 (あね)	お姉さん (ねえ)
younger brother	弟 (おとうと)	弟さん (おとうと)
younger sister	妹 (いもうと)	妹さん (いもうと)
brothers and sisters	兄弟 (きょうだい)	ご兄弟 (きょうだい)
grandfather	祖父 (そふ)	お祖父さん (じい)
grandmother	祖母 (そぼ)	お祖母さん (ばあ)
husband	主人 (しゅじん)	ご主人 (しゅじん)
wife	つま	おくさん
child/children	子供 (こども)	お子さん (こ)

Note that 子供, 兄弟, 家族 and 両親 can be used in general statements.
こども きょうだい かぞく りょうしん

日本の子供はよくあそびます。   *Japanese children play a lot.*
こども

ハワイには日本人の家族がたくさんいます。   *There are many Japanese*
かぞく   *families in Hawaii.*

Activity 1

Look at the family trees. Note that each family member is represented by a letter.
Now, form groups of three. One of you will write the letters A through T in
random order on a piece of paper and read a letter on the list. The other two will
give the kinship term that corresponds to the letter. Remember to say 私の〜 or
山田さんの〜. Whoever calls out the correct term first gets a point. The person
with the most points wins. Take turns reading the letters.

Example: The dealer says *H.* Player 1 says 私の 弟 first. Player 1 gets a point.
おとうと

私の家族   山田さんのご家族
かぞく   かぞく

Supplementary Vocabulary: 親族 (Kinship terms)
しんぞく

	Your own family member (humble form)		Someone else's family member (polite form)	
cousin	いとこ	従兄弟	いとこさん	従兄弟さん
nephew	おい	甥	おいごさん	甥子さん
uncle	おじ	叔父／伯父	おじさん	叔父さん／伯父さん
aunt	おば	叔母／伯母	おばさん	叔母さん／伯母さん
relatives	しんせき	親戚	ごしんせき	ご親戚
niece	めい	姪	めいごさん	姪子さん
grandchild	まご	孫	おまごさん	お孫さん

B. 人   People

あたま
head

目
め
eye

かお
face

耳
みみ
ear

はな
nose

口
くち
mouth

手
て
hand/arm

足
あし
leg

> ### Activity 2
>
> Work with in class. Everyone claps their hands twice and immediately after that, your instructor will say a body part in Japanese. Touch the part he/she says.

> ### Activity 3
>
> "Simon Says." Work with a partner. Using the vocabulary in this chapter, take turns calling out and identifying parts of the body in Japanese.

Supplementary Vocabulary: からだ   The Body

あご	顎	chin
うで	腕	arm
おなか		belly
からだ	体	body
くちびる	唇	lip(s)
くび	首	neck
こし	腰	waist
せなか	背中	back
どう	胴	torso, trunk, body
つめ	爪	nail
のど	咽	throat
は	歯	tooth
ひげ	髭	mustache, beard
ほっぺた		cheek
まつげ	睫	eyelash
まゆげ	眉毛	eyebrow
ゆび	指	finger

C. からだのとくちょう   Physical features

せが高い	tall (height)
せがひくい	short (height)
手がながい	have long reach
足がみじかい	have short legs
かおがまるい	have a round face
かおがほそながい	have a narrow face
かおが四角い	have a square face
目があおい	have blue eyes
口が小さい	have a small mouth
はなが高い	have a big nose
かっこいい	good-looking
かみがくろい	have black hair
ブロンド	blond hair
ふとっている	fat, chubby
やせている	thin

おぼえていますか。

きれい（な）　ちゃいろい　あかい　しろい　みどり

Activity 4

Write your guess for the opposite of each attribute listed below.

1. せがひくい　　　　＿＿＿＿＿＿＿＿＿＿＿＿＿＿
2. ふとっている　　　＿＿＿＿＿＿＿＿＿＿＿＿＿＿
3. かみがくろい　　　＿＿＿＿＿＿＿＿＿＿＿＿＿＿
4. かおが小さい　　　＿＿＿＿＿＿＿＿＿＿＿＿＿＿
5. 足がみじかい　　　＿＿＿＿＿＿＿＿＿＿＿＿＿＿
6. 手がながい　　　　＿＿＿＿＿＿＿＿＿＿＿＿＿＿
7. 口が小さい　　　　＿＿＿＿＿＿＿＿＿＿＿＿＿＿
8. はなが高い　　　　＿＿＿＿＿＿＿＿＿＿＿＿＿＿
9. 耳が大きい　　　　＿＿＿＿＿＿＿＿＿＿＿＿＿＿
10. あたまが小さい　　＿＿＿＿＿＿＿＿＿＿＿＿＿＿

Activity 5

Take a moment to think about your own physical features. Then state as many as you can in sixty seconds.

D. Verbs used with clothing and accessories

シャツを<u>きる</u>	put on a blouse
スカートを<u>はく</u>	put on a skirt
くつを<u>はく</u>	put on shoes
ぼうしを<u>かぶる</u>	put on a hat
めがねを<u>かける</u>	put on glasses
イヤリングを<u>する</u>	put on earrings
うでどけいを<u>する</u>	put on a wristwatch

おぼえていますか。

コート	ジャケット	シャツ	ジーンズ	スーツ
ストッキング	セーター	Ｔシャツ	ドレス	ネクタイ
ネックレス	パンツ／ズボン	ふく	ゆびわ	ベルト

Activity 6

Classify the above articles of clothing and accessories that are used with the following verbs:

Verbs	Articles of clothing and accessories
きる	
はく	
する	

E. せいかくとのうりょく   Personality and ability

親切 (な) しんせつ	kind
あかるい	cheerful
かわいい	cute, adorable
あたまがいい	smart, intelligent
日本語が分かる	understand Japanese
スポーツが<u>上手</u> (な) じょうず	good at sports

おぼえていますか。

やさしい	おもしろい	たのしい	いい	つまらない	むずかしい
さびしい	げんきな	りっぱな	しずかな	にぎやかな	

Activity 7

しつもんに日本語でこたえて下さい。

1. お父さんはどんな人ですか。
2. お母さんはどんな人ですか。
3. どんな人が好きですか。
4. 一番いい友達はどんな人ですか。

Supplementary Vocabulary: せいかく　Personality

うちき（な）	内気（な）	shy, introverted
きがつよい	気が強い	strong-minded
きがながい	気が長い	patient
きがはやい	気が早い	impatient, hasty, rash
きがみじかい	気が短い	short-tempered
きがよわい	気が弱い	weak-minded
くらい	暗い	somber, nerdy
たんき（な）	短気（な）	short-tempered
のんびりしている		easygoing, carefree

F. しごととちい　Work and social status

～と　けっこんする	to get married
～に　すむ	to reside
～に　つとめる	to get a job at
会社員	business person
小学生	elementary school student
中学生	middle school student

おぼえていますか。

しごと　学生　大学生　大学院生　高校　高校生

Activity 8

しつもんに日本語でこたえて下さい。

1. けっこんしたいですか。いつけっこんしたいですか。
2. 今、どこにすんでいますか。
3. どんなところにすみたいですか。
4. 日本の会社につとめたいですか。
5. どんなところにつとめたいですか。
6. ご家族に小学生がいますか。中学生がいますか。高校生がいますか。
7. お父さんは／お母さんはどこかにつとめていますか。

Supplementary Vocabulary: Occupations

いしゃ	医者	medical doctor
エンジニア		engineer
かんごし	看護士	nurse, medical assistant
きょうし	教師	teacher
こうむいん	公務員	government official
サラリーマン		white-collar worker (from the Japanese term "salary man")
じえいぎょう	自営業	self-employed
だいがくきょうじゅ	大学教授	college professor
はいしゃ	歯医者	dentist
べんごし	弁護士	lawyer
マネージャー		manager

G.　としと人数　Age and number of people

	～人 (～ people)	～さい (～ years old)
何	なんにん	（お）いくつ／なんさい
〇		れいさい
一	※　ひとり	※　いっさい
二	※　ふたり	にさい
三	さんにん	さんさい
四	※　よにん	よんさい
五	ごにん	ごさい
六	ろくにん	ろくさい
七	※　しちにん	※　ななさい
八	はちにん	※　はっさい
九	きゅうにん	きゅうさい
十	じゅうにん	※　じゅっさい ※　じっさい
百	ひゃくにん	ひゃくさい
千	せんにん	
一万	いちまんにん	

Note: 四人家族 means *a family of four including yourself.* 兄弟が二人います however, means that you have two brothers and sisters excluding yourself.

Activity 9

Sing a version of this popular counting rhyme in Japanese!

ひ　とりふ　たり　さんにんいるよ　　よにんご　にん　ろくにんいるよ

しち　にん　はち　にん　きゅう　にん　いる　よ　　じゅう　にん　のこ　ども　　た

ちー　　　へーイ!
（右手の掌を振り上げ　回れ右）

Activity 10

Form groups of varying sizes according to the directions your instructor calls out.
Try to join each group as quickly as possible so that you won't be left behind.

Example:　

Activity 11

Write down three numbers on a piece of paper. Your instructor will call out an
age. Cross out a number if it corresponds to what you hear. Whoever crosses out
all the numbers first wins.

Activity 12

しつもんに日本語でこたえて下さい。

1. この大学には学生が何人ぐらいいますか。
2. この大学には先生が何人ぐらいいますか。
3. 日本語の先生は何人いますか。
4. 日本語の学生が何人ぐらいいますか。
5. 今、きょうしつにクラスメートが何人いますか。
6. ご兄弟がいますか。何人いますか。
7. 何人家族ですか。

Activity 13

Work in groups of five or six. Make up a number representing a classmate's age, write it down on a piece of paper, and tape it to the back of someone else in your group. Take turns asking about your ages. Then line up from the "youngest" to the "oldest."

Activity 14

The following table lists typical age ranges for children and young adults who attend school or day care in Japan. The information about Japan is provided. Fill in the information about your country and compare the two.

Example: 日本では　れいさいから三さいの子供がたくじしょに行きます。

アメリカでは／も、〜さいから〜さいの子供がたくじしょ
に行きます。

	日本	
たくじしょ (nursery)	0 さいから　　3 さい	（　　）さいから　（　　）さい
ほいくえん (day care center)	0 さいから　　6 さい	（　　）さいから　（　　）さい
ようちえん (kindergarten)	3 さいから　　6 さい	（　　）さいから　（　　）さい
小学校 しょう	6 さいから　　12 さい	（　　）さいから　（　　）さい
中学校	12 さいから　　15 さい	（　　）さいから　（　　）さい
高校	15 さいから　　18 さい	（　　）さいから　（　　）さい
大学	18 さいから　　22 さい	（　　）さいから　（　　）さい

Activity 15

しつもんに日本語でこたえて下さい。

1. お父さんはおいくつですか。
2. お母さんはおいくつですか。
3. 〜さんは、今何さいですか。

ダイアローグ

はじめに　　**Warm Up**

A. しつもんに日本語でこたえて下さい。

1. 何人家族ですか。
2. お兄さんがいますか。お姉さんはどうですか。
3. 妹さんがいますか。弟さんはどうですか。

私の家族は五人家族です。　*There are five people in my family*

上田さんの友達の川口さんがあそびに来ています。上田さんと
川口さんは、上田さんのへやにいます。

川口：　あ、あのしゃしん、上田さんのご家族ですか。

上田：　ええ、そうです。これが父で、これが母です。

川口：　かっこいいお父さんですね。それにとてもきれいなお母さん
　　　　ですね。

上田：　ああ、でも、父も母も四十九さいなんですよ。

川口：　そうですか。とてもわかく見えますけど。

上田：　父はくるまの会社につとめていて、母は英語の先生なんです。

川口：　そうなんですか。じゃあ、この帽子をかぶっている男の子は
　　　　弟さんですか。

上田：　ええ、そうです。なまえはデービッドで、今、小学三年生です。

川口：　かわいいですね。じゃあ、この人はお姉さんですか。

上田：　いいえ、それは妹のパムです。パムはまだ十七さいなんですが、
　　　　パムのほうが私よりせが高くて大きいから、よく年上に
　　　　見られるんですよ。

川口：　そうなんですか。

DIALOGUE PHRASE NOTES

- It is rude to refer to people using これ, それ, あれ, but you can do so when you talk about a person in a photograph or drawing because they are not actual human beings.
- わかく見えます means *look young*. わかい means *young*, and it is usually used for teenagers or adults but not for children.
- 年上に見られる means *to be mistaken for an older (sibling)*.

ダイアローグの後で

1. Look at the picture of a family tree on page 138. Using it as an example, draw Ms. Ueda's family tree.
2. Based on the dialogue, complete the following paragraphs using appropriate words and phrases.

上田さんの家族は五人家族です。お父さんとお母さんと＿＿＿＿＿＿＿＿
と＿＿＿＿＿＿＿＿＿がいます。上田さんの＿＿＿＿＿＿＿＿＿は四十九さいで、
くるまの会社につとめています。上田さんの＿＿＿＿＿＿＿＿＿＿＿＿も
四十九さいです。＿＿＿＿＿＿＿＿＿＿＿は　英語の先生です。上田さんの
＿＿＿＿＿＿＿＿＿のなまえは＿＿＿＿＿＿＿で、高校生ですが、せがとても高
いです。上田さんの＿＿＿＿＿＿＿＿＿のなまえはデービッドで、小学校の
＿＿＿＿＿＿＿＿＿です。とてもかわいいです。

日本の文化
ぶん か

日本の家族
か ぞく

According to a 2005 government survey, about 60 percent of Japanese families fall under the category of nuclear families, and 27 percent are single-person households. Only 13 percent are three-generation families.

Since the end of World War II, the number of children in a Japanese family has decreased substantially. The average for 2006 was only 1.3 children per household, compared with 2.0 for the same year in the U.S. and France. Some reasons for the decline are economic; others are social, such as later marriages and a lack of support for women to continue to work after having children. According to 2005 statistics from the Japanese

Ministry of Health, Labor and Welfare, the average age for a man to marry was 29.8 years. For a woman, it was 28 years. Nearly 90 percent of women work before getting married, but only 65 percent continue to work after marriage. After a child is born, the percentage plummets to a scant 23 percent. Traditionally, wives are expected to take care of the house and children, even

while holding down a job. Despite recent efforts to update traditional roles, the current support infrastructure, such as day-care facilities and baby-sitting services, is still inadequate to allow many women to work.

Conversely, Japanese husbands are expected to support the family financially, and they tend to work long hours. For example, according to a 2004 ILO survey, over 28 percent of Japanese workers logged more than 50 hours a week, which is much higher than the European average of 1.4 to 15.5 percent or the U.S. average of 20 percent. Although some companies offer parental leave for men in addition to maternity leave, new fathers rarely take advantage of this benefit, as it would lower their income significantly, could inconvenience their co-workers, and might even affect chances for promotion.

Despite these pressures, the divorce rate in Japan is extremely low. Until 1972, it was less than one percent. After climbing to a high of 2.3 percent in 2002, the rate as of 2005 declined to under 2.1 percent.

ウチとソト **Insiders and Outsiders**

The Japanese rarely praise members of their own family when they are talking to someone outside the family. They are very conscious of the distinction between "in-groups" (ウチ) and "out-groups" (ソト). It is very important to be polite to those who are not in one's in-group, and praising members of your own family—the primary in-group—is considered impolite. Accordingly, you may often hear a Japanese man complaining that his wife is not good at cooking when in fact she is an excellent cook, or you may hear a woman say that her husband is impractical and inept at household matters. Similarly, boasting about yourself is considered socially inappropriate.

Within one's own family, お父さん, お母さん, お兄さん, お姉さん

and similar terms are used to address senior members. First names are used only to address younger members. A daughter or son would address their mother as お母さん, お母ちゃん (ちゃん being the more familiar form), or ママ (Mom); older brothers as お兄さん or お兄ちゃん; and a younger sister named Michiko as みち子ちゃん. Senior members tend to refer to themselves using their kinship terms when talking to a younger member of the family. Instead of using their first names with their children, parents usually call each other お父さん／パパ (Dad, Papa), and お母さん／ママ.

In addition, Japanese forms of address do not distinguish between biological parents and stepparents. Using the Japanese equivalent of terms such a stepfather and stepmother can imply a distant relationship between the stepchild and the stepparents, so both biological and stepparents are addressed in the same way.

文法
ぶんぽう

I. Stating the order within a family using 番（目）
め

Expressing the order within a family using 番（目）
め

番（目）converts cardinal numbers into ordinal numbers, and it is used to describe
め

one's standing in his/her family such as:

一番上	oldest (*literally,* the first from the top, the highest)
上から二番目 め	second oldest (*literally,* the second from the top, the second highest)
まん中	right in the middle
下から二番目 め	second youngest (*literally,* the second from the bottom, the second lowest)
一番下	youngest (*literally,* the first from the bottom, the lowest)

The pronunciation of numbers preceding ばん（め）is regular and follows the same
pattern as the pronunciaiton for counter 〜まい.

	〜番（目）(ordinal, 〜 th)		
		め	
何	なんばん（め）	六	ろくばん（め）
一	いちばん（め）	七	ななばん（め）
二	にばん（め）	八	はちばん（め）
三	さんばん（め）	九	きゅうばん（め）
四	よんばん（め）	十	じゅうばん（め）
五	ごばん（め）	百	ひゃくばん（め）

家本： 私の家族は五人家族です。
いえもと　　　　　か ぞく　　にん か ぞく
> *My family consists of five members.*

小山： そうですか。ゆみ子さんは何番目ですか。
こ やま　　　　　　　　　　　　　こ　　　　め
> *Where do you come in the family* (literally, *what order are you), Yumiko?*

家本： 一番上です。
いえもと
> *I am the oldest.*

小山： そうですか。じゃあ、一番下はだれですか。
こ やま
> *I see. Who is the youngest?*

家本： 妹のみかです。みかは、今十五さいです。
いえもと　いもうと
> *My younger sister Mika. She is fifteen years old now.*

Note that the term for *only child* is 一人っ子.
ひとり　こ

話してみましょう

Activity 1

Take turns asking your classmates how many people are in their family. Then compare the results. Whose family is the largest or the smallest? Discuss the advantages and disadvantages of coming from large and small families.

Example:　A:　〜さんのご家族は何人家族ですか。

　　　　　　B:　四人家族です。

　　　　　or　母と私と妹が二人います。

Activity 2

Work in groups of four or five. Take turns asking your classmates how many siblings they have and their order in the family. Then compare the results. Who is the oldest or the youngest?

Example:　A:〜さんはご兄弟がいますか。

　　　　　　B:はい、二人います。

　　　　　　A:〜さんは何番目ですか。

　　　　　　B:私は一番上です。

Activity 3

Work with a partner. Take turns describing your family members in terms of name and age, and complete the table with your partner's descriptions.

Example:　私の家族は三人家族です。兄が一人います。なまえは
　　　　　　トーマスで、二十五さいです。父のなまえはジョンです。今、
　　　　　　五十二さいです。

ご兄弟	おなまえ	〜さい

ご両親	おなまえ	〜さい

II. Describing a resultant state using verb て - form ＋ いる

The verb て - form + いる describes a state (of being) that is the result of a past action. For example, めがねをかける means to put on (glasses), and めがねをかけている means as the result of putting glasses on, the person is now wearing them.

めがねをかける　　　　　　　　めがねをかけている

Similarly, けっこんする means to get married whereas けっこんしている means to be married.

Action: けっこんする (get married)	Resultant state: けっこんしている (is married)

Action: ふとる (gain weight)	Resultant state: ふとっている (is fat)

山本：　田中さんはめがねをかけていますか。
　　　　Does Ms. Tanaka wear glasses?

チョイ：　いいえ、めがねはかけていませんが、イヤリングを
　　　　　　していますよ。
　　　　　No, she doesn't, but she wears earrings.

NOTES

- The past form 〜ていました describes a (resultant) state at a specified time in the past.
  たくさん食べて、ふとりました。
  I ate a lot and gained some weight.

  私は小さい時、ふとっていました。
  　　　　とき
  I was fat (chubby) when I was small.

● 〜ている can be used to describe a person who wears something habitually.

田中さんはよくジーンズをはいています。
Mr. Tanaka often wears jeans.

山田さんはいつもネクタイをしています。
Mr. Yamada always wears a tie.

● The verbs すむ and つとめる are usually used with 〜ている. The particle に is used to indicate a location, company or organization.

私はとうきょうにすんでいます。
I live in Tokyo.

山田さんはアパートにすんでいました。
Mr. Yamada used to live (was living) in an apartment.

ぼくはじょうとう大学につとめています。
I work for Joto University.

話してみましょう

Activity 1

Describe what each person is wearing, using the verb ている form.

Example:　さとうさんはスーツをきています。そして、ネクタイを
　　　　　しています。

さとうさん　　山本さん　　こんどうさん　　木村さん
　　　　　　　　　　　　　　　　　　　　　むら

Activity 2

Work with a partner. Pick a classmate and have your partner guess who it is by asking what the person is wearing, using はい／いいえ questions.

Example:　A:　その人は帽子をかぶっていますか。
　　　　　　　　　ぼう　し
　　　　　B:　いいえ、かぶっていません。
　　　　　A:　その人はスカートをはいていますか。
　　　　　B:　はい、はいています。

Activity 3

Your instructor will ask the class to walk around the classroom observing what the others are wearing. When he/she tells the class to stop, each student will stand back to back with the person who is closest and describe his/her clothing. How many items can you describe correctly?

Example:　〜さんはあかいセーターをきていて、ジーンズを
　　　　　はいています。

Activity 4

Work with a series of partners. Take turns finding out where your classmates have lived up until now. Note that 〜 の時 means *at the time of* 〜 or *when I*
とき
was / am 〜 .

Example:　A:　〜さんは、今、どこにすんでいますか。

　　　　　B:　ハリソン・ホールにすんでいます。

　　　　　A:　ずっと *(for a long time)* そこにすんでいますか。

　　　　　B:　いいえ、高校の時は 両親の家にすんでいました。
　　　　　　　　　　　　　りょうしん　うち

　　　　　A:　そうですか。ご両親はどこにすんでいますか。
　　　　　　　　　　　りょうしん

　　　　　B:　バーリントンにすんでいます。

III. Describing physical appearance and skills using ～は ～が

The ～は ～が construction is used to describe the characteristics of a variety of things such as people, places, and other physical objects. This chapter introduces how ～は ～が can be used to describe people's physical appearance, skills, and personality.

A. Describing physical appearance

The construction "person は body parts が adjectives" is used to describe a person's physical appearance.

山下さんは	はなが	高いです。	*Mr. Yamashita has a large nose.*
リーさんは	目が	ちゃいろいです。	*Ms. Li has brown eyes.*
上田さんは	かみが	ながいです。	*Ms. Ueda has long hair.*
キムさんは	かおが	四角いです。	*Mr. Kim has a square face.*

本木： あの人はせが高くて、足がながくて、かっこいいですね。
That person over there is good-looking. She is very tall, and has long legs.

山口： ああ、あの人はモデルですからね。
Oh yes, that's because she is a model.

B. Describing skills and ability

～は ～が can be used with other personal traits such as personality and ability. In the following example, いい and 上手 are adjectives and 分かる is an intransitive verb. Unlike a transitive verb, an intransitive verb does not take a direct object or the direct object marker を. Instead, the particle が is used.

チョイさんは	あたまが	いいです。	*Mr. Choi is smart.*
石田さんは	テニスが	上手です。	*Mr. Ishida is good at tennis.*
山田さんは	フランス語が	分かります。	*Mr. Yamada understands French.*

田口： あの人は日本語が分かりそうですね。
That person over there appears to understand Japanese.

三上： ええ、でも、あまり上手じゃなさそうです。
Yes, but it does not look like he is good at it.

NOTES

- Like 好き and きらい, the plain present affirmative form of a verb + の can be used with 上手.

  アリソンさんはうたをうたうのが上手です。
  Allison is good at singing songs.

話してみましょう

Activity 1

Using the following chart listing various physical characteristics, describe the persons named.

Example: 私

私はせがひくいですが、手と足はながいです。

かおがまるくて、かみがながいです。そして、目もはなも口も小さいです。

からだ	大きい　小さい					
せ	高い　ひくい					
手	ながい　みじかい　きれい					
足	ながい　みじかい　きれい					
かお	まるい　四角い　ほそながい　たまごがた (egg-shaped)					
かみ	ながい　みじかい　くろい　あかい　ちゃいろい　ブロンド					
目	大きい　小さい　あおい　ちゃいろい　くろい　みどり					
はな	大きい　小さい　高い　ひくい					
口	大きい　小さい					

1. 私
2. 父
3. 母
4. 一番いい友達
5. Other members of your family

Activity 2

Work with a partner. Pick one face in the drawing and describe it to your partner. Have him/her identify the face by the number on the illustration.

Example:　この人はかおがまるいです。
　　　　　この人は目が大きいです。

Activity 3

Work with a partner. Draw a person's face. Then, describe the face to your partner. Your partner will try to draw the face according to your description. Compare the two faces.

Example:　この人はかおがほそながくて、目が小さいです。

（め）

Activity 4

Work with the class. Find out which languages your classmates can speak, who knows the most languages, and any other talents they may have. List the information you obtain in the chart.

Example:

1. A：　〜さんはどんなことばが分かりますか。

   B：　かんこく語が分かります。

   A：　そうですか。かっこいいですね。

2. A：　〜さんはどんなことをするのが上手ですか。

（じょうず）

   B：　かんじを書くのが上手です。

（じょうず）

   A：　そうですか。いいですね。私はかんじを書くのが上手じゃないんです。

（じょうず）

クラスメートの　なまえ	ことば　(language)	上手なこと（じょうず）

IV. Describing people and things using nouns and modifying clauses

A noun may be modified by another noun, an adjective, or a modifying clause. The modifier always comes before the noun. In a noun-modifying clause, the verb must be in the plain form. The negative forms of adjectives and the copula verb must be in the plain form as well.

ブロンドの	かみ	*blond hair*
日本のくるまじゃない	くるま	*a car that is not a Japanese car*
きれいな	家 うち	*a clean house*
きれいじゃない	家 うち	*a house that is not clean*
りょうりが上手な じょうず	人	*a person who is good at cooking*
そうじが上手じゃない じょうず	人	*a person who is not good at cleaning*
小さい	くつ	*small shoes*
小さくない	くつ	*not so small shoes*
かみがながい	人	*a person who has long hair*
かみがながくない	人	*a person who does not have long hair*
英語が分かる えい	人	*a person who understands English*
新聞をよく読む	人	*a person who often reads the paper*
けっこんしている	人	*a person who is married*
けっこんしていない	人	*a person who is not married*

ホン： 田中さんのお母さんはどの方ですか。
かあ　　　　かた
Which (person) is Mr. Tanaka's mother?

木村： あそこにいる人ですよ。せが高くてかみがながい人です。
むら
(She is) the person over there—the tall person with long hair.

ホン： ああ、 あの方ですか。とてもきれいな方ですね。
かた　　　　　　　　　　　　かた
Oh, that person? She's very beautiful, isn't she?

木村： 本当にそうですね。
むら　ほんとう
Indeed.

話してみましょう

Activity 1

Look at the drawing and answer the questions using a noun-modifying clause wherever appropriate.

さとうさん　　山本さん　　こんどうさん　　木村さん
むら

Example: さとうさんはどの人ですか。

スーツをきている人です。

1. さとうさんはどの人ですか。

2. こんどうさんはどの人ですか。

3. 木村<ruby>村<rt>むら</rt></ruby>さんはどの人ですか。

4. 山本さんはどの人ですか。

5. ジーンズをはいている人は木村さんですか。

6. ネックレスをしている人はどの人<ruby>むら<rt></rt></ruby>ですか。

7. めがねをかけている人はこんどうさんですか。

Activity 2

Fruit Basket. Work with the class. Arrange your chairs in a circle so that everybody except for one person has a place to sit. That person stands in the center of the circle and calls out a physical descriptor. Anyone who fits the description must move to another seat. Whoever is left without a seat then takes the center and calls out another descriptor.

Example: The person in the center says: めがねをかけている人
People who wear glasses must move to another seat.

Activity 3

Take turns finding out how many in the class fall into the categories listed in the chart. Then check your answers with each other. Note that 私のデータでは means *according to my data.*

Example: 1. A: 〜さんはけっこんしていますか。

B: いいえ、していません。

2. A: けっこんしている人は何人いますか。

B: 二人います。／ぜんぜんいません。

A: そうですか。私のデータでは一人です。

	はい	いいえ
けっこんしている		
お姉さんがいる		
妹 さんがいる		
一人っ子だ		
りょうにすんでいる		
スポーツが上手だ		
スペイン語が分かる		

Activity 4

Work in groups of four. One student thinks of a classmate but does not say his/her name. The other members ask questions about his/her characteristics to find out who he or she is. They can ask up to six questions. Anyone who guesses the answer after the first question receives six points. After the second question, he/she receives five points. If no one is able to get the correct answer after the sixth question, the person who has chosen the name receives six points. The person who earns the most points wins.

Example:　A:　女の人ですか。
　　　　　　　おんな
　　　　　　B:　はい。
　　　　　　C:　かみがながい人ですか。
　　　　　　B:　いいえ、かみはみじかいです。
　　　　　　D:　じゃあ、ブロンドですか。
　　　　　　B:　いいえ、ちゃいろいかみの人です。

Activity 5

With a partner, take turns asking what kind of person appeals to each of you. Have your partner describe the person in terms of physical appearance, personality, interests, and ability, using noun modifiers. Take turns. Take detailed notes on the information that your partner gives you.

Example:　A:　スミスさんはどんな人が好きですか。
　　　　　　B:　せが高くて、かみがブロンドの人が好きです。
　　　　　　　　そして、やきゅうが上手な人がいいですね。
　　　　　　　　　　　　　　　じょうず
　　　　　　　　おいしいものを食べるのが好きな人もいいですね。
　　　　　　A:　せいかくは (personality) どんな人がいいですか。
　　　　　　B:　そうですね。あたまがよくて、やさしい人がいいですね。

Activity 6

You are a dating consultant looking for the best match for your partner from the previous activity. Take turns asking about your classmates' favorite types. They will give information about their previous partner's preferences.

Example:　A:　どの人のデータ (data) がありますか。
　　　　　　B:　スミスさんのデータがあります。
　　　　　　A:　スミスさんはどんな人が好きなんですか。
　　　　　　B:　せが高くて、かみがブロンドの人が好きです。
　　　　　　　　そして、あたまがよくて、やさしい人が好きです。

V. Expressing opinions using 〜とおもう

〜とおもう expresses the speaker's opinion about things or events. The subject of おもう, the speaker, is often deleted. The clause before とおもう must end in the plain form.

Copula verb			
ご主人は	会社員だと	おもいます。	I think her husband is a businessman.
ご主人は	日本人じゃないと	おもいます。	I think her husband is not Japanese./ I don't think her husband is Japanese.
い - adjectives			
上田さんは	かわいいと	おもいます。	I think Ms. Ueda is cute.
このテストは	むずかしくないと	おもいます。	I think this test isn't difficult./ I don't think this test is difficult.
な - adjectives			
先生は	とても親切だと	おもいます。	I think my teacher is very kind.
弟は	さしみが好きじゃないと	おもいます。	I think my younger brother doesn't like sashimi./ I don't think my younger brother likes sashimi.
Verbs			
友田さんは	けっこんしていると	おもいます。	I think Mr. Tomoda is married.
山田さんは	明日来ないと	おもいます。	I think Ms. Yamada is not coming tomorrow./I don't think Mr. Yamada is coming tomorrow.

The speaker can be specified for emphasis to clarify the context.

私はアリソンさんは明日来るとおもいます。
I think Allison is coming tomorrow.

私はこの本はいいとおもいます。
I think this book is good.

When the subject of the main clause is someone other than the speaker, the form おもっている is used instead of おもう.

トムさんは足がながいと　<u>おもっています</u>。

<u>Tom thinks</u> he has long legs.

トムさんは足がながいと　<u>おもいます</u>。

<u>I think</u> Tom has long legs.

木村さんはふとっていないと　<u>おもっています</u>。

<u>Mr. Kimura doesn't think</u> he is fat.

木村さんはふとっていないと　<u>おもいます</u>。

<u>I don't think</u> Mr. Kimura is fat.

ペギーさんは和食は高いと　<u>おもっています</u>。

<u>Peggy thinks</u> Japanese food is expensive.

私も和食は高いと　<u>おもいます</u>。

<u>I also think</u> that Japanese food is expensive.

To form an information question, use a question word and end the sentence and か. To ask for a general impression or opinion, use 〜をどうおもいますか, what do you think of 〜.

高田：　このクラスでだれが一番せが高いとおもいますか。
　　　　Who do you think is the tallest in this class?

キム：　イアンさんが一番高いとおもいます。
　　　　I think Ian is the tallest.

さとう：　どの新聞がいいとおもいますか。
　　　　　Which newspaper do you think is good?

もり：　朝日新聞がいいとおもいます。
　　　　I think Asahi Newspaper is good.

ゆみ：　田中さんをどうおもいますか。
　　　　What do you think of Ms. Tanaka?

トム：　ちょっとしずかだけど、いい人だとおもいます。
　　　　I think she's rather quiet but a nice person.

石田：　この本、どうおもいますか。
　　　　What do you think of this book?

大川：　むずかしくて、あまりおもしろくないとおもいます。
　　　　I think it's difficult and not very interesting.

石田：　ぼくもそうおもうんですよ。
　　　　I think so, too!

NOTES

- The plain form とおもう cannot express the speaker's wish or intention without an additional suffix attached to the verb. You will learn how to express intentions in Nakama 2.

  日本に行くとおもいます。
  I think (someone, in context) is going to Japan.

  キムさんは日本に行くとおもいます。
  I think Ms. Kim is going to Japan.

- 〜たいとおもいます to express a wish is often used instead of たいです in conversation, because it sounds softer and more polite.

  私は日本に行きたいとおもいます。
  I would like to go to Japan.

  キムさんは日本に行きたいとおもっています。
  Ms. Kim would like to go to Japan.

話してみましょう

Activity 1

A friend of Mr. Ishida is thinking about applying to your school. Answer his/her questions using plain form +とおもう.

Example: 〜さんの大学は大きいですか。

   いいえ、あまり大きくないとおもいます。

1. 〜さんの大学には日本人がたくさんいますか。
2. 大学があるまちには日本のレストランがありますか。
3. 大学のじゅぎょうは大変ですか。
   <ruby>大変<rt>たいへん</rt></ruby>
4. どんな大学ですか。
5. 大学があるまちはどんなまちですか。

Activity 2

Work with a partner. Look at the following pictures and guess what kind of people they show.

Example:　A:　この男の子はどんな子だとおもいますか。
　　　　　　　　　おとこ　こ　　　　　　　　　こ

　　　　　　B:　げんきな子だとおもいます。
　　　　　　　　　　　　こ

　　　　　or　げんきそうな子だとおもいます。
　　　　　　　　　　　　　　　こ

1　　　　　　　　2　　　　　　　　3

4　　　　5　　　　6　　　　7

Activity 3

Work with a partner. Think about the strengths (ちょうしょ) of each one of your classmates and write down your opinions using ～とおもう.

Example:　A:　スミスさんのちょうしょは何だとおもいますか。
　　　　　　B:　そうですね。スミスさんはかんじがとても上手だ
　　　　　　　　　　　　　　　　　　　　　　　　　　　　　じょうず
　　　　　　　　とおもいますね。
　　　　　　A:　ええ、私もそうおもいます。

Activity 4

Work with the class. Think of a famous person or cartoon figure, and write out a description, including your opinion of the person or character. After reading your description to the class, have them guess who it is.

Example:　A:　この人は高いところが好きだとおもいます。そして、
　　　　　　　　スポーツが上手だとおもいます。あかいマスク (mask) を
　　　　　　　　　　　　じょうず
　　　　　　　　していて、あかくてあおいスーツをきています。
　　　　　　B:　スパイダーマンですか。
　　　　　　A:　はい、そうです。

聞く練習
れんしゅう

上手な聞き方
じょうず　　かた

Using one's background knowledge about a person

Besides visual cues, background knowledge about a person such as his/her age, sex, and occupation can help you to understand better what is being said or asked.

練習
れんしゅう

Look at the photo below. Then listen to each question and circle the letter of the answer you think is correct. The questions will be repeated.

1.　a　　　　b　　　　c　　　　d

2.　a　　　　b　　　　c　　　　d

3.　a　　　　b　　　　c　　　　d

私たちの家族　Our family
かぞく

テープを聞いて、家系図 (family tree) を書いて下さい。そして、「はい」
　　　　　　　かけいず
か「いいえ」にまるをつけて下さい。(Then circle はい if a statement below
is true or いいえ if it is false.)

1. 中山あやかさんの家族
　　　　　　　　　　かぞく

家系図
かけいず

```
┌─────────────────────────────────────┐
│                                     │
│                                     │
│                                     │
│                                     │
│                                     │
│                                     │
└─────────────────────────────────────┘
```

はい　　　いいえ　　　　中山さんはお兄さんがいます。
　　　　　　　　　　　　　　　　　にい
はい　　　いいえ　　　　中山さんの弟さんはせが高いです。
　　　　　　　　　　　　　　　　　おとうと
はい　　　いいえ　　　　中山さんのお母さんはびょういんに
　　　　　　　　　　　　　　　　　かあ
　　　　　　　　　　　　つとめています。
はい　　　いいえ　　　　中山さんのお姉さんは大学生です。
　　　　　　　　　　　　　　　　　ねえ

2. 吉田けい子さんの家族
　　よしだ　こ　　　　かぞく

家系図
かけいず

```
┌─────────────────────────────────────┐
│                                     │
│                                     │
│                                     │
│                                     │
│                                     │
└─────────────────────────────────────┘
```

はい　　　いいえ　　　　けい子さんは兄弟がいます。
　　　　　　　　　　　　　　　こ　　きょうだい
はい　　　いいえ　　　　けい子さんのお祖父さんは七十五さいです。
　　　　　　　　　　　　　　　こ　　じい
はい　　　いいえ　　　　けい子さんのお父さんはふとっています。
　　　　　　　　　　　　　　　こ　　　とう

聞き上手 話し上手
じょうず　　　 じょうず

上手な話し方
じょうず　　 かた

Being modest about yourself and your family

As noted earlier in this chapter, the Japanese generally refrain from praising or bragging about their families. Again, if someone praises a family member, they usually deny the compliment or try to steer the conversation in another direction. For example, when someone says to a Japanese person that his mother is beautiful, he will say something like *No, she isn't.* or *Do you really think so?* This is not an attempt to milk the compliment, and may seem strange to people from cultures where praise is received in a straightforward manner. In Japan, however, it is best to observe this protocol. If you receive a compliment in Japanese, try using the following standard replies:

いいえ、そんなことありません／ないですよ。
No, that isn't the case.

いいえ、まだまだです。
No, I still have a long way to go.

練習
れんしゅう

Work with a partner. Respond to each compliment appropriately. Ask your instructor to check your manner of delivery.

1. ～さんは日本語が上手ですね。
　　　　　　　　　　 じょうず
2. ～さんのお母さんはとてもきれいな方ですね。
　　　　　　か あ　　　　　　　　　　　 かた
3. ～さんはあたまがいいですね。
4. ～さんは足がながくて、かっこいいですね。
　　　　　 あし
5. ～さんのおじいさんはりっぱな方ですね。
　　　　　　　　　　　　　　　　 かた
6. ～さんの家は大きくてりっぱですね。
　　　　　 うち

漢字
かんじ

Kanji derived from pictures (3)

(Rice field and an strong arm came to mean *male*.)

(女, "female" with breasts came to mean *mother*.)

(An axe and a strong hand → *man* → *father*)

(A person with a big head → *bigger brother*)

(A pig under a roof. → *house*. Pigs were important livestock.)

男 男	male, man	一 冂 冂 用 田 男 男		
	おとこ ダン	女の人と男の子がいます。 おんな　　おとこ こ		
女 女	female, woman	〈 女 女 女 女 女		
	おんな ジョ	山本さんは帽子をかぶった女の人です。 　　　　ぼうし　　　　　おんな		
目 目	eye	一 冂 冃 目 目		
	め モク	目がわるいです。　上から二番目です。 め　　　　　　　　　　　　　　　め		
口 口	mouth	一 冂 口		
	くち・ぐち コウ	口が小さいです。　　川口 くち　　　　　　　　　ぐち		

国 ごく
町 まち
写真 sashin
言 ながい

耳足 手 父 母

| 耳 | 耳 | ear
みみ　ジ | 一　丁　下　下　�　耳　耳　耳　耳　耳
私は耳があまりよくありません。
<small>みみ</small> |

| 足 | 足 | foot, leg
あし　ソク | 丨　ロ　口　尸　足　足　足
ジョンはせが高くて、足がながいです。
<small>あし</small> |

| 手 | 手 | hand
て　シュ | ノ　二　三　手　手　手
手がきれいですね。　テニスが上手です。
<small>て</small>　　　　　　　<small>じょうず</small> |

| 父 | 父 | father
ちち・とう | ノ　ハ　ク　父
父のなまえはジョンです。　お父さん
<small>ちち</small>　　　　　　　<small>とう</small> |

| 母 | 母 | mother
はは　・　かあ | く　ム　Ц　母　母　母　母　母
母のしごとは高校の先生です。　お母さん
<small>はは</small>　　　　　　　<small>かあ</small> |

| 姉 | 姉 | older sister
あね・ねえ　シ | く　女　女　女　女`　姉　姉　姉　姉　姉
姉は私より三さい上です。　お姉さん
<small>あね</small>　　　　　　　<small>ねえ</small> |

| 兄 | 兄 | older brother
あに・にい　ケイ　キョウ | 丨　ロ　口　尸　兄
兄が一人います。　お兄さん　兄弟
<small>あに</small>　<small>ひとり</small>　　　<small>にい</small>　<small>きょうだい</small> |

| 妹 | 妹 | younger sister
いもうと　マイ | く　女　女　女　女　妖　妹　妹
妹はいません。
<small>いもうと</small> |

| 弟 | 弟 | younger brother
おとうと　ダイ | 丶　丷　丛　兰　弟　弟　弟　弟
弟は四時にアルバイトに行きます。　兄弟
<small>おとうと</small>　　　　　　　　<small>きょうだい</small> |

| 家 | 家 | house
いえ・（うち）　カ | 丶　宀　宀　宁　宇　宇　家　家　家　家
父は七時ごろ家に帰ります。　新しい家
<small>ちち</small>　　　　<small>うち</small>　　　　　<small>いえ</small> |

| 族 | 族 | tribe
ゾク | 亠　方　方　方　扩　扩　斿　族　族　族
私の家は四人家族です。
<small>うち</small>　<small>にんかぞく</small> |

| 両 | 両 | both
リョウ | 一　冂　両　両　両　両
両親はニューヨークにすんでいます。
<small>りょうしん</small> |

| 親 | 親 | parent
おや　　シン | 両親はアメリカが好きです。　親切な人
りょうしん　　　　　　　　　　しんせつ |

子

| 子 | 子 | child
こ　　シ | 男の子が三人います。　母のなまえは「よし子」です。
おとこ　こ　さんにん　　　　はは　　　　　　　　こ |

読めるようになった漢字
かん　じ

男の人　男の子　女の人　女の子　目　〜番目　口　耳　足　手
　　　　　　　　　　　　　　　　　　　め

上手　父　お父さん　お祖父さん　祖父　母　お母さん　お祖母さん
じょうず　　　　　　　　じ　い　　　そ　ふ　　　　　　　　　　　ば　あ

祖母　姉　お姉さん　兄　お兄さん　妹　弟　兄弟　家族　私の家
そ　ば

両親　親切　子供　お子さん　一人っ子　帽子　いい方　一人　二人
　　　しんせつ　ども　　　　　　ひとり　こ　ぼうし　　　かた　　ひとり　　ふたり

三人　何人　ご主人　会社員　真ん中　四角い　小学生　小学校
にん　　にん　しゅじん　かいしゃいん　ま　なか　しかく　　しょう　　　しょう

日本人のなまえ：家本　小山　田口　山口　三上　吉田
　　　　　　　　　　いえもと　こやま　たぐち　やまぐち　みかみ　よしだ

練習
れんしゅう

Read the following sentences written in a mixture of **hiragana, katakana,** and **kanji.**

1. 父は先週の月曜日に川につりに行きました。弟はえいがを見に行きました。私と母は家にいました。

2. 中山さんのお父さんはせが高くて、目が大きいですね。

3. 妹は小学生で、弟は中学一年生です。

4. 高田：「ご兄弟は何人いますか。」

   川口：「三人います。」

5. めがねをかけている女の人が山田さんのお姉さんで、スーツをきている人がお兄さんです。

6. 山本：「川口さんは何人家族ですか。」

   川口：「両親と弟の四人家族です。」

7. 田中さんのお子さんは目が大きくて、口が小さくて、とてもかわいいですよ。

8. 本田さんの親子はよくにていますね。(にている = *resemble*)

9. A:「あの男の人は手と足がながくて、スタイルがいいですねえ。」

    B:「そうですか。あの人は、私の兄なんですよ。」

10. 父はこのごろ耳がとおくなりました。(耳がとおい = *hard of hearing*)

読む練習
れんしゅう

Creating charts and figures

People usually read with a specific purpose in mind, such as to gather specific information or to skim for the main ideas. When reading an assignment, you might jot down only the information that you need. If you organize your notes systematically, you may understand the assignment better and retain the information longer. One way to organize material is to make charts or tables.

練習
れんしゅう

A. Review the dialogue on pages 394-95 and complete the following table.

上田さんの家族	なまえ	しごと	Physical appearance

B. Now read the following passage. It was written by Ms. Ueda, but some of the information is different from what the dialogue contains on pages 394-95. Circle the discrepancies or write them on a separate piece of paper. Don't worry about any unfamiliar words or **kanji** you may encounter.

上田さんの家族

私の家族は五人家族です。父は四十五歳の会社員で、銀行に勤めています。父は目があまりよくないので、たいていめがねをかけています。ゴルフが大好きで、日曜日にはよくゴルフに行きます。母は四十三歳で、大学で英語を教えています。背があまり高くないので、たいていハイヒールの靴を履いています。母はとても優しくて明るい人です。弟のトムは十三歳で、中学生です。背が高くて、目がとても大きいです。スポーツは好きなんですが、勉強がきらいなので、こまります。そして、妹の名前はパムです。パムは背が高くありませんが、とてもかわいいです。頭がよくて、勉強もスポーツも大好きな高校一年生です。

C. Underline all the sentence and clause connectors in the above passage.

D. Describe your ideal family (りそうの家族). Use the following questions as cues.

1. 何人家族がいいですか。

2. 子供は何人がいいですか。

3. どんな子供がいいですか。

4. お父さんとお母さんはどんな人ですか。

5. どんなところにすみたいですか。

6. お父さんは／お母さんはどんなしごとをしますか。

総合練習
そうごうれんしゅう

Work with the class. Your instructor will give you a card similar to the one in the example below. It will have a description of two people, A and B. You are A. You are looking for B. Go around the class and ask your classmates questions using B's description. After you find B, check his/her identity card against yours.

Example:

Features	A Your identity	B The person you are looking for
かみ	ながい	くろい
目	あおい	みどり
すんでいる	とうきょう	ニューヨーク
上手	日本語	英語 えい

A: その人はかみがくろいですか。

B: はい、くろいです。

A: その人は目があおいですか。

B: いいえ、あおくありません。

A: そうですか。それじゃあ、また。

(Go to a different person.)

ロールプレイ

1. You are introducing a member of your family to your instructor. Your instructor will praise the person. Respond appropriately.
2. You are looking for a new roommate. Tell your partner what type of person you are looking for and ask for help.

Chapter 11

第
<ruby>十<rt>だい</rt></ruby>
一
<ruby>課<rt>か</rt></ruby>

きせつと天気
Seasons and Weather
<ruby>天気<rt>てんき</rt></ruby>

Objectives	Describing the weather
Vocabulary	Weather, climate, temperature, compass directions
Dialogue	寒いですね。 *It's cold.* さむ
Japanese Culture	Japan's climate
Grammar	I. Expressing ongoing and repeated actions using the て- form of verbs + いる
	II. Plain past forms and casual speech
	III. Describing characteristics of places, objects, and time using 〜は 〜が
	IV. Expressing manner of action or outcome of a change using the adverbial forms of adjectives and noun + に
	V. Expressing uncertainty using 〜でしょう, 〜かもしれない, and 〜かな
Listening	Understanding the organization of prepared speech
Communication	Expressing agreement and solidarity using ね and も
Kanji	Component shapes of **kanji** 1—Introduction 天 気 雨 雪 風 晴 温 度 東 西 南 北 寒 暑 多 少 冷
Reading	Getting used to vertical writing

単語
たん

Nouns

あき	秋	fall, autumn
あめ	雨	rain
かぜ	風	wind
きおん	気温	air temperature
きこう	気候	climate
きせつ	季節	season
きた	北	north
きょねん	去年	last year
くも	雲	cloud
くもり	曇り	cloudy
けさ	今朝	this morning
ことし	今年	this year
さいきん	最近	recent, recently
たいふう	台風	typhoon
つゆ	梅雨	rainy season
てんき	天気	weather
てんきよほう	天気予報	weather forecast
なつ	夏	summer
なんせい	南西	southwest
なんとう	南東	southeast
にし	西	west
にわかあめ	にわか雨	shower (rain)
のち	後	after
はる	春	spring
はれ	晴れ	sunny weather
ひがし	東	east

ふゆ	冬	winter
ほう	方	direction
ほくせい	北西	northwest
ほくとう	北東	northeast
マイナス		minus
みなみ	南	south
ゆうがた	夕方	evening
ゆき	雪	snow
よる	夜	night

う -verbs

あがる	上がる	to rise, to go up
くもる	曇る	to become cloudy
さがる	下がる	to fall, to go down
しる	知る	to come to know　しっている to know しらない　don't know
つづく	続く	to continue
ふく	吹く	to blow
ふる	降る	to fall

る -verbs

はれる	晴れる	to become sunny

い -adjectives

あたたかい	暖かい／温かい	warm　暖かい (air temperature)　温かい (other objects such as water, food, heart, etc.)
あつい	暑い／熱い	hot　暑い (air temperature) 熱い (other objects such as water, food, heart, etc.)
さむい	寒い	cold
すずしい	涼しい	cool
つよい	強い	strong
はやい	早い	early

よわい	弱い	weak
むしあつい	蒸し暑い	humid
わるい	悪い	bad

な -adjectives

きゅう（な）	急（な）	sudden, きゅうに suddenly
いや（な）	嫌（な）	unpleasant, yuck

Suffixes

～ど	～度	degree, temperature
～がつ	～月	month

Expressions

～のち～		after, あめのちはれ sunny after rain
ほんとう（に）/ ほんと（に）	本当（に）	truly, really, indeed
		ほんと（に） is more conversational than ほんとう（に）

単語の練習
たん　　れんしゅう

A. 天気予報　　Weather forecast
てんきよほう

晴れ
は
sunny

くもり
cloudy

雨
あめ
rain, rainy

雪
ゆき
snow, snowy

晴れのちくもり
は
sunny then cloudy

くもり時々雨
ときどきあめ
cloudy with occasional rain

Activity 1

Write the readings of the following weather symbols.

1	**2**	**3**	**4**
5	**6**	**7**	**8**
9	**10**	**11**	**12**
13	**14**	**15**	**16**
17	**18**	**19**	**20**
21	**22**	**23**	**24**

Supplementary Vocabulary: Nouns to indicate regions

たいへいようがわ	太平洋側	Pacific ocean side (east side) of Japan
にほんかいがわ	日本海側	Sea of Japan side (west side) of Japan
さんがくぶ	山岳部	mountain area (in any country)
にしかいがん	西海岸	West coast region (USA)
ちゅうせいぶ	中西部	Midwest region (USA)
なんぶ	南部	South region (USA)
なんせいぶ	南西部	Southwest region (USA)
ひがしかいがん	東海岸	East coast region (USA)

Supplementary Vocabulary: Nouns expressing weather

おんど	温度	temperature
かし	華氏	Fahrenheit
きあつ	気圧	air pressure
こうすいりょう	降水量	amount of precipitation
さいこうきおん	最高気温	highest temperature
さいていきおん	最低気温	lowest temperature
しつど	湿度	humidity
せっし	摂氏	Celsius
てんきず	天気図	weather map

B. 天気　Weather
てん き

暑い あつ	hot	晴れる は	to clear up
寒い さむ	cold	くもる	to become cloudy
すずしい	cool	風がふく かぜ	wind blows
あたたかい	warm	雨がふる あめ	to rain
むし暑い あつ	humid	雪がふる ゆき	to snow
天気がいい てん き	good weather	にわか雨がふる あめ	sudden showers
天気がわるい てん き	bad weather	台風が来る たいふう	a typhoon comes
くもが多い おお	cloudy	梅雨になる つ ゆ	the rainy season comes
風がつよい かぜ	strong winds	大雨がふる おおあめ	heavy rain falls
風がよわい かぜ	mild winds	大雪がつづく おおゆき	heavy snow continues

おぼえていますか。

多い おお	少ない すく	少し すこ	冷たい つめ

Notes

- Both 寒い and 冷たい mean *cold*, but 寒い refers to cold temperatures, as in 今日は寒い (*It is cold today*). On the other hand, 冷たい refers to objects that are cold, e.g., 水が冷たい, 風が冷たい.

- 梅雨 refers to the rainy season particular to Japan. It usually starts in early June and ends in mid-July.

Supplementary Vocabulary: 天気の言葉（てんき ことば）

あらし	嵐	storm
あられ		hail
いなびかり	稲光り	lightening
かみなり	雷	thunder
きり	霧	fog
こうずい	洪水	flood
こさめ	小雨	light rain
たつまき	竜巻	tornado
つなみ	津波	tidal wave, tsunami
どしゃぶり	どしゃ降り	downpour
ハリケーン		hurricane
ひでり	日照り	drought
ふぶき	吹雪	snowstorm
みぞれ		sleet
ゆうだち	夕立ち	evening shower

Activity 2

Imagine that the following chart shows tomorrow's weather in some of the major cities in the world. そして、下のしつもんに日本語でこたえて下さい。

Example: 明日、カイロの天気はいいですか。
ええ、明日は晴れますよ。

まち	東京（とうきょう）	ニューヨーク	モスクワ	シドニー	カイロ
天気（てんき）					
気温（きおん）	61.9/48.9° F 16.6/9.4° C	49.8/39.0° F 9.9/3.9° C	34.7/26° F 1.5/-3.3° C	75.2/58.1° F 24/14.5° C	98.2/60.3° F 36.8/15.7° C
風（かぜ）	SSW 5 mph	NE 20 mph	NE 15 mph	SE 10 mph	E 3 mph

1. 明日、モスクワは天気がいいですか。
2. 東京は明日晴れますか。ニューヨークはどうですか。
3. 明日、どこで雨がふりますか。
4. シドニーとカイロとどちらの方が暑いですか。
5. ニューヨークと東京とどちらの方が寒いですか。
6. どこがあたたかいですか。
7. どこがすずしいですか。
8. 明日、東京は風がつよいですか。ニューヨークはどうですか。
9. カイロは風がつよいですか。よわいですか。
10. モスクワではつよい風がふきますか。

Activity 3

Select the item that describes recent weather in your area.

1. 寒い／すずしい／あたたかい／暑い／むし暑い
2. 天気がいい／天気がよくない
3. いやな天気がつづく／いやな天気がつづかない
4. 雨がぜんぜんふらない／雨があまりふらない／雨が時々ふる
5. 雨がよくふる／毎日雨がふる
6. にわか雨が多い／にわか雨が少ない
7. 雪がぜんぜんふらない／雪があまりふらない／雪が時々ふる
8. 雪がよくふる／毎日雪がふる
9. 大雪になる／大雪にはならない
10. よく風がふく／あまり風がふかない
11. 風がつよい／風がよわい

Activity 4

Describe the recent weather in your area using your answers from Activity 2. It is unnecessary to use all of your responses, but make sure that your description is cohesive.

Example: このへんは、さいきん天気がよくて、むし暑いです。雨は ぜんぜんふりません。そして、風もあまりありません。

C. きせつ Seasons

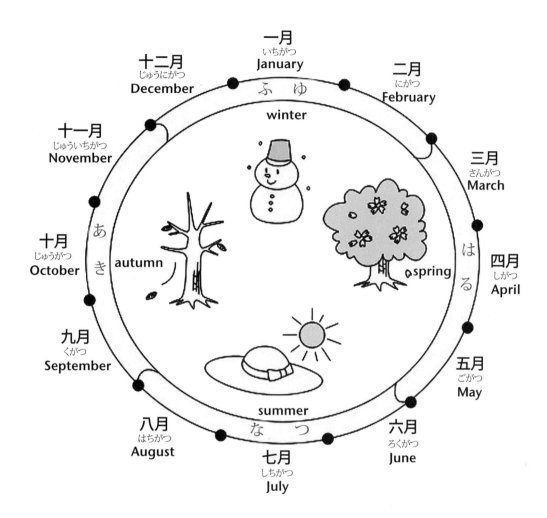

Activity 5

Complete the following statements about Japanese seasons.

Example: 日本では、六月に梅雨がはじまって、七月におわります。

1. 日本では＿＿＿＿＿＿にはるがはじまって、＿＿＿＿＿＿におわります。

2. 日本では＿＿＿＿＿＿になつがはじまって、＿＿＿＿＿＿におわります。

3. 日本では＿＿＿＿＿＿にあきがはじまって、＿＿＿＿＿＿におわります。

4. 日本では＿＿＿＿＿＿にふゆがはじまって、＿＿＿＿＿＿におわります。

5. このへんは＿＿＿＿＿＿にはるがはじまって、＿＿＿＿＿におわります。

6. このへんは＿＿＿＿＿＿になつがはじまって、＿＿＿＿＿におわります。

7. このへんは＿＿＿＿＿＿にあきがはじまって、＿＿＿＿＿におわります。

8. このへんは＿＿＿＿＿＿にふゆがはじまって、＿＿＿＿＿におわります。

Activity 6

For each season, write five things that describe where you live.

Example: このへんは　ふゆに雪がたくさんふります。
_{ゆき}

はる	
なつ	
あき	
ふゆ	

D. 気温　**Air temperature**
_{き　おん}

気温が下がる　　air temperature falls
_{き おん　さ}

気温が上がる　　air temperature rises
_{き おん　あ}

何度	なんど
－1度	マイナスいちど
0度	れいど
1度	いちど
2度	にど
3度	さんど
4度	よんど
5度	ごど
6度	ろくど
7度	なゝど、しちど
8度	はちど
9度	きゅうど、くど
10度	じゅうど

Japan uses the Celsius scale for temperature, and the metric system for other measurements. The following table shows equivalent temperatures for Celsius and Fahrenheit.

せっし (Celsius)	かし (Fahrenheit)
0℃	32℉
10℃	50℉
20℃	68℉
30℃	86℉
40℃	104℉

Activity 7

しつもんに日本語でこたえて下さい。

1. 今の気温は何度ぐらいですか。

2. 今朝の気温は何度ぐらいでしたか。

3. あさから何度ぐらい気温が上がりましたか。

4. 今晩、何度ぐらいまで気温が下がるとおもいますか。

5. 寒い日は何度ぐらいまで気温が下がりますか。

6. 暑い日は何度ぐらいまで気温が上がりますか。

7. せっし (Celsius) 0 度はかし (Fahrenheit) 何度ですか。

8. かし (Fahrenheit) 0 度はせっし (Celsius) 何度ですか。

Activity 8

Using your answers from Activity 5, give a short description of your town in its four seasons.

E.　方角　Compass directions

〜の方　toward 〜

北の方　to the north

Activity 9

Write the appropriate direction word in each blank.

Example:　オーストラリアは日本の＿＿南＿＿にあります。
　　　　　　　　　　　　　　　　みなみ

1. カナダはアメリカの＿＿＿＿＿＿にあります。

2. 日本はかんこくの＿＿＿＿＿＿にあります。

3. メキシコはアメリカの＿＿＿＿＿＿にあります。

4. フランスはスペインの＿＿＿＿＿＿にあって、ドイツの＿＿＿＿にあります。

5. 中国はかんこくの＿＿＿＿＿＿にあります。
　　ごく

Activity 10

えを見て、しつもんに日本語でこたえて下さい。

1. このまちの北の方には何がありますか。南の方には何がありますか。
　　　　　　きた　ほう　　　　　　　　みなみ　ほう

2. 学校はどこにありますか。

3. 学校の東の方に何がありますか。西の方に何がありますか。
　　　　ひがし　ほう　　　　　　　　にし　ほう

4. こうえんはどこにありますか。

5. 図書館はどこにありますか。
　　と　かん

6. えきの北には何がありますか。
　　　　きた

ダイアローグ

はじめに

しつもんに日本語でこたえて下さい。

1. 今日のお天気はどうですか。

2. ふゆの寒い日の気温は何度ぐらいですか。

3. ふゆのあたたかい日の気温は何度ぐらいですか。

寒いですね。 *It's cold.*

鈴木道子さんは石田さんにきょうしつで会いました。

鈴木： あ、石田さん。おはよう。

石田： あ。鈴木さん。寒いね。

鈴木： ええ、今日は風がつよいから。

石田： たしかに、今晩は雪かな。

鈴木： そうね。くもってるから、ふるかもしれないね。

石田： でも、まだ十一月だよ。

鈴木： そうね。今年はいつもよりはやく寒くなりそうね。ざんねんだけど。

石田： いやだなあ。

先生がきょうしつにいらっしゃいました。
(*The professor has come to the classroom.*)

鈴木： あ、先生。おはようございます。

先生： あ、鈴木さん、石田くん。おはよう。寒いね。

石田： ええ、それにくもっていますね。

先生： そうだね。雪がふりそうな天気だね。

鈴木さんはまどのそとを見ました。雪がふっています。

鈴木： あ、先生、雪がふっていますよ。

先生： 本当だね。みんな風邪ひかないように気をつけるんだよ。

DIALOGUE PHRASE NOTES

- たしかに means *certainly*.
- いつもより means ～ *than usual*.
- いやだなあ means *unpleasant*.
- みんな風邪ひかないように気をつける means *Everybody, take care so that you don't catch cold*. 風邪 means *cold*. Note that the **kanji** is different from 風, *wind*.

ダイアローグの後で

1. The following manga frames are scrambled—they are not in the order described in the dialogue. Read the dialogue and unscramble the frames by writing their correct order in the box located in the upper right corner of each frame.

2. しつもんに日本語でこたえて下さい。

1. 今、何月ですか。時間はいつごろですか。

2. 今どんな天気ですか。
   てんき

3. 天気予報によると今日の天気はどうですか。
   てんき よほう   てんき

4. 石田さんはふゆが好きだとおもいますか。
   いし

3. Work with a partner. The following conversation is a simplified version of the dialogue. You meet each other in the classroom in the morning. Decide on a season and the weather, and complete the following conversation using appropriate phrases.

A: あ、_____さん。おはよう。

B: あ、_____さん。今日は_____ね。

A: ええ、_____ね。

B: _____かもしれないね。

A: そうだね。

日本の文化
ぶん か

気候   Climate
き こう

Japan lies in the temperate zone and has four distinct seasons. The climate is predominantly temperate, but it varies from subarctic to subtropical because

the country extends so far from north to south. Southeast winds blow across Japan from the Pacific in summer, bringing humidity to the Pacific side of the country (たいへいようがわ). The northwest winds blow across from continental Asia in winter, bringing sunny and dry weather to the Pacific Ocean side but heavy snow to the Japan Sea side (日本海側).
に ほんかいがわ

Between June and July, there is a period of predominantly rainy weather, called tsuyu (梅雨), in all parts of
つ ゆ
Japan except 北海道 . Typhoons (台風) occur most frequently from August
ほっかいどう   たいふう
through October.

Japan's climate is further divided into six principal zones because of its geographical features. On the northernmost island, 北海道 ,
ほっかいどう
spring and summer are short, and it is cool with little rain throughout the year. Although precipitation is not heavy, winters are severe with deep snow banks from November through April.

The Japan Sea side of the northern main island, such as 北陸 region and the east coast of
ほくりく
東北 , experiences heavy snowfall in the winter,
とうほく
but it is cooler than the Pacific Ocean side in

the summer. The Pacific Ocean side, such as 関東, 東海, and きんき, is
generally sunny, cold, and dry in winter, but the summer is hot and humid.

Temperatures in the central highland region, 中部, range widely between
summer and winter, and between day and night, although precipitation is
generally light.

Southwestern regions such as 四国, 中国 and 九州 tend to have mild
weather throughout the year, especially in せとないかい (Seto-Inland Ocean)
area, the area surrounded by these three regions.

The southern islands, おきなわ and いしがきじま, have a subtropical
climate and are known for high temperatures and precipitation throughout the
year. The rainfall is heavy during 梅雨, and 台風 are very common.

文法
ぶんぽう

> ## I. Expressing ongoing and repeated actions using the て - form of verbs + いる

In Chapter 10, you learned the verb て- form + いる, which expresses resultant state. This interpretation is common for verbs used to express wearing clothes or accessories.

田中さんはめがねをかけている。　*Mr. Tanaka has glasses on.*

田中さんはネクタイをしている。　*Mr. Tanaka has a tie on.*

Also, if the verb indicates an instantaneous change of state or transfer (e.g., 行く, けっこんする), then the verb て-form + いる will express a resultant state.

田中さんはけっこんしている。　*Mr. Tanaka is married.*

田中さんは高校につとめている。　*Mr. Tanaka works for a high school.*

田中さんは学校に行っている。　*Mr. Tanaka has gone to school and is there.*

田中さんはここに来ている。　*Mr. Tanaka has come here and is here now.*

田中さんはその人をしっている。　*Mr. Tanaka knows that person.*

今日は晴れている。
　は　　　　　　　　　　　　*It is sunny today.*

くもっている。　*It is cloudy.*

In the above example, the て-form of the verb しる (*to come to know*) , しっている (*to know*), expresses the result of one's discovery of information.

In addition to this usage, the verb て-form + いる can express ongoing action and repeated action. This chapter introduces these two usages of the verb て-form + いる.

A. Ongoing action

The verb て-form + いる can express ongoing action when used with certain action verbs. The verbs indicate activities that take place for a period of time. For example, the act of eating, drinking, raining, etc., can take place for a long time.

石田さんはおすしを<u>食べている</u>。
　いし　　　　　　　　　　　　　　　*Mr. Ishida is eating sushi.*

石田さんはおちゃを<u>飲んでいる</u>。
　いし　　　　　　　　　　　　　　　*Mr. Ishida is drinking tea.*

石田さんは本を<u>読んでいる</u>。
　いし　　　　　　　　　　　　　　　*Mr. Ishida is reading.*

雨が<u>ふっている</u>。
あめ　　　　　　　　　　*It is raining.*

風が<u>ふいている</u>。
かぜ　　　　　　　　　　*The wind is blowing.*

The verb て-form + いる is often contracted to the verb て-form + る in conversation (in both formal and casual styles).

ドレスを<u>きています</u>。	ドレスを<u>きてます</u>。
けっこん<u>しています</u>。	けっこん<u>してます</u>。
しゅくだいを<u>しています</u>。	しゅくだいを<u>してます</u>。
さとみさんを<u>しっている</u>。	さとみさん、<u>しってる</u>。
ごはんを<u>食べている</u>。	ごはん、<u>食べてる</u>。

い dropped in casual

かおり：何、しているの。　　　*What are you doing?*

まさお：しゅくだい、してるんだ。　*I am doing homework.*

リン：どうしたんですか。
What's wrong?

鈴木：雨がふっているんですが、かさがないんです。
すず　あめ
It's raining but I don't have an umbrella.

リン：そうですか。じゃあ、私のくるまで行きませんか。
I see. Well, why don't we take my car?

鈴木：いいんですか。
すず
Is that okay?

リン：ええ、どうぞ。
Yeah, sure.

B. Repeated action

Many verbs, including action verbs or change-of-state verbs, can be used to express habitual action with the verb て-form + いる.

鈴木さんはよくあかいジャケットをきている。
すず
Ms. Suzuki often wears a red jacket.

田中さんは時々バスでびょういんへ行っています。
　　　　ときどき
Mr. Tanaka sometimes goes to hospital by bus.

毎週土曜日にテニスをしています。
I play tennis every Saturday.

健一：　ブラウンさんはよくサングラスをかけているけど、どうして？
けん
Ms. Brown often wears sunglasses, but why?

道子：　サラは目がよわいからよ。
みち
Because Sarah has weak eyes.

健一：　そうなんだ。
けん
Oh, I see.

話してみましょう

Activity 1

Make sentences from the following expressions using the verb て -form + いる.
Then say whether the sentence indicates an ongoing action or a resultant state.

Example: ごはんを食べる

ごはんを食べています。   Ongoing action

1. 雪がふる

ゆき
2. くもる
3. 気温が下がる
き おん さ
4. 本を読む
5. 家に帰る
6. つよい風がふく
かぜ
7. 手紙を書く
て がみ
8. 気温が三十度まで上がる。
き おん ど あ

Activity 2

Work with a partner. Your partner will write a name for each person in the
picture. Ask your partner who is who by describing what the people are doing.

Example: A: コーヒーを飲んでいる人はだれですか。

B: スミスさんです。

Activity 3

Work with a partner. Think of five actions, then act them out and have your partner guess what you are doing by asking questions using 〜ている.

Example: You act as though you are drinking coffee.

A: おちゃを飲んでいるんですか。

B: いいえ。

A: コーヒーを飲んでいるんですか。

B: はい。

Activity 4

Work as a class. Ask your classmates what kinds of things they practiced or learned recently for fun or personal improvement.

Example: A: さいきん、どんなことをよくしていますか。

B: テニスをよくしています。

なまえ	さいきんよくしていること

II.   Plain past forms and casual speech

The plain forms are used in a variety of structures and contexts in Japanese. For example, they are used in the structure ので (*because*) in Chapter 7, 〜んです in Chapter 8, から and けど in Chapter 9, and とおもう and noun modification in Chapter 10. So far the plain present forms have been used with these structures, but the plain past forms can be used with all of them. This chapter introduces the plain past forms of verbs and adjectives. It also introduces another usage of the plain form, namely casual and self-directed speech.

Plain past forms

1. Plain past affirmative form

The plain past affirmative form of the verbs is formed by taking the て-form of a verb and replacing it with た (or だ).

Verb types	Dictionary form	て -form	Plain past affirmative form
う -verb	つづく (to continue)	つづい<u>て</u>	つづい<u>た</u> (continued)
	読む (to read)	読ん<u>で</u>	読ん<u>だ</u> (read)
る -verb	晴れる (to become sunny)	晴れ<u>て</u>	晴れ<u>た</u> (became sunny)
	食べる (to eat)	食べ<u>て</u>	食べ<u>た</u> (ate)
Irregular verb	する (to do)	し<u>て</u>	し<u>た</u> (did)
	来る (to come)	来<u>て</u>	来<u>た</u> (came)

The plain past affirmative form of い-adjectives is formed by deleting です from the polite past affirmative form.

Dictionary form	Polite past affirmative form	Plain past affirmative form
暑い (hot)	暑<u>かったです</u>	暑<u>かった</u> (was hot)
いい (good)	<u>よかったです</u>	<u>よかった</u> (was good)

The plain past affirmative form of な-adjective and the copula verb is formed by adding った to the plain present affirmative form.

	Dictionary form	Polite past affirmative form	Plain past affirmative form
な -adjective	好き (like)	好きだ	好き<u>だった</u> (liked)
	元気 (healthy)	元気だ	元気<u>だった</u> (was healthy)
Noun + copula	台風 (typhoon)	台風だ	台風<u>だった</u> (was typhoon)
	くも (cloud)	くもだ	くも<u>だった</u> (was a cloud)

2. Plain past negative form

The plain past negative form of the verbs and adjectives of all types is formed by replacing the plain present negative ending ない with なかった.

	Dictionary form	Plain present negative form	Plain past negative form
う-verb	行く (to go)	行か<u>ない</u>	行か<u>なかった</u> (didn't go)
	飲む (to drink)	飲ま<u>ない</u>	飲ま<u>なかった</u> (didn't drink)
	ある (to exist)	<u>ない</u>	<u>なかった</u> (didn't exist)
る-verb	起きる (to get up)	起き<u>ない</u>	起き<u>なかった</u> (didn't get up)
	食べる (to eat)	食べ<u>ない</u>	食べ<u>なかった</u> (didn't eat)
Irregular verb	する (to do)	し<u>ない</u>	し<u>なかった</u> (didn't do)
	来る (to come)	来<u>ない</u>	来<u>なかった</u> (didn't come)
い-adjective	わるい (bad)	わるく<u>ない</u>	わるく<u>なかった</u> (wasn't bad)
	いい (good)	よく<u>ない</u>	よく<u>なかった</u> (wasn't good)
な-adjective	元気 (healthy)	元気じゃ<u>ない</u>	元気じゃ<u>なかった</u> (wasn't healthy)
	きれい (pretty)	きれいじゃ<u>ない</u>	きれいじゃ<u>なかった</u> (wasn't pretty)
Noun + Copula	雪 (snow)	雪じゃ<u>ない</u>	雪じゃ<u>なかった</u> (wasn't snow)
	南 (south)	南じゃ<u>ない</u>	南じゃ<u>なかった</u> (wasn't south)

梅雨が<u>ながかったので</u>、今年のなつはむし暑いとおもいます。
Because the rainy season was long, I think this summer will be humid.

いい天気が<u>つづかなかったので</u>、ざんねんでした。
I was disappointed because the nice weather did not last long.

風が<u>冷たかったから</u>、ジャケットをきました。
I put on a jacket because the wind was cold.

元気が<u>よくなかったから</u>、家にいました。
I stayed home because the weather was not good.

お母さんは親切<u>だったけど</u>、お父さんはあまり話しませんでした。
The mother was kind but the father did not talk much.

そのアパートは<u>きれいじゃなかったけど</u>、安かったです。
The apartment was not very clean but cheap.

<u>元気そうだったけど</u>、本当は病気でした。
He looked healthy, but he was actually sick.

去年の三月は<u>あたたかかったとおもいます</u>。
I think last March was warm.

図書館はまちの北の方に<u>あった</u>とおもいます。
<small>と かん</small>　　　<small>きた ほう</small>
I think the library is on the north side of the town.

今年の梅雨はあまり<u>ながくなかった</u>んです。
<small>こ と し</small>　<small>つ ゆ</small>
This year's rainy season was not very long.

あれは台風<u>じゃなかった</u>んです。
<small>たいふう</small>
That was not a typhoon.

昨日<u>ふった</u>大雪ででんしゃがストップしました。
<small>き のう</small>　　　　<small>おおゆき</small>
The train stopped because of the heavy snow that fell yesterday.

日本へ<u>帰った</u>友達にメールを書きました。
　　　　　　　<small>だち</small>
I wrote a letter to a friend who went back to Japan.

Plain forms in casual conversation

Plain forms are used in conversations among close friends and family members, because the plain forms indicate closeness, intimacy, and carefree attitudes. On the other hand, です／ます indicates that the speaker is more aware of the listener's presence and intends to maintain a proper social distance.

The use of plain and polite forms is not always determined by the degree of formality. For example, in relatively casual situations such as a home party and going out after work, a person may use です／ます toward someone who holds a higher social status or someone who is much older, in order to show respect. In this situation, です／ます signals that the speaker is aware of the social difference and does not consider his/her interlocutor a true equal. Conversely, the social superior may use the plain form toward the junior interlocutor in order to show close carefree attitudes. Also, it is very common for two people of the same age group who meet for the first time to start conversation in です／ます forms but switch to plain forms as the conversation progresses. In other words, the choice between です／ます and the plain form depends on the speaker's perception about his/her social relationship with his/ her interlocutor. For this reason, it is common for a teacher to use the plain form to show familiarity to his/her students while the students use です／ます toward the teachers to show respect in the same conversational context.

子供：お母さん、かさ、いるよ。　*Mom, I need an umbrella.*
<small>ども</small>
お母さん：え、どうして？　　　　*Why?*

子供：雨、ふってるよ。　　　　*It's raining.*
<small>ども</small>　<small>あめ</small>
お母さん：ええっ！　　　　　　　*Oh, really?*

In answering a yes-no question, use うん (the casual form of はい or ええ) or ううん (the casual form of いいえ).

Mr. Li and Ms. Ueda are friends:

リー：ねえ、上田さん、今日いそがしい？
Hey, Ms. Ueda, are you busy today?

上田：<u>ううん</u>、ひまだけど。
No, not really.

学生：先生、少し寒くありませんか。　*Professor, isn't it a bit cold here?*

先生：<u>うん</u>、ほんとに寒いね。　*Yeah, it's really cold.*

学生：ヒーター、入れましょうか。　*Shall I turn on the heater?*

先生：うん、そうして。　*Yes, please.*

NOTES

- The thematic particle は、the subject particle が, and the direct object particle を are not used in conversations often.

  今日、すずしいね。　*It's cool today.*

  あ、雪、ふってる。　*Gee, it's snowing.*

  雨、ふった。　*It rained.*

- In casual conversation, the question marker か is often omitted in questions. It usually has a rising intonation toward the end.

  リー：寒い？　*Are you cold?*

  上田：うん、ちょっと寒い。　*Yes, a little bit.*

  リー：これ、きる？　*Do you want to put this on?*

  上田：ありがとう。　*Thank you.*

- The copular verbs だ and だ in な- adjective are also deleted in questions. Deleting だ before particles like ね and よ makes the speech sound feminine.

  リー：大丈夫？　*Are you OK?*

  上田：うん、大丈夫（だ）よ。　*Yes, I am.*

  リー：あの人、学生？　*Is he a student?*

  上田：うん、学生（だ）よ。　*Yes, he is.*

- The plain form of んです is んだ or の. In questions の is usually used. In statements, both の and んだ can be used.

  上田：昨日どうしたの？　*What happened yesterday?*

  リー：あ、病気で寝てたんだ。　*I got sick and stayed in bed.*

- 〜てください is 〜て:

  リー：わるいけど、あれとって。　*Sorry, but can you take that?*

  上田：ああ、いいよ。　*Sure.*

話してみましょう

Activity 1

The following conversations take place between two acquaintances. Change the style so that the conversation takes place between close friends.

Example: A: 昨日<ruby>昨日<rt>きのう</rt></ruby>はすずしかったですね。

    B: ええ。

    A: 昨日<ruby>昨日<rt>きのう</rt></ruby>はすずしかったね。

    B: ええ／うん。

1. A: 先週の火曜日は休みでしたか。

  B: いいえ、じゅぎょうはありましたよ。

2. A: 昨日は本当にあつかったですね。

  B: ええ、気温が三十五度まで上がりましたからね。

3. A: 今朝、雨がふっていましたか。

  B: いいえ、ふりませんでしたよ。昨日のばん、雪がふっていましたけど。

4. A: 去年のはるは寒い日がつづきましたけど、今年はあたたかい日が多くていいですね。

  B: そうですね。去年の三月と四月は気温がぜんぜん上がりませんでしたから、寒かったですね。

5. A: 昨日の台風は大きかったですね。

  B: ええ、雨はあまり多くありませんでしたけど、風がとてもつよかったですね。

Activity 2

Work with a partner. One person restates the following questions using the plain form, and the other person responds to them using 〜とおもいます。

Example:　日本のなつをどうおもいますか。

　　　　　A: 日本のなつ（を）どうおもう。

　　　　　B: そう（だ）ね。アメリカよりむし暑いとおもう。

1. 今朝の気温は何度ぐらいでしたか。

2. 今日は気温が何度ぐらいまで上がりますか。

3. 昨日のばんは気温が何度ぐらいまで下がりましたか。

4. 昨日と今日とどちらの方があたたかいですか。

5. 昨日と一昨日とどちらの方があたたかかったですか。

Activity 3

Work with partner. Ask and answer questions using the sentences provided.

Example:　今までいろいろなえいがを見ましたが、〜が一番おもしろかったです。
　　　　　(いろいろな = various)

　　　　　A: 今まで見たえいがの中で何が一番おもしろかったですか。

　　　　　B: 〜です。

1. 今までいろいろなところに行きましたが、〜が一番たのしかったです。

2. 今までいろいろなりょうりを食べましたが、〜が一番おいしかったです。

3. 今までいろいろな本を読みましたが、〜が一番おもしろかったです。

4. 今までいろいろな先生に会いましたが、〜先生が一番よかったです。

5. 今までいろいろなアルバイトをしましたが、〜が一番大変でした。

	パートナーのこたえ
一番たのしかったところ	
一番おいしかったりょうり	
一番おもしろかった本	
一番よかった先生	
一番大変だったアルバイト	

III. Describing characteristics of places, objects, and time using 〜は〜が

In addition to describing physical appearance, as you learned in Chapter 10, 〜は 〜が is used to describe other characteristics or to comment on things and concepts. The particle は indicates what the rest of the sentence is going to be about. You can interpret 〜は as as for 〜.

十二月は雨が少ない。	*We have little rain in December.*
あきは食べものがおいしい。	*Food tastes good in fall.*
ふゆは水が冷たい。	*Water is cold in winter.*
ハワイは気候がいい。	*Hawaii has a nice climate.*
東京はものが高い。	*Things are expensive in Tokyo.*
日本は山が多い。	*Japan is mountainous.*
まどは南の方がいい。	*The south (side) is good for a window.*
和食は天ぷらがおいしい。	*When it comes to Japanese food, tempura is good.*
山は富士山が一番だ。	*Mt. Fuji is No.1 of all mountains.*
ここは水がきれいだ。	*The water is clean here.*

リー：今日は風がつよいね。	*The wind is strong today.*
上田：ほんと。	*Indeed.*

山中：このへんはどのきせつがいいですか。
  Which season is the best around here?

高山：はるが一番きれいですね。

  Spring is the nicest.

話してみましょう

⬢ **Activity 1**

しつもんに日本語でこたえて下さい。

Example: アメリカはどのまちが一番好きですか。
    ニューヨークが一番好きです。

1. 〜さんの大学は何がゆうめいですか。
2. 〜さんは何が上手ですか。
3. 〜さんのまちはどのきせつが一番いいですか。
4. アメリカはどの大学が一番大きいですか。
5. 先生はどんな人がいいですか。
6. 日本語は何が大変ですか。むずかしいですか。

Activity 2

The following charts indicate average temperature or precipitation in various cities. Describe the climate in each city, using 〜は〜が . Find similarities among different cities.

Example: 東京は八月が暑いです。　　シンガポールは雨が多いです。
とうきょう　　あつ　　　　　　　　　　　　　あめ　おお

Activity 3

Work with a partner. Choose a town you like. One person will ask the following questions about his /her partner's favorite town and take notes. Then write a short description about the partner's favorite town using the 〜は〜 が forms. Speak casually.

Example:　A: 〜さん、どのまちが好き？

B: メルボルンが好きだね。

A: そう。メルボルンのどんなところが好きなの？

B: メルボルンはこうえんが多くてきれいだから。
おお

A: いいねえ。じゃあ、気候はどう？
きこう

B: そう（だ）ね。なつは暑いけど、ふゆはあまり寒くないよ。
あつ　　　　　　　　さむ

〜さんが好きなまちはメルボルンです。メルボルンはこうえんがたくさんあって、きれいです。なつは暑いですが、ふゆは寒くありません。
あつ　　　　　　さむ

1. 〜さんはどのまちが好きですか。
2. どうしてそのまちが好きなんですか。
3. そのまちの気候はどうですか。
きこう
4. そのまちはどのきせつがいいですか。どうしてですか。
5. そのまちは何がゆうめいですか。どこがおもしろいですか。

Activity 4

Work in groups of three or four. One person will select a city in the box without telling the rest of the group. The others will take turns asking questions about various characteristics of the city to find out which it is.

ニューヨーク	シカゴ	アンカレッジ
ホノルル	デンバー	ロサンゼルス
アテネ	ローマ	シドニー
東京 <small>とうきょう</small>	きょうと	ロンドン

Example:　A: そのまちは古いたてものが多いですか。

B: いいえ。

C: くるまや人が多いですか。

B: ええ、多いです。

D: そのまちは日本にありますか。

B: ええ。

C: 東京<small>とうきょう</small>ですか。

B: はい、そうです。

> ## IV. Expressing manner of action or outcome of a change using the adverbial forms of adjectives and noun + に

The く- form of い- adjectives and the に- form of な- adjectives modify verbs. They are called adverbial forms.

Adjective type	Dictionary form	Adverbial form
い -adjective	おもしろ<u>い</u>	おもしろ<u>く</u>
な -adjective	きれい	きれい<u>に</u>

The adverbial forms modify a verb indicating how an action takes place.

	<u>元気に</u>	あるいて下さい。	*Please walk cheerfully.*
かんじを	<u>上手に</u>	書いた。	*I wrote kanji skillfully (beautifully).*
雪が	<u>しずかに</u>	ふっている。	*It is snowing quietly (softly).*
雨が	<u>きゅうに</u>	ふった。	*It rained suddenly.*
	<u>あかるく</u>	わらう。	*to smile brightly (cheerfully)*
今日は	<u>はやく</u>	起きた。	*I woke up early (or quickly).*
風が	<u>やさしく</u>	ふいていた。	*The wind was blowing gently yesterday.*

They are also used to express change of state or outcome. The adverbial form + する means "to make something/someone into ～," and the adverbial form + なる means "to become ～."

子供を	<u>先生に</u>	する	*(Parents) make a child into a teacher.*
子供が	<u>先生に</u>	なる	*A child becomes a teacher.*
	<u>しずかに</u>	する	*to make (something/someone) quiet*
	<u>しずかに</u>	なる	*to become quiet*
じゅぎょうを	<u>おもしろく</u>	する	*(A teacher) makes the class interesting.*
じゅぎょうが	<u>おもしろく</u>	なる	*A class becomes interesting.*

お母さん：	へや、きれいにしてね。	*Clean this room.*
子供：	は〜い。	*Okay./Yes.*

川田： くるまを新しくしたんですよ。
I got a new car.

山下： ええっ、新しいくるまを買ったんですか。
What? You bought a brand-new car?

川田： いいえ。くるまは古いんですけど、さいきん買ったんです。
No, the car is old, but I got it recently.

話してみましょう

Activity 1

しつもんに日本語でこたえて下さい。

Example: なつはあさ何時ごろあかるくなりますか。
五時ごろあかるくなります。

1. なつは何時ごろくらくなりますか。
2. ふゆは何時ごろあかるくなりますか。
3. ふゆは何時ごろくらくなりますか。
4. このへんはいつごろ寒くなりますか。
5. このへんはいつごろあたたかくなりますか。
6. ふゆの気温温は何度ぐらいになりますか。
7. なつの気温は何度ぐらいになりますか。

Activity 2

Describe the following pictures using the adverbial forms of adjectives.

Example: 風がつよくふいています。

Example   1   2

3   4   5

6

Activity 3

Work with a partner. Your partner first draws a face without showing it to you, then gives you instructions on how to draw this face. Compare the two faces when you are done. Use casual speech.

Example: A: かおを大きく書いて。まるく書いて。

B draws a big round face.

A: そして、目を小さく書いて。はなはみじかく書いて。

B draws small eyes and a short nose.

Activity 4

A home remodeling expert is trying to make suggestions to make a room more comfortable. Help the expert make suggestions by completing the sentences using the adverbial form of adjective + する or noun + にする.

Example: かべ (wall) がきれいじゃないから、きれいにしましょう。

1. 押し入れがせまいから、＿＿＿＿＿＿＿＿＿＿＿＿＿。
2. このへやは小さいから、＿＿＿＿＿＿＿＿＿＿＿＿＿。
3. まどが少ないから、＿＿＿＿＿＿＿＿＿＿＿＿＿。
4. ドアが古いから、＿＿＿＿＿＿＿＿＿＿＿＿＿。
5. トイレがくらいから、＿＿＿＿＿＿＿＿＿＿＿＿＿。

Activity 5

Discuss the results of the remodeling performed in Activity 4.

Example: かべをきれいにしたので、へやがあかるくなりました。

V. Expressing uncertainty using 〜でしょう, 〜かもしれない, and 〜かな

〜でしょう, 〜かもしれない, and 〜かな express the speaker's conjecture, but they vary in degree of certainty and the intended interlocutor. All of these expressions are preceded by the plain form of verbs and adjectives. However, with な- adjectives and the copula verb, だ is deleted.

Verb くもる (*to become cloudy*)

	Probably	Maybe	I wonder
Present affirmative	くもるでしょう	くもる かもしれない	くもるかな
Present negative	くもらないでしょう	くもらない かもしれない	くもらないかな
Past affirmative	くもったでしょう	くもった かもしれない	くもったかな
Past negative	くもらなかった でしょう	くもらなかった かもしれない	くもらなかったかな

い- adjective 寒い (*cold*)

	Probably	Maybe	I wonder
Present affirmative	寒いでしょう	寒いかもしれない	寒いかな
Present negative	寒くないでしょう	寒くない かもしれない	寒くないかな
Past affirmative	寒かったでしょう	寒かった かもしれない	寒かったかな
Past negative	寒くなかった でしょう	寒くなかった かもしれない	寒くなかったかな

な- adjective いや (*unpleasant*)

	Probably	Maybe	I wonder
Present affirmative	いやでしょう	いや かもしれない	いやかな
Present negative	いやじゃない でしょう	いやじゃない かもしれない	いやじゃないかな
Past affirmative	いやだった でしょう	いやだった かもしれない	いやだったかな
Past negative	いやじゃなかった でしょう	いやじゃなかった かもしれない	いやじゃなかったかな

Noun + copula verb

	Probably	**Maybe**	**I wonder**
Present affirmative	風でしょう かぜ	風かもしれない かぜ	風かな かぜ
Present negative	風じゃない かぜ でしょう	風じゃない かぜ かもしれない	風じゃないかな かぜ
Past affirmative	風だった かぜ でしょう	風だった かぜ かもしれない	風だったかな かぜ
Past negative	風じゃなかった かぜ でしょう	風じゃなかった かぜ かもしれない	風じゃなかったかな かぜ

〜でしょう／だろう　probably, I suppose

〜でしょう indicates probability or conjecture. It can be used for future and past events or actions. The probability expressed by でしょう ranges from probably to must be/must have been. 〜でしょう is often used in weather forecasts.

いい天気でしょう。 てんき	*It will probably be good weather.*
にぎやかでしょう。	*It will probably be lively.*
東京はくもり時々雨でしょう。 とうきょう　　　ときどきあめ	*It will be cloudy with occasional rain in Tokyo.*
よこはまは雨でしょう。 あめ	*It will be rainy in Yokohama.*

In addition, 〜でしょう can be used with a rising intonation to ask for confirmation. This usage of 〜でしょう is rather casual and should not be used toward someone in a superior status.

そとはむし暑いでしょう。 あつ	*It is humid outside, don't you think?*
あの人は上田さんでしょう。	*That's Ms. Ueda over there, isn't it?*

The question form of 〜でしょう, 〜でしょうか is used for questions that are more polite than those ending in 〜ですか.

あのう、えきはどこでしょうか。	*Excuse me, but where is the station? (more polite)*
あのう、えきはどこですか。	*Excuse me, but where is the station?*
今、何時でしょうか。	*Do you have the time? (more polite)*
今、何時ですか。	*What time is it now?*

田中：明日の天気はどうでしょうか。 　　　あした　てんき	*How will tomorrow's weather be?*
川口：さあ、よく分かりませんが。	*Well, I'm not sure.*
鈴木：田中さんは来ますか。 すず	*Is Mr. Tanaka coming?*
川口：雨だから、たぶん来ないでしょう。 　　　あめ	*It's raining, so he probably won't come.*

NOTES

- でしょう is sometimes used with たぶん (*perhaps*).

  たぶん雨<ruby>雨<rt>あめ</rt></ruby>でしょう。　*It will probably rain*

- The plain form of でしょう is だろう. When 〜だろう is used in a question such as あの人は日本人だろうか, it can be interpreted as a self-directed question: *I wonder if that person is Japanese.* The polite speech version, あの人は日本人でしょうか, would be consistently interpreted as being a polite question.

〜かもしれない　　**might**

〜かもしれない also indicates probability or conjecture and can be used for future and past events or actions. The probability expressed by かもしれない is about 50% or lower.

石田<rt>いし</rt>：　にわか雨<rt>あめ</rt>がふりそうですね。
　　　　It looks like we will have a shower.

チョイ：　そうですね。くもが多<rt>おお</rt>いから、ふるかもしれませんね。
　　　　I agree. It's very cloudy, so it might rain.

イアン：　あの人は山田先生でしょうか。
　　　　Is that person (perhaps) Professor Yamada?

本田：　さあ、どうでしょうね。Tシャツ、きてるから、学生
　　　かもしれませんよ。
　　　　Well, I am not sure. He is wearing a T-shirt, so he may be a student.

〜かな　　**I wonder 〜 (Casual speech)**

〜かな is used when the speaker asks himself/herself about something. Since it expresses the speaker's monologue question, *I wonder 〜*, it cannot be used as someone else's monologue questions such as *he/she wonders 〜*. Also, it indicates present tense and cannot be used in cases such as *I wondered 〜* or *he/she wondered 〜*.

台風<rt>たいふう</rt>かな。	*I wonder if it is a typhoon.*
そとは寒<rt>さむ</rt>いかな。	*I wonder if it is cold outside.*
今晩<rt>ばん</rt>は気温<rt>きおん</rt>が下<rt>さ</rt>がるかな。	*I wonder if the temperature will fall tomorrow.*

〜かな is not used as a straightforward question to others like 〜でしょうか but can be used to solicit the listener's answer indirectly. However, it should not be used toward someone of superior status, because it is used in fairly informal speech.

アリス：　今日も雨かな。
　　　　　I wonder if it will rain today, too.

健一：　ううん。昨日のばん、ふったから、今日は大丈夫だよ。
　　　　　No. It won't because we had rain last night.

道子：　これは石田さんのかな。リーさんのかな。
　　　　　I wonder if this is Mr. Ishida's or Mr. Li's.

ふみえ：　さあ、よく分からないけど。イニシャルが T.I. だから、石田さんのかもしれないね。
　　　　　Well, I don't know, but it might be Mr. Ishida's because the initials are T.I.

古田：　上田さんは来るかな。　*I wonder if Ms. Ueda is coming.*

山下：　さあ、どうかな。　　　*Well, I wonder that, too.*

Notes

- In feminine speech 〜かしら is used instead of かな.

  大雪になるかしら。　*I wonder if the snow will get heavy* (feminine).

話してみましょう

Activity 1

Convert the following questions into monologue questions using 〜かな.

Example:　今年のなつは暑いですか。

今年のなつは暑いかな。

1. 去年の八月は暑い日が多かったですか。
2. 今年のふゆは寒いでしょうか。
3. 去年は雨がたくさんふりましたか。
4. 去年のふゆは雪が少なかったでしょうか。
5. 一昨年のふゆはあまり寒くありませんでしたか。
6. 今年のなつは暑くなりますか。

Activity 2

Work with a partner. The following chart shows today's weather forecast for various cities. One person asks a question using the words in 1-8 and 〜でしょう. The other person answers the questions, using 〜でしょう or 〜かもしれません.

Example: 東京／いい天気

A: 東京はいい天気でしょうか。

B: いいえ、天気はあまりよくないでしょう。

東京／雨

A: 今日東京は雨がふるでしょうか。

B: そうですね。東京は雨がふるかもしれませんね。

	東京	アラスカ	ニューヨーク	シドニー	ロサンゼルス
天気	くもり	雪	くもりのち雨	晴れ	くもり時々晴れ
気温	59° F 15° C	-4° F -20° C	41° F 5° C	91.4° F 33° C	77° F 25° C
雨	50%	0%	80%	0%	30%
雪	0%	100%	15%	0%	0%

1. 東京／あたたかい
2. アラスカ／雪
3. ニューヨーク／寒い
4. ニューヨーク／雨
5. シドニー／晴れる
6. ロサンゼルス／あたたかい
7. ロサンゼルス／雨
8. シドニー／むし暑い

Activity 3

Using the state of Illinois (イリノイしゅう , しゅう = *state*) as a reference point, ask your classmates where other states are in respect to Illinois. Your classmates will answer using direction words and ～でしょう , ～かもしれない , or ～と おもう depending on their level of certainty. Tally the results.

Example: A: イリノイしゅうの北に何しゅうがありますか。
                  きた　　　なに

          B: ウィスコンシンしゅうがあるでしょう／

              かもしれません／とおもいます。

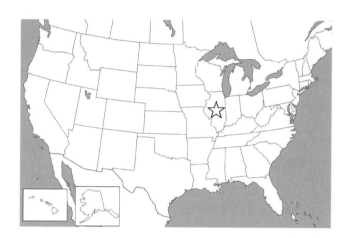

Activity 4

Work with a partner. Look at the following weather map and say what seems to be happening weather-wise in various places. Use casual speech.

Example: 今日、テキサスはいい天気になるでしょう。
                       てん き

	HI	Lo	Otlk	HI	Lo	Otlk
		Today		Tomorrow		
Atlanta	71	55	clr	68	56	cdy
Baltimore	61	44	cdy	64	48	cdy
Boston	49	41	cdy	56	41	m
Buffalo	51	33	cdy	45	41	clr
Charlotte, N.C.	73	50	cdy	75	56	cdy
Cincinnati	70	45	cdy	48	40	cdy
Columbus, Ohio	68	45	cdy	46	40	cdy
Dallas-Ft Worth	84	56	clr	75	43	cdy
Dayton	68	45	cdy	45	40	cdy
Denver	52	25	clr	38	22	cdy
Detroit	52	31	cdy	44	38	cdy
Grand Rapids	52	30	m	41	37	cdy
Greensboro, N.C.	68	48	cdy	73	53	cdy
Hartford Spgfld	54	39	cdy	55	41	m
Honolulu	79	69	cdy	80	70	cdy
Houston	88	65	cdy	75	58	cdy
Indianapolis	70	46	m	51	39	cdy
Los Angeles	64	47	clr	66	50	cdy
Louisville	72	52	cdy	57	44	cdy
Memphis	81	59	cdy	61	47	cdy
Miami Beach	83	64	cdy	83	65	cdy
Nashville	77	54	cdy	58	47	cdy
New Orleans	74	63	cdy	74	63	cdy
New York City	60	45	cdy	59	47	m

聞く練習
<ruby>れんしゅう</ruby>

上手な　聞き方
<ruby>かた</ruby>

Understanding the organization of prepared speech

Unlike face-to-face conversations, news reports and weather forecasts are based on prepared text and hence do not have much redundant information. It is thus very important to understand the information the first time. Luckily, prepared speech usually has a set pattern. Being aware of the organization of speech helps you to identify when to pay attention and to what. For example, news reports usually start with what happens, to whom, where, and when. The details come later.

聞く前に
<ruby>まえ</ruby>

Write an outline of the organization of a weather report. Include the types of information provided and their order.

天気予報を聞く　　Listening to weather forecasts
<ruby>てん　き　よ ほう</ruby>

聞いてみましょう

Listen to the following weather forecasts. Then complete the chart, in English, by writing in the weather as well as high and low temperatures for each city listed.

言葉のリスト
<ruby>こと ば</ruby>

最高気温　　highest temperature　　　さいてい気温　　lowest temperature

	天気予報 (Example)	天気予報 1	天気予報 2	天気予報報 3
まち	きょうと	東京	よこはま	きょうと
天気	雪			
気温	1度／－1度			

聞いた後で
<ruby>あと</ruby>

しつもんに日本語でこたえて下さい。

1. 天気予報 1のきせつはいつですか。
2. そのきせつの東京と～さんのまちとどちらの方が寒いですか。
3. 天気予報 2のきせつはいつですか。
4. そのきせつのよこはまと～さんのまちとどちらの方があたたかいですか。
5. 天気予報 3のきせつはいつですか。
6. ～さんのまちでは、そのきせつに雨がたくさんふりますか。

聞き上手　話し上手

Expressing agreement and solidarity using ね and も

Conversation is like two people playing catch. Both people need to throw the ball in a way that is easy for the other person to catch. To facilitate conversation, it is important to give feedback and show a willingness to participate in the conversation.

Expressing agreement or emphasizing similarity is one way to show your support to the listener. This will help to create a sense of sharing or solidarity. In Japanese, two particles, ね and も, are often used to show agreement. For example, the particle ね in Ms. Suzuki's speech below indicates that she is requesting a confirmation of her impression about the weather. The particle ね in Mr. Yamamoto's speech indicates that he agrees with Ms. Suzuki's assertion that it is humid today.

鈴木：　今日はむし暑いですね。　　　　*It's humid today, isn't it?*

山本：　ええ、本当に暑いですね。　　*It certainly is.*

Similarly, the particle も in the following example emphasizes agreement between Ms. Suzuki and Mr. Yamamoto and indicates what they have in common.

鈴木：私はいぬが好きです。　　　　　　　　*I like dogs.*

山本：そうですか。ぼくもいぬが好きなんですよ。　*Really? So do I.*

Even if you disagree with a person, it is good to start off by agreeing about something before stating a disagreement. Starting a conversation with a disagreement often sounds rude or cold.

鈴木：　今年は雪が多いですね。　　　*It has snowed a lot this year.*

山本：　本当によくふりますね。でも、去年より少ないかもしれませんね。

It's really snowed a lot, hasn't it? But, it may be less than last year.

練習

1. Listen to people expressing their opinions. For each person, first express your agreement using ね and も. Then express your disagreement, but (1) show your support by using ね and も, and (2) articulate the point on which you disagree.
2. Work with a partner. Your partner will express opinions about class, school, weather, a particular hobby, parents. Agree with him/her using ね and も.
3. Work with a partner. Your partner will again express opinions about class, school, weather, a hobby or parents, but this time, show your support for his/her opinion using ね and も, and then express your disagreement.
4. The following conversation is unnatural. Make it more natural by using ね and も.

A:　今日は。おでかけですか。

B:　今日は。ええ、今日は暑いから、およぎに行くんです。

A:　そうですか。今日は本当に暑いです。私はおよぎに行きたいです。明日は暑いでしょうか。

B:　さあ、よく分かりませんが、むし暑いから、よるは雨がふるかもしれません。

A:　そうですか。じゃあ、少しすずしくなるでしょうか。

B:　そうおもいます。

漢字
かん じ

Component shapes of kanji 1 – Introduction

Many **kanji** consist of more than one component. Certain components appear in many different **kanji**. Some of them are **kanji** by themselves while others are not. Since the number of these component shapes is much smaller than the number of **kanji**, approximately 300 in total, they serve as organizers and aid in memorizing.

   The term *radical* (部首) is traditionally used to refer to components of
ぶ しゅ
characters. The concept of radicals was developed to classify and index a large number of **kanji**. In modern Japanese, a little over 200 radicals are used to index kanji. A radical is assigned to every **kanji**. Although radicals are very useful in studying **kanji**, they are sometimes deceptive. For example, the radical of 家 is 宀 , but the radical of 字 is 子 .

   In this book, we use the term *component shape* to refer to any shape that repeatedly appears as part of **kanji** (e.g., 寸 , 口 , 又 , 月 , 宀 , etc.). Some component shapes are **kanji** by themselves, while some others only appear in other **kanji**. There are about 300 such shapes, which include all of the shapes used as radicals.
Some of the component shapes indicate the meaning (or meaning category) of **kanji**. For example, if a **kanji** contains 日 , it is likely that the meaning of the **kanji** is related to day or sun. Some other component shapes may indicate an on-reading of **kanji**.

   Component shapes appear in various places within **kanji**, but some shapes have a strong tendency to appear in fixed locations such as the left, the right, the top, or the bottom of the character. The following is a list of major types of component shapes based on where they are found within the character.

Type *	Example		Use Example
へん (left side)	イ	meaning: person	休　体　住
つくり (right side)	冓	on-reading: /kou/	講　構　購
かんむり (top)	宀	meaning: roof	家　寒い
きゃく (bottom)	儿	meaning: leg	兄　見　先　元
たれ (top to left)	疒	meaning: sickness	病　痛　疲
かまえ (enclosure)	門	meaning: gate	間　聞　閉
くにがまえ (enclosure)	囗	meaning: border	回　国
にょう (left to bottom)	辶	meaning: walk, round	週　道　進　近

＊ These names are used to label radicals.

天天	heaven テン	一 一 于 天
		明日の天気はいいでしょう。 あした　てんき

気気	spirit, mind キ	ノ ノ 气 气 気 気 気 気
		昨日は天気がよくありませんでした。 きのう　てんき

雨雨	rain あめ　ウ	一 一 厅 币 币 雨 雨 雨 雨 雨
		雨がしずかにふっています。 あめ

雪雪	snow ゆき　セツ	一 一 厂 戸 示 雪 雪 雪 雪
		明日は大雪です。 あした　おおゆき

風風	wind かぜ　フウ	ノ 几 几 凡 同 同 風 風 風 風 風
		風がつよいです。　台風が来ます。 かぜ　　　　　たいふう

晴晴	to clear, fine は（れる）セイ	日 日一 日十 日キ 晴 晴 晴 晴 晴
		ずっと晴れていて、雨がふりません。 は　　　　　　あめ

温温	warm あたた（かい）オン	氵 氵 氵冂 氵曰 氵曰 温 温 温 温
		先週は気温が35度まで上がりました。 きおん　ど　あ

度度	degree ド	丶 广 广 庐 庐 庐 度 度
		おふろの温度は42度ぐらいです。 おんど　ど

東東	east ひがし　トウ	一 一 戸 戸 自 車 東 東
		まちの東の方にこうえんがあります。 ひがし　ほう

西西	west にし　セイ	一 一 冂 丙 西 西
		きょうとは東京の西にあります。 とうきょう　にし

南南	south みなみ　ナン	一 十 ナ 内 内 南 南 南 南
		南のうみはとてもきれいで温かいです。 みなみ　　　　　　　　あたた

北北	north きた　ホク	一 十 才 北 北
		ほっかいどうは日本の北の方にあります。 きた　ほう

読めるようになった漢字

天気　天気予報　天ぷら　気温　気候　雨　梅雨　にわか雨　雪　風

台風　晴れる　温かい　温度　何度　東　西　南　南東　南西　北

北東　北西　寒い　暑い　多い　少ない　冷たい　上がる　下がる

去年　今朝　今年　方　夕方　本当に　少し

日本人のなまえ：川田

練習

1. 東京の天気は雨のち晴れです。ごごには気温が二十五度まで上がるでしょう。

2. 今晩は北の風がつよいですが、明日は南東の風になって、よわくなるでしょう。

3. 西の方が暗いですから、晴れないでしょう。

4. なつは暑くて、ふゆは寒いです。雪もたくさんふります。

5. ひるごはんの時は人が多いですが、そのあとは少なくなります。

6. 大阪は東京の西にあります。せんだいは東京の北です。

7. 今日はあたたかかったけど、明日は雨がふるそうだから、気温が下がって、寒くなるかもしれないね。

読む練習
れんしゅう

上手な読み方
かた

Getting used to vertical writing

Japanese text can be written either horizontally or vertically. In vertical writing, text is read from top to bottom, right to left. Japanese newspaper articles are written vertically, including the weather forecast. Popular magazines and literary works are also usually written vertically. Texts requiring scientific symbols, equations, formulas, and foreign words, such as science textbooks, language texts, and computer magazines, tend to be written horizontally.

練習
れんしゅう

1. Mark the beginning and end of each of the following short paragraphs.

メルボルンに給水制限？

メルボルンでは十三年ぶりに給水制限がしかれる可能性が大きいと見られている。

一五〇年ぶりの低雨量を記録したメルボルン供給ダムの水量は、七二％と去年の同時期の九五％を大幅に下回り、関係者もこの状態を深刻に受け止めている様子。

メルボルン水道局のベイリー氏は、市民に対し節水に協力してくれるよう積極的に呼びかけている。

ちなみに、年間平均降雨量六三九ミリに対し、去年の降雨量はわずか三五九ミリだった。

2. Rewrite the following text vertically in two or more lines.

東京は今日は晴れ時々くもりで、ごぜんちゅうは少し寒いですが、
とうきょう　　　　　　　　　ときどき
ごごには十度ぐらいになるでしょう。よるになって、雨がふる
でしょう。この雨はあしたのごごまでつづくでしょう。

読む前に
<small>まえ</small>

1. The numbers in the following map represent various regions in Japan. Read the description of each region below and write the number that matches the description. Note that しま means *island*.

山陰 <small>さんいん</small>	本州にあります。大阪の西で、四国の北です。かんこくにちかいです。
北海道 <small>ほっかいどう</small>	日本で一番北にあるしまです。
関東 <small>かんとう</small>	本州にあります。東京の近くです。
近畿 <small>きんき</small>	本州にあります。東京の南です。大阪やきょうとがあります。四国にちかいです。
九州 <small>きゅうしゅう</small>	四国の南西にあるしまです。
北陸 <small>ほくりく</small>	本州にあります。東京の北西の方です。
本州 <small>ほんしゅう</small>	日本で一番大きいしまです。
東北 <small>とうほく</small>	本州にあります。東京の北の方です。
東海 <small>とうかい</small>	本州にあります。東京の少し南の方です。
四国 <small>しこく</small>	日本にある四つのしまの中で一番小さいしまです。

新聞の天気予報　A weather forecast in a newspaper

前線を伴った低気圧が日本海から東北東に進み、全国的に天気はくずれる。本州の日本海側は四国、九州、朝から雨、関東、東北、北陸も午後から雨になる。山陰地方の海岸では所々で雷雨を伴い風も強まる。北海道は雪から雨、沖縄も晴れ後曇りで、昼過ぎから雨。

読んだ後で

A. After reading the above weather forecast, choose the weather map that corresponds to the forecast.

1

2

3

B. しつもんに日本語でこたえて下さい。

1. 四国にすんでいる人は今日かさをもって、出かけた方がいいですか。

2. 九州にすんでいる人は今日どんなふくをきて、出かけた方がいいですか。

3. 北海道にすんでいる人は今日はかさをもって、出かけた方がいいですか。

C. An out-of-town friend is planning to visit you for a week and has asked what the weather is like now. Compose an e-mail message to your friend giving details about the forecast for each of the next seven days. Information should include high and low temperatures, the chance of precipitation, and so forth.

総合練習
そうごうれんしゅう

明日のお天気
あした

You are a TV meteorologist forecasting tomorrow's weather. Work with a partner to create a map of your country and region. As you make your forecast, add the appropriate weather symbols and temperatures to your map. Give your weather report to the class.

ロールプレイ

Work with a series of partners to act out the following role play activities.

1. You are talking to your roommate. You are planning to go out tonight, but the weather is getting worse. Ask your roommate what he/she knows about tonight's weather.
2. You meet your neighbor on your way to school. Yesterday was a cold, rainy day, but the weather today is nice. Greet him/her and make small talk.
3. A typhoon is approaching your city. It is getting windy and starting to rain hard. Discuss these weather conditions with a partner.
4. Walk around the classroom. As soon as your instructor names a season, pair up with a classmate, greet him/her as if you have bumped into one another on the street, and chat about the weather.

Chapter 12

第
十
二
課
だい・い・に・か

年中行事
ねんちゅうぎょうじ
Annual Events

Objectives	Describing seasonal holidays and yearly events
Vocabulary	Dates, years, other time expressions, attractions and leisure activities, and memorable events
Japanese Culture	National holidays and annual events
Dialogue	子供の時の上田さん *Ms. Ueda as a child* ども とき
Grammar	I. Talking about time using noun/adjective + 時, duration + 前/後 とき まえ ご
	II. Talking about past experiences using 〜たことがある; listing representative activities using 〜たり〜たりする
	III. Expressing frequency using time-span に frequency / duration / amount
	IV. Expressing hearsay using the plain form + そうだ
	V. Using noun modifying clauses in the past and present
Listening	Taking turns in conversation
Communication	Phrases for filling in pauses
Kanji	Which one should I use, kanji or kana? 春 夏 秋 冬 朝 昼 晩 午 前 後 去 昨 供 元 思 明 回
Reading	Understanding the format of a postcard

単語
たん

Nouns

うみ	海	ocean, sea
おととし	一昨年	the year before last
おもいで	思い出	memories
がいこく	外国	foreign countries
がっき	学期	semester, quarter いちがっき one semester はるがっき spring semester/quarter
かぶき	歌舞伎	kabuki (Japanese traditional performing art)
きもの	着物	traditional Japanese clothes, kimono
キャンプ		camping
きょうかい	教会	church
クリスマス		Christmas
けんか		fight, quarrel けんかをする to fight
こんげつ	今月	this month
しょうがつ	正月	the New Year (often used with the polite prefix お，おしょうがつ)
じんじゃ	神社	Shinto shrine
すいぞくかん	水族館	aquarium
せんげつ	先月	last month
ちゅうがく	中学	junior high school (shortened form of 中学校)
デート		dating, デートする go out on a date
てら	寺	Buddhist temple (often used as おてら)
どうぶつえん	動物園	zoo
とき	時	when, at the time of 〜 (子供の時 when I was a child) ども
はくぶつかん	博物館	museum
バレンタインデー		St. Valentine's Day
ハロウィン		Halloween
はんとし	半年	a half year
ひこうき	飛行機	airplane
びじゅつかん	美術館	art museum

プレゼント		present, gift
まつり	祭り	festival (often used as おまつり)
ミュージカル		musical
やまのぼり	山登り	mountain climbing
ゆうえんち	遊園地	amusement park
らいげつ	来月	next month

う -verbs

なく	泣く	to cry
のる	乗る	to get on, to ride (ひこうきに　のる　get on a plane)
もらう		to receive, to get

Irregular verbs

| しつれんする | 失恋する | to be disappointed in love |

Adverbs

| はじめて | 初めて | for the first time |

Particles

| なあ | | A particle of exclamation to express desires or feelings without addressing anyone in particular. Used in casual speech. |

Suffixes

〜かい	〜回	〜 times
〜かげつ	〜か月	counter for months
〜ご	〜後	from 〜, after 〜 (三年ご three years from now)
〜しゅうかん	〜週間	for 〜 weeks
〜ど	〜度	〜 times
〜にち	〜日	day
〜ねん	〜年	specific year (1996年), counter for year (十年)
〜まえ	〜前	〜 ago　(一年まえ one year ago)

Expressions

| えーと | | Well, Let's see . . . |
| あけましておめでとうございます。 | 明けましておめでとうございます。 | Happy New Year |

単語の練習
たん　　　れんしゅう

A. 日にち　Days of the month

日	月	火	水	木	金	土
		一日 ついたち *	二日 ふつか	三日 みっか	四日 よっか	五日 いつか
六日 むいか	七日 なのか	八日 ようか	九日 ここのか	十日 とおか	十一日 じゅういち にち	十二日 じゅうに にち
十三日 じゅうさん にち	十四日 じゅう よっか	十五日 じゅうご にち	十六日 じゅうろく にち	十七日 じゅうしち にち	十八日 じゅうはち にち	十九日 じゅうく にち
二十日 はつか	二十一日 にじゅう いちにち	二十二日 にじゅうに にち	二十三日 にじゅう さんにち	二十四日 にじゅう よっか	二十五日 にじゅうご にち	二十六日 にじゅう ろくにち
二十七日 にじゅう しちにち	二十八日 にじゅう はちにち	二十九日 にじゅうく にち	三十日 さんじゅう にち	三十一日 さんじゅう いちにち		

NOTE

- いちにち means *one day*; ついたち means the *first of the month*. Both are written as 一日 in **kanji** but the context makes the reading clear. The other expression of dates can be used for the duration of time. For example, ふつか may mean the *second day of the month* or *two days*, depending on context.

おぼえていますか。

何月　一月　二月　三月　四月　五月　六月　七月　八月　九月
十月　十一月　十二月

Activity 1

Work with the class. Ask your classmates about their birthdays, and put them in the following charts.

Example: A: スミスさんのお誕生日はいつですか。

B: 一月一日です。

月	日にちと名前
一月	一日　スミスさん
二月	
三月	
四月	
五月	
六月	
七月	
八月	
九月	
十月	
十一月	
十二月	

B. とくべつな日　Special days

お正月	New Year's Day
クリスマス	Christmas
バレンタイン・デー	St. Valentine's Day
ハロウィン	Halloween

Supplementary Vocabulary: アメリカの休日　US holidays
きゅうじつ

マーティン・ルーサー・キング・デー	Martin Luther King, Jr. Day
プレジデンツ・デー	President's Day
イースター	Easter
どくりつきねんび　　独立記念日	Independence Day
メモリアルデー	Memorial Day
レーバーデー	Labor Day
コロンブス・デー	Columbus Day
ハヌカ	Hanukkah

Activity 2

Work with a partner. Ask your partner about the dates of holidays this year.

Example:　A: 今年のハヌカ (Hanukkah) はいつですか。
　　　　　B: 十二月十一日です。

C. ほかの時間のいい方　Other time expressions

	日	週	月	年
～ before last ～	1 day before yesterday	N/A	N/A	一昨年 おととし year before last
Last	2 Yesterday	5	先月 せんげつ last month	8
This	3 Today	6	今月 こんげつ this month	9
Next	4 Tomorrow	7	来月 らいげつ next month	来年 next year

Activity 3

Fill in the blanks in the above table with appropriate time expressions that you have learned in previous chapters.

Activity 4

しつもんに日本語でこたえて下さい。

1. 今月は何月ですか。
   こんげつ

2. 来月は何月ですか。

3. 先月は何月でしたか。
   せんげつ

4. 今年は何年ですか。

5. 来年は何年ですか。

6. 一昨年は何年でしたか。
   お と と し

7. 去年は何年でしたか。
   きょ

D. 時間のながさ　Duration of time

～度／回 かい (times)	～週間 しゅうかん (for ～ week)	～か月 げつ (for ～ month)	～年 (year)
いちど／いっかい	いっしゅうかん	いっかげつ	いちねん
にど／にかい	にしゅうかん	にかげつ	にねん
さんど／さんかい	さんしゅうかん	さんかげつ	さんねん
よんかい	よんしゅうかん	よんかげつ	よねん
ごかい	ごしゅうかん	ごかげつ	ごねん
ろっかい	ろくしゅうかん	はんとし ／ろっかげつ	ろくねん
ななかい	ななしゅうかん	ななかげつ	しちねん
はちかい ／はっかい	はっしゅうかん	はちかげつ ／はっかげつ	はちねん
きゅうかい	きゅうしゅうかん	きゅうかげつ	きゅうねん ／くねん
じゅっかい	じゅっしゅうかん	じゅっかげつ	じゅうねん

Notes

- ～度 refers to frequency and temperature up to 3. Beyond that, it usually refers to temperature only.

- ～年 indicates both the specific point of time, as in 2008年 (*the year 2008*), and the duration of time as in 八年 (*for 8 years*).

- When ～かい is written as the **kanji** 階, it refers to *floor levels*, as in Chapter 8, but when it is written as 回, it refers to *frequency*. There are some differences between them in terms of pronunciation as well. For example, the first mora is pronounced with a low pitch and the following mora have high pitch when the expression refers to a floor level, such as いっかい, にかい, and さんかい, but this is not the case with the frequency, as in いっかい、にかい、さんかい. Also, *3rd floor* is pronounced さんがい or さんかい but *3 times* is さんかい. On the other hand, *8th floor* is usually pronounced はちかい but *8 times* can be はちかい or はっかい.

- Instead of the western (Gregorian) calendar, the Japanese frequently use the current Emperor's era to refer to a certain year. For example, へいせい五年 is 1993. Recent eras are: 明治 (1868 -1912), 大正 (1912-1926), しょうわ (1926-1989), and へいせい (1989-).

Activity 5

Tell the year the following events occurred. If you do not know the answer, ask your classmates.

1. コロンブス（Columbus）がアメリカに来た。

2. アメリカがイギリスからどくりつした (became independent) 。

3. アメリカで夏のオリンピックがあった。

4. アメリカで冬のオリンピックがあった。

5. 第二次世界大戦 (WWII) がはじまった。

6. 第二次世界大戦 (WWII) がおわった。

7. ベトナムせんそう (Vietnam War) がおわった。

8. イラクせんそう (Iraq War) がはじまった。

Activity 6

しつもんに日本語でこたえて下さい。

1. 夏休みは何か月ありますか。冬休みはどうですか。春休みは？

2. 一学期は何週間ありますか。

3. 今週は何度学校に来ますか。

4. 今年、何度えいがを見ましたか。

5. 今月、何度じゅぎょうが休みになりましたか。

E. めいしょとレジャー　Attractions and leisure activities

Activity 7

Identify the picture that depicts each of the buildings and activities in the list by writing the number corresponding to the picture.

<u>1</u>.	はくぶつかん	museum	__.	ゆうえんち	amusement park
__.	ミュージカル	musical	__.	教会 きょうかい	church
__.	水族館 すいぞくかん	aquarium	__.	うみ	sea
__.	山のぼり	mountain climbing	__.	（お）てら	temple
__.	旅行 りょこう	travel	__.	じんじゃ	shrine
__.	びじゅつかん	art museum	__.	（お）まつり	festival
__.	かぶき	kabuki	__.	キャンプ	camping
__.	がいこく	foreign country	__.	どうぶつえん	zoo

おぼえていますか。

図書館　こうえん　たいいくかん　えいが　コンサート
（と）（かん）
パーティ　　ピクニック　　休みの日

Activity 8

Work with a partner. Ask each other whether you have been to any of the places
or attractions or have participated in them this year.

Example:　A:　今年、はくぶつかんに行きましたか。
　　　　　　B:　ええ、行きました。
　　　　　　A:　何度ぐらい行きましたか。
　　　　　　　　　（ど）
　　　　　　B:　一度／一回行きました。
　　　　　　　　（ど）　（かい）

	今年行った／見に行った／した	～度／回 （かい）
はくぶつかん		
びじゅつかん		
水族館 （すいぞくかん）		
どうぶつえん		
ゆうえんち		
教会 （きょうかい）		
おてら／てら		
じんじゃ		
うみ		
がいこく		
ミュージカル		
おまつり／まつり		
山のぼり		
かぶき		
旅行 （りょこう）		
キャンプ		

F. 思い出　Memories

きものをきる
to put on kimono

飛行機にのる
to get on a plane

プレゼントをもらう
to receive a present

デートする
to go on a date

けんかをする
to have a fight, a quarrel

しつれんする
to be disappointed in love

なく
to cry

おぼえていますか。

おふろに入る　和食を食べる　およぐ　出かける

Activity 9

Work in a group of three or four. One person acts out the activity in the list, and the rest of the group will try to guess what it is.

Activity 10

Complete the following statements using 〜さいの時 (*when I was 〜 years old*).

1. ＿＿＿＿＿＿＿の時、はじめて (for the first time) 人を好きになりました。

2. ＿＿＿＿＿＿＿の時、はじめて外国人と話しました。

3. ＿＿＿＿＿＿＿の時、はじめて飛行機にのりました。

4. ＿＿＿＿＿＿＿の時、はじめてデートをしました。

5. ＿＿＿＿＿＿＿の時、はじめて友達とけんかしました。

6. ＿＿＿＿＿＿＿の時、しつれんしました。

7. ＿＿＿＿＿＿＿の時、高いプレゼントをもらいました。

ダイアローグ

はじめに

A. しつもんに日本語でこたえて下さい。

1. 子供の時、どんな子供でしたか。

2. 小学校の時、よくどんなことをしましたか。

3. 中学の時、よくどんなことをしましたか。

4. 高校の時、よくどんなことをしましたか。

B. Work with a partner. Ask your partner about his/her childhood memories.

Example:　A:　〜さんは子供の時、どんな子供だったの？

B:　そう（だ）ね。とても元気だったけど、よくなく子供だったんだ／の。

子供の時の上田さん　*Ms. Ueda as a child*

道子さんはたんすの上のしゃしんを見ています。(*Michiko is looking at a picture on the chest.*)

道子：　あら、これ、アリス？

上田：　ええ、そうよ。

道子：　かわいい。何さい？

上田：　そうね。それは、七さいの誕生日の時にとったしゃしんなの。

道子：　そう、アリスはどんな子供だったの？

上田：　そうね。父や母によると、明るくて元気な子供だったそうよ。

道子：　へえ、そうなんだ。

上田：　ええ、スポーツが好きだったから、いつもそとであそんでた。

道子：　そうなの。

上田：　で、道子はどんな子供だったの？

道子：　そうね。私も小さい時は、よくうみにあそびに行ったり、山に
　　　　ハイキング行ったりしてたから、けっこうかっぱつだったかな。
　　　　けど、中学や高校の時は、いつもべんきょうしてた。

上田：　そうか。日本はじゅけんがあるからね。

道子：　え、ないの、アメリカじゃ。

上田：　SAT や ACT はあるけど、じゅけんはないのよ。だから、
　　　　じゅけんべんきょうもしたこと、ないの。

道子：　そう。いいなあ。

上田：　だから、高校の時は、よくパーティに行ったり、友達と
　　　　えいがを見たりしたんだ。

道子：　いいなあ。私もアメリカの学校に行きたかった。

上田：　でも、大学はアメリカの方がずっと大変だよ。

道子：　あ、そうか。じゃあ、おなじことね。

DIALOGUE PHRASE NOTES

- けっこう means *quite* and かっぱつ means *active.*

- ないの、アメリカじゃ。 This is an inverted sentence of アメリカじゃないの, but it does not mean *it is not America.* In this sentence, じゃない is not the negative form of だ. Instead, it consists of じゃ and ない. じゃ is a contraction for では where で refers to the place of action and は is a topic marker. ない is the negative form of ある. Therefore this sentence means: *Doesn't it exist in the U.S.?*

- じゅけん means "entrance examination."

- 私もアメリカの学校に行きたかった。 Literally, *I wanted to go to a U.S. school,* and in this context, it means *I wish I had gone to a U.S. school.*

- おなじ means *same,* and おなじこと means *the same thing.*

ダイアローグの後で

A. Complete the chart with information about Ms. Ueda's and Michiko's childhoods.

	どんな子供でしたか。	よくどんなことをしましたか。
アリス		
道子		

日本の文化
ぶんか

A. National holidays.

There are fourteen national holidays in Japan. Visit the *Nakama 1* student website to learn more about these holidays.

1月1日	元日 がんじつ	New Year's Day
1月第2月曜日 だい	成人の日 せいじん	Coming-of-Age Day
2月11日	建国記念の日 けんこくきねん	National Foundation Day
3月21日	春分の日 しゅんぶん	Vernal Equinox Day
4月29日	昭和の日 しょうわ	Emperor Showa's (Hirohito; 1901–1989) birthday / ゴールデン・ウイーク (Golden Week).
5月3日	憲法記念日 けんぽうきねん	Constitution Day
5月4日	みどりの日	Green Day
5月5日	子供の日 ども	Children's Day
7月第3月曜日 だい	海の日 うみ	Ocean Day
9月第3月曜日 だい	敬老の日 けいろう	Day of the Elderly
9月23日	秋分の日 しゅうぶん	Autumnal Equinox Day
10月第2月曜日 だい	体育の日 たいいく	Health and Sports Day.
11月3日	文化の日 ぶんか	Culture Day
11月23日	勤労感謝の日 きんろうかんしゃ	Labor and Harvest Day
12月23日	天皇誕生日 てんのうたんじょう	Emperor Akihito's Birthday

B. Seasonal events and celebrations.

Besides national holidays, the Japanese celebrate a variety of seasonal events: February 3rd is called 節分 , and it is the first day of spring according to the old lunar calendar. On this day, people throw soybeans inside and outside their

house while saying "おに (devils) はそと、ふく (luck) はうち" to keep out evil sprits and allow only good luck into the house.

On バレンタインデー it is the women who give men chocolate. Men reciprocate a month later with candies, marshmallows, and white chocolate on ホワイトデー (March 14).

March 3 is ひなまつり (Girl's Day), and people display dolls depicting ancient wedding ceremonies to express their wish for daughters to grow up to be gentle, beautiful women.

The Japanese national flower is the cherry blossom, and it blooms throughout Japan during late March to early April, when TV news programs provide daily forecasts on the blossoms. Bus tours travel to the best cherry blossom regions, and schoolchildren, college students, and corporate groups alike picnic under the blossoms. This eating, drinking, singing, and dancing under the cherry trees is called お花見 (*flower watching*) .
はなみ

July 7 is considered one of the most romantic days and is called 七夕 . According to Chinese mythology, it is the one day a year when two star-crossed
たなばた
lovers, separated by the Milky Way, meet. Schoolchildren write their wishes on small pieces of paper and tie them on bamboo trees to celebrate this day.

Around the middle of July, the rainy season ends, and the summer festival season starts. Many of the major festivals are held between July and August throughout Japan, especially during the period surrounding おぼん (August 13–15). It is a Buddhist festival in honor of deceased relatives and ancestors, and many people go back to their hometowns to greet their ancestors and family, similar to Thanksgiving break in the U.S. In addition to Golden Week, おぼん is one of the three major holiday seasons in Japan.

Starting in the middle of December, many people organize the end-of-the year party called 忘年会 . The Japanese also celebrate クリスマス as
ぼうねんかい
a romantic day for couples and a party day for children and families. After December 29, most companies close until January 4. Traditionally, to prepare for the new year, people launch a major house or office cleaning and pay off personal debts during this period.

文法
ぶんぽう

> ## I. Talking about time using noun/adjective + 時, とき
> duration + 前／後
> まえ ご

When you want to express a period of time in your life rather than a date, a day of the week, or a specific time, you can create a phrase using 時 (when), 前 (before) とき まえ and 後 (after). Grammatically they are nouns so they can be modified by a noun, ご adjective, or a clauselike noun modification. This chapter introduces 時 with respect とき to nouns and adjectives and 前／後 in relation to counterexpressions. まえ ご

A. Noun/adjectives + 時 (*when, at the time of* ~) とき

時 can be modified by a noun in the form of noun の noun (時) or adjective + noun. とき とき The particle に for a time expression can be used with ～時. とき

子供の時 どども とき	*When I was a child*
小学校の時 とき	*When I was in elementary school*
十一さいの時 とき	*When I was eleven*
ひまな時 とき	*When I have free time*
いやな時 とき	*When I am annoyed*
元気な時 げんき とき	*When I am healthy*
いそがしい時 とき	*When I am busy*
寒い時 とき	*When I am cold*
小さい時 とき	*When I was small*

The negative ending ない is grammatically an い -adjective, so it can be combined with 時 just like other い -adjectives. とき

病気じゃない時 びょうき とき	*When I am not sick*
ひまじゃない時 とき	*When I do not have free time*
いそがしくない時 とき	*When I am not busy*

ウィル： いつアメリカに来たんですか。
When did you come to the United States?

あつ子： 高校の時に来ました。 とき
It was when I was in high school.

キム：　ひまな時<ruby>時<rt>とき</rt></ruby>はよくいぬのさんぽをします。
I often walk my dog when I am free.

スミス：　そうですか。どんないぬですか。
I see. What kind of dog do you have?

B. Duration + 前<ruby><rt>まえ</rt></ruby>／後<ruby><rt>ご</rt></ruby>

Duration + 前<ruby><rt>まえ</rt></ruby> indicates *ago* or *before*; it is used with the particle of time, に .

三年前に日本に行きました。　　　*I went to Japan three years ago.*

一か月前にけっこんしました。　*I got married a month ago.*

Duration + 後<ruby><rt>ご</rt></ruby> indicates *later* or *after*, and it can be used with に .

三日後に会いましょう。　*I will see you three days from now.*

一年後に日本に行きました。　　　*I went to Japan a year later.*

ジョン：　ホンコンへはいつ行ったの？
When did you go to Hong Kong?

ひろし：　二か月ぐらい前<ruby><rt>まえ</rt></ruby>。
About two months ago.

ジョン：　どうだった？
How was it?

ひろし：　おもしろかったけど、ちょっと暑くて大変<ruby>大変<rt>たいへん</rt></ruby>だった。
It was fun, but it was a bit too hot and that was hard to take.

ジョン：　今度はいつ行くの。
When are you going again?

ひろし：　半年後<ruby><rt>ご</rt></ruby>だと思<ruby><rt>おも</rt></ruby>う。
I think it will be six months from now.

ジョン：　そうか。いいなあ。
I see. That is nice.

NOTE

- ぐらい can be used with 前<ruby><rt>まえ</rt></ruby> and 後<ruby><rt>ご</rt></ruby>. It is used right after the duration and before 前<ruby><rt>まえ</rt></ruby> or 後<ruby><rt>ご</rt></ruby>. When ぐらい used with 後<ruby><rt>ご</rt></ruby>, the pronunciation of the **kanji** 後 becomes あと.

  その人に四日<ruby>四日<rt>よっか</rt></ruby>ぐらい前<ruby><rt>まえ</rt></ruby>に会った。 *I met the person about four days ago.*

  その人に一年ぐらい後<ruby><rt>あと</rt></ruby>に会った。 *I met the person about a year later.*

話してみましょう

> **Activity 1**

Answer the following questions using 〜 時(とき).

Example:　　　どんな時(とき)にセーターをきますか。
　　　　　　　寒(さむ)い時(とき)にきます。

1. どんな時(とき)に家(いえ)でゆっくりしますか。
2. どんな時(とき)になきますか。
3. どんな時(とき)に友達(ともだち)にメールを書(か)きますか。
4. どんな時(とき)は時間(じかん)がありませんか。
5. どんな時(とき)にびょういんへ行(い)きますか。

> **Activity 2**

Work with a partner. Ask what he/she does on the occasions listed below.

Example:　A:　ひまな時(とき)に何(なに)をしますか。
　　　　　B:　家(いえ)でテレビを見(み)ます。
　　　　　A:　〜さんはひまな時(とき)に何(なに)をしますか。
　　　　　B:　たいてい友達(ともだち)と電話(でんわ)で話(はな)します。

	すること
ひまな時(とき)	
暑(あつ)い時(とき)	
寒(さむ)い時(とき)	
うれしい時(とき)	
かなしい時(とき)	
さびしい時(とき)	

Activity 3

Work with a partner. Your partner is a psychic. Ask him/her about your future.

Example:　A: 私はこれから何をするでしょうか。

　　　　　B: 二か月後に、だれかを好きになるでしょう。

　　　　　　 そして、半年後にけっこんするでしょう。

Activity 4

Work with a partner. Ask your partner about places where he/she visited in the past six months and for how long.

Example:　A: どんなところに行きましたか。

　　　　　B: シカゴに行きました。

　　　　　A: そうですか。いいですね。いつ行ったんですか。

　　　　　B: 三週間前です。

　　　　　A: そうですか。何日ぐらいシカゴにいましたか。

　　　　　B: そうですね。二日いました。

どこ	いつ	どのくらい

II. Talking about past experiences using 〜たことがある; listing representative activities using 〜たり〜たりする

The plain past affirmative form 〜た can be used in various structures in Japanese. This chapter introduce two commonly used structures, namely 〜たことがある and 〜たり〜たりする.

A. Talking about past experiences using 〜たことがある

The construction 〜たことがある is used to express an experience one has had in the past. In contrast, 〜ました simply expresses a past action. The absence of any experience is expressed by 〜たことが／はない.

私はミュージカルを<u>見たことがあります</u>。
I have seen a musical.

私はミュージカルを<u>見たことがありません</u>。
I have never seen a musical.

私はミュージカルを<u>見ました</u>。
I saw a musical.

私はミュージカルを<u>見ませんでした</u>。
I did not see a musical.

The construction 〜たことがある is usually used to talk about experience in the not-so-recent past and not about something that took place as recently as 昨日 (きのう) or 一昨日 (おととい).

一昨年 (おととし) 中国 (ごく) に行ったことがあります。
I had the experience of going to China two years ago.

一昨日 (おととい) 中国 (ごく) に行きました。
I went to China the day before yesterday.

チョイ： 田中さんは英語 (えい) が上手ですね。
Mr. Tanaka is good at English, isn't he?

山本： ああ、田中さんは小さい時 (とき) 、がいこくにすんでいたことがあるそうですよ。
Well, I heard that he lived in a foreign country when he was small.

チョイ： ああ、それで、上手なんですね。
I see, that's why he is so good.

B. Listing representative activities using 〜たり〜たりする

The construction 〜たり〜たりする is used to list representative activities. It is similar to や in Chapter 7, which is used to list nouns and noun phrases.

食べたり飲んだりしました。
I ate and drank. (Literally, I did things like eating and drinking.)

新聞を読んだり、ざっしを見たりします。
I do things like reading newspapers and browsing through magazines.

新聞やざっしを読みます。
I read newspapers and magazines. (etc.)

川口：　きょうとに行ったことがありますか。
　　　　　Have you ever to Kyoto?

ワット：えぇ、ありますよ。じつは、先月行ったんです。
　　　　　Yes, I have. In fact, I went there last month?

川口：　そうなんですか。どうでしたか、きょうとは？
　　　　　Is that so? How was it?

ワット：とてもたのしかったですよ。おてらやじんじゃを見たり、
　　　　　買いものをしたりしました。
　　　　　It was really fun. I saw temples and shrines and did shopping.

キム：　子供の時、よく何したの？
　　　　　What kinds of things did you do when you were a child?

一也：　どうぶつえんに行ったり、ゆうえんちであそんだりしたよ。
　　　　　I did things like going to the zoo and playing at the amusement park.

話してみましょう

Activity 1

Look at the drawings on the following page and make up questions asking whether someone has ever done these things.

Example:　Picture #1
はな (*flowers*) をもらったことがありますか。

Activity 2

Bingo. Work with the class. Ask whether your classmates have done the things in the Bingo chart. Write the name of the person when he/she answers with yes. The first one to complete a row or column with different names wins.

さしみを食べる	ゴルフをする	日本で教会へ 行く きょうかい	ゆびわを もらう
おてらを見る	日本のざっしを 読む	山のぼりをする	日本人と 日本語で話す
きものをきる	スペイン語を べんきょうする	しつれんして、 なく	ふとんで寝る
はくぶつかんに 行く	くるまを買う	ハワイのうみで およぐ	先生を好きに なる

Activity 3

Look at Mr. Jones's personal history and make sentences that express what kinds of activities he did at different stages in his life.

Example: ジョーンズさんは小学校の時、よくアニメを見たり、こうえんで
やきゅうをしたりしました。

	よくしたこと
1990 12/3　誕生日 たんじょう	
1996〜2001　小学校	どうぶつえんへ行く。こうえんでやきゅうをする。アニメを見る。
2001〜2004　中学	うみへおよぎに行く。キャンプをする。うたをうたう。ケーキを作る。
2004〜2007　高校	アルバイトを する。しゃしんをとる。えをかく。びじゅつかんに行く。デートする。
今　　　大学	べんきょうする。アルバイトをする。日本人とチャット (chat) で話す。ドライブに行く。

Activity 4

Work with a partner. Ask what kinds of activities he/she did at different times in his/her life.

Example: A: 小学校の時、よくどんなことをしましたか。
B: そうですね。友達の家にあそびに行ったり、
　　　だち
　　　父とどうぶつえんに行ったりしました。

	よくしたこと / よくすること
小学校	
中学	
高校	
今	

Activity 5

Work in groups of three or four. Think about a place, such as a park, department store, supermarket, and so on. Describe to the rest of the group what people do at that place and make them guess what that place is.

Example:　A: ここでジェットコースターにのったり、メリーゴーランドに
　　　　　　　　のったりします。

　　　　　　B: ゆうえんちですか。

　　　　　　A: はい、そうです。

Activity 6

Work with a partner. Ask your partner what kinds of places he/she has been to for a vacation, when, and what he/she did there, using plain forms. Then report the result using polite forms.

Example:　A: 〜さんは　どんなところにあそびに行ったことがあるの？

　　　　　　B: ボストンに行ったことがあるけど。

　　　　　　A: いいなあ。いつ行ったの？

　　　　　　B: 二年前に行ったんだ／の。

　　　　　　A: ボストンでは、どんなことしたの？

　　　　　　B: びじゅつかんに行ったり古い教会を見たりしたよ。

　　　　　〜さんは二年前にボストンへ行ったことがあります。

　　　　　ボストンではびじゅつかんに行ったり、古い教会を見たりしました。

III. Expressing frequency using time-span に frequency / duration /amount

Use of the time-span に with frequency /duration expresses how often, how long, or how much one does a certain thing within a specified time.

	Time frame	Particle	Frequency / duration	
私は	一日 いちにち	に	二時間ぐらい	べんきょうします。

I study for about two hours a day.

The time frame can be specified by any expression that specifies a duration of time such as 〜分 (*minute*) , 〜時間 (*hour*), 〜日 (*day*), 〜週間 (*week*), 〜か月 (*month*), and 年 (*year*) .

五分に	一度	トイレに行く。	*I go to the restroom every five minutes.*
一時間に	三回 かい	電話が来る。 でん	*I receive a call three times in an hour.*
二日に ふつか	一度	プールでおよぐ。	*I swim in a pool every other day.*
一週間に	十時間ぐらい	テレビを見る。	*I watch TV for about ten hours a week.*
一か月に	十五万円ぐらい	いる。	*I need 150,000 yen in a month.*
半年に	一度	旅行に出かける。 りょ	*I go on a trip every six months.*
一年に	三か月ぐらい	休みがある。	*I have a vacation for about three months a year.*
十年に	一度	会う。	*I see (him) once in every ten years.*

東山：　教会へはよく行きますか。
ひがしやま　きょうかい
Do you often go to church?

中西：　ええ、一週間に一度行きます。
なかにし
Yes, I go there once a week.

イアン：　どのぐらい本を読むんですか。
How many books do you read?

チョイ：　そうですね。一週間に三さつぐらい読みますね。
Let's see, about three books a week.

イアン：　すごいですね。
Wow!

話してみましょう

Activity 1

Rephrase the following sentences using the frequency or quantity and time frame in the right column.

Example:

	Frequency / Quantity	Time frame
水族館に行きます。 すいぞくかん	About twice	1 year

一年に二回／二度ぐらい水族館に行きます。
かい　　　　　　　　　　　すいぞくかん

	Frequency/Quantity	Time frame
1．およぎに行きます。	once	2 weeks
2．デートをします。	twice	1 week
3．びょういんに行きます。	once	2 months
4．テレビを見ます。	30 minutes	1 day
5．アルバイトをします。	once	2 days
6．おまつりがあります。	4 times	1 year
7．メールを読みます。	3 times	1 day
8．山のぼりをします。	once	1 month

Activity 2

Work with a partner. Find out how often he/she does the following things. Compare this information with your own lifestyle.

Example: A: 一週間にどのぐらいうんどうしますか。
　　　　　　 B: そうですね。一週間に三回／三度ぐらいします。
　　　　　　　　　　　　　　　　　　かい

うんどうをします／一週間	
アルバイトをします／一週間	
べんきょうします／一日	
寝ます／一日	
友達と出かけます／一週間 だち	

Activity 3

Work with your class. First find out which classmates do not live with their parents. Then ask them how often they get together with their parents, on what occasions, and what sorts of things they do together.

Example: A: ご両親と一緒にすんでいますか。

B: いいえ、一人ですんでいます。

A: そうですか。じゃあ、ご両親とご兄弟にはよく会いますか。

B: そうですね。一年に三回ぐらい会います。

A: そうですか。どんな時に会うんですか。

B: クリスマスやお正月や夏休みですね。

A: そうですか。じゃあ、ご家族とどんなことをしますか。

B. 旅行に行ったり、食事をしたりします。

名前 なまえ	Frequency	Occasion	Activity

IV. Expressing hearsay using the plain form + そうだ

A construction using the stem of the verb + そうだ was introduced in Chapter 9; it expresses the speaker's conjecture based on a direct observation.

おまつりは　<u>おもしろ</u>　　　　そうだ。　*The festival looks interesting.*

おまつりは　<u>おもしろくなさ</u>　そうだ。　*The festival does not look interesting.*

This chapter introduces a different type of そうだ, which takes the plain form of verbs and adjectives. It expresses hearsay and it means *I heard* or *I have heard.*

おまつりは　<u>おもしろい</u>　　　　そうだ。　*I've heard that the festival is interesting.*

おまつりは　<u>おもしろくない</u>　そうだ。　*I've heard the festival is not interesting.*

In addition to the present form, 〜そうだ for hearsay is used with the plain past forms.

おまつりは　<u>おもしろかった</u>　　　そうだ。　*I've heard that the festival was interesting.*

おまつりは　<u>おもしろくなかった</u>　そうだ。　*I've heard the festival was not interesting.*

Also, 〜そうだ in this usage is often used with 〜によると (according to 〜).

> スミスさんによると、ハロウィンはアメリカのおまつりだそうだ。
> *According to Mr. Smith, (I heard that) Halloween is an American festival.*

> 田中さんによると、キムさんは来年けっこんするそうです。
> *According to Mr. Tanaka, (I heard that) Mr. Kim is getting married next year.*

木村：　クリスマスにハワイ旅行に行ったそうですね。
　　　　I heard that you went on trip to Hawaii during Christmas.

リー：　ええ、二十三日から五日行きました。
　　　　Yes. I went there for five days starting the 23rd.

木村：　いいですね。私はハワイへは行ったことがないんですよ。
　　　　Nice. I've never been to Hawaii.

NOTE

- It may be difficult to distinguish the そうだ meaning *it looks like* from the そうだ indicating hearsay with い-adjectives, because they can sound very similar. So it is essential to pay attention to pronunciation.

おいし<u>そう</u>ですね。　　*It looks delicious.*
おいし<u>い</u>そうですね。　*I heard that it is delicious.*

話してみましょう

▶ **Activity 1**

You heard some things about Ms. Tanaka. Make a sentence that reports what you have heard.

Example:　田中さんは小さい時よく寝る子供でした。

　　　　　田中さんは小さい時よく寝る子供だったそうです。

1. 田中さんは大学院の学生です。
2. 田中さんは中学の時よく山のぼりをしました。
3. 田中さんはしゃしんをとるのが好きです。
4. 田中さんはがいこくにすんでいたことがあります。
5. 田中さんは先週かぶきを見に行きました。
6. かぶきは少しむずかしかったけど、おもしろかったです。

▶ **Activity 2**

Work in a group of four or five. The instructor tells something to a member from each team. They then go back to their respective team and take turns whispering the information only to the next person on the team. The last person of each team will come to the board and write the information.

Example:　〜さんから本をもらいました。

　　　　　先生は〜さんから本をもらったそうです。

Activity 3

Work with a partner. Choose one person from the list (or choose yourself) and pretend you are that person. Your partner interviews you. He/She will take detailed notes. Reverse the roles and repeat.

Example: A: アメリカの大統領 (President) は今どこにすんでいますか。
　　　　　　だいとうりょう

　　　　　　B: ホワイトハウスにすんでいます。

有名人のリスト
ゆうめい

アメリカの大統領 だいとうりょう	ジョージ・ワシントン
ブラッド・ピット	リンカーン
ジャネット・ジャクソン	ウィリアム王子 (Prince William) 　　　　　おうじ
コロンブス	ダイアナひ (Princess Diana)
スーパーマン	マーティン・ルーサー・キング
バットマン	イチロー

Activity 4

Work in a group of three or four. Report to the group about your interview from Activity 3 without revealing the name of the interviewee. The rest of the group will try to guess who the interviewee was.

Example: この人はアメリカ人じゃないそうです。そして、旅行がとても
　　　　　　　　　　　　　　　　　　　　　　　　　　　りょ
　　　　　　好きだったそうです。

V. Using noun modifying clauses in the past and present

Chapter 10 introduced the noun modifying clause (see p. 406). The modifying clause is in the plain form, and it immediately precedes the noun to be modified. This chapter expands the use of this structure in two ways. First, the modifying clause can be in the past tense as long as it is in plain form.

たのしかった	ミュージカル	*the musical that was fun*
先月キャンプに来た	人	*the person who came to the campsite last month*
けんかをした	友達	*the friend who had a fight*
昨日来なかった	学生	*the student who did not come yesterday*

Second, the subject of the verb in a modifying clause is marked by が. The topic marker は does not appear in a modifying clause.

山田さんが　よく話す思い出	*the memory that Mr. Yamada often talks about*
弟が　昨日行ったおてら	*the temple that my younger brother went to yesterday*
母が　好きだったかぶき	*the kabuki that my mother liked*
姉が　好きなおんがく	*the music that my elder sister likes*

The subject marker が is often replaced by the particle の when the modifying clause is very short.

母が／の　好きだったきもの	*the kimono that my mother liked*
母が　子供の時に好きだったきもの	*the kimono that my mother liked when she was a child*
父が／の　行った水族館	*the aquarium that my father went to*
父が　キムさんと行ったびじゅつかん	*the art museum that my father went to with Mr. Kim.*

Use the present tense when a modifying clause describes a characteristic of a person or thing, although the sentence is in the past tense.

私は　よく食べる子供でした。	*I was a child who ate a lot.*
田中さんは　せが高い人でした。	*Mr. Tanaka was the person who was tall.*

話してみましょう

Activity 1

Read each statement and make up a question that asks for the underlined thing, place, or person.

Example: 田中さんは今月どこかに行きました。

田中さんが今月行ったところはどこですか。

1. 川本さんは昨日何か食べました。
2. 川口さんは昨日だれかに電話をかけました。
3. 金田さんは一昨日だれかとデートをしました。
4. 東山さんは昨日どこかで本を買いましたか。
5. 大田さんは昨日何か飲みました。
6. 中西さんのねこはどこかにいます。
7. 月本さんは来月だれかに会います。
8. 古川さんは何か作ります。

Actvity 2

Work with a partner. Ask what kinds of things your partner did, using the given verbs. Then, for each thing ask how it was.

Example: A: ねえ、どんなものを食べたことがある？

B: アイスクリームの天ぷらを食べたことがあるよ。

A: どうだった？

B: う〜ん、あまりおいしくなかった。

	もの／ところ	どうでしたか。
食べる		
飲む		
行く		
見る		
聞く		

Activity 3

Work with a new partner. Convey the information you collected in Activity 2 to your new partner by using noun modifying clauses.

Example: 〜さんが食べたものはアイスクリームの天ぷらですが、

〜さんが食べたアイスクリームの天ぷらはあまり
おいしくなかったそうです。

Activity 4

Work in a group of three or four. One person defines one of the items in the list, and the others try to figure it out. The person who correctly guesses the most items is the winner.

Example: A: 先生とべんきょうするへやです。

B: きょうしつですか。

A: はい、そうです。

図書館　先生　学生　子供　お母さん　やきゅう　デパート　おてら
スーパー　じんじゃ　ゆうびんきょく　えんぴつ　ノート
ゆうえんち　小学校　がいこく　クリスマス　ハロウィン　教会
はくぶつかん　山　うみ

Activity 5

Work with the class. Ask each other what kind of children your classmates were.

Example: A: キムさんはどんな子供でしたか。

B: よくあそんで、よく食べる子供でした。

名前	どんな子供

MORE ABOUT CASUAL SPEECH

Some expressions like かな are used only in casual speech. Another common sentence final particle is なあ. It expresses the speaker's surprise, admiration, or desires without addressing anyone in particular. It is used both in monologues and dialogues. In general, it is considered a male speech pattern, but women often use it in casual conversation, especially in monologues. The fact that なあ can be used in the first monologue below can imply that the speaker is less aware of the presence of the listener. Therefore, women may choose to use 〜ね if addressing someone in conversation.

きれいだなあ。	*It is beautiful!*
きれいだね。	*It's beautiful, isn't it?*
きれいねえ。	*It's beautiful! / it is beautiful, isn't it?*

Do not use なあ with polite forms such as です and ます, as the use of なあ with these forms is characteristic of the speech of middle-aged men, called おじさんことば.

Another expression that you hear often is すごく (*very*). It can be used instead of とても, though とても can be used in both formal and casual speech.

すごくきれい！　*Very pretty*

The adjective すごい can be used in casual speech as well. It can be used to describe an extremely positive or negative situation, and it means *great, amazing, awful,* or *horrible,* depending on the context.

聞く練習
れんしゅう

上手な聞き方

Taking turns in conversation

One important rule in conversation is taking turns, or allowing only one person to speak at a time. Body language, introductory remarks, and silence are some ways to signal who should speak next. Of course, not everyone waits for a turn to speak. In fact, many times you may hear two or more conversations going on at the same time in one group.

練習
れんしゅう

Listen to the conversations and decide which one breaks the rule of turn-taking. Write a check mark next to the conversation.

Conversation 1_____   Conversation 2 _____

日本の思い出
おも   で

言葉のリスト
ことば

北海道	Hokkaido
ほっかいどう	
雪まつり	Snow Festival
よこはま	Yokohama

These students are talking about their experiences in Japan. Listen to their descriptions and complete the following chart in English. You may not understand every detail, but try to get the gist of each speech.

	いつ行きましたか。	どんなことがありましたか。どんなことをしましたか。
チョンさん		
モリルさん		
クリシュナさん		

聞き上手話し上手

Phrases for filling in pauses

Speaking always involves false starts, paraphrases, and pauses. Even native speakers do not speak in fluent and complete sentence all the time. In English one often says *um, uh, let's see,* or *well* to fill in pauses. In Japanese, expressions like あのう,そうですね and えーと serve as conversational "fillers." This usage of あのう differs from that of あのう、すみません, which is used to get someone's attention. あのう is commonly inserted between phrase and utterance breaks to give some time for the speaker to put his thoughts into words. When あのう is used, the speaker is aware of the listener's presence. えーと is also used to fill in time between phrases, but it is used for the sake of speaker and does not imply the speaker's awareness of the listener's presence. For this reason, using えーと frequently, especially toward your superior, is rather rude because you may give an impression that you do not pay much attention to the listener when you speak. In any case, overuse of these fillers can break the natural flow of conversation, so one should be careful not to do so.

> 山本：　休みによくどんなことをしますか。
> 木村：　そうですね。テニスをしたり、およぎに行ったり、それから、
> むら　　　あのう、えいがを見たりしますね。

練習
れんしゅう

1. Listen to the conversation as you read the following text, which does not include any fillers. Write in the fillers as you listen.

   > ゆかり：　クリスマス、どうだった？
   > ケイト：　とてもたのしかった。みんなでコロラドにスキーに
   > 　　　　　行ったんだ。
   > ゆかり：　ほんと。いいなあ。
   > ケイト：　うん、でね。アスペンに行ったんだけど、とまった
   > 　　　　　ホテルがすごくりっぱで、へやもひろくて、ほんとに
   > 　　　　　よかった。
   > ゆかり：　そう。よかったね。スキーはどうだったの？
   > ケイト：　ああ、スキーは、私、あまり好きじゃないから、
   > 　　　　　しなかったんだ。だから、毎日おいしいもの
   > 　　　　　食べたり、パーティしたり、あそんでたのよ。
   > ゆかり：　そうか。いいなあ。

2. Work with a partner. Ask your partner a question that requires a long answer such as a description of his/her apartment, friend, or past experience. Practice using conversation fillers.

漢字
かんじ

Which one should I use, kanji or kana?

There are several words in Japanese that can be written in **kanji** but are usually expressed in **hiragana** or **katakana**. For example、ここ、そこ、あそこ、and どこ can be written as 此処、其処、彼処、and 何処, respectively. The choices between ひらがな or 漢字 for such words are made by convention. That is, words like the こそあど expressions are commonly written in **kana** but you may see the **kanji** versions in novels, for example. Similarly, おいしい is more likely to be written in **kana** instead of as 美味しい. On the other hand, the word 寒い is usually written in **kanji** though さむい is possible. It is impossible to know which words are more likely to be written in **kanji** and which are not at this point, but keep in mind that writing every available **kanji** is not necessarily appropriate.

In general, the more **kanji** are used, the more formal or difficult a piece of writing will look. Therefore, official documents addressed to the public may not contain many **kanji** in order to make it look familiar to the general public, whereas an academic journal may contain a large number of **kanji**. A good text is said to have about 30% of the characters written in **kanji** and will not contain more than 40%. For this reason, writing as many **kanji** as possible just for the sake of using **kanji** is not considered appropriate.

In some situations, **kanji** cannot be used even when available. For example, こと is a noun, meaning an *intangible thing*, and can be written with the **kanji** 事. However, when it is used as a part of a grammar expression, such as ことがある, it must be written in **hiragana**. Similarly, ある can be expressed with the **kanji** 有る but it must be written in **hiragana** in the phrase ことがある. Also、いる (*exist*) can be written with the **kanji** 居る, but this character is never used in the expression 〜ている. The **kanji** for the verbs 行く and 来る are commonly used when these words appear as as the main verb in a sentence, but are not used for the expressions 〜ていく／てくる, which are introduced in volume 2 of *Nakama*.

| 春 春 | spring
はる　シュン | 一 二 三 宇 夫 表 春 春 春 |
| | | 春は雨が多いです。
はる |

| 夏 夏 | summer
なつ　カ | 一 一 一 一 一 一 一 一 一 |
| | | 日本の夏は暑いです。
なつ |

| 秋 秋 | autumn, fall
あき　シュウ | ノ 二 千 禾 禾 利 利 秒 秋 |
| | | 秋の山はとてもきれいです。
あき |

Kanji		Meaning / Reading	Stroke order	
冬	冬	winter ふゆ　トウ	ノ　ク　タ　冬　冬	
			冬は寒いから、時々雪がふります。 _{ふゆ}　　　　　_{ときどき}	
朝	朝	morning あさ　チョウ	十　サ　古　古　車　朝　朝　朝　朝	
			日曜日の朝、おそくまで寝るのが好きです。 　　　　_{あさ}	
昼	昼	noon, daytime ひる　チュウ	つ　コ　尸　尺　尺　尽　昼　昼	
			母が昼ごはんを作りました。 　　_{ひる}	
晩	晩	evening バン	日　日　日′　日″　晩　晩　晩　晩　晩	
			明日の晩ごはんは天ぷらです。 　　　_{ばん}	
午	午	noon ゴ	ノ　ー　二　午	
			午前　　　月曜日の午後、両親と家族が来ます。 _{ごぜん}　　　　　　_{ごご}	
前	前	before, front まえ　ゼン	丶　ソ　ソ　ソ　前　前　前　前　前	
			午前中にしゅくだいをします。　中学の前　名前 _{ごぜんちゅう}　　　　　　　　　_{まえ}　_{なまえ}	
後	後	after, later あと/うし(ろ) のち　ゴ	ノ　ク　彳　彳　彳′　彳′　後　後　後	
			午後は暑かったです。一か月ぐらい後　つくえの後ろ _{ごご}　　　　　　　　　_{あと}　　　_{うし}	
去	去	to leave, past さ(る)　キョ	一　十　土　去　去	
			去年、南アメリカに行きました。 _{きょ}	
昨	昨	last ~ (yesterday, year) サク	丨　冂　日　日　日′　旷　昨　昨	
			一昨年日本に行きました。　昨日 _{おととし}　　　　　　　_{きのう}	
供	供	attendant, companion とも／ども　キョウ	ノ　イ　仁　什　供　供　供　供	
			子供が二人います。 　_{ども}	
元	元	origin, former もと　ゲン	一　二　テ　元	
			父は元気です。　元気なお母さん 　_{げんき}　　　_{げんき}	
思	思	to think おも(う)　シ	丨　冂　冊　田　田　田　思　思　思	
			昨日の朝は風がつよかったと思います。 _{きのう}　_{あさ}　　　　　　　　_{おも}	

明	明	bright, light あか（るい）　メイ	一　冂　月　日　日　明　明　明	
			明るいへや　　明日　　明るい人 　あか　　　　あした　　あか	

回	回	times, frequency まわ（る）　カイ	一　冂　冂　冋　回　回	
			私の弟は一か月に十回ぐらいラーメンを食べます。 　　　　　　　　　　　　かい	

読めるようになった漢字
　　　　　　　　かんじ

春　夏　秋　冬　朝　朝ご飯　　今朝　　毎朝　　昼ご飯　　晩ご飯　　今晩
　　　　　　　　　　　　はん　　　　　　　　　　　　はん　　　　はん

毎晩　午前　午後　二日前　三日後　名前　　後　去年　昨年　昨日
　　　　　　　　　　　　　　　　　な　　　のち

一昨年　子供　元気　思う　思い出　明るい　明日　一回　二回
　　　　　　　　　　　おも　　で

三回　一週間　二度　時　今月　正月　先月　来月　中学　今度
　　　　　　　　とき　　　　　　　　　　　　　　　こん　ど

学期　教会　水族館　外国人　後ろ　半年　飛行機
がっき　きょうかい　すいぞくかん　がいこくじん　　　はんとし　ひこうき

明けましておめでとうございます
あ

日本人の名前：川本　月本　中西　東山　古
な　まえ　　かわもと　つきもと　なかにし　ひがしやま　ふる

練習
れんしゅう

Read the following sentences.

1. 来年の春から夏まで日本にいます。
2. 冬の朝はとても寒くて、水が冷たかったです。
3. 夏は午前中はあまり暑くありませんが、午後はとても暑いです。
4. 昨日の晩、その子供は何時ごろ寝ましたか。
5. 去年の秋にきょうとに行きました。十月だったと思います。
6. おばあさんは明るくて、とても元気です。
7. 一年に二回、日本に帰ります。
8. 三年前に一度日本に行ったことがあります。その一か月後に
   タイへ行きました。
9. 教会の後ろに何がありますか。

読む練習
れんしゅう

上手な読み方

Understanding the format of a postcard

Japanese postcards （葉書） are usually written vertically. In vertical writing, text is
は がき
read from right to left. The stamp is at the upper left corner of the front of the
card. Under the stamp, the sender's name and address are written. Write the sender's
zip code in the small boxes at the lower left corner. The addressee's address should
be written on the right side with the zip code in the boxes at the top of the card, and
his/her name should be in the center of the card. Use さま (様), a formal version of
さん , after the addressee's name.

On the back of the card, it is not necessary to write the name of the sender or
addressee. The card usually contains a short greeting phrase, a body, a short closing
phrase, and a date.

Seven-digit postal code

Sender's address and name

Recipient's name

Recipient's address

Date

Main text

練習
れんしゅう

The most important greeting card in Japan is probably the New Year's card
(ねんがじょう). New Year's cards are exchanged not only among friends and
relatives, but also among businesses, neighbors, students, and teachers. Look at the
following New Year's card and identify the sender's and addressee's address, name,
and zip code. Then identify the greeting phrases.

葉書　(A postcard)
はがき

読む前に

A. しつもんに日本語でこたえて下さい。

1. 絵葉書 (*picture postcard*) をもらったことがありますか。
   えはがき

2. いつ友達に絵葉書を書きますか。
   だち　えはがき

3. 絵葉書にはどんなことを書きますか。
   えはがき

言葉のリスト
ことば

前略　　　　opening phrase (lit. ommited)
ぜんりゃく

ひっこす　　to move

[handwritten margin note: りょこうがいしゃ ryokoogaisha (travel agency)]

前略、上田さん。

Sidney Harbour, NWS
Australia

AFFIX
STAMP
HERE

ADDRES

Ms. Alice Ueda

10-1-Nishi Shinjuku

Shinjuku, Tokyo 160-0007

Japan

☐ ☐ ☐ ☐　POST

お元気ですか。私は今オーストラリアのシドニーに来ています。三か月前にアメリカからひっこしました。今、日本の旅行会社につとめています。オーストラリアには日本からあそびに来る人がたくさんいるので、とてもいそがしいですが、週末はビーチでのんびりしたり、どうぶつえんにコアラを見に行ったりします。上田さんはオーストラリアに来たことがありますか。今度ぜひあそびにきてください。

三月三日

山本ちひろ

読んだ後で   Comprehension

A. しつもんに日本語でこたえて下さい。

1. この葉書_{はがき}をもらった人はだれですか。

2. この葉書_{はがき}を書いた人はだれですか。

3. この人は四か月前どこにすんでいたと思いますか。

4. この人は今どこで何をしていますか。

5. この人はどうして葉書_{はがき}を書きましたか。

B. In Japan, it is common to send greeting cards on New Year's day and in the middle of summer and winter. New Year's cards must be sent so that they will arrive on January 1. The post office has a pre-set period when people can send cards to have them delivered on New Year's day. New Year's cards go on sale in November, and those sold in the post office come with prizes ranging from stamp sheets to televisions. You can also use regular postcards, but you need to write 年賀 to indicate that it is a New Year's card.

No New Year's card should be sent to a person who has lost an immediate family member or close relative during the past year. Instead, a winter greeting card (寒中見舞い) is sent in the middle of January.

Summer greeting cards (暑中見舞い) are sent to friends and acquaintances to inquire about the addressee's health in the summer heat and to tell news about yourself. Summer greeting cards sent after August 8 are called 残暑見舞い (*greetings in the lingering heat*) because this date indicates the beginning of autumn according to the old lunar calendar.

There are fixed expressions used in these cards. The following are some of the common expressions used in each type of card:

New Year's cards

Greeting phrases

明けましておめでとうございます。

Happy New Year

新年おめでとうございます。

Happy New Year

昨年は大変お世話になりありがとうございました。

Thank you for all your kind help throughout last year.

今年もどうぞよろしくおねがいします。

I hope for your continuous favor this year.

Winter greeting cards

Greeting phrases

寒中お見舞い申し上げます。

Sending you midwinter greetings.

Summer greeting cards

Greeting phrases

暑中お見舞い申し上げます。
しょちゅう　みま　もう　あ
Sending you midsummer greetings.

残暑お見舞い申し上げます。
ざんしょ　みま　もう　あ
Sending you late summer greetings.

1. Work with a partner. Read the following cards, and identify the type of each card, the sender, and the sender's recent news, if any.

暑中お見舞い申し上げます

梅雨が明けて急に暑くなりましたが、
お元気ですか。私はしごとで いそが
しい毎日をすごしています。お元気で
お過ごしください。

Before おぼん　山下友子

残暑お見舞い申し上げます

まだ暑い日が続きますが、お元気ですか。
先週は秋田のねぶた祭りを見にいきました。
夏バテしないようお体にお気をつけください。

山田みさ子

after おぼん

寒中お見舞い申し上げます

寒い日が続いていますが、お元気
ですか。ここは先週はじめて雪が
ふりました。
これから寒くなると思いますが、
お体に気をつけて下さい。

川口　新

2. Write summer and New Year's greeting cards to your friends following the examples on the previous page.

総合練習
そうごうれんしゅう

A. 私はだれですか

1. Work in a group of three or four. First, complete the following paragraph with your own information as in the example. Then, interview each other and write memos about other members in your group.

Example: 私の名前はスーザン・ロスです。私はシカゴから来ました。
誕生日は六月二十五日です。私は子供の時はしずかな子供
でした。よく本を読んだり、おんがくを聞いたりしました。
一か月に一度ピアノのレッスンに行きました。私はフランスに
行ったことがあります。十五さいの時でした。フランスに
友達がいたからです。

私の名前は＿＿＿＿＿＿＿＿＿＿＿です。私は＿＿＿＿＿＿＿＿＿か
ら来ました。誕生日は＿＿＿＿＿＿＿＿です。私は子供の時
＿＿＿＿＿＿＿＿＿＿子供でした。＿＿＿＿＿＿＿＿＿＿＿＿たり、
＿＿＿＿＿＿＿＿＿＿＿＿＿＿たりしました。＿＿＿＿＿＿＿に
＿＿＿＿＿＿＿＿＿＿＿＿＿＿＿＿＿＿ました。
＿＿＿＿＿＿＿＿＿＿＿＿＿＿＿＿＿＿＿＿＿＿＿＿こと
があります。＿＿＿＿＿＿＿＿＿＿＿時でした。＿＿＿＿＿＿＿＿
＿＿＿＿＿＿＿＿＿からです。

Sample interview questions

Q: どこから来ましたか。

Q: 子供の時、どんな子供でしたか。

Q: 子供の時、どんなことをしましたか。

Q: どんなことをしたことがありますか。何さいの時でしたか。
どうしてしたんですか。

2. Work in a group. Each group chooses a person and describes the person, except for the name, to the entire class by using そうです for hearsay. The class will try to figure out which member of the group is being described.

Member 1: この人は子供の時、しずかな子供だったそうです。

Member 2: この人はフランスに行ったことがあるそうです。

Member 3: この人は十五さいの時にフランスに行ったことがあるそうです。

Member 4: この人は子供の時、本を読んだり、おんがくを聞いたりしたそうです。

Note that the person chosen to be described must still use そうです although he/she will be talking about himself/herself.

B. ロールプレイ

1. You are talking with your Japanese friend about your childhood. Describe what sort of things you did or didn't do.
2. Talk about the best vacation you ever had. What happened? Why was it so special?
3. You are attending a college reunion. Talk about what sort of things you did in college.

APPENDIX A

PITCH ACCENTS

Whereas Enlish uses stress (or loudness) for accent, Japanese uses two relative pitches: high and low. Standard Japanese has the following rules.

1. The first mora (or syllable) and the second mora must have different pitches. Thus, a word always begins with either a low-high or a high-low combination.

2. Once the pitch goes low, it will never go up within a word.

3. For an N-mora word, there are N + 1 accent patterns. This becomes obvious when a particle follows a noun.

Common patterns

One-mora word

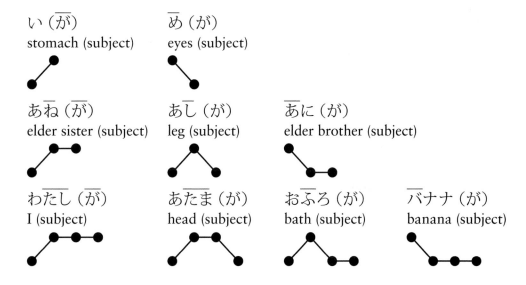

APPENDIX B
VERB CONJUGATIONS

			Irregular Verb	Irregular Verb	る - verb	う - verb
Dictionary Form			くる (to come)	する (to do)	たべる (to eat)	いく (to go)
Plain	Present	Affirmative	くる	する	たべる	いく
		Negative	こない	しない	たべない	いかない
	Past	Affirmative	きた	した	たべた	いった
		Negative	こなかった	しなかった	たべなかった	いかなかった
Polite	Present	Affirmative	きます	します	たべます	いきます
		Negative	きません	しません	たべません	いきません
	Past	Affirmative	みました	しました	たべました	いきました
		Negative	きません でした	しません でした	たべません でした	いきません でした
Volitional	Plain		こよう	しよう	たべよう	いこう
	Polite		きましょう	しましょう	たべましょう	いきましょう
Potential	Plain		こられる	できる	たべられる	いける
	Polite		こられます	できます	たべられます	いけます
Conditional			くれば	すれば	たべれば	いけば
て - form			きて	して	たべて	いって

う - verb	う - verb	う - verb	う - verb	う - verb
およぐ (to swim)	かえる (to go home)	かく (to write)	のむ (to drink)	はなす (to talk)
およぐ	かえる	かく	のむ	はなす
およがない	かえらない	かかない	のまない	はなさない
およいだ	かえった	かいた	のんだ	はなした
およがなかった	かえらなかった	かかなかった	のまなかった	はなさなかった
およぎます	かえります	かきます	のみます	はなします
およぎません	かえりません	かきません	のみません	はなしません
およぎました	かえりました	かきました	のみました	はなしました
およぎませんでした	かえりませんでした	かきませんでした	のみませんでした	はなしませんでした
およごう	かえろう	かこう	のもう	はなそう
およぎましょう	かえりましょう	かきましょう	のみましょう	はなしましょう
およげる	かえれる	かける	のめる	はなせる
およげます	かえれます	かけます	のめます	はなせます
およげば	かえれば	かけば	のめば	はなせば
およいで	かえって	かいて	のんだ	はなして

APPENDIX C
ADJECTIVE AND COPULA CONJUGATIONS

			い - adjective おおきい (big)	な - adjective しずか（な）(quiet)	Copula だ / です (be)
Plain	Present	Affirmative	おおきい	しずかだ	N だ
		Negative	おおきくない	しずかじゃない	N じゃない
	Past	Affirmative	おおきかった	しずかだった	N だった
		Negative	おおきくなかった	しずかじゃなかった	N じゃなかった
Polite	Present	Affirmative	おおきいです	しずかです	N です
		Negative	おおきくないです / おおきくありません	しずかじゃないです / しずかじゃありません	N じゃないです / N じゃありません
	Past	Affirmative	おおきかったです	しずかでした	N でした
		Negative	おおきくなかったです / おおきくありませんでした	しずかじゃなかったです / しずかじゃありませんでした	N じゃなかったです / N じゃありませんでした
		Prenominal	おおきい（だいがく）		
		Conditional	おおきければ		
		て - form	おおきくて		

APPENDIX D
COUNTERS AND TIME EXPRESSIONS

Common Counters			
General Counter 〜つ	**People** 〜にん	**Bound Objects** (book, magazine, etc.) 〜さつ	**Cylindrical Objects** (pen, umbrella, etc.) 〜ほん
1 ひとつ	ひとり	いっさつ	いっぽん
2 ふたつ	ふたり	にさつ	にほん
3 みっつ	さんにん	さんさつ	さんぼん
4 よっつ	よにん	よんさつ	よんほん
5 いつつ	ごにん	ごさつ	ごほん
6 むっつ	ろくにん	ろくさつ	ろっぽん
7 ななつ	しちにん	ななさつ	ななほん
8 やっつ	はちにん	はっさつ	はっぽん
9 ここのつ	くにん	きゅうさつ	きゅうほん
10 とお	じゅうにん	じゅっさつ じっさつ	じゅっぽん じっぽん
11 じゅういち	じゅういちにん	じゅういっさつ	じゅういっぽん
12 じゅうに	じゅうににん	じゅうにさつ	じゅうにほん

			Specific Time	
	Month ～がつ	Day ～にち	Time (o'clock) ～じ	Time (minute) ～ふん
1	いちがつ	ついたち	いちじ	いっぷん
2	にがつ	ふつか	にじ	にふん
3	さんがつ	みっか	さんじ	さんぷん
4	しがつ	よっか	よじ	よんぷん、よんふん
5	ごがつ	いつか	ごじ	ごふん
6	ろくがつ	むいか	ろくじ	ろっぷん
7	しちがつ	なのか	しちじ	ななふん、しちふん
8	はちがつ	ようか	はちじ	はっぷん、はちふん
9	くがつ	ここのか	くじ	きゅうぷん
10	じゅうがつ	とおか	じゅうじ	じゅっぷん、じっぷん
11	じゅういちがつ	じゅういちにち	じゅういちじ	じゅういっぷん
12	じゅうにがつ	じゅうににち	じゅうにじ	じゅうにふん
14		じゅうよっか (14)		
20		はつか (20)		
24		にじゅうよっか (24)		

	Year ~ねん	Month ~かげつ	Extent Week ~しゅうかん	Day ~にち	Hour ~じかん
1	いちねん	いっかげつ	いっしゅうかん	いちにち	いちじかん
2	にねん	にかげつ	にしゅうかん	ふつか (かん)	にじかん
3	さんねん	さんかげつ	さんしゅうかん	みっか (かん)	さんじかん
4	よねん	よんかげつ	よんしゅうかん	よっか (かん)	よじかん
5	ごねん	ごかげつ	ごしゅうかん	いつか (かん)	ごじかん
6	ろくねん	ろっかげつ	ろくしゅうかん	むいか (かん)	ろくじかん
7	しちねん ななねん	ななかげつ	ななしゅうかん	なのか (かん)	しちじかん
8	はちねん	はちかげつ はっかげつ	はっしゅうかん	ようか (かん)	はちじかん
9	きゅうねん くねん	きゅうかげつ	きゅうしゅうかん	ここのか (かん)	くじかん
10	じゅうねん	じゅっかげつ じっかげつ	じゅっしゅうかん じっしゅうかん	とおか (かん)	じゅうじかん
11	じゅういちねん	じゅういっかげつ	じゅういっしゅうかん	じゅういちにち (かん)	じゅういちじかん
12	じゅうにねん	じゅうにかげつ	じゅうにしゅうかん	じゅうににち (かん)	じゅうにじかん
14				じゅうよっか (かん) (14)	
20				はつか (かん) (20)	
24				にじゅうよっか (かん) (24)	

APPENDIX E

DEMONSTRATIVE WORDS （こ そ あ ど）

	こ series	そ series	あ series	ど series
	Close to both speaker and listener	Closer to listener than to speaker; moderately away from both	Away from both speaker and listener	Interrogative
Adjective	この〜 (this 〜)	その〜 (that 〜)	あの〜 (that 〜)	どの〜 (which 〜)
Pronoun	これ (this thing)	それ (that thing)	あれ (that thing)	どれ (which thing)
Location	ここ (this place)	そこ (that place)	あそこ (that place)	どこ (where)
Direction	こちら (this way)*	そちら (that way)	あちら (that way)	どちら (which way)
Manner	こう (this way)	そう (that way)	ああ (that way)	どう (how)

* こちら can be used for "this person" (polite)

APPENDIX F
KANJI LIST

No.	Kanji	Ch.	Kun-reading	On-reading	Examples
1	大	4	おお (きい)	ダイ	大学、大きい、大学院、大学院生
2	学	4	まな (ぶ)	ガク、ガッ	学生、学校、学生、〜学
3	校	4		コウ	学校、高校
4	先	4	さき	セン	先生、先週
5	生	4	なま、う (まれる)	セイ	学生、先生、一年生、留学生、生活
6	山	5	やま	サン、ザン	山川さん、富士山 、山の上
7	川	5	かわ、がわ	セン	小川さん、川中さん、ミシシッピー川
8	田	5	た	デン	上田さん、田中さん
9	人	5	ひと	ジン、ニン	日本人
10	上	5	うえ、かみ	ジョウ	テーブルの上
11	中	5	なか	チュウ	へやの中 、中国
12	下	5	した、下 (さい)	カ、ゲ	まどの下、いって下さい
13	小	5	ちい (さい)	ショウ	小さいへや
14	日	5	ひ、び	ニチ、ニ、ジツ、カ	日本、 昨日、今日、明日
15	本	5	もと	ホン、ボン、ポン	山田さんの本、日本

No.	Kanji	Ch.	Kun-reading	On-reading	Examples
16	今	6	いま	コン	今、何時ですか。、今週、今日 _{いま なんじ こんしゅう きょう}
17	私	6	わたし、わたくし	ン	私は日本人です。 _{わたし}
18	月	6	つき	ゲツ、ガツ	月、月曜日 _{げつようび}
19	火	6	ひ	カ	火曜日 _{かようび}
20	水	6	みず	スイ	水曜日 _{すいようび}
21	木	6	き	モク	木曜日 _{もくようび}
22	金	6	かね	キン	金曜日 _{きんようび}
23	土	6	つち	ト、ド	土曜日 _{どようび}
24	曜	6		ヨウ	日曜日 _{にちようび}
25	何	6	なに、なん		何曜日、何ですか。、何時ですか。 _{なんようび なん なんじ}
26	週	6		シュウ	今週の週末、先週 _{こんしゅう しゅうまつ せんしゅう}
27	末	6	すえ	マツ	週末 _{しゅうまつ}
28	休	6	やす（む）	キュウ	休みの日 _{やす ひ}
29	時	7	とき	ジ	一時、二時半、五時間べんきょうします _{いちじ にじはん ごじかん} 。その時 _{とき}
30	間	7	あいだ	カン	時間がありません。 _{じかん}
31	分	7	わ（ける）・ わ（かる）	フン・ブン ・プン	二十分、分かりました。 _{にじゅっぷん わ}
32	半	7		ハン	毎日六時半におきます。 _{まいにちろくじ はん}
33	毎	7		マイ	毎週シカゴにいきます。毎日、毎月 _{まいしゅう まいにち まいつき}
34	年	7	とし	ネン	三年生、毎年 _{さんねんせい まいとし}
35	好	7	す（き）	コウ	テニスが好きです。 _す
36	語	7	かた（る）	ゴ	日本語、フランス語ではなします。 _{にほんご ご}
37	高	7	たか（い）	コウ	古い高校、高い山 _{ふる こうこう たか}
38	番	7		バン	やさいが一番好きです。 _{いちばん}

No.	Kanji	Ch.	Kun-reading	On-reading	Examples
39	方	7	かた	ホウ	サッカーの方がフットボールより好きです。
40	新	7	あたら（しい）	シン	新しいレストラン
41	古	7	ふる（い）	コ	カラオケで古いうたをうたいます。
42	安	7	やす（い）	アン	今日はやさいが安いです。
43	友	7	とも	ユウ	友達とかいものにいくのが好きです。
44	一	8	ひと（つ）	イチ	一つ、一本、いぬが一匹います。
45	二	8	ふた（つ）	ニ	りんごが二つあります。二さつ、二本
46	三	8	みっ（つ）	サン	けしゴムを三つかいました。　三本
47	四	8	よ・よん・よっ（つ）	シ	四つ、四時、ビールが四本あります。
48	五	8	いつ（つ）	コ	五つ、ベルトが五本あります。
49	六	8	むっ（つ）	ロク・ロッ	六つ、六時、えんぴつが六本あります。
50	七	8	なな（つ）	シチ	七時、七本、オレンジが七つあります。
51	八	8	やっ（つ）	ハチ・ハッ	八つ、八時、ペンが八本あります。
52	九	8	ここの（つ）	キュウ・ク	九つ、九時、バナナが九本あります。
53	十	8	とう	ジュウ・ジュッ	靴下が十あります。　十本、十時
54	百	8		ヒャク・ビャク・ピャク	二百、三百、六百
55	千	8		セン・ゼン	二千、三千、八千、千円
56	万	8		マン	一万円、百万円
57	円	8		エン	五十円、このセーターは、7800円です。
58	店	8	みせ	テン	大きい店、店の人
59	行	9	い（く）	コウ	来年日本に行きます。
60	来	9	く（る）	ライ	いつアメリカに来ますか。来週は来ない

No.	Kanji	Ch.	Kun-reading	On-reading	Examples
61	帰	9	かえ（る）	キ	たいてい七時にうちに帰ります。
62	食	9	た（べる）	ショク	あさごはんを食べてください。学食
63	飲	9	の（む）	イン	ビールを二本飲みました。
64	見	9	み（る）	ケン	えいがを見に行きませんか。
65	聞	9	き（く）	ブン	インターネットでラジオを聞く、新聞
66	読	9	よ（む）	ドク	本を読むのが好きです。
67	書	9	か（く）	ショ	てがみをあまり書きません。
68	話	9	はな（す）	ワ	友達と日本語で話すのが好きです。
69	出	9	で（る）・で（かける）・だ（す）	シュッ	銀座に出かけます。
70	会	9	あ（う）	カイ	人と会って、カフェで話をします。
71	買	9	か（う）	バイ	買い物が好きです。
72	起	9	お（きる）	キ	毎朝六時に起きます。
73	寝	9	ね（る）	シン	十二時ごろ寝ます。
74	作	9	つく（る）	サク	ばんごはんはカレーを作りましょう。
75	入	9	はい（る）・い（れる）	ニュウ	はこに入ります。店に入ります。
76	男	10	おとこ	ダン	女の人と男の子がいます。
77	女	10	おんな	ジョ	山本さんは帽子をかぶった女の人です。
78	目	10	め	モク	目がわるいです。上から二番目です。
79	口	10	くち・ぐち	コウ	口が小さいです。　川口
80	耳	10	みみ	ジ	私は耳があまりよくありません。
81	足	10	あし	ソク	ジョンはせが高くて、足がながいです。

No.	Kanji	Ch.	Kun-reading	On-reading	Examples
82	手	10	て	シュ	手がきれいですね。テニスが上手です。
83	父	10	ちち・とう	フ	父のなまえはジョンです。お父さん
84	母	10	はは・かあ	ボ・モ	母のしごとは高校の先生です。お母さん
85	姉	10	あね・ねえ	シ	姉は私より三さい上です。お姉さん
86	兄	10	あに・にい	ケイ・キョウ	兄が一人います。お兄さん　兄弟
87	妹	10	いもうと	マイ	妹 はいません。
88	弟	10	おとうと	ダイ	弟 は四時にアルバイトにいきます。兄弟
89	家	10	いえ・うち	か	父は七時ごろ家に帰ります。
90	族	10		ゾク	私の家は四人家族です。
91	両	10		リョウ	両親はニューヨークにすんでいます。
92	親	10	おや	シン	両親はアメリカが好きです。親切な人
93	子	10	こ	シ	男の子が三人います。母のなまえは「よし子」です。
94	天	11		テン	明日の天気はいいでしょう。
95	気	11		キ	昨日は天気がよくありませんでした。
96	雨	11	あめ	ウ	雨がしずかにふっています。
97	雪	11	ゆき	セツ	明日は大雪です。
98	風	11	かぜ	フウ	風がつよいです。台風が来ます。
99	晴	11	は（れる）	セイ	ずっと晴れていて、雨がふりません。
100	温	11	あたた（かい）	オン	先週は気温が35度まで上がりました。
101	度	11		ド	おふろの温度は42度ぐらいです。
102	東	11	ひがし	トウ	まちの東の方にこうえんがあります。
103	西	11	にし	セイ	きょうとは東京の西にあります。

No.	Kanji	Ch.	Kun-reading	On-reading	Examples
104	南	11	みなみ	ナン	南のうみはとてもきれいで温かいです。
105	北	11	きた	ホク	ほっかいどうは日本の北にあります。
106	寒	11	さむ（い）	カン	カナダのふゆは寒いです。
107	暑	11	あつ（い）	ショ	東京のなつはむし暑いです。
108	多	11	おお（い）	タ	シンガポールは雨が多いです。
109	少	11	すく（ない）・すこ（し）	ショウ	このまちは人が少ないです。
110	冷	11	つめ（たい）	レイ	暑いから冷たいものを飲みましょう。
111	春	12	はる	シュン	春は雨が多いです。
112	夏	12	なつ	カ	日本の夏は暑いです。
113	秋	12	あき	シュウ	秋の山はとてもきれいです。
114	冬	12	ふゆ	トウ	冬は寒いから、時々雪がふります。
115	朝	12	あさ	チョウ	日曜日の朝、おそくまで寝るのが好きです。
116	昼	12	ひる	チュウ	母が昼ごはんを作りました。
117	晩	12		バン	明日の晩ごはんは天ぷらです。
118	午	12		ゴ	月曜日の午後、両親と家族が来ます。午前
119	前	12	まえ	ゼン	午前中にしゅくだいをします。中学の前名前
120	後	12	あと/うし（ろ）のち	ゴ	午後は暑かったです。一か月ぐらい後つくえの後ろ
121	去	12	さ（る）	キョ	去年南アメリカにいきました。
122	昨	12		サク	一昨年日本にいきました。昨日
123	供	12	とも/ども	キョウ	子供が二人います。
124	元	12	もと	ゲン	父は元気です。元気なお母さん
125	思	12	おも（う）	シ	昨日の朝は風がつよかったと思います。

No.	Kanji	Ch.	Kun-reading	On-reading	Examples
126	明	12	あか（るい）	メイ	明るいへや、明日、明るい人 あか　　　　あした　あか
127	回	12	まわ（る）	カイ	私の弟は一か月に十回ぐらいラーメンを 食べます。　　　　　　　　かい
111	春	12	はる	シュン	春は雨が多いです。 はる
112	夏	12	なつ	カ	日本の夏は暑いです。 　　　なつ
113	秋	12	あき	シュウ	秋の山はとてもきれいです。 あき
114	冬	12	ふゆ	トウ	冬は寒いから、時々雪がふります。 ふゆ　　　　　ときどき
115	朝	12	あさ	チョウ	日曜日の朝、おそくまで寝るのが好きで 　　　　あさ す。
116	昼	12	ひる	チュウ	母が昼ごはんを作りました。 　　ひる
117	晩	12		バン	明日の晩ごはんは天ぷらです。 　　　ばん
118	午	12		ゴ	月曜日の午後、両親と家族が来ます。午 　　　　ごご　　　　　　　　　　　　ご 前 ぜん
119	前	12	まえ	ゼン	午前中にしゅくだいをします。中学の前名 ごぜん　　　　　　　　　　　　　　まえ な 前 まえ
120	後	12	あと/うし（ろ ）のち	ゴ	午後は暑かったです。一か月ぐらい後つ ごご　　　　　　　　ご くえの後ろ
121	去	12	さ（る）	キョ	去年南アメリカにいきますた。 きょねん
122	昨	12		サク	一昨年日本にいきました。昨日 おととし　　　　　　　　きのう
123	供	12	とも/ども	キョウ	子供が二人います。 　ども
124	元	12	もと	ゲン	父は元気です。元気なお母さん 　　げんき　げんき
125	思	12	おも（う）	シ	昨日の朝は風がつよかったと思います。 きのう　あさ　　　　　　　　　　おも
126	明	12	あか（るい）	メイ	明るいへや、明日、明るい人 あか　　　　あした　あか
127	回	12	まわ（る）	カイ	私の弟は一か月に十回ぐらいラーメンを 食べます。　　　　　　　　かい

JAPANESE-ENGLISH GLOSSARY

This glossary contains all Japanese words that appear in the vocbulary list of each chapter. They are listed according to **gojuuon-jun** (Japanese alphabetical order). Each entry follows this format: word written in kana, word written in kanji, part of speech, English meaning, and chapter number where the word first appears. If the chapter number is followed by the letter P, the word is designated as supplementary vocabulary. Other abbreviations are identical to the labels used in each chapter's vocabulary list.

adv.	adverb	*conj.*	conjunction	*q. word*	question word
い-*adj.*	い-adjective	*inter.*	interjection	*pref.*	prefix
な-*adj.*	な-adjective	*count.*	counter	*suf.*	suffix
う-*v.*	う-verb	*n.*	noun	*part.*	particle
る-*v.*	る-verb	*exp.*	expression	*cop. v.*	copula verb
irr. v.	irregular verb	*demo.*	demonstrative	*number*	number

あ

アイスクリーム　*n.* ice cream, 9

あいます（会います）　う-*v.* (to) meet, 6

あおい（青い）　い-*adj.* blue, 4

あかい（赤い）　い-*adj.* red, 4

あがってください（上がって下さい。）*exp.* Please come in., 5

あがる（上がる）　う-*v.* to rise; to go up, 11

あかるい（明るい）　い-*adj.* bright, 5; cheerful, 10

あき（秋）　*n.* fall, autumn, 11

アクセサリー　*n.* accessories, 8

あけましておめでとうございます。（明けましておめでとうございます。）　*exp.* Happy New Year, 12

あさ（朝）　*n.* morning, 3

あさごはん（朝御飯）　*n.* breakfast, 3

あさって（明後日）　*n.* the day after tomorrow, 3

あし（足）　*n.* leg, foot, 10

アジアけんきゅう（アジア研究）　*n.* Asian studies, 2

あした（明日）　*n.* tomorrow, 3

あそこ　*demo.* over there; that place (far away from both speaker and listener), 4

あそびます（遊びます）　う-*v.* (to) play, 6

あたたかい（温かい）　い-*adj.* warm, 9

あたたかい（暖かい／温かい）　い-*adj.* warm, 11

あたま（頭）　*n.* head, あたまがいい smart, intelligent, 10

あたらしい（新しい）　い-*adj.* new, 4

あつい（熱い）　い-*adj.* hot (in temperature), 9

あつい（暑い／熱い）　い-*adj.* hot, 11

あに（兄）　*n.* older brother (the speaker's), 10

あね（姉）　*n.* older sister (the speaker's), 10

あの　*demo.* that Noun over there, 5

あのう　*inter.* uh, well, 2

アパート　*n.* apartment, 4

あびます（浴びます）　る-*v.* (to) take (a shower)　シャワーを　あびます take a shower.
　The dictionary form is あびる., 3

あぶら（油 / 脂）　*n.* oil あぶらが　おおい fatty, oily, 9

あまい（甘い）　い-*adj.* sweet, 9

あまり　*adv.* very (always used with a negative form), 4

あめ（雨）　*n.* rain, rainy, 11

アメリカ　*n.* America, U.S., 2

ありがとうございます。　*exp.* Thank you., 1

あります　う-*v.* (to) be held, (to) have　The dictionary form is ある., 3

あるいて（歩いて）*exp.* on foot , 5

あるきます（歩きます）　う-*v.* (to) walk　The dictionary form is あるく., 6

アルバイト　*n.* part time job , 6

あれ　*demo.* that object over there; that, 4

あれは　にほんごで　なんと　いいますか。　*exp.* How do you say that (over there) in Japanese?, 1

い

いい　い-*adj.* good, 4

いいえ　*inter.* no, don't mention it, you're welcome, 2

いいえ、そうじゃありません *exp.* No, that's not so., 2

いいえ、そんなことはありません。　*exp.* No, that's not the case, 10

いいえ、まだまだです。　*exp.* No, I still have a long way to go, 10

いいえ、わかりません。*exp.* No, I don't understand it., 1

いいます（言います）　う-*v.* (to) say, 6

いかが　*q. word* how (polite form of どう), 8

いきます（行きます）　う-*v.* (to) go　The dictionary form is いく., 3

イギリス　*n.* England, 2

いくつ　*q. word* how many, 8

いくつ　*q. word* How old 〜 ? おいくつ　polite form of いくつ, 10

いくら　*q. word* how much (money), 8

いす（椅子）*n.* chair, 5

いそがしい（忙しい）　い-*adj.* busy, 6

イタリア　*n.* Italy, 9

いち（一）　*number* one, 3

いちじ（一時）　*time exp.* one o'clock, 2

いちねんせい（一年生）　*n.* freshman, first-year student　(The suffix せい may be dropped), 2

いつ　*q. word* when, 3

いっしょに（一緒に）　*adv.* together, 6

いって　ください。　*exp.* Please say it. / Repeat after me., 1

いつも　*adv.* always, 3

いぬ（犬）　*n.* dog, 5

いま（今）　*adv.* now, 2

います　る-*v.* to be; to exist (used for an animate beings). Dictionary form is いる., 4

いもうと（妹）　*n.* younger sister (the speaker's), 10

いもうとさん（妹さん）　*n.* younger sister (someone else's), 10

いや（な）　な-*adj.* unpleasant, 11

イヤリング　*n.* earring, 8
いらっしゃい。　*exp.* Welcome! Come in., 5
いらっしゃいませ。　　*exp.* Welcome, 8
いる（要る）　う*-v.* to need something, 9
いれる（入れる）　る*-v.* to put, 8

う

うえ（上）　*loc. n.* on; above; over, 5
うしろ（後ろ）　*loc. n.* behind; back of, 5
うた（歌）　*n.* song, 7
うたう（歌う）　う*-v.* to sing, 7
うち（家）　*n.* home, 3
うでどけい（腕時計）　*n.* wristwatch, 8
うどん　*n.* Japanese wheat noodles, 9
うみ（海）　*n.* ocean, sea, 12
うりば（売り場）　*n.* department, section (of a store), 8
うれしい（嬉しい）　い*-adj.* happy, 6
うんどう（運動）*n.* (physical) exercises, 6

え

え（絵）　*n.* picture, 5
エアロビクス　*n.* aerobics, 7
えいが（映画）　*n.* movie, 3
えいご（英語）　*n.* English, 2
えーと　*exp.* Well, Let's see. . . , 12
えき（駅）　*n.* station, 4
〜えん（〜円）　*count.* counter for Japanese currency, 8
えんぴつ（鉛筆）　*n.* pencil, 4

お

お〜　*pref.* polite prefix おなまえ　polite form of なまえ (name), 2
おいしい　い*-adj.* delicious, good, tasty, 7
おおい（多い）　い*-adj.* a lot, much, 9
おおきい（大きい）　い*-adj.* big, 4
おおきい　こえで　いってください。*exp.* Please speak loudly. (Teacher's request), 1
おおきい　こえで　おねがいします。*exp.* Please speak loudly. (Student's request), 1
オーストラリア　n. Australia, 2
おかあさん（お母さん）　*n.* mother (someone else's), 10
おきます（起きます）　る*-v.* (to) get up, (to) wake up　　The dictionary form is おきる., 3
おくさん（奥さん）　*n.* wife (someone else's), 10
おこさん（お子さん）　*n.* child (someone else's), 10
（お）さしみ（御刺身）　*n.* sashimi (fillet of fresh raw fish, such as tuna) (usually used with お at the beginning), 9
おじいさん（お祖父さん）　*n.* grandfather (someone else's), 10
おしいれ（押し入れ）　*n.* Japanese-style closet; storage space, 5

おじゃまします (お邪魔します。)　*exp.* Thank you. (literally, *I will intrude on you*) (said before going inside someone's house or apartment), 5

(お) すし (御寿司)　*n.* sushi (usually used with お at the beginning), 9

おちゃ (お茶)　*n.* tea, green tea, 7

おとうさん (お父さん)　*n.* father (someone else's), 10

おとうと (弟)　*n.* younger brother (the speaker's), 10

おとうとさん (弟さん)　*n.* younger brother (someone else's), 10

おとこ (男)　*n.* male, おとこの人 man, 10

おととい (一昨日)　n. the day before yesterday, 3

おととし (一昨年)　*n.* the year before last year, two years ago, 12

おにいさん (お兄さん)　*n.* older brother (someone else's), 10

おねえさん (お姉さん)　*n.* older sister (someone else's), 10

おばあさん (お祖母さん)　*n.* grandmother (someone else's), 10

おはよう。　*exp.* Good morning. / Hello. (casual), 1

おはようございます。　*exp.* Good morning. / Hello., 1

おふろ (お風呂)　*n.* bath, 3

おもいで (思い出)　*n.* memories, 12

おもしろい (面白い)　い-*adj.* interesting, 6

およぎます (泳ぎます)　う-*v.* (to) swim, 6

オレンジ　*n.* orange, 7

おわる (終わる)　う-*v.* to end, 7

おんがく (音楽)　n. music, 6

おんな (女)　*n.* female おんなの人 woman, おんなのこ girl, 10

か

か　*part.* question marker, 2

〜かい (〜階)　*count.* counter for floors of a building, 8

〜かい (〜回)　*suf.* times, 12

がいこく (外国)　*n.* foreign countries, 12

かいしゃいん (会社員)　*n.* businessman, 10

かいて ください。　*exp.* Please write., 1

かいもの (買い物)　n. shopping, 6

かえります (帰ります)　う-*v.* (to) return, (to) go home　The dictionary form is かえる, 3

かう (買う)　う-*v.* to buy, 7

かお (顔)　*n.* face, 10

かかります　う-*v.* to take (time), it costs, 5

かきます (書きます)　う-*v.* (to) write, 6

がくしょく (学食)　*n.* school cafeteria (a shortened form of 学生しょくどう), 5

がくせい (学生)　*n.* student, 2

がくせいかいかん (学生会館)　*n.* student union, 5

〜かげつ (〜か月)　*suf.* counter for month, 12

かけます　る-*v.* (to) make (a phone call)　でんわを かけます, 6

かける　る-*v.* to put on (glasses), 10

かさ (傘)　*n.* umbrella, 8

かぜ (風)　*n.* wind, 11

かぞく (家族)　*n.* family, the speaker's family, 10

〜かた（〜方）　*suf.* person, polite form of 人 but cannot stand alone and needs a modifier いいかた (nice person), 10

かたい（固い）　い *-adj.* hard, tough, 9

〜がつ（〜月）　*suf.* month, 11

がっき（学期）　*n.* semester, quarter いちがっき one semester はるがっき spring semester/ quarter, 12

かっこいい　い *-adj.* good-looking, neat, 10

がっこう（学校）　*n.* school, 3

かなしい（悲しい）　い *-adj.* sad, 6

カナダ　*n.* Canada, 2

かばん（鞄）　*n.* luggage, bag, 4

カフェ　*n.* coffee shop, café (more recent word), 4

かぶき（歌舞伎）　*n.* kabuki (Japanese traditional performing art), 12

かぶる　う *-v.* ot put on (a hat, a cap), 10

かみ（髪）　*n.* hair, 10

かようび（火曜日）　*n.* Tuesday, 3

から　*part.* from, 5

〜から　きました。　*exp.* came from 〜 [casual], 2

からい（辛い）　い *-adj.* spicy, 9

カラオケ　*n.* Karaoke, sing-along, 7

カレーライス　*n.* curry and rice dish. An abbreviated form is カレー, 9

カロリー　*n.* calorie, 9

かわ（川）　*n.* river, 5

かわいい（可愛い）　い *-adj.* cute, adorable, 10

かんこく（韓国）　*n.* South Korea, 2

き

き（木）　*n.* tree, 5

きいて　ください。　*exp.* Please listen., 1

きいろい（黄色い）　い *-adj.* yellow, 4

きおん（気温）　*n.* air temperature, 11

ききます（聞きます／聴きます）　う *-v.* (to) ask; (to) listen to, 6

きこう（気候）　*n.* climate, 11

きせつ（季節）　*n.* season, 11

きた（北）　*n.* north, 11

きっさてん（喫茶店）　*n.* coffee shop (more traditional word), 4

きのう（昨日）　*n.* yesterday , 3

きます（来ます）　*irr. v.* (to) come, 3

きもの（着物）　*n.* traditional Japanese clothes, kimono, 12

キャンプ　*n.* camping, 12

きゅう、く（九）　*number* nine, 3

きゅう（な）（急（な））　な *-adj.* sudden きゅうに suddenly, 11

きょう（今日）　*n.* today, 3

きょうかい（教会）　*n.* church, 12

きょうかしょ（教科書）　*n.* textbook, 4

きょうしつ（教室）　*n.* classroom, 5

きょうだい (兄弟)   *n.* sibling, 10
きょねん (去年)   *n.* last year, 11
きらい (な)(嫌い (な))   な -*adj.* dislike, hate, 7
きる (着る)   る -*v.* to put on (sweater, shirt, jacket), 10
きれい (な)   な-*adj.* clean; pretty; neat, 4
ぎんこう (銀行)   *n.* bank, 4
きんようび (金曜日)   *n.* Friday, 3

く

くじ (九時)   *time exp.* nine o'clock, 2
くだもの (果物)   *n.* fruit, 7
くち (口)   *n.* mouth, 10
くつ (靴)   *n.* shoes, 8
クッキー   *n.* cookie, 9
くつした (靴下)   *n.* socks, 8
くも (雲)   *n.* cloud, 11
くもり (曇り)   *n.* cloudy, 11
くもる (曇る)   う -*v.* to become cloudy, 11
くらい (暗い)   い-*adj.* dark, 5
〜ぐらい、〜くらい   *suf.* about duration, quantity, 5
クラシック   *n.* classical music, 7
クラス   *n.* class, 3
クリスマス   *n.* Christmas, 12
くるま (車)   *n.* car, 5
くろい (黒い)   い-*adj.* black, 4

け

けいえいがく (経営学)   *n.* management/business administration, 2
ケーキ   *n.* cake, 9
ゲーム   *n.* game, 6
けさ (今朝)   *n.* this morning, 11
けしゴム (消しゴム)   *n.* eraser, 4
けっこん (結婚)   *n.* marriage,   〜とけっこんする to marry 〜 , けっこんしている to be married, 10
げつようび (月曜日)   *n.* Monday, 3
けんか   *n. fight, quarrel*   けんかをする to fight, 12
げんき (な)(元気 (な))   な-*adj.* healthy, cheerful, lively (person), 6

こ

こ (子)   *n.* child, おとこのこ boy, おんなのこ girl, 10
〜ご (〜語)   *suf.* language   にほんご Japanese language, 2
〜ご (〜後)   *suf.* from 〜 , after 〜 (3 年ご three years from now), 12
ご〜 (御〜)   *pref.* polite prefix   ごちゅうもん, 9
ご (五)   *number* five, 3
こうえん (公園)   *n.* park, 4
こうがく (工学)   *n.* engineering, 2

こうこう（高校） *n.* high school, 2
こうちゃ（紅茶） *n.* black tea, 7
コート *n.* coat, 8
こうばん（交番） *n.* police box, 4
コーヒー *n.* coffee, 3
コーラ *n.* cola, 7
ごかぞく（ご家族） *n.* family (someone else's), 10
ごきょうだい（ご兄弟） *n.* siblings (someone else's), 10
こくばん（黒板） *n.* blackboard, chalkboard, 5
ここ *demo.* here; this place, 4
ごご（午後） *n.* p.m., afternoon, 2
ごじ（五時） *time exp.* five o'clock, 2
ごしゅじん（ご主人） *n.* husband (someone else's), 10
ごぜん（午前） *n.* a.m., forenoon, morning, 2
こちら *n.* this person, this way, 2
こちらこそ。 *exp.* It is I who should be saying that. Thank YOU., 2
こと *n.* thing (intangible), 7
ことし（今年） *n.* this year, 11
こども（子供） *n.* child, 10
この *demo.* this Noun, 5
このへん（この辺） *n.* this area, 4
ごはん（御飯） *n.* meal, cooked rice, 3
ごめんください（御免下さい。） *exp.* Excuse me; Anyone home?, 5
ゴルフ *n.* golf, 7
これ *demo.* this object, this, 4
これは　にほんごで　なんと　いいますか。 *exp.* How do you say this in Japanese?, 1
〜ごろ *suf.* about 〜 (used only with a time expression), 3
こん〜（今〜） *pref.* this こんしゅう、こんばん, 3
こんげつ（今月） *n.* this month, 12
コンサート *n.* concert, 6
こんしゅう（今週） *n.* this week, 3
こんど（今度） *n.* next time, 6
こんにちは。 *exp.* Good afternoon. / Hello., 1
こんばん（今晩） *n.* tonight, 3
こんばんは。 *exp.* Good evening. / Hello., 1
コンビニ *n.* convenience store, 4
コンピュータ *n.* computer, 5

さ
〜さい（〜歳 / 才） *suf.* 〜 years old, 10
さいきん（最近） *n.* recent, recently (it can be used as an adverb), 11
さかな（魚） *n.* fish, 7
さがる（下がる） う -*v.* to fall; to go down, 11
〜さつ（〜冊） *count.* counter for bound objects (e.g. books, magazines), 8
ざっし（雑誌） *n.* magazine, 6
さびしい（寂しい） い -*adj.* lonely, 6

さむい（寒い）　い-adj. cold, 11
サラダ　n. salad, 9
さようなら。／さよなら。　exp. Good-bye., 1
〜さん　suf. Mr./Mrs./Miss/Ms. 〜, 1
さん（三）　number three, 3
さんじ（三時）　time exp. three o'clock, 2
サンドイッチ　n. sandwich, 9
ざんねん（な）（残念（な））　な-adj. sorry, regrettable, 6
さんねんせい（三年生）　n. junior, third-year student (The suffix せい may be dropped.), 2
さんぽ（散歩）　n. (to take) a walk　さんぽ（を）　します to take a walk, 6

し

〜じ（〜時）　suf. 〜 o'clock, 2
ジーンズ　n. jeans, 8
しかくい（四角い）　い-adj. square, 10
〜じかん　suf. 〜 hours, 5
しごと（仕事）　n. job, 6
じしょ（辞書）　n. dictionary, 4
しずか（な）（静か（な））　な-adj. quiet, 5
した（下）　loc. n. under; beneath, 5
しちじ（七時）　time exp. seven o'clock, 2
しつもん（質問）　n. question　しつもん（を）します (to) ask a question, 6
しつれいします。　exp. Good-bye. / Excuse me., 1
じてんしゃ（自転車）　n. bicycle, 5
します　irr. v. (to) do　The dictionary form is する, 3
じゃあ、また。　exp. See you later. (literally, Well then, again.), 1
ジャケット　n. jacket, 8
しゃしん（写真）　n. photograph, 5
ジャズ　n. jazz, 7
シャツ　n. shirt, 8
シャワー　n. shower, 3
じゅう（十）　number ten, 3
じゅういちじ（十一時）　time exp. eleven o'clock, 2
〜しゅうかん（〜週間）　suf. for 〜 weeks, 12
じゅうじ（十時）　time exp. ten o'clock, 2
ジュース　n. juice, 7
じゅうにじ（十二時）　time exp. twelve o'clock, 2
しゅうまつ（週末）　n. weekend, 3
じゅぎょう（授業）　n. class, course, 3
しゅくだい（宿題）　n. homework, 3
しゅじん（主人）　n. husband (the speaker's), 10
しゅっしん（出身）　n. one's native country, hometown, birthplace, alma mater, 2
しゅみ（趣味）　n. hobby, 7
しょう〜（小〜）　pref. elementary, 小学生 elementary school student, 小学校 elementary
　school, 10

しょうがつ（正月）　*n.* the New Year often used with the polite prefix お，　おしょうがつ，　12

じょうず（な）（上手（な））　な *-adj.* good at, skillful, 10

ジョギング　*n.* jogging, 6

しょくじ（食事）　*n.* dining, 7

しょくじする（食事する）　*irr. v.* to dine, 7

しょくひん（食品）　*n.* food, 8

しょっぱい　い *-adj.* salty, 9

しる（知る）　う *-v.* to come to know, しっている to know, しらない don't know, 11

しろい（白い）　い *-adj.* white, 4

〜じん（〜人）　*suf.* 〜 nationality アメリカじん, 2

しんしふく（紳士服）　*n.* menswear, 8

じんじゃ（神社）　*n.* Shinto shrine, 12

しんせつ（な）（親切（な））　な *-adj.* kind, 10

しんぶん（新聞）　*n.* newspaper, 6

す

すいぞくかん（水族館）　*n.* aquarium, 12

すいようび（水曜日）　*n.* Wednesday, 3

スーツ　*n.* suit, 8

スーパー　*n.* supermarket, 4

スープ　*n.* soup, 9

スカート　*n.* skirt, 8

すき（な）（好き（な））　な *-adj.* like, 7

スキー　*n.* skiing, ski, 7

すきでもきらいでもありません（好きでも嫌いでもありません。）　*exp.* I don't like or dislike it, 7

すくない（少ない）　い *-adj.* a little bit, 9

すこし（少し）　*adv.* a little, a few, 8

すずしい（涼しい）　い *-adj.* cool, 11

すっぱい（酸っぱい）　い *-adj.* sour, 9

ステーキ　*n.* steak, 9

ストッキング　*n.* stockings, pantyhose, 8

スパゲティ　*n.* spaghetti, 9

スペイン　*n.* Spain, 2

スポーツ　*n.* sport, 7

ズボン　*n.* trousers (primarily men's), 8

（あのう、）すみません。*exp.* (Eh,) Excuse me., 1

すみません。*exp.* I am sorry. / Excuse me., 1

すむ（住む）　う *-v.* to reside, 〜にすんでいる to live in 〜, 10

する　*irr. v.* to put on (accessories), 10

せ

せ（背）　*n.* back (part of the body); height (of a person), 10

〜せい（〜生）　*suf.* 〜 student だいがくせい　college student いちねんせい　freshman, 2

せいかつ（生活）　*n.* life, living, 3

セーター   *n.* sweater, 8
セール   *n.* sale, 8
セット   *n.* a Western-style fixed menu, 9
ぜひ（是非）   *adv.* I'd love to, by all means, 6
せまい（狭い）   い-*adj.* cramped; narrow, 5
ゼロ（ゼロ）   *number* zero, 3
せんげつ（先月）   *n.* last month, 12
せんこう（専攻）   *n.* major, 2
せんしゅう（先週）   *n.* last week, 3
せんせい   *n.* Teacher, 1
〜せんせい   *suf.* Professor 〜, 1
ぜんぜん（全然）   *adv.* not at all (used with negative form of verb), 3
せんたく（洗濯）   *n.* laundry, 6
ぜんぶで（全部で）   *exp.* all together, 8

そ

そうじ（掃除）   *n.* cleaning, 6
そうじゃないです   *exp.* No, that's not so., 2
そうですか   *exp.* Is that so? I see., 2
そこ   *demo.* there; that place (close to the listener or slightly removed from both speaker and listener), 4
そと（外）   *loc. n.* outside, 5
その   *demo.* that Noun, 5
そば（蕎麦）   *n.* Japanese buckwheat noodles, 9
そふ（祖父）   *n.* grandfather (the speaker's), 10
ソファ   *n.* sofa, 5
そぼ（祖母）   *n.* grandmother (the speaker's), 10
それ   *demo.* that object; that (close to the listener or slightly removed from both speaker and listener), 4
それから   *conj.* and, in addition, then, 7
それは　にほんごで　なんと　いいますか。   *exp.* How do you say that in Japanese?, 1

た

だい〜（大〜）   *pref.* very much, 大すき like very much, 7
たいいくかん（体育館）   *n.* gym, 5
だいがく（大学）   *n.* college, university, 2
だいがくいんせい（大学院生）   *n.* graduate student, 2
だいがくせい（大学生）   *n.* college student, 2
だいじょうぶ（な）（大丈夫（な））   な-*adj.* all right, no problem, 6
たいてい   *adv.* usually, 3
たいふう（台風）   *n.* typhoon, 11
たいへん（な）（大変（な））   な-*adj.* tough, 6
たいわん（台湾）   *n.* Taiwan, 2
たかい（高い）   い-*adj.* tall, high, 4
たかい（高い）   い-*adj.* expensive, 7
たくさん   *adv.* a lot, many, much, 8
たてもの（建物）   *n.* building, structure, 4
たとえば（例えば）   *conj.* for example, 7

たのしい（楽しい）　い-*adj.* fun, 6
たべます（食べます）　る-*v.* (to) eat　The dictionary form is たべる., 3
たべもの（食べ物）　*n.* food, 7
たまご（卵／玉子）　*n.* egg, 7
だれ　*q. word* who, 4
たんじょうび（誕生日）　*n.* birthday, 8
たんす（箪笥）　*n.* chest; drawers, 5

ち

ちいさい（小さい）　い-*adj.* small, 4
チーズ　*n.* cheese, 9
ちか（地下）　*n.* basement　ちかいっかい first basement floor, 8
ちかく（近く）　*loc. n.* near; vicinity, 5
チキン　*n.* chicken, 9
ちち（父）　*n.* father (the speaker's), 10
チャーハン　*n.* Chinese style fried rice, 9
ちゃいろい（茶色い）　い-*adj.* brown, 4
ちゅう〜（中〜）　*pref.* middle, 中学生 middle school student, 中学校 middle school/junior high school, 10
ちゅうがく（中学）　*n.* junior high school (shortened form of 中学校), 12
ちゅうかりょうり（中華料理）　*n.* Chinese cooking, 9
ちゅうごく（中国）　*n.* China, 2
ちゅうもん（注文）　*n.* order, 9
ちゅうもんする（注文する）　*irr. v.* to order, 9
チョコレート　*n.* chocolate, 9
ちょっと　*adv.* a little, a few (more casual than すこし), 8
ちょっと　つごうが　わるくて（ちょっと都合が悪くて。）*exp.* I'm a little busy. (literally, *Sorry, it's a little inconvenient.*), 6
ちょっと　ようじが　あって（ちょっと用事があって。）*exp.* Sorry, I have some errands/ business to attend to., 6

つ

〜つ　*count.* general counter (Japanese origin number), 8
つぎ（次）　*n.* next, 3
つくえ（机）　*n.* desk, 5
つくる（作る）　う-*v.* to make, 7
つづく（続く）　う-*v.* to continue, 11
〜って　なんですか。*exp.* What does 〜 mean?, 1
〜って　いいます。　*exp.* Colloquial version of 〜と　いいます。, 2
つとめる（勤める）　る-*v.* to become employed, 〜につとめている to be employed at, work for 〜 , 10
つま（妻）　*n.* wife (of speaker), 10
つまらない　い-*adj.* boring, 6
つめたい（冷たい）　い-*adj.* cold, 9
つゆ（梅雨）　*n.* rainy season, 11
つよい（強い）　い-*adj.* strong, 11

つり（釣り）　*n.* fishing, 7

て

て（手）　*n.* hand, 10

で　*part.* at, in, on, etc. (location of action or event)　としょかんで　べんきょうします。, 3

で　*part.* by means of, by, with, 5

Ｔシャツ　*n.* T-shirt, 8

デート　*n.* dating, 12

デートする　*irr. v.* to go out on a date, 12

テーブル　*n.* table, 5

ていしょく（定食）　*n.* Japanese or Asian-styled dish set, 9

〜ている　*aux. v.* resultant state, 10

でかけます（出かけます）　る-*v.* (to) go out, 6

てがみ（手紙）　*n.* letter, 6

デザート　*n.* dessert, 9

です　*cop. v.* (to) be, 2

テスト　*n.* test, 4

テニス　*n.* tennis テニスを　します to play tennis, 6

デパート　*n.* department store, 4

でも　*conj.* but, 7

てら（寺）　*n.* Buddhist temple, (often used as おてら), 12

テレビ　*n.* TV, 3

てんき（天気）　*n.* weather, 11

てんきよほう（天気予報）　*n.* weather forecast, 11

てんぷら（天麩羅／天ぷら）　*n.* tempura (fish, shrimp, and vegetables battered and deep-fried), 9

でんわ（電話）　*n.* telephone, 5

でんわばんごう（電話番号）　*n.* telephone number, 3

と

と　*part.* with, together with (association), 6

と　*part.* and (exhaustive listing), 6

〜と　いいます。／〜って　いいます。　*exp.* You call it 〜. / You say 〜, 1

〜ど（〜度）　*suf.* degree, 11

〜ど（〜度）　*suf.* times, 12

ドア　*n.* door, 5

トイレ　*n.* toilet; restroom, 5

どういたしまして。　*exp.* You are welcome., 1

どうして　*q. word* why, 7

トースト　*n.* toast, 9

どうですか。　*exp.* How about 〜 ?, 7

どうぶつえん（動物園）　*n.* zoo, 12

どうも　*adv.* very, 4

どうも　ありがとう　*adv.* Thank you very much, 4

どうも　すみません　*adv.* I'm very sorry, 4

とき（時）　*n.* when, at the time of 〜　　（子供の時 when I was a child）, 12

ときどき（時々）　*adv.* sometimes, 3
とけい（時計）　*n.* clock; watch, 5
どこ　*q. word* where, 2
ところ（所）　*n.* place, 5
とし（年）　*n.* age; としうえ elder, older; ととした younger, 10
としょかん（図書館）　*n.* library, 3
どちら　*q. word* where (more polite than どこ), which way, 2
とても　*adv.* very (always used with an affirmative form), 4
となり（隣）　*loc. n.* next to, 5
どの　*demo.* which Noun, 5
どのぐらい、どのくらい　*exp.* how long, how much, how many, 5
トマト　*n.* tomato, 7
ともだち（友達）　*n.* friend, 6
どようび（土曜日）　*n.* Saturday, 3
ドライブ　*n.* driving (pleasure driving), 7
とる（撮る）　う -v. to take (a photograph), しゃしんを　とる , 7
とる（取る）　う -v. to take, get, 8
どれ　*q. word* which one, 4
ドレス　*n.* dress, 8
どんな　*q. word* what kind of, 4

な

なあ　*part.* A particle of exclamation to express desires or feelings without addressing anyone in particular. Used in casual speech, 12
なか（中）　*loc. n.* in; inside, 5
ながい（長い）　い -adj. long, 10
なく（泣く）　う -v. to cry, 12
なつ（夏）　*n.* summer, 11
なな、しち（七）　*number* seven, 3
なに／なん（何）　*q. word* what, 2
なまえ（名前）　*n.* name, 2
なんせい（南西）　*n.* southwest, 11
なんとう（南東）　*n.* southeast, 11

に

に（二）　*number* two, 3
に　*part.* at, on, in (point in time)　10 じに　ねます。, 3
に　*part.* to (goal, activity + に) クラスに　いきます。, 3
に　*part.* in order to; for (purpose), 6
に　*part.* to (goal, receiver), 6
〜に　する　*exp.* to decide on 〜 , 9
にがい（苦い）　い -adj. bitter, 9
にぎやか（な）（賑やか（な））　な -adj. lively (place or event), 6
にく（肉）　*n.* meat, 7
にし（西）　*n.* west, 11
にじ（二時）　*time exp.* two o'clock, 2

〜にち（〜日）　*suf.* day, 12
にちようび（日曜日）　*n.* Sunday, 3
にねんせい（二年生）　*n.* sophomore, second-year student (The suffix せい may be dropped.), 2
にほん（日本）　*n.* Japan, 2
にわかあめ（にわか雨）　*n.* (rain) shower, 11
〜にん（〜人）　*suf.* 〜 people, 10
にんじん　*n.* carrot, 7

ね

ネクタイ　*n.* tie, 8
ねこ（猫）　*n.* cat, 5
ネックレス　*n.* necklace, 8
ねます（寝ます）　る -*v.* (to) go to bed　The dictionary form is ねる., 3
〜ねん（〜年）　*suf.* year　いちねん first year, 2
〜ねん（〜年）　*suf.* specific year (2008 年), counter for year（十年）, 12

の

の　*part.* noun modifier marker (of), ('s), 2
ノート　*n.* notebook, 4
のち（後）　*n.* after, 11
〜のち〜　*exp.* after　あめのちはれ sunny after rain, 11
のみます（飲みます）　う -*v.* (to) drink　The dictionary form is のむ., 3
のみもの（飲み物）　*n.* drinks, 7
のる（乗る）　う -*v.* to get on, to ride（ひこうきに　のる　get on a plane）, 12

は

は　*part.* topic marker, 2
〜は　ありませんか。　*exp.* Do you have 〜 ? / Do you carry 〜 ? (lit, Isn't there 〜 ?), 8
〜は　にほんごで　なんと　いいますか。*exp.* How do you say 〜 in Japanese?, 1
パーティ　*n.* party, 6
はい（ええ）、そうです。*exp.* Yes, that's so., 2
はい、わかりました。*exp.* Yes, I understand it., 1
はい／ええ　*inter.* yes, 2
ハイキング　*n.* hiking, 7
はいります（入ります）　う -*v.* (to) take (a bath), (to) enter　The dictionary form is はいる.
　おふろに　はいります　take a bath., 3
はく　う -*v.* to put on (skirt, pants, socks), 10
はくぶつかん（博物館）　*n.* museum, 12
はこ（箱）　*n.* box, 8
はじまる（始まる）　う -*v.* to begin, 7
はじめまして。〜です。どうぞ　よろしく。*exp.* How do you do? I am 〜 . Pleased to meet you., 1
はじめて（初めて）　*adv.* for the first time, 12
バス　*n.* bus, 5
バスケットボール　*n.* basketball (abbreviated as バスケット or バスケ), 7
はち（八）　*number* eight, 3
はちじ（八時）　*time exp.* eight o'clock, 2

はな (鼻)   *n.* nose, 10
はなします (話します)   う-*v.* (to) talk, 6
バナナ   *n.* banana, 7
はは (母)   *n.* mother (the speaker's), 10
はやい (速い)   い-*adj.* fast; quick, 5
はやい (早い)   い-*adj.* early, 11
はる (春)   *n.* spring, 11
はれ (晴れ)   *n.* sunny, 11
はれる (晴れる)   る-*v.* to become sunny, 11
バレンタインデー   *n.* St. Valentine's Day, 12
ハロウィン   *n.* Halloween, 12
はん (半)   *time exp.* half past いちじはん 1:30, 2
はん (〜半)   *suf.* half past, 2
ばん (晩)   *n.* night, evening, 3
パン   *n.* bread, 9
〜ばん (め)(〜番 (目))   *suf.* 〜 th (ordinal), 10
ばんごはん (晩御飯)   *n.* supper, dinner, 3
パンツ   *n.* (primarily women's) trousers, shorts, 8
はんとし (半年)   *n.* a half year, 12
ハンドバッグ   *n.* handbag, 8
ハンバーガー   *n.* hamburger, 9

ひ
ビーフ   *n.* beef, 9
ビール   *n.* beer, 7
ひがし (東)   *n.* east, 11
〜ひき (〜匹)   *count.* counter for fish and small four-legged animals, 8
ひくい (低い)   い-*adj.* low, カロリーがひくい low in calories, 9
ピクニック   *n.* picnic, 6
ひこうき (飛行機)   *n.* airplane, 12
ピザ   *n.* pizza, 9
びじゅつかん (美術館)   *n.* art museum, 12
ビジネス   *n.* business, 2
ひだり (左)   *loc. n.* to the left; left side, 5
ヒップホップ   *n.* hip-hop music, 7
ビデオ   *n.* video, 5
ひと (人)   *n.* person, 5
ひとりっこ (一人っ子)   *n.* only child, 10
ひま (な)(暇 (な))   な-*adj.* free, idle, unscheduled, 6
びょういん (病院)   *n.* hospital, 4
ひる (昼)   *n.* afternoon, 3
ビル   *n.* building, 4
ひるごはん (昼御飯)   *n.* lunch, 3
ひろい (広い)   い-*adj.* spacious; wide, 5

ふ

プール　*n.* pool, 6

ふく（服）　*n.* clothing, 8

ふく（吹く）　う -*v.* to blow, 11

ふじんふく（婦人服）　*n.* woman's clothing, 8

フットボール　*n.* (American) football（アメフト）, 7

ふとる（太る）　う -*v.* to gain weight、ふとっている　to be fat, 10

ふとん（布団）　*n.* futon, 5

ふゆ（冬）　*n.* winter, 11

フライドチキン　*n.* fried chicken, 9

ブラウス　*n.* blouse, 8

フランス　*n.* France, 2

ふる（降る）　う -*v.* to fall, 11

ふるい（古い）　い -*adj.* old, 4

プレゼント　*n.* present, 12

ブロンド（ブロンド）　*n.* blond, 10

～ふん（～分）　*count.* ～ minute, (for) ～ minute, 3

ぶんがく（文学）　*n.* literature, 2

ぶんぼうぐ（文房具）　*n.* stationery, 8

へ

へ　*part.* to (direction)　がっこうへ　いきます。, 3

ベッド　*n.* bed, 5

へや（部屋）　*n.* room, 5

ベルト　*n.* belt, 8

ペン　*n.* pen, 4

べんきょう（勉強）　*n.* study, 3

べんきょうします（勉強します）　*irr. v.* (to) study　The dictionary form is べんきょうする, 3

ほ

ほう（方）　*n.* direction, 11

ぼうし（帽子）　*n.* hat, cap, 8

ポーク　*n.* pork, 9

ボールペン　*n.* ball point pen, 4

ぼく（僕）　*pron.* I (normally used by males), 2

ほくせい（北西）　*n.* northwest, 11

ほくとう（北東）　*n.* northeast, 11

ほそながい（細長い）　い -*adj.* long/elongated, 10

ポップス　*n.* pop music, 7

～ほん（～本）　*count.* counter for long, cylindrical objects (e.g. pen, pencil, bottle), 8

ほん（本）　*n.* book, 3

ほんだな（本棚）　*n.* bookshelf, 5

ほんとうに / ほんとに（本当に）　*adv.* truly, really, indeed　（ほんとに is more conversational than ほんとうに）, 11

ほんや（本屋）　*n.* bookstore, 4

ま

〜まい（〜枚）　*count.* counter for thin objects (e.g. paper, shirts, plates), 8
まい〜（毎〜）　*pref.* every　まいしゅう　まいあさ　まいばん　まいにち, 3
まいあさ（毎朝）　*n.* every morning, 3
まいしゅう（毎週）　*n.* every week, 3
マイナス　*n.* minus, 11
まいにち（毎日）　*n.* every day, 3
まいばん（毎晩）　*n.* every night, 3
まえ（前）　*loc. n.* in front of; in the front, 5
〜まえ（〜前）　*suf.* 〜 ago　（一年まえ one year ago）, 12
まち（町）　*n.* town, 4
まちます（待ちます）　う-*v.* (to) wait, 6
まつり（祭り）　*n.* festival (often used as おまつり）, 12
まで　*part.* until, to, 5
まど（窓）　*n.* window, 5
まるい（丸い）　い-*adj.* round, 10
まんなか（真ん中）　*n.* center, middle, middle child, 10

み

みぎ（右）　*loc. n.* to the right, 5
みじかい（短い）　い-*adj.* short (length), 10
みず（水）　*n.* water, 7
みせ（店）　*n.* store, shop, 8
みせる（見せる）　る-*v.* to show, 8
みて　ください。　*exp.* Please look at it., 1
みなみ（南）　*n.* south, 11
みます（見ます）　る-*v.* (to) see, (to) watch　The dictionary form is みる., 3
みみ（耳）　*n.* ear, 10
ミュージカル　*n.* musical, 12
ミルク　*n.* milk, 7

む

むしあつい（蒸し暑い）　い-*adj.* humid, 11
むずかしい（難しい）　い-*adj.* difficult, 6

め

め（目）　*n.* eye, 10
メール　*n.* email, 6
めがね（眼鏡）　*n.* glasses, 10
メキシコ　*n.* Mexico, 2

も

も　*part.* similarity marker (also, too), 2
もう　*adv.* a little 〜, 8
もう　いちど　いってください。　*exp.* Please say it again. (Teacher's request), 1
もう　いちど　おねがいします。　*exp.* Please say it again. (Student's request), 1

もう　すこし　ゆっくり　おねがいします。 *exp.* Please say it slowly., 1
もくようび (木曜日)　*n.* Thursday, 3
もっと　*adv.* more, 7
もの (物)　*n.* thing (tangible), 5
もらう　う -*v.* to receive, to get, 12

や

や　*part.* and (when listing examples), 7
〜や (〜屋)　*suf.* store (e.g. ほんや bookstore), 4
やきゅう (野球)　*n.* baseball, 7
やさい (野菜)　*n.* vegetable, 7
やさしい (易しい、優しい)　い -*adj.* easy, kind, 6
やさしい　ことばで　いってください。(やさしい　言葉で　言って下さい。)　*exp.*
　　Please say it in easier words, 8
やすい (安い)　い -*adj.* inexpensive, 7
やすみ (休み)　*n.* rest; absence, a day off, 6
やすみのひ (休みの日)　*n.* a day off; holiday, 6
やせる　る -*v.* to lose weight, やせている　to be thin, 10
やま (山)　*n.* mountain, 5
やまのぼり (山登り)　*n.* mountain climbing, 12
やわらかい (柔らかい)　い -*adj.* soft , 9

ゆ

ゆうえんち (遊園地)　*n.* amusement park, 12
ゆうがた (夕方)　*n.* evening, 11
ゆうびんきょく (郵便局)　*n.* post office, 4
ゆうめい (な)(有名 (な))　な -*adj.* famous, 4
ゆき (雪)　*n.* snow, snowy, 11
ゆっくり　*adv.* slowly, ゆっくりします, to relax; to, 6
ゆびわ (指輪)　*n.* ring, 8

よ

ようしょく (洋食)　*n.* western style cuisine, 9
〜ようび (〜曜日)　*suf.* days of the week, 3
よく　*adv.* often, well, 3
よこ (横)　*loc. n.* next to; at the side of, 5
よじ (四時)　*time exp.* four o'clock, 2
よねんせい (四年生)　*n.* senior, fourth-year student (The suffix せい may be dropped.), 2
よびます (呼びます)　う -*v.* (to) call (someone); (to) invite, 6
よみます (読みます)　う -*v.* (to) read　The dictionary form is よむ., 3
よる (夜)　*n.* night, 11
よわい (弱い)　い -*adj.* weak, 11
よん、し (四)　*number* four, 3
よんで ください。 *exp.* Please read., 1

ら

ラーメン　*n.* ramen, Chinese noodles in soup, 9
らいげつ (来月)　*n.* next month, 12
ライス　*n.* rice, 9
らいねん (来年)　*adv.* next year, 2
ラップ　*n.* rap music, 7
ラボ (ラボ)　*n.* laboratory, 5
ランチ　*n.* lunch, lunch set A- ランチ Lunch set A, 9
ランチ　*n.* lunch, set lunch (Western style), 9

り

りっぱ (な)(立派 (な))　な-*adj.* fine; splendid, 4
りゅうがくせい (留学生)　*n.* foreign student, 2
りょう　*n.* dormitory, 4
りょうしん (両親)　*n.* parents, 6
りょうり (料理)　*n.* meal; cuisine りょうりをします to fix a meal, 6
りょこう (旅行)　*n.* traveling, 7
りんご　*n.* apple, 7

れ

れい (零)　number zero, 3
れきし (歴史)　*n.* history, 2
レストラン　*n.* restaurant, 4
レタス　*n.* lettuce, 7

ろ

ろく (六)　*number* six, 3
ろくじ (六時)　*time exp.* six o'clock, 2
ロック　*n.* rock and roll, 7

わ

ワイン　*n.* wine, 7
わかりましたか。　*exp.* Do you understand it?, 1
わかる (分かる)　う-*v.* to understand, 日本語がわかる to understand Japanese, 10
わしょく (和食)　*n.* Japanese cuisine (にほんりょうり), 9
わたし (私)　*pron.* I (used by both males and females), 2
わるい (悪い)　い-*adj.* bad, 11

を

を　*part.* direct object marker　ほんを　よみます。, 3
～を　おねがいします　（～をお願いします）　*exp.* I would like to have ～, 9
～を　ください　（～を下さい）　*exp.* Please give me ～, 8

ENGLISH-JAPANESE GLOSSARY

A

a day off; holiday　やすみのひ (休みの日)　*n.*, 6
a little　ちょっと　*adv.*, 8
a little 〜　もう　*adv.*, 8
a little bit　すくない (少ない)　い -*adj.*, 9
a little, a few　すこし (少し)　*adv.*, 8
a lot, many, much　たくさん　*adv.*, 8
a lot, much　おおい (多い)　い -*adj.*, 9
a.m., forenoon, morning　ごぜん (午前)　*n.*, 2
about 〜 (used only with a time expression)　〜ごろ suf., 3
about duration, quantity　〜ぐらい suf., 5
accessories　アクセサリー　*n.*, 8
aerobics　エアロビクス　*n.*, 7
after　のち (後)　*n.*, 11
after　〜のち〜　*exp.*, 11
afternoon　ひる (昼)　*n.*, 3
age　とし (年)　*n.*, 10
〜 ago　(一年まえ one year ago)　〜まえ (〜前)　*suf.*, 12
air temperature　きおん (気温)　*n.*, 11
airplane　ひこうき (飛行機)　*n.*, 12
all right, no problem　だいじょうぶ (な)(大丈夫 (な))　な -*adj.*, 6
all together　ぜんぶで (全部で)　*exp.*, 8
always　いつも *adv.*, 3
America, U.S.　アメリカ *n.*, 2
amusement park　ゆうえんち (遊園地)　*n.*, 12
and (exhaustive listing)　と *part.*, 6
and (when listing examples)　や　*part.*, 7
and, in addition, then　それから　*conj.*, 7
apartment　アパート *n.*, 4
apple　りんご　*n.*, 7
aquarium　すいぞくかん (水族館)　*n.*, 12
art museum　びじゅつかん (美術館)　*n.*, 12
Asian studies　アジアけんきゅう (アジア研究) *n.*, 2
(to) ask; (to) listen to　ききます (聞きます / 聴きます)　う -*v.*, 6
at, in, on, etc. (location of action or event)　としょかんで　べんきょうします。　で *part.*, 3
at, on, in (point in time)　10 じに　ねます。　に *part.*, 3
Australia　オーストラリア *n.*, 2

B

back (part of the body); height (of a person)　せ (背)　*n.*, 10
bad　わるい (悪い)　い -*adj.*, 11
ball point pen　ボールペン *n.*, 4

banana　バナナ　*n.*, 7
bank　ぎんこう (銀行)　*n.*, 4
baseball　やきゅう (野球)　*n.*, 7
basement　ちか (地下)　*n.*, 8
basketball　バスケットボール　*n.*, 7
bath　おふろ (お風呂)　*n.*, 3
(to) be　です　*cop. v.*, 2
(to) be held, (to) have　The dictionary form is ある．ありますう *-v.*, 3
(to) become cloudy　くもる (曇る)　う *-v.*, 11
(to) become employed　つとめる (勤める)　る *-v.*, 10
(to) become sunny　はれる (晴れる)　る *-v.*, 11
bed　ベッド　*n.*, 5
beef　ビーフ　*n.*, 9
beer　ビール　*n.*, 7
(to) begin　はじまる (始まる)　う *-v.*, 7
behind; back of　うしろ (後ろ)　*loc. n.*, 5
belt　ベルト　*n.*, 8
bicycle　じてんしゃ (自転車)　*n.*, 5
big　おおきい (大きい)　い *-adj.*, 4
birthday　たんじょうび (誕生日)　*n.*, 8
bitter　にがい (苦い)　い *-adj.*, 9
black　くろい (黒い)　い *-adj.*, 4
black tea　こうちゃ (紅茶)　*n.*, 7
blackboard, chalkboard　こくばん (黒板)　*n.*, 5
blond　ブロンド (ブロンド)　*n.*, 10
blouse　ブラウス　*n.*, 8
(to) blow　ふく (吹く)　う *-v.*, 11
blue　あおい (青い)　い *-adj.*, 4
book　ほん (本)　*n.*, 3
bookshelf　ほんだな (本棚)　*n.*, 5
bookstore　ほんや (本屋)　*n.*, 4
boring　つまらない　い *-adj.*, 6
box　はこ (箱)　*n.*, 8
bread　パン　*n.*, 9
breakfast　あさごはん (朝御飯)　*n.*, 3
bright　あかるい (明るい)　い *-adj.*, 5
brown　ちゃいろい (茶色い)　い *-adj.*, 4
Buddhist temple (often used as おてら)　てら (寺)　*n.*, 12
building　ビル　*n.*, 4
building, structure　たてもの (建物)　*n.*, 4
bus　バス　*n.*, 5
business　ビジネス　*n.*, 2
businessman　かいしゃいん (会社員)　*n.*, 10
busy　いそがしい (忙しい)　い *-adj.*, 6
but　でも　*conj.*, 7

(to) buy　かう（買う）　う-v., 7
by means of, by, with　で part., 5

C

cake　ケーキ　n., 9
(to) call (someone); (to) invite　よびます（呼びます）　う-v., 6
calorie　カロリー　n., 9
came from ～ [casual]　～から　きました。 exp., 2
camping　キャンプ　n., 12
Canada　カナダ n., 2
car　くるま（車）　n., 5
carrot　にんじん　n., 7
cat　ねこ（猫）　n., 5
center, middle, middle child　まんなか（真ん中）　n., 10
chair　いす（椅子）　n., 5
cheerful　あかるい（明るい）　い-adj., 10
cheese　チーズ　n., 9
chest; drawers　たんす（箪笥）　n., 5
chicken　チキン　n., 9
child　こども（子供）　n., 10
child (someone else's)　おこさん（お子さん）　n., 10
child　こ（子）　n., 10
China　ちゅうごく（中国）　n., 2
Chinese cooking　ちゅうかりょうり（中華料理）　n., 9
Chinese style fried rice　チャーハン　n., 9
chocolate　チョコレート　n., 9
Christmas　クリスマス　n., 12
church　きょうかい（教会）　n., 12
class　クラス　n., 3
class, course　じゅぎょう（授業）　n., 3
classical music　クラシック　n., 7
classroom　きょうしつ（教室）　n., 5
clean; pretty; neat　きれい（な）　な-adj., 4
cleaning　そうじ（掃除）　n., 6
climate　きこう（気候）　n., 11
clock; watch　とけい（時計）　n., 5
clothing　ふく（服）　n., 8
cloud　くも（雲）　n., 11
cloudy　くもり（曇り）　n., 11
coat　コート　n., 8
coffee　コーヒー n., 3
coffee shop (more traditional word)　きっさてん（喫茶店）　n., 4
coffee shop, café (more recent word)　カフェ n., 4
cola　コーラ　n., 7
cold　さむい（寒い）　い-adj., 11
cold　つめたい（冷たい）　い-adj., 9

college student　だいがくせい（大学生）　*n.*, 2
college, university　だいがく（大学）　*n.*, 2
(to) come　きます（来ます）　*irr. v.*, 3
(to) come to know　しる（知る）　う *-v.*, 11
computer　コンピュータ　*n.*, 5
concert　コンサート　*n.*, 6
(to) continue　つづく（続く）　う *-v.*, 11
convenience store　コンビニ　*n.*, 4
cookie　クッキー　*n.*, 9
cool　すずしい（涼しい）　い *-adj.*, 11
counter for bound objects (e.g. books, magazines)　〜さつ（〜冊）　*count.*, 8
counter for fish and small four-legged animals　〜ひき（〜匹）　*count.*, 8
counter for floors of a building　〜かい（〜階）　*count.*, 8
counter for Japanese currency　〜えん（〜円）　*count.*, 8
counter for long, cylindrical objects (e.g. pen, pencil, bottle)　〜ほん（〜本）　*count.*, 8
counter for month　〜かげつ（〜か月）　*suf.*, 12
counter for thin objects (e.g. paper, shirts, plates)　〜まい（〜枚）　*count.*, 8
counter, general (Japanese origin number)　〜つ　*count.*, 8
cramped; narrow　せまい（狭い）　い *-adj.*, 5
(to) cry　なく（泣く）　う *-v.*, 12
curry and rice dish　カレーライス　*n.*, 9
cute, adorable　かわいい（可愛い）　い *-adj.*, 10

D

dark　くらい（暗い）　い *-adj.*, 5
dating　デート　*n.*, 12
day　〜にち（〜日）　*suf.*, 12
the day after tomorrow　あさって（明後日）　*n.*, 3
the day before yesterday　おととい（一昨日）　*n.*, 3
days of the week　〜ようび（〜曜日）　*suf.*, 3
(to) decide on　〜.　〜に　する　*exp.*, 9
degree　〜ど（〜度）　*suf.*, 11
delicious, good, tasty　おいしい　い *-adj.*, 7
department　うりば（売り場）　*n.*, 8
department store　デパート　*n.*, 4
desk　つくえ（机）　*n.*, 5
dessert　デザート　*n.*, 9
dictionary　じしょ（辞書）　*n.*, 4
difficult　むずかしい（難しい）　い *-adj.*, 6
(to) dine　しょくじする（食事する）　*irr. v.*, 7
dining　しょくじ（食事）　*n.*, 7
direct object marker　ほんを　よみます。　を *part.*, 3
direction　ほう（方）　*n.*, 11
dislike, hate　きらい（な）（嫌い（な））　な *-adj.*, 7
(to) do　The dictionary form is する　します *irr. v.*, 3
Do you have 〜 ? / Do you carry 〜 ? (lit., Isn't there 〜 ?)　〜は　ありませんか。　*exp.*, 8

Do you understand it?　わかりましたか。　*exp.*, 1
dog　いぬ（犬）　*n.*, 5
door　ドア　*n.*, 5
dormitory　りょう　*n.*, 4
dress　ドレス　*n.*, 8
(to) drink　The dictionary form is のむ.　のみます（飲みます）　う*-v.*, 3
drinks　のみもの（飲み物）　*n.*, 7
driving (pleasure driving)　ドライブ　*n.*, 7

E

ear　みみ（耳）　*n.*, 10
early　はやい（早い）　い*-adj.*, 11
earring　イヤリング　*n.*, 8
east　ひがし（東）　*n.*, 11
easy, kind　やさしい（易しい, 優しい）　い*-adj.*, 6
(to) eat　The dictionary form is たべる.　たべます（食べます）　る*-v.*, 3
egg　たまご（卵 / 玉子）　*n.*, 7
eight　はち（八）　*number*, 3
eight o'clock　はちじ（八時）　*time exp.*, 2
elementary　しょう～（小～）　*pref.*, 10
eleven o'clock　じゅういちじ（十一時）　*time exp.*, 2
e-mail　メール　*n.*, 6
(to) end　おわる（終わる）　う*-v.*, 7
engineering　こうがく（工学）　*n.*, 2
England　イギリス　*n.*, 2
English　えいご（英語）　*n.*, 2
eraser　けしゴム（消しゴム）　*n.*, 4
evening　ゆうがた（夕方）　*n.*, 11
every　まいしゅう　まいあさ　まいばん　まいにち　まい～（毎～）　*pref.*, 3
every day　まいにち（毎日）　*n.*, 3
every morning　まいあさ（毎朝）　*n.*, 3
every night　まいばん（毎晩）　*n.*, 3
every week　まいしゅう（毎週）　*n.*, 3
(Eh,) Excuse me.　（あのう、）すみません。　*exp.*, 1
Excuse me; Anyone home?　ごめんください（御免下さい。）　*exp.*, 5
A particle of exclamation　なあ　*part.*, 12
exercise (physical)　うんどう（運動）　*n.*, 6
expensive (Chapter 4: high, tall)　たかい（高い）　い*-adj.*, 7
eye　め（目）　*n.*, 10

F

face　かお（顔）　*n.*, 10
(to) fall (as rain or snow)　ふる（降る）　う*-v.*, 11
fall, autumn　あき（秋）　*n.*, 11
(to) fall; to go down　さがる（下がる）　う*-v.*, 11
family (someone else's)　ごかぞく（ご家族）　*n.*, 10

family, the speaker's family　かぞく（家族）　*n.*, 10
famous　ゆうめい（な）（有名（な））　な-*adj.*, 4
fast; quick　はやい（速い）　い-*adj.*, 5
father (someone else's)　おとうさん（お父さん）　*n.*, 10
father (the speaker's)　ちち（父）　*n.*, 10
female　おんな（女）　*n.*, 10
festival (often used as おまつり)　まつり（祭り）　*n.*, 12
fight, quarrel　けんか　*n.*, 12
fine; splendid　りっぱ（な）（立派（な））　な-*adj.*, 4
fish　さかな（魚）　*n.*, 7
fishing　つり（釣り）　*n.*, 7
five　ご（五）　*number*, 3
five o'clock　ごじ（五時）　*time exp.*, 2
food　しょくひん（食品）　*n.*, 8
food　たべもの（食べ物）　*n.*, 7
(American) football (アメフト)　フットボール　*n.*, 7
for ～ weeks　～しゅうかん（～週間）　*suf.*, 12
for example　たとえば（例えば）　*conj.*, 7
for the first time　はじめて（初めて）　*adv.*, 12
foreign countries　がいこく（外国）　*n.*, 12
foreign student　りゅうがくせい（留学生）　*n.*, 2
four　よん、し（四）　*number*, 3
four o'clock　よじ（四時）　*time exp.*, 2
France　フランス　*n.*, 2
free, idle, unscheduled　ひま（な）（暇（な））　な-*adj.*, 6
freshman, first-year student (The suffix せい may be dropped.)　いちねんせい（一年生）　*n.*, 2
Friday　きんようび（金曜日）　*n.*, 3
fried chicken　フライドチキン　*n.*, 9
from　から　*part.*, 5
from ～, after ～　～ご（～後）　*suf.*, 12
fruit　くだもの（果物）　*n.*, 7
fun　たのしい（楽しい）　い-*adj.*, 6
futon　ふとん（布団）　*n.*, 5

G

(to) gain weight　ふとる（太る）　う-*v.*, 10
game　ゲーム　*n.*, 6
(to) get on, to ride　のる（乗る）　う-*v.*, 12
(to) get up, (to) wake up　The dictionary form is おきる．おきます（起きます）　る-*v.*, 3
glasses　めがね（眼鏡）　*n.*, 10
(to) go　The dictionary form is いく．いきます（行きます）　う-*v.*, 3
(to) go out　でかけます（出かけます）　る-*v.*, 6
(to) go out on a date　デートする　*irr. v.*, 12
(to) go to bed　The dictionary form is ねる．ねます（寝ます）　る-*v.*, 3
golf　ゴルフ　*n.*, 7
good　いい　い-*adj.*, 4

Good afternoon. / Hello. こんにちは。 *exp.*, 1
good at, skillful じょうず (な) (上手 (な)) *な -adj.*, 10
Good evening. / Hello. こんばんは *exp.*, 1
good-looking, neat かっこいい *い -adj.*, 10
Good morning. / Hello. おはようございます。 *exp.*, 1
Good morning. / Hello. (casual) おはよう。 *exp.*, 1
Good-bye. さようなら。／さよなら。 *exp.*, 1
Good-bye. / Excuse me. しつれいします。 *exp.*, 1
graduate student だいがくいんせい (大学院生) *n.*, 2
grandfather (someone else's) おじいさん (お祖父さん) *n.*, 10
grandfather (the speaker's) そふ (祖父) *n.*, 10
grandmother (someone else's) おばあさん (お祖母さん) *n.*, 10
grandmother (the speaker's) そぼ (祖母) *n.*, 10
gym たいいくかん (体育館) *n.*, 5

H

hair かみ (髪) *n.*, 10
half past はん (～半) *suf.*, 2
half past いちじはん 1:30 はん (半) *time exp.*, 2
a half year はんとし (半年) *n.*, 12
Halloween ハロウィン *n.*, 12
hamburger ハンバーガー *n.*, 9
hand て (手) *n.*, 10
handbag ハンドバッグ *n.*, 8
happy うれしい (嬉しい) *い -adj.*, 6
Happy New Year あけましておめでとうございます。(明けましておめでとうございます。)
     exp., 12
hard, tough かたい (固い) *い -adj.*, 9
hat, cap ぼうし (帽子) *n.*, 8
head あたま (頭) *n.*, 10
healthy, cheerful, lively (person) げんき (な) (元気 (な)) *な -adj.*, 6
here; this place ここ *demo.*, 4
high school こうこう (高校) *n.*, 2
hiking ハイキング *n.*, 7
hip-hop music ヒップホップ *n.*, 7
history れきし (歴史) *n.*, 2
hobby しゅみ (趣味) *n.*, 7
home うち (家) *n.*, 3
homework しゅくだい (宿題) *n.*, 3
hospital びょういん (病院) *n.*, 4
hot あつい (暑い / 熱い) *い -adj.*, 11
hot (in temperature) あつい (熱い) *い -adj.*, 9
～ hours ～じかん *suf.*, 5
how (polite form of どう) いかが *q. word*, 8
How about ～? どうですか。 *exp.*, 7
How do you do? I am ～. Pleased to meet you. はじめまして。～です。どうぞよろしく。 *exp.*, 1

How do you say ～ in Japanese?　～は　にほんごで　なんと　いいますか。 *exp.,* 1
How do you say that (over there) in Japanese? あれは　にほんごで　なんと　いいますか。 *exp.,* 1
How do you say that in Japanese? それは　にほんごで　なんと　いいますか。 *exp.,* 1
How do you say this in Japanese? これは　にほんごで　なんと　いいますか。 *exp.,* 1
how long, how much, how many　どのぐらい／どのくらい　*exp.,* 5
how many　いくつ　*q. word,* 8
how much (money)　いくら　*q. word,* 8
How old ～?　いくつ　*q. word,* 10
humid　むしあつい（蒸し暑い）　*い -adj.,* 11
husband (someone else's)　ごしゅじん（ご主人）　*n.,* 10
husband (the speaker's)　しゅじん（主人）　*n.,* 10

I

I (normally used by males)　ぼく（僕）　*pron.,* 2
I (used by both males and females)　わたし（私）　*pron.,* 2
I am sorry. / Excuse me.　すみません。　*exp.,* 1
I'd love to, by all means　ぜひ（是非）　*adv.,* 6
I don't like or dislike it.　すきでもきらいでもありません（好きでも嫌いでもありません。）　*exp.,* 7
I'm a little busy. (literally, *Sorry, it's a little inconvenient.*)　ちょっと　つごうが　わるくて（ちょっと都合が悪くて。）*exp.,* 6
I'm very sorry　どうも　すみません　*adv.,* 4
I would like to have ～.　～を　おねがいします（～をお願いします）　*exp.,* 9
ice cream　アイスクリーム　*n.,* 9
in; inside　なか（中）　*loc. n.,* 5
in front of; in the front　まえ（前）　*loc. n.,* 5
in order to; for (purpose)　に　*part.,* 6
inexpensive　やすい（安い）　*い -adj.,* 7
interesting　おもしろい（面白い）　*い-adj.,* 6
Is that so? I see.　そうですか　*exp.,* 2
It is I who should be saying that. Thank YOU.　こちらこそ。　*exp.,* 2
Italy　イタリア　*n.,* 9

J

jacket　ジャケット　*n.,* 8
Japan　にほん（日本）　*n.,* 2
Japanese buckwheat noodles　そば（蕎麦）　*n.,* 9
Japanese cuisine（にほんりょうり）　わしょく（和食）　*n.,* 9
Japanese or Asian-styled dish set　ていしょく（定食）　*n.,* 9
Japanese-style closet; storage space　おしいれ（押し入れ）　*n.,* 5
Japanese wheat noodles　うどん　*n.,* 9
jazz　ジャズ　*n.,* 7
jeans　ジーンズ　*n.,* 8
job　しごと（仕事）　*n.,* 6
jogging　ジョギング　*n.,* 6
juice　ジュース　*n.,* 7

junior, third-year student (The suffix せい may be dropped.) さんねんせい（三年生） *n.*, 2

junior high school (shortened form of 中学校) ちゅうがく（中学） *n.*, 12

K

kabuki (Japanese traditional performing art) かぶき（歌舞伎） *n.*, 12

Karaoke, sing-along カラオケ *n.*, 7

kind しんせつ（な）（親切（な）） な-*adj.*, 10

L

laboratory ラボ（ラボ） *n.*, 5

language にほんご Japanese language 〜ご（〜語） *suf.*, 2

last month せんげつ（先月） *n.*, 12

last week せんしゅう（先週） *n.*, 3

last year きょねん（去年） *n.*, 11

laundry せんたく（洗濯） *n.*, 6

leg, foot あし（足） *n.*, 10

letter てがみ（手紙） *n.*, 6

lettuce レタス *n.*, 7

library としょかん（図書館） *n.*, 3

life, living せいかつ（生活） *n.*, 3

like すき（な）（好き（な）） な-*adj.*, 7

literature ぶんがく（文学） *n.*, 2

lively (place or event) にぎやか（な）（賑やか（な）） な-*adj.*, 6

lonely さびしい（寂しい） い-*adj.*, 6

long ながい（長い） い-*adj.*, 10

long/elongated ほそながい（細長い） い-*adj.*, 10

(to) lose weight やせる る-*v.*, 10

low ひくい（低い） い-*adj.*, 9

luggage, bag かばん（鞄） *n.*, 4

lunch ひるごはん（昼御飯） *n.*, 3

lunch, luch set ランチ *n.*, 9

lunch, set lunch (Western style) ランチ *n.*, 9

M

magazine ざっし（雑誌） *n.*, 6

major せんこう（専攻） *n.*, 2

(to) make つくる（作る） う-*v.*, 7

(to) make (a phone call) でんわを　かけます　かけます る-*v.*, 6

male おとこ（男） *n.*, 10

management/business administration けいえいがく（経営学） *n.*, 2

marriage けっこん（結婚） *n.*, 10

meal, cooked rice ごはん（御飯） *n.*, 3

meal; cuisine りょうりをします to fix a meal りょうり（料理） *n.*, 6

meat にく（肉） *n.*, 7

(to) meet あいます（会います） う-*v.*, 6

memories おもいで（思い出） *n.*, 12

menswear   しんしふく（紳士服）   *n.*, 8
Mexico   メキシコ *n.*, 2
middle   ちゅう〜（中〜）   *pref.*, 10
milk   ミルク   *n.*, 7
minus   マイナス   *n.*, 11
〜 minute, (for) 〜 minute   〜ふん（〜分）   *count.*, 3
Monday   げつようび（月曜日）   *n.*, 3
month   〜がつ（〜月）   *suf.*, 11
more   もっと   *adv.*, 7
morning   あさ（朝）   *n.*, 3
mother (someone else's)   おかあさん（お母さん）   *n.*, 10
mother (the speaker's)   はは（母）   *n.*, 10
mountain   やま（山）   *n.*, 5
mountain climbing   やまのぼり（山登り）   *n.*, 12
mouth   くち（口）   *n.*, 10
movie   えいが（映画）   *n.*, 3
Mr./Mrs./Miss/Ms. 〜   〜さん *suf.*, 1
museum   はくぶつかん（博物館）   *n.*, 12
music   おんがく（音楽）   *n.*, 6
musical   ミュージカル   *n.*, 12

N

name   なまえ（名前）   *n.*, 2
〜 nationality アメリカじん   〜じん（〜人）   *suf.*, 2
(one's) native country   しゅっしん（出身）   *n.*, 2
near; vicinity   ちかく（近く）   *loc. n.*, 5
necklace   ネックレス   *n.*, 8
(to) need something   いる（要る）   う -*v.*, 9
new   あたらしい（新しい）   い-*adj.*, 4
newspaper   しんぶん（新聞）   *n.*, 6
next   つぎ（次）   *n.*, 3
next month   らいげつ（来月）   *n.*, 12
next time   こんど（今度）   *n.*, 6
next to   となり（隣）   *loc. n.*, 5
next to; at the side of   よこ（横）   *loc. n.*, 5
next year   らいねん（来年）   *adv.*, 2
night, evening   ばん（晩）   *n.*, 3
night   よる（夜）   *n.*, 11
nine   きゅう、く（九）   *number*, 3
nine o'clock   くじ（九時）   *time exp.*, 2
no, don't mention it, you're welcome   いいえ   *inter.*, 2
No, I don't understand it.   いいえ、わかりません。   *exp.*, 1
No, I still have a long way to go.   いいえ、まだまだです。   *exp.*, 10
No, that's not so.   いいえ、そうじゃありません   *exp.*, 2
No, that's not so.   （そうじゃないです）   *exp.*, 2
No, that's not the case.   いいえ、そんなことはありません。   *exp.*, 10

north　きた（北）　*n.*, 11
northeast　ほくとう（北東）　*n.*, 11
northwest　ほくせい（北西）　*n.*, 11
nose　はな（鼻）　*n.*, 10
not at all (used with negative form of verb)　ぜんぜん（全然）　*adv.*, 3
notebook　ノート *n.*, 4
noun modifier marker (of), ('s)　の *part.*, 2
now　いま（今）　*adv.*, 2

O

ocean, sea　うみ（海）　*n.*, 12
〜 o'clock　〜じ（〜時）　*suf.*, 2
often; well　よく *adv.*, 3
oil　あぶら（油／脂）　*n.*, 9
old　ふるい（古い）　*い-adj.*, 4
older brother (someone else's)　おにいさん（お兄さん）　*n.*, 10
older brother (the speaker's)　あに（兄）　*n.*, 10
older sister (someone else's)　おねえさん（お姉さん）　*n.*, 10
older sister (the speaker's)　あね（姉）　*n.*, 10
on; above; over　うえ（上）　*loc. n.*, 5
on foot　あるいて（歩いて）*exp.*, 5
one　いち（一）　*number*, 3
one o'clock　いちじ（一時）　*time exp.*, 2
only child　ひとりっこ（一人っ子）　*n.*, 10
orange　オレンジ　*n.*, 7
order　ちゅうもん（注文）　*n.*, 9
(to) order　ちゅうもんする（注文する）　*irr. v.*, 9
outside　そと（外）　*loc. n.*, 5
over there; that place (far away from both speaker and listener)　あそこ *demo.*, 4

P

p.m., afternoon,　ごご（午後）　*n.*, 2
parents　りょうしん（両親）　*n.*, 6
park　こうえん（公園）　*n.*, 4
part time job　アルバイト *n.*, 6
party　パーティ　*n.*, 6
pen　ペン *n.*, 4
pencil　えんぴつ（鉛筆）　*n.*, 4
〜 people　〜にん（〜人）　*suf.*, 10
person　ひと（人）*n.*, 5
person, polite form of 人　〜かた（〜方）　*suf.*, 10
photograph　しゃしん（写真）　*n.*, 5
picnic　ピクニック *n.*, 6
picture　え（絵）　*n.*, 5
pizza　ピザ　*n.*, 9
place　ところ（所）　*n.*, 5

(to) play　あそびます（遊びます）　う-v., 6
Please come in.　あがってください（上がって下さい。）　exp., 5
Please give me ～.　～を　ください（～を下さい）　exp., 8
Please listen.　きいて　ください。　exp., 1
Please look at it.　みて　ください。　exp., 1
Please read.　よんで　ください。　exp., 1
Please say it. / Repeat after me.　いって　ください。　exp., 1
Please say it again. (Student's request)　もう　いちど　おねがいします。　exp., 1
Please say it again. (Teacher's request)　もう　いちど　いってください。　exp., 1
Please say it in easier words.　やさしい　ことばで　いってください。（やさしい　言葉で
　　言って下さい。）　exp., 8
Please say it slowly.　もう　すこし　ゆっくり　おねがいします。　exp., 1
Please speak loudly. (Student's request)　おおきい　こえで　おねがいします。　exp., 1
Please speak loudly. (Teacher's request)　おおきい　こえで　いってください。　exp., 1
Please write.　かいて　ください。　exp., 1
police box　こうばん（交番）　n., 4
polite prefix　　おふろ　　お（御～）　pref., 3
polite prefix おなまえ　polite form of なまえ (name)　お～ pref., 2
polite prefix　ご～（御～）　pref., 9
pool　プール n., 6
pop music　ポップス　n., 7
pork　ポーク　n., 9
post office　ゆうびんきょく（郵便局）　n., 4
present　プレゼント　n., 12
Professor ～　～せんせい　suf., 1
(to) put　いれる（入れる）　る-v., 8
(to) put on (a hat, a cap)　かぶる　う-v., 10
(to) put on (accessories)　する　irr-v., 10
(to) put on (glasses)　かける　る-v., 10
(to) put on (skirt, pants, socks)　はく　う-v., 10
(to) put on (sweater, shirt, jacket)　きる（着る）　る-v., 10

Q

question　しつもん（を）します (to) ask a question　しつもん（質問）　n., 6
question marker　か part., 2
quiet　しずか（な）（静か（な））　な-adj., 5

R

rain, rainy　あめ（雨）　n., 11
rainy season　つゆ（梅雨）　n., 11
ramen, Chinese noodles in soup　ラーメン　n., 9
rap music　ラップ　n., 7
(to) read　The dictionary form is よむ. よみます（読みます）　う-v., 3
(to) receive, to get　もらう　う-v., 12
recent, recently　さいきん（最近）　n., 11
red　あかい（赤い）　い-adj., 4

to reside　すむ（住む）　う-*v.*, 10
rest; absence, a day off　やすみ（休み）　*n.*, 6
restaurant　レストラン　*n.*, 4
resultant state　〜ている　aux. *v.*, 10
(to) return, (to) go home　The dictionary form is かえる．かえります（帰ります）　う-*v.*, 3
rice　ライス　*n.*, 9
ring　ゆびわ（指輪）　*n.*, 8
river　かわ（川）　n., 5
(to) rise; to go up　あがる（上がる）　う-*v.*, 11
rock and roll　ロック　*n.*, 7
room　へや（部屋）　*n.*, 5
round　まるい（丸い）　い-*adj.*, 10

S

sad　かなしい（悲しい）　い-*adj.*, 6
salad　サラダ　*n.*, 9
sale　セール　*n.*, 8
salty　しょっぱい　い-*adj.*, 9
sandwich　サンドイッチ　*n.*, 9
sashimi　（お）さしみ（御刺身）　*n.*, 9
Saturday　どようび（土曜日）　*n.*, 3
(to) say　いいます（言います）　う-*v.*, 6
school　がっこう（学校）　*n.*, 3
school cafeteria　がくしょく（学食）（a shortened form of 学生しょくどう）*n.*, 5
season　きせつ（季節）　*n.*, 11
See you later. (literally, *Well then, again.*)　じゃあ、また。*exp.*, 1
(to) see, (to) watch　The dictionary form is みる．みます（見ます）　る-*v.*, 3
semester, quarter　がっき（学期）　*n.*, 12
senior, fourth-year student (The suffix せい may be dropped.)　よねんせい（四年生）　*n.*, 2
seven　なな、しち（七）　*number*, 3
seven o'clock　しちじ（七時）　*time exp.*, 2
Shinto shrine　じんじゃ（神社）　*n.*, 12
shirt　シャツ　*n.*, 8
shoes　くつ（靴）　*n.*, 8
shopping　かいもの（買い物）　*n.*, 6
short (length)　みじかい（短い）　い-*adj.*, 10
(to) show　みせる（見せる）　る-*v.*, 8
shower　シャワー　*n.*, 3
(rain) shower　にわかあめ（にわか雨）　*n.*, 11
sibling　きょうだい（兄弟）　*n.*, 10
siblings (someone else's)　ごきょうだい（ご兄弟）　*n.*, 10
similarity marker (also, too)　も　*part.*, 2
(to) sing　うたう（歌う）　う-*v.*, 7
six　ろく（六）　*number*, 3
six o'clock　ろくじ（六時）　*time exp.*, 2
skiing, ski　スキー　*n.*, 7

skirt　スカート　*n.*, 8

slowly, ゆっくりします, to relax; to　ゆっくり　*adv.*, 6

small　ちいさい (小さい)　い-*adj.*, 4

snow, snowy　ゆき (雪)　*n.*, 11

socks　くつした (靴下)　*n.*, 8

sofa　ソファ　*n.*, 5

soft　やわらかい (柔らかい)　い-*adj.*, 9

sometimes　ときどき (時々)　*adv.*, 3

song　うた (歌)　*n.*, 7

sophomore, second-year student (The suffix せい may be dropped.)　にねんせい (二年生)　*n.*, 2

sorry, regrettable　ざんねん (な)(残念 (な))　な-*adj.*, 6

Sorry, I have some errands/business to attend to.　ちょっと　ようじが　あって (ちょっと用事があって。)　*exp.*, 6

soup　スープ　*n.*, 9

sour　すっぱい (酸っぱい)　い-*adj.*, 9

south　みなみ (南)　*n.*, 11

South Korea　かんこく (韓国)　*n.*, 2

southeast　なんとう (南東)　*n.*, 11

southwest　なんせい (南西)　*n.*, 11

spacious; wide　ひろい (広い)　い-*adj.*, 5

spaghetti　スパゲティ　*n.*, 9

Spain　スペイン　*n.*, 2

specific year (2008年), counter for year (十年)　〜ねん (〜年)　*suf.*, 12

spicy　からい (辛い)　い-*adj.*, 9

sport　スポーツ　*n.*, 7

spring　はる (春)　*n.*, 11

square　しかくい (四角い)　い-*adj.*, 10

St. Valentine's Day　バレンタインデー　*n.*, 12

station　えき (駅)　*n.*, 4

stationery　ぶんぼうぐ (文房具)　*n.*, 8

steak　ステーキ　*n.*, 9

stockings, pantyhose　ストッキング　*n.*, 8

store (e.g. ほんや　bookstore)　〜や (〜屋)　*suf.*, 4

store, shop　みせ (店)　*n.*, 8

strong　つよい (強い)　い-*adj.*, 11

student　がくせい (学生)　*n.*, 2

Student union　がくせいかいかん (学生会館)　*n.*, 5

〜 student だいがくせい　college student いちねんせい　freshman 〜せい (〜生)　*suf.*, 2

study　べんきょう (勉強)　*n.*, 3

(to) study　The dictionary form is べんきょうする　べんきょうします (勉強します)　*irr. v.*, 3

sudden　きゅう (な)(急 (な))　な-*adj.*, 11

suit　スーツ　*n.*, 8

summer　なつ (夏)　*n.*, 11

Sunday　にちようび (日曜日)　*n.*, 3

sunny　はれ (晴れ)　*n.*, 11

supermarket　スーパー　*n.*, 4

supper, dinner　ばんごはん（晩御飯）　*n.*, 3

sushi (usually used with お at the beginning)　（お）すし（御寿司）　*n.*, 9

sweater　セーター　*n.*, 8

sweet　あまい（甘い）　い -*adj.*, 9

(to) swim　およぎます（泳ぎます）　う -*v.*, 6

T

table　テーブル　*n.*, 5

Taiwan　たいわん（台湾）　*n.*, 2

(to) take, get　とる（取る）　う -*v.*, 8

(to) take (a bath), (to) enter. The dictionary form is はいる. おふろに はいります　take a bath.
　　はいります（入ります）　う -*v.*, 3

(to) take (a photograph), しゃしんを　とる　とる（撮る）　う -*v.*, 7

(to) take (a shower)　シャワーを　あびます　take a shower. The dictionary form is あびる.
　　あびます（浴びます）　る -*v.*, 3

to take (time), it costs　かかります　う -*v.*, 5

(to) talk　はなします（話します）　う -*v.*, 6

tall, high　たかい（高い）　い -*adj.*, 4

tea, green tea　おちゃ（お茶）　*n.*, 7

Teacher　せんせい　*n.*, 1

telephone　でんわ（電話）　*n.*, 5

telephone number　でんわばんごう（電話番号）　*n.*, 3

tempura (fish, shrimp, and vegetables battered and deep-fried)　てんぷら（天麩羅 / 天ぷら）
　　n., 9

ten　じゅう（十）　*number*, 3

ten o'clock　じゅうじ（十時）　*time exp.*, 2

tennis テニスを　します　to play tennis　テニス　*n.*, 6

test　テスト　*n.*, 4

textbook　きょうかしょ（教科書）　*n.*, 4

〜 th　(ordinal)　〜ばん（め）（〜番（目））　*suf.*, 10

Thank you.　ありがとうございます。*exp.*, 1

Thank you. (literally, *I will intrude on you*) (said before going inside someone's house or apartment)
　　おじゃまします（お邪魔します。）*exp.*, 5

Thank you very much　どうも　ありがとう　*adv.*, 4

that noun　その　*demo.*, 5

that noun over there　あの　*demo.*, 5

that object over there; that　あれ　*demo.*, 4

that object; that (close to the listener or slightly removed from both speaker and listener) それ *demo.*, 4

the New Year　しょうがつ（正月）　*n.*, 12

the year before last year, two years ago　おととし（一昨年）　*n.*, 12

there; that place (close to the listener or slightly removed from both speaker and listener) そこ *demo.*, 4

thing (intangible)　こと　*n.*, 7

thing (tangible)　もの（物）　*n.*, 5

this 〜　こんしゅう、こんばん　こん〜（今〜）　pref., 3

this area　このへん（この辺）　*n.*, 4

this month　こんげつ（今月）　*n.*, 12
this morning　けさ（今朝）　*n.*, 11
this noun　この　*demo.*, 5
this object, this　これ　*demo.*, 4
this person, this way　こちら　*n.*, 2
this week　こんしゅう（今週）　*n.*, 3
this year　ことし（今年）　*n.*, 11
three　さん（三）　*number*, 3
three o'clock　さんじ（三時）　*time exp.*, 2
Thursday　もくようび（木曜日）　*n.*, 3
tie　ネクタイ　*n.*, 8
times　〜ど（〜度）　*suf.*, 12
times　〜かい（〜回）　*suf.*, 12
to (direction)　がっこうへ　いきます。　へ *part.*, 3
to (goal, activity + に)　クラスに　いきます。　に *part.*, 3
to (goal, receiver)　に *part.*, 6
to be; to exist (used for an animate beings).　Dictionary form is いる.　います　*る-v.*, 4
to the left; left side　ひだり（左）　*loc. n.*, 5
to the right　みぎ（右）　*loc. n.*, 5
toast　トースト　*n.*, 9
today　きょう（今日）　*n.*, 3
together　いっしょに（一緒に）　*adv.*, 6
toilet; restroom　トイレ　*n.*, 5
tomato　トマト　*n.*, 7
tomorrow　あした（明日）　*n.*, 3
tonight　こんばん（今晩）　*n.*, 3
topic marker　は *part.*, 2
tough　たいへん（な）（大変（な））　*な-adj.*, 6
town　まち（町）　*n.*, 4
traditional Japanese clothes, kimono　きもの（着物）　*n.*, 12
traveling　りょこう（旅行）　*n.*, 7
tree　き（木）　*n.*, 5
trousers (primarily men's)　ズボン　*n.*, 8
(primarily women's) trousers, shorts　パンツ　*n.*, 8
truly, really, indeed　ほんとうに / ほんとに（本当に）　*adv.*, 11
T-shirt　Tシャツ　*n.*, 8
Tuesday　かようび（火曜日）　*n.*, 3
TV　テレビ *n.*, 3
twelve o'clock　じゅうにじ（十二時）　*time exp.*, 2
two　に（二）　*number*, 3
two o'clock　にじ（二時）　*time exp.*, 2
typhoon　たいふう（台風）　*n.*, 11

U

uh, well　あのう *inter.*, 2
umbrella　かさ（傘）　*n.*, 8

under; beneath　した（下）　*loc. n.*, 5
(to) understand　わかる（分かる）　う-*v.*, 10
unpleasant　いや（な）　な-*adj.*, 11
until, to　まで　*part.*, 5
usually　たいてい　*adv.*, 3

V

vegetable　やさい（野菜）　*n.*, 7
very　どうも　*adv.*, 4
very (always used with a negative form)　あまり　*adv.*, 4
very (always used with an affirmative form)　とても　*adv.*, 4
very much, 大すき like very much　だい〜（大〜）　*pref.*, 7
video　ビデオ　*n.*, 5

W

(to) wait　まちます（待ちます）　う-*v.*, 6
(to) walk　あるきます（歩きます）　う-*v.*, 6
(to take) a walk　さんぽ（を）　します　to take a walk　さんぽ（散歩）　*n.*, 6
warm　あたたかい（温かい）　い-*adj.*, 9
warm　あたたかい（暖かい／温かい）　い-*adj.*, 11
water　みず（水）　*n.*, 7
weak　よわい（弱い）　い-*adj.*, 11
weather　てんき（天気）　*n.*, 11
weather forecast　てんきよほう（天気予報）　*n.*, 11
Wednesday　すいようび（水曜日）　*n.*, 3
weekend　しゅうまつ（週末）　*n.*, 3
Welcome.　いらっしゃいませ。　*exp.*, 8
Welcome! Come in.　いらっしゃい。　*exp.*, 5
Well, let's see. . .　えーと　*exp.*, 12
west　にし（西）　*n.*, 11
western style cuisine　ようしょく（洋食）　*n.*, 9
a Western-style fixed menu　セット　*n.*, 9
what　なに／なん（何）　*q. word*, 2
What does 〜 mean?　〜って　なんですか。　*exp.*, 1
what kind of　どんな　*q. word*, 4
when　いつ　*q. word*, 3
when, at the time of 〜　とき（時）　*n.*, 12
where　どこ　*q. word*, 2
where (more polite than どこ), which way　どちら　*q. word*, 2
which Noun　どの　*demo.*, 5
which one　どれ　*q. word*, 4
white　しろい（白い）　い-*adj.*, 4
who　だれ　*q. word*, 4
why　どうして　*q. word*, 7
wife (someone else's)　おくさん（奥さん）　*n.*, 10
wife (the speaker's)　つま（妻）　*n.*, 10

wind　かぜ（風）　*n.*, 11
window　まど（窓）　*n.*, 5
wine　ワイン　*n.*, 7
winter　ふゆ（冬）　*n.*, 11
with, together with (association)　と　*part.*, 6
wristwatch　うでどけい（腕時計）　*n.*, 8
(to) write　かきます（書きます）　う-*v.*, 6

Y

year　いちねん first year　～ねん（～年）　*suf.*, 2
～ years old　～さい（～歳／才）　*suf.*, 10
yellow　きいろい（黄色い）　い-*adj.*, 4
yes　はい／ええ　*inter.*, 2
Yes, I understand it.　はい、わかりました。　*exp.*, 1
Yes, that's so.　はい（ええ）、そうです。　*exp.*, 2
yesterday　きのう（昨日）　*n.*, 3
You are welcome.　どういたしまして。　*exp.*, 1
You call it ～/You say ～　～と　いいます。／～って　いいます。　*exp.*, 1
younger brother (someone else's)　おとうとさん（弟さん）　*n.*, 10
younger brother (the speaker's)　おとうと（弟）　*n.*, 10
younger sister (someone else's)　いもうとさん（妹さん）　*n.*, 10
younger sister (the speaker's)　いもうと（妹）　*n.*, 10

Z

zero　ゼロ、れい（ゼロ、零）　*number*, 3
zoo　どうぶつえん（動物園）　*n.*, 12

INDEX